Ireland's Great Famine
Popular Politics

Ireland's Great Famine of 1845–52 was among the most devastating food crises in modern history. A country of some eight-and-a-half-million people lost one million to hunger and disease and another million to emigration. According to land activist Michael Davitt, the starving made little or no effort to assert 'the animal's right of existence,' passively accepting their fate. But the poor did resist. In word and deed, they defied landlords, merchants and agents of the state: they rioted for food, opposed rent and rate collection, challenged the decisions of those controlling relief works and scorned clergymen who attributed their suffering to the Almighty. The essays collected here examine the full range of resistance in the Great Famine and illuminate how the crisis itself transformed popular politics. Contributors include distinguished scholars of modern Ireland and emerging historians and critics. This book is essential reading for students of modern Ireland and the global history of collective action.

Enda Delaney is Professor of Modern History at the University of Edinburgh.

Breandán Mac Suibhne is Associate Professor of History at Centenary College, New Jersey.

Routledge Studies in Modern European History

1 **Facing Fascism**
The Conservative Party and the European Dictators 1935–1940
Nick Crowson

2 **French Foreign and Defence Policy, 1918–1940**
The Decline and Fall of a Great Power
Edited by Robert Boyce

3 **Britain and the Problem of International Disarmament**
1919–1934
Carolyn Kitching

4 **British Foreign Policy 1874–1914**
The Role of India
Sneh Mahajan

5 **Racial Theories in Fascist Italy**
Aaron Gilette

6 **Stormtroopers and Crisis in the Nazi Movement**
Activism, Ideology and Dissolution
Thomas D. Grant

7 **Trials of Irish History**
Genesis and Evolution of a Reappraisal 1938–2000
Evi Gkotzaridis

8 **From Slave Trade to Empire**
European Colonisation of Black Africa 1780s-1880s
Edited by Olivier Pétré-Grenouilleau

9 **The Russian Revolution of 1905**
Centenary Perspectives
Edited by Anthony Heywood and Jonathan D. Smele

10 **Weimar Cities**
The Challenge of Urban Modernity in Germany
John Bingham

11 **The Nazi Party and the German Foreign Office**
Hans-Adolf Jacobsen and Arthur L. Smith, Jr.

12 **The Politics of Culture in Liberal Italy**
From Unification to Fascism
Axel Körner

13 **German Colonialism, Visual Culture and Modern Memory**
Edited by Volker M. Langbehn

14 **German Colonialism and National Identity**
Edited by Michael Perraudin and Jürgen Zimmerer

15 **Landscapes of the Western Front**
Materiality during the Great War
Ross J. Wilson

16 **West Germans and the Nazi Legacy**
Caroline Sharples

17 **Alan S. Milward and a Century of European Change**
Edited by Fernando Guirao, Frances M. B. Lynch, and Sigfrido M. Ramírez Pérez

18 **War, Agriculture, and Food**
Rural Europe from the 1930s to the 1950s
Edited by Paul Brassley, Yves Segers and Leen Van Molle

19 **Totalitarian Dictatorship**
New Histories
Edited by Daniela Baratieri, Mark Edele and Giuseppe Finaldi

20 **Nurses and Midwives in Nazi Germany**
The "Euthanasia Programs"
Edited by Susan Benedict and Linda Shields

21 **European Border Regions in Comparison**
Overcoming Nationalistic Aspects or Re-Nationalization?
Edited by Katarzyna Stokłosa and Gerhard Besier

22 **The Red Brigades and the Discourse of Violence**
Revolution and Restoration
Marco Briziarelli

23 **History, Memory, and Trans-European Identity**
Unifying Divisions
Aline Sierp

24 **Constructing a German Diaspora**
The "Greater German Empire," 1871–1914
Stefan Manz

25 **Violence, Memory, and History**
Western Perceptions of Kristallnacht
Edited by Colin McCullough and Nathan Wilson

26 **Turkey and the Rescue of European Jews**
I. Izzet Bahar

27 **Antifascism After Hitler**
East German Youth and Socialist Memory, 1949–1989
Catherine Plum

28 **Fascism and Ideology**
Italy, Britain, and Norway
Salvatore Garau

29 **Hitler's Brudervolk**
The Dutch and the Colonization of Occupied Eastern Europe, 1939–1945
Geraldien von Frijtag Drabbe Künzel

30 **Alan S. Milward and Contemporary European History**
Collected Academic Reviews
Edited by Fernando Guirao and Frances M.B. Lynch

31 **Ireland's Great Famine and Popular Politics**
Edited by Enda Delaney and Breandán Mac Suibhne

Ireland's Great Famine and Popular Politics

Edited by Enda Delaney
and Breandán Mac Suibhne

NEW YORK AND LONDON

First published 2016
by Routledge
605 Third Avenue, New York, NY 10017

and by Routledge
2 Park Square, Milton Park, Abingdon, Oxon OX14 4RN

First issued in paperback 2021

Routledge is an imprint of the Taylor & Francis Group, an informa business

Publisher's Note
The publisher has gone to great lengths to ensure the quality of this reprint but points out that some imperfections in the original copies may be apparent.

Library of Congress Cataloging-in-Publication Data
Ireland's Great Famine and popular politics / edited by Enda Delaney and Breandán Mac Suibhne.
pages cm. — (Routledge studies in modern European history ; 31)
Includes bibliographical references and index.
ISBN 978-0-415-83630-2 (hardback) — ISBN 978-1-315-87955-0 (ebook)
1. Ireland—History—Famine, 1845–1852. 2. Ireland—Politics and government—1837–1901. 3. Famines—Political aspects—Ireland—History—19th century. 4. Famines—Social aspects—Ireland—History—19th century. 5. Poor—Ireland—History—19th century. 6. Government, Resistance to—Ireland—History—19th century. 7. Political culture—Ireland—History—19th century. 8. Social change—Ireland—History—19th century. 9. Ireland—Social conditions—19th century. I. Delaney, Enda, 1971– II. Mac Suibhne, Breandán.
DA950.7.I725 2017
941.5081—dc23 2015025851

ISBN 13: 978-1-03-209819-7 (pbk)
ISBN 13: 978-0-415-83630-2 (hbk)

Typeset in Sabon
by Apex CoVantage, LLC

Contents

Figures

Maps

Tables

Editors' Introduction

'To Assert Even the Animal's Right of Existence'

Enda Delaney and Breandán Mac Suibhne

> There is possibly no chapter in the wide records of human suffering and wrong so full of shame—measureless, unadulterated, sickening shame—as that which tells us of (it is estimated) a million of people including, presumably, two hundred thousand adult men, lying down to die in a land out of which forty-five millions' worth of food was being exported, in one year alone, for rent the product of their own toil and making no effort, combined or otherwise, to assert even the animal's right of existence—the right to live by the necessities of its nature. It stands unparalleled in human history, nothing approaching to it in the complete surrender of all the ordinary attributes of manhood by almost a whole nation, in the face of an artificial famine.
>
> Michael Davitt, *The Fall of Feudalism in Ireland; or, The Story of the Land League Revolution* (London and New York, 1904), 47–48

For Michael Davitt, the passivity of the poor during Ireland's Great Famine was an article of faith: the Famine dead were 'slaves who . . . died like sheep, without leaving on record one single redeeming trait of courageous manhood to the credit of their memories'.[1] And yet, when he wrote of that passivity in *The Fall of Feudalism in Ireland* (1904), it had been a common rhetorical device in the land agitation that he himself had set in train a quarter century earlier. At the very commencement of that agitation, in June 1879, Charles Stewart Parnell, addressing a large crowd of tenants in a field outside Westport, County Mayo, had invoked the Famine years as a warning of the fate that awaited those who did not resist the landlords:

> A fair rent is a rent the tenant can reasonably pay according to the times, but in bad times a tenant cannot be expected to pay as much as he did in good times, three or four years ago. If such rents are insisted upon, a repetition of the scenes of 1847 and 1848 will be witnessed. Now, what must we do in order to induce the landlords to see the position? You must show the landlords that you intend to hold a fair grip on your homesteads and lands. You must not allow yourselves to be dispossessed as you were dispossessed in 1847.[2]

Davitt was to return to the theme repeatedly, and with force. Passivity in the Famine was a central element in one of his most powerful speeches, an emotive oration, delivered to a crowd numbered at 20,000 by some reporters, in his birthplace, Straide, County Mayo, on 1 February 1880. Standing on a platform erected on the very site of the house from which his family had been evicted in September 1850 and which he, as a child of four, had watched being 'burned down by agents of the landlord, assisted by agents of the law'[3]—and conscious too that 'in the memory of many now listening to my words' the then depopulated district had been loud with the laughter of children—he had stressed that 'every nerve would have to be strained to stave off, if possible, the horrible fate which befell our famine-slaughtered kindred in 1847 and 1848'. He had grown up, he said, in 'a strange land', listening to 'accounts of famine and sorrow, of deaths from landlordism, of coffinless graves, of scenes':

> On highway's side, where oft were seen
> The wild dog and the vulture keen
> Tug for the limbs and gnaw the face
> Of some starved child of our Irish race.

And he proceeded to deplore the 'abrogation of our manhood' in those years, and how smallholders 'stood by like a flock of frightened sheep, timid and terrified, unable to prevent this human bird of prey [the landlord] from devouring their own and their children's substance'.[4] Famine-time passivity, real or imagined, had become a call to action.

Mention of the passivity of the poor in the face of catastrophe can be found in nationalist and republican writing before the Land War. Still, it was from 1879 that it became a commonplace that made a deep impression on subsequent scholarly work. The Famine years, Kevin B. Nowlan argued in a contribution to the Revisionist compendium, *The Great Famine: Studies in Irish History* (1956), were 'conspicuous for their tranquility rather than their turbulence'.[5] Certainly, 'tranquility' is well-documented in the Famine; however, acceptance was considered a virtue of the 'deserving poor', and so it is most frequently encountered in appeals for support by people involved in the administration of relief, including agents of charities and members of relief committees, particularly clergymen.[6] 'Turbulence', actual and apprehended, greatly concerned police and policy makers, landlords and large farmers, merchants and mealmongers: a far-from-passive poor are evident in their correspondence, reports and statistical series. Significantly too, the urban and rural poor who emerge from the memoirs of people who witnessed the Famine, and oral histories collected from the generations that came after them, were not passive, or at least not always so. They held meetings to demand employment. They rioted and plundered food stores, resisted and rebuked rent and rate collectors, and the police-protected agents, bailiffs and sheriffs who came to evict them, and they verbally and physically attacked their social superiors and those state officials who they understood to be compounding their suffering.[7]

In the six decades since the publication of Nowlan's essay, historians have come to see patterns of resistance in Ireland in the mid- to late-1840s as broadly consistent with those observed in other famine-afflicted times and places. Specifically, protest, 'combined and otherwise', in Davitt's phrase, is now perceived to have been vigorous in the first two years of the crisis, that is, from the end of 1845 through to the autumn of 1847, but to have lost energy as starvation bit, disease spread and a fever of emigration took hold. Apathy and despair, historians argue, were more general in the latter stages of the Famine.[8] Davitt's focus on the 'animal's right of existence'—though not his conclusion that it was not asserted—was apposite, however. Years after the horror of it all, it was the feral politics of the famished—a politics beyond protest and resistance—that haunted many people: they remembered the fittest being first to the pot; families converting to obtain food or employment; children deserted by parents, women by men, the ill and the old by the able; and poor men grabbing the land of poorer widows.[9] Historians are becoming more attentive to these aspects of the Famine. Souperism—its extent and the motivation of converters and converted—is now much better understood; so too are other dark issues, such as forestalling, prostitution and 'famine's darkest secret', cannibalism.[10]

For some, the memory of what hunger drove people to do would define their own lives. Jeremiah O'Donovan Rossa, like Davitt a Fenian, was once a guest in the hotel of Tom Curley of Ballinasloe, County Galway, in Troy, New York. They talked of 'the bad times' in Ireland, and Curley asked him if he ever 'felt the hunger'. 'I told him I did not', Rossa wrote, 'but that I felt something that was worse than the hunger; that I felt it still; and that was—the degradation into which want and hunger will reduce human nature'.

> I told him of that Sunday evening in Ross when I went home to my dinner, and my mother had no dinner for me; I told him how I had one penny piece in my pocket; I told him how I went out and bought for it a penny bun, and how I stole to the back of the house and thievishly ate that penny bun without sharing it with my mother and my sister and my brothers. I am proud of my life, one way or another; but that penny bun is a thorn in my side; a thorn in the pride of my life; it was only four ounces of bread—for bread was four pence (eight cents) a pound at the time—but if I ever feel any pride in myself, that little loaf comes before me to humble me; it also comes before me to strengthen me in the determination to destroy that tyranny that reduces my people to poverty and degradation, and makes them what it is not natural for them to be. I know it is not in my nature to be niggardly and selfish. I know that if I have money above my wants, I find more happiness and satisfaction in giving it to friends who want it than in keeping it. But that penny-bun

> affair clashes altogether against my own measurement of myself, and stands before me like a ghost whenever I would think of raising myself in my own estimation. I suppose it was the general terror and alarm of starvation that was around me at the time that paralyzed my nature, and made me do what I am now ashamed to say I did.[11]

Yet if there were people, like O'Donovan Rossa, who were ashamed of what hunger had made them do, there were others who felt shame at what they had not been able to do 'in the years of the Famine'—feed themselves and their children, and bury their people according to custom.

Shame, then, had real sources and shame had its uses, as evidenced by O'Donovan Rossa's polemic and that of Davitt. The historian R.V. Comerford concluded that 'the dominant feeling left behind by the Famine was not a desire for self-government but a sense of embarrassment and inadequacy.'[12] It is a curious conclusion, given that the Fenians were claiming 80,000 members by the early 1860s, but more particularly as it insinuates that a 'sense of embarrassment and inadequacy' is somehow incompatible with a 'desire for self-government' when they are, in fact, intimately connected: without the capacity to feel shame for one's 'nation', most especially at its lacking a state, there is no nationalism. The passivity of the poor—the source of Davitt's 'measureless, unadulterated, sickening shame'—was one 'nationalist myth' that Revisionism was happy not to 'debunk'. But that other source of shame—the eaten bread that was never forgotten, the forestalling and the land grabbing—is no less vital to the history of 'the bad times' than an awareness that the poor apprehended their likely fate and acted to avert it, for, in Ó Gráda's words, 'ignoring the shame and the guilt leaves the way open for a version of famine history in which the descendants of those who survived all become vicarious victims'.[13] An apprehension of what O'Donovan Rossa termed 'the degradation into which want and hunger will reduce human nature' keeps the poor from being entirely stripped of age, gender, culture and class: it reminds us that not all suffer equally in famine. At the same time, as the critic Maud Ellmann has observed, 'there is something about hunger, or more specifically about the *spectacle* of hunger, that deranges the distinction between self and other', and so, paradoxically, bringing into view the degradation of human nature in the Great Famine—the nastiness and the brutishness of it all—recovers the humanity of all who suffered.[14] And it is possible to bring that degradation into view—to achieve some understanding of what happened to those real human beings who constituted the Irish poor—without losing sight of the economic, ideological and political factors that led to mass mortality and mass migration, and central here, in the long-term and the short, must be the 'connection to England' that Davitt and O'Donovan Rossa had hoped to break.

Still, at base, there remains the poor's own desire for 'cultural dignity and self-respect', registered, in agrarian societies, by not begging, by supporting parents in old age, by being charitable to neighbors and strangers, and by achieving 'minimal standards of culturally acceptable conduct' at seasonal festivals, weddings and, particularly, wakes and funerals—and not meeting those standards, as happened in Ireland in the Famine, was a source of great and enduring shame. With that mindset in view, James C. Scott has recently argued, that in a 'local face-to-face community', the political implications of dire poverty are not purely 'a matter of calories and cash and the calculations of risk that they impel', but 'a *local* claim for dignity and respect'.[15] Certainly, in the years of the Famine, such local claims flashed in efforts to prevent the removal of provisions from districts where the poor were hungry and attempts to compel forestallers to lower their prices and sell food in small quantities. They were discernible too in struggles to ameliorate conditions on public works and at soup kitchens, and in opposition to usury, eviction and rate collection. But while Scott is undoubtedly correct when he says that 'there is no *purely* abstract experience of class in a small face-to-face community' (italics added), the poor were by no means oblivious to the supra-local dimensions of a crisis that pitted *na huaisle*, the gentry, and *na boic mhóra*, the great and the good, against *na daoine*, the people, *na daoine bochta*, the poor, and 'the working classes'—a phrase encountered with some frequency in the years of the Famine—and they located it too in a long history of colonial oppression.[16]

•

This collection's concern is popular politics broadly defined, that is, non-élite action ('combined and otherwise'), the ideas that animated it, and the state and social groups toward which it was directed. It comprises essays that illuminate accommodation and resistance and the memory and the representation of them, as well as shifts in rural society, not least the consolidation of holdings and the 'improvement' of estate management, that were, in places, bitterly contested in the period of post-Famine adjustment.

The heroic phase in the historiography of the Great Famine that began with K.H. Connell's *The Population of Ireland, 1700–1845* (1951) ended in the late 1980s with benchmark publications by the historians James S. Donnelly, Jr. and Kerby A. Miller and the economists Joel Mokyr and Cormac Ó Gráda.[17] Despite some significant studies of disparate aspects of the crisis in the intervening years—including, in the 1990s, major books in social, administrative and political history and, in the last few years, three well-received narratives—historians have not been overly interested in the Great Famine.[18] There are a dozen History departments in Ireland's colleges and universities, but only one (Queen's University Belfast) has today (2015) a faculty member for whom the crisis that long defined the country has been a major research focus, and much of the innovative and insightful recent work on Famine-related issues has been produced by critics, economists, anthropologists and geographers.[19] Moreover, the scholarship remains preoccupied with what was done *to and for the poor*—by landlords, charities and the state. To the extent that the essays gathered here encourage scholars, particularly historians, to consider what the poor did *to and for each other*—and to do so without losing sight of the broader political and economic context—this collection will have realized one of its objectives.

NOTES

1. Michael Davitt, *The Fall of Feudalism in Ireland; or, The Story of the Land League Revolution* (London, 1904), 53. For recent work on Davitt, see Laurence Marley, *Michael Davitt: Freelance Radical and Frondeur* (Dublin, 2007), Carla King, *Michael Davitt* (Dublin, 2009), and the various essays in Fintan Lane and Andrew G. Newby, eds., *Michael Davitt: New Perspectives* (Dublin and Portland, 2009). On Davitt's perspective on the Great Famine, see Scott Brewster and Virginia Crossman, 'Re-writing the Famine: Witnessing in Crisis', in Scott Brewster, Virginia Crossman, Fiona Beckett and David Alderson, eds., *Ireland in Proximity: History, Gender, Space* (London and New York, 1999), 42–58, esp. 48–50; James S. Donnelly, Jr., 'Constructing the Memory of the Famine, 1850–1900', in his *The Great Irish Famine* (Phoenix Mill, 2001), 209–45, esp. 222, 233, 235, 240. Also see Carla King, ed., *Michael Davitt: Collected Writings, 1868–1906* (Bristol, 2001).
2. *Freeman's Journal*, 9 June 1879, quoted in Davitt, *Fall of Feudalism*, 154.
3. For Davitt's account of his family's eviction, see his remarkable *Times-Parnell Commission: Speech Delivered by Michael Davitt in Defence of the Land League* (London, 1890), 201–02, where he further illuminates the profound impact of stories which his parents, particularly his mother, told of the Famine:

    > I remember, though I was but a child, we went to the workhouse a few miles away, and we were refused admission because my mother would not submit to certain conditions which were imposed upon all those who sought the shelter of those abodes of misery and degradation; and I recollect many and many a time in our English home listening to her stories of the famine years. One fact contained in one of those stories made such an impression upon my mind that it had largely to do with the circumstance of my having started the land agitation in Mayo in 1879. I remember hearing from her a graphic account of how 300 poor people who had died of starvation round about where I was born, between Straide and Swinford, had been thrown into one pit in the corner of the workhouse yard, without coffin, without sermon, without anything which denotes respect for the dead; and so great an impression did this make upon me in my youthful days in Lancashire that when I visited Swinford twenty-five years afterwards, I went to the very spot where these bodies had been so buried, without asking anyone to direct me to the place.

4. *Freeman's Journal*, 2 February, 3 February 1880. Davitt's 'Speech at Straide' appeared in many books on oratory. For his own recollection of it, see *Fall of Feudalism*, 202–03.
5. Kevin B. Nowlan, 'The Political Background', in R.D. Edwards and T.D. Williams, eds., *The Great Famine: Studies in Irish History, 1845–1852* (Dublin, 1956), 131–206, 136. Nowlan's essay was conceived as a discussion of the 'Course of the Famine'; see Cormac Ó Gráda, 'Making Famine History in Ireland in the 1940s and 1950s', in his *Ireland's Great Famine: Interdisciplinary Perspectives* (Dublin, 2006), 234–50, 237.

6. On the representation of 'victims of the Famine', see Margaret Kelleher, *The Feminization of Famine: Expressions of the Inexpressible* (Cork, 1997), especially chs. 1–2.
7. For one lower-class memoir of the Famine, see Hugh Dorian, *The Outer Edge of Ulster: A Memoir of Social Life in Nineteenth-Century Donegal,* ed. Breandán Mac Suibhne and David Dickson (Dublin, 2000), and for oral histories of the Famine, many gathered from the children of people who lived through it, see the important samplers compiled by Cathal Póirtéir: *Famine Echoes* (Dublin, 1995) and *Glórtha ón Ghorta: Béaloideas na Gaeilge agus an Gorta Mór* (Baile Átha Cliath, 1996). For a careful consideration of the utility of those materials for the history of the Famine, see Cormac Ó Gráda, *An Drochshaol: Béaloideas agus Amhráin* (Baile Átha Cliath, 1994), esp. 17–19, 24–26; for an English-language version, see 'Famine Memory', in idem, *Black '47 and Beyond: The Great Irish Famine in History, Economy and Memory* (Princeton, NJ, 2000), 194–225.
8. On patterns of resistance and social unrest in famine, see Cormac Ó Gráda, *Famine: A Short History* (Princeton, NJ, 2009), 45–89, esp. 55, and idem, *Eating People is Wrong and Other Essays on Famine, Its Past, and Its Future* (Princeton, NJ, 2015), 1. On resistance during the Great Famine, see Mary Daly, *The Famine in Ireland* (Dundalk, 1986), 85–87; Christine Kinealy, *The Great Irish Famine: Impact, Ideology and Rebellion* (Houndmills, 2002), 182–210; Kerby A. Miller, *Emigrants and Exiles: Ireland and the Irish Exodus to North America* (Oxford, 1985), 290–91; and, most especially, Andrés Eiríksson, 'Food Supply and Food Riots', in Cormac Ó Gráda, ed., *Famine 150: Commemorative Lecture Series* (Ballsbridge, 1997), 67–94; and John Cunningham's contribution to this volume. S. J. Connolly, 'The Great Famine and Irish Politics', in Cathal Póirtéir, ed., *The Great Irish Famine* (Dublin, 1995), 34–49, is not particularly concerned with 'politics outside the electoral system', but reiterates (42) the view that 'there was more violence than is sometimes recognised, especially during 1845–6, before prolonged distress had weakened the will to protest'. For coincident protests in Europe, see Pedro Díaz Marín, 'Subsistence Crisis and Popular Protest in Spain: The *Motines* of 1847', in Cormac Ó Gráda, Richard Paping, and Eric Vanhuate, eds., *When the Potato Failed: Causes and Effects of the Last European Subsistence Crisis, 1845–1850* (Turnhout, 2007), 267–92.
9. Such issues are central to the stories collected by the Irish Folklore Commission in the mid-twentieth century: see Póirtéir, ed., *Famine Echoes*, and idem, *Glórtha an Ghorta.* Also see Patricia Lysaght, 'Women and the Great Famine: Vignettes from the Irish Oral Tradition', in Arthur Gribben, ed., *The Great Famine and the Irish Diaspora in America*, with an Introduction by Ruth-Ann Harris (Amherst, 1999), 21–47.
10. On souperism, see Irene Whelan, 'The Stigma of Souperism', in Póirtéir, ed., *Great Irish Famine*, 135–54; on prostitution, see Cormac Ó Gráda, 'Famine in Dublin City', in his *Black '47 and Beyond*, 157–93, esp. 178–82; and on cannibalism, see idem, *Eating People is Wrong*, ch. 1. For some thoughts on the 'gray zone' of the Great Famine, see Breandán Mac Suibhne, 'A Jig in the Poorhouse', *Dublin Review of Books* (April 2013); http://www.drb.ie/essays/a-jig-in-the-poorhouse. An edited extract of this essay has since appeared in translation as 'La Zone Grise, le Gros Mot, et de Nouvelles Manières de le Raconter: Quelques Histoires Récentes de la Grande Famine', traduit de l'anglais par Chloé Lacoste, *Révue Française de Civilisation Britannique*, 19, 2 (2014), 213–38. Also see Miller, *Emigrants and Exiles*, 290–91; Joe Lee, 'Famine as History', in Ó Gráda, ed., *Famine 150*, 159–75, esp. 167–69, and 172.

11. [Jeremiah] O'Donovan Rossa, *Rossa's Recollections, 1838 to 1898. Memoirs of an Irish Revolutionary*, with an Introduction by Seán Ó Lúing (New York, 1898), 122–23.
12. R.V. Comerford, *The Fenians in Context: Irish Politics and Society, 1848–82* (Dublin, 1998), 21. For a dissenting view, see Anthony McNicholas, *Politics, Religion and the Press: Irish Journalism in Mid-Victorian England* (Bern, 2007), 284. Connolly, 'The Great Famine and Irish Politics', 49, notes the suggestion that, 'in the short term . . . the catastrophe may well have weakened nationalist politics, casting doubt on the feasibility of the goal of a self-governing prosperous Ireland', but he concludes that, 'in the longer term, there can be little doubt but that the crisis contributed substantially to the growth of nationalist sentiment'.
13. Ó Gráda, 'Famine Memory', 212.
14. Maud Ellmann, *The Hunger Artists: Starving, Writing and Imprisonment* (London, 1993), 54. Also see Luke Gibbons, *Limits of the Visible: Representing the Great Hunger* (Cork, 2015).
15. James C. Scott, 'Introduction', in *Decoding Subaltern Politics: Ideology, Disguise, and Resistance in Agrarian Politics* (New York, 2013), 1–6, 6; italics in original.
16. Scott, 'Introduction', 6. For the phrase 'working classes', see a printed poster, drafted and distributed by a nail-maker, calling a meeting in Ramelton in September 1846 to consider 'the condition of the Working Classes, on the approaching season of destitution, arising from the entire failure of the POTATO Crop, and *the utter want of any public employment*', National Archives of Ireland, Outrage Papers, 1846/7/25875; it is reproduced in Dorian, *Outer Edge of Ulster*, 221.
17. Here, we have in mind Donnelly's contribution to *A New History of Ireland, V: Ireland under the Union, I, 1801–70* (Oxford, 1989); Miller, *Emigrants and Exiles*; Joel Mokyr, *Why Ireland Starved: A Quantitative and Analytical History of the Irish Economy, 1800–1850* (London and New York, 1983); and Cormac Ó Gráda, *Ireland before and after the Famine: Explorations in Economic History, 1800–1925* (Manchester, 1988). Enduring works from that heroic phase include Cecil Woodham-Smith's magisterial *The Great Hunger: Ireland: 1845–1849* (London, 1962) and the sociologist Samuel Clark's *Social Origins of the Irish Land War* (Princeton, NJ, 1979).
18. In social history, see Robert James Scally, *The End of Hidden Ireland: Rebellion, Famine and Emigration* (Oxford, 1995); in administrative history, see Christine Kinealy, *This Great Calamity: The Irish Famine, 1845–52* (Dublin, 1994); and in political history, see Peter Gray, *Famine, Land and Politics: British Government and Irish Society* (Dublin, 1999). For three recent narratives, see Enda Delaney, *The Curse of Reason: The Great Irish Famine* (Dublin, 2012), retitled for the second edition as *The Great Irish Famine: A History in Four Lives* (Dublin, 2014); John Kelly, *The Graves are Walking: The Great Famine and the Saga of the Irish People* (London and New York, 2012); and Ciarán Ó Murchadha, *The Great Famine: Ireland's Agony* (London and New York, 2011).
19. Colm Tóibín, 'The Irish Famine', in Colm Tóibín and Diarmaid Ferriter, *The Irish Famine: A Documentary* (London, 1998), 3–42, remains a most suggestive reflection on the Great Famine and its scholarship; no less important is David Lloyd, 'The Indigent Sublime: Specters of Irish Hunger', *Representations*, 92, 1 (2005), 152–85, reprinted in his *Irish Times: Temporalities of Modernity* (Dublin, 2008), 39–72. For important work in Economics, see Timothy W. Guinnane, *The Vanishing Irish: Households, Migration, and the Rural Economy, 1850–1914* (Princeton, NJ, 1997), Martin Turner, *After*

the Famine: Irish Agriculture, 1850–1914 (Cambridge, 2002) and Ó Gráda, *Black '47 and Beyond*; and in Geography, David P. Nally, *Human Encumbrances: Political Violence and the Great Irish Famine* (Notre Dame, 2011) and William J. Smyth's contributions to John Crowley, William J. Smyth and Mike Murphy, eds., *Atlas of the Great Irish Famine, 1845–52* (Cork, 2012). For interventions by critics, see the useful select bibliographies compiled by Margaret Kelleher ('Famine'; accessed 2 June 2015; last modified 27 November 2013) and Marguérite Corporaal ('Writing of the Irish Famine'; accessed 2 June 2015; last modified 30 July 2014), and accessible at Oxford Bibliographies Online. To both bibliographies might be added Seamus Deane, 'National Character and the Character of Nations', in his *Strange Country: Modernity and Nationhood in Irish Writing since 1790* (Oxford, 1999), 49–99.

1 ' 'Tis Hard to Argue Starvation into Quiet'

Protest and Resistance, 1846–47[1]

John Cunningham

Toward the end of a life that began in County Mayo in the Great Famine, the Fenian and land activist Michael Davitt (1846–1906) wrote of his 'measureless, unadulterated, sickening shame' at the 'wholesale cowardice of the men who saw food leave the country, and turned and saw their wives and little ones sicken and die . . . making no effort, combined or otherwise, to assert the animal's right of existence—the right to live by the necessities of its nature'.[2] Davitt's judgment was severe, but his impression of the impoverished people of Ireland during the Famine has been the predominant one. Passivity and submissive resignation remain the key motifs of monuments, and they are the staples of oratory at remembrance ceremonies, such as the National Famine Commemoration of 2012, when Taoiseach Enda Kenny referred to 'mere hints of humans, carrying their most precious possession: their children, blue-black and bloated from hunger and fever'.[3]

If an alignment of ecological and ideological forces in the late 1840s denied the poorest three million of the Irish the means of survival, posterity has deprived the same people of agency. But not all of them were passive all of the time. Indeed, many participated in collective actions of protest and resistance. An illustration published in the *Pictorial News* of a demonstration in Dungarvan, County Waterford, in October 1846 provides a striking visual record of one such act of resistance; led by a man bearing a pole with a loaf of bread impaled upon it, the demonstrators were asserting that there was food in their community, but that high prices had pushed it beyond their reach, and they were appealing for it to be sold at fair prices. Here, the concern is to probe the intentions of the men and women involved in such protests, and to make an assessment of their impact.

'THEY CONSIDER IT JUST . . .': SEPTEMBER 1846

In the latter half of September 1846, a number of demonstrations took place in the Decies in the western part of County Waterford. Crowds of laborers, many hundreds in number, gathered outside the houses of farmers to demand refunds of rent that they had paid for their potato gardens.[4] 'The crop having failed’, explained the Dungarvan resident magistrate, ‘they consider it just to obtain their money’.[5] Baron Stuart de Decies (previously Henry Villiers Stuart MP) advised Dublin Castle that an estimated two hundred people who had followed a ringleader to the door of Glenard House demanding ‘the repayment of conacre rent money’ was ‘only a portion of the crowd he led through the parish on the same day for the purpose of coercing in a similar manner the farmers of the district’.[6] Police sub-inspectors at Ballinamult and at Cappoquin reported that crowds of fifteen hundred and five hundred, respectively, were ‘calling on farmers’ to demand reimbursement. Intimidated, many farmers ‘promised to pay up’.[7] Around Dungarvan, laborers told farmers ‘that unless the money be refunded by a given day, they will come back and thrash as much corn . . . as will not alone pay the conacre tenant, but likewise compensate him for seed, labour, &c.’. Cognizant that ‘many such cases’ went unreported, a magistrate ordered the arrest of twelve ‘captains’—a term applied to leaders of factions and agrarian secret societies—but there were difficulties in identifying these men, because their *modus operandi* was to have ‘strangers’ convey their demands.[8] Thomas Fitzgerald, who had found himself in a position to observe the movement, reported that they ‘appeared altogether strangers to this side of the country. They advanced with regularity and order . . . armed mostly with sticks. There was no appearance of intoxication among them’.[9] Another witness detailed visits which the crowd paid to several farmers:

> Darby Brien, Ballymacart, was attacked in a violent manner, dragged about, and compelled to pay back to . . . his workmen £1.5.0. They then visited David Hourigan. Having told them he had no money, they threw down part of a stack of corn and said they would take it in lieu of the money. They then marched him to the old chapel, and on his promising to have it on Tuesday next, he was allowed to return home. They next visited Darby Harty of Hacketstown, took the half-door of his house, and demanded that £2.8.0 be refunded his workmen. Harty saw his own workmen among them. They threatened if he did not pay it Monday next they would take away his corn and murder him. . . . They also called to Mary Fegan, Glenwilliam, assaulted her, and threatened to visit her again if she did not refund David Foley £6 before Sunday next.[10]

The nature of conacre laborers’ relationships with such farmers can be glimpsed in a number of pre-Famine parliamentary enquiries. For instance, evidence from twenty-three Waterford informants to the Poor Inquiry of 1836 indicates that the overwhelming majority of laborers were paid, either in full or more commonly in part, in conacre or ‘dairy ground’ on which to plant potatoes. According to William Villiers Stuart (brother of Stuart de Decies), ‘the conacre when taken by the labourer from the farmer employing him is generally charged against his labour; and . . . very little money passes between the parties'. A Protestant clergyman observed that laborers around Lismore were paid in provisions and conacre 'much above the market price', and that when the crop failed the only alternatives were 'to beg or go to law'.[11] An equally indignant Waterford clergyman, giving evidence to the Devon Commission in 1844, judged 'the treatment of the labourers by the farmers more severe than the treatment of the farmers by the landlords'. Other witnesses to the Commission further illuminated these relationships. An auctioneer advised that farmers paid between £2 and £3 for land that they sublet in conacre for £4 to £6, that the laborer paid 'this off by his labour at 6d per day', and that in 'trying to clear off this charge he is constantly yoked to the farmer's employment'. Similar figures for rent and wage rates were given by other witnesses, indicating that it would have taken a Waterford laborer approximately two hundred days' labor to pay for an acre of 'dairy ground'.[12]

Waterford, then, was not unlike north Leinster, where William O'Reilly, a landlord near Ardee, observed: 'Every class in this country oppresses the class below it until you come to the most wretched class. . . . There are no exactions practiced on their superiors that they do not practice upon those below them'.[13] Indeed, by the eve of the Famine, the position of laborers was worse than it had been a decade or so earlier, not least as they were increasingly being obliged to pay rent in advance. Land agent James Galwey of Carrick-on-Suir explained: 'Formerly the tenants could distrain for the potatoes if they were not paid; now the people [conacre sub-tenants] must go to the usurers to get it, or pawn their clothes, to enable them to pay the money in hand for the half acre'.[14]

Such exploitative relationships had resulted in extensive and violent class-based conflict in east Munster. A secret society of laborers, the Caravats, had come into conflict with the Shanavests, representing the interests of better-off tenant farmers in the first decade of the nineteenth century. In the 1830s, these factions were succeeded by Poleens and Gows.[15] In considering the inheritors of the Caravat and Poleen tradition in September 1846, the *Waterford Mail* lamented that while the 'mutineers are well-known to the farmers whom they visited', no steps were being taken to prosecute them.[16] The O'Connellite *Waterford Freeman* was more understanding:

> We do not wish to defend the late disturbances in this and the adjoining counties; at the same time, we cannot speak harshly of them. 'Tis hard to argue starvation into quiet. . . . If we cannot meet their demand with a concession of food, we must not hastily deny their claims. Irritation to the feelings must not be added to the pressure on the stomach. The present time calls for a sacrifice of individual opinion—for the exercise of a boundless benevolence—for the promptings of a generous patriotism; it calls also for a lenient administration of the law.[17]

Sympathy for the cottiers was also expressed at a number of public meetings in Waterford. Moreover, it is clear that some concession with regard to conacre was being canvassed in the wider region as the wave of protest was building in September 1846. At a ‘numerous’ meeting attended by landlords, priests, farmers and laborers at Castlelyons, near Fermoy, County Cork, on 15 September, a Catholic priest asked that the predicament of laborers, in particular, be considered, and the meeting unanimously adopted the following resolution moved by a farmer named Towell: ‘That the conacre being the basis of the contract between the farmers and their labourers and the potato crop—the produce of the land—having entirely failed, a new arrangement of their relations is imperatively and immediately needed’. A resolution along the same lines was adopted by the Relief Committee of the Ballyhard district.[18] In short, then, even a cursory analysis of the conacre laborers’ protests in Waterford must restore consciousness and agency to those now frequently remembered as ‘mere hints of human beings’, and their collective action may be numbered among those movements of protest characterized by Alain Badiou as ‘interesting failures’.[19]

A MORAL ECONOMY?

The wave of demonstrations by Waterford conacre laborers was but one of many different movements of protest in the course of the Great Famine. Indeed, there were protests too by people belonging to classes above the laboring poor. For instance, tenant farmers mobilized for forgiveness of rents and poor rates. In one remarkable demonstration in September 1846, a thousand Protestant farmers marched from Arva, County Cavan, to Ballinalee, County Longford, to support the demand for rent reductions made by a predominantly Catholic tenantry.[20] As for interventions by the laborer and cottier class intended to shift the attitude of local notables or the policy of governmental agencies, they were mainly in relation to ensuring a supply of food. However, there were also militant collective acts aimed at securing and retaining employment.

To the extent that they have discussed Famine protests, historians have tended to treat them as elemental ‘rebellions of the belly’—almost physiological responses to food deprivation—rather than as efforts to enforce justice.[21] There have been exceptions, notably Andrés Eiríksson, whose research on Counties Clare and Limerick uncovered considerable evidence of social protest informed by a sense of ‘moral economy’ in the early stages of the Famine.[22] This study, drawing principally on ‘outrage’ reports for late 1845 and all of 1846, concerns protests throughout the entire country, and broadly supports Eiríksson’s findings in this regard.

The concept of a moral economy, as elaborated by E.P. Thompson, has informed much of the historiography of popular protest.[23] Based on his analysis of the eighteenth-century English crowd, Thompson’s moral economy was essentially a social contract, which protected working families and the poor from the vagaries of the provisions market. Several historians have since illuminated the operation of comparable arrangements in eighteenth-century Ireland.[24] For instance, there were laws against monopolistic practices (engrossing, forestalling and regrating) in marketplaces; there were laws regulating the assize of bread; there were legal prohibitions on food exports, on distilling and on the feeding of grain to cavalry horses during periods of scarcity. Popular protests drew occasional attention to failures to enforce such laws, to provide customary entitlements or to show consideration when conditions were adverse. With the growing hegemony of doctrines of political economy placing an emphasis on free trade, official intervention in the marketplace became ideologically unacceptable to governing élites. Poor people continued to expect protection and consideration, however, and showed this by mobilizing at times of scarcity, sometimes to insist that the authorities enforce the law or comply with custom, and sometimes to themselves enforce the law or custom. Notwithstanding the use of terms like 'riot' and 'mob', such protests were usually relatively peaceful and restrained, exemplified by *taxation populaire*, whereby the populace seized over-priced or otherwise controversial foodstuffs, sold them in the public marketplace at what was considered to be a 'fair price', and then paid over that price to the owner. Scrupulosity of this character conveyed the message that the crowd was the moral actor, reinstating equitable dealing where unscrupulous merchants or traders had been taking advantage of scarcity to secure excessive profits at the expense of the poor.[25]

The historian Joe Lee has suggested that disputes about conacre contracts sometimes 'served as a surrogate form of food riot' in Ireland.[26] Certainly, the west Waterford protests described above exhibited features of a Thompsonian 'moral economy of the poor', and if there was intimidation, there was little violence. In one instance an item of property (a half-door belonging to Darby Hart) was impounded as collateral, but those deemed to be malefactors were afforded opportunities of making restitution. The confidence of those involved that they had combined for a moral purpose was underlined by their assembling in broad daylight, and in their conveying the recalcitrant farmer David Hourigan to a sacred site cum public place, the old chapel, to make a formal undertaking to refund his laborers within a week.

FOOD EXPORTS

Food prices were an obvious concern of the poor in periods of scarcity. Hence, in bad seasons, the purpose of much collective action was to disrupt the removal of foodstuffs from a community or to prevent speculators from securing opportunistic profits at the expense of consumers. Urban and village crowds in many parts of Ireland impeded the loading of ships and barges, while country people obstructed farmers taking their produce to sell in town. If the authorities had to be alert to the possibility of unrest during periods of scarcity, compromises were frequently reached with anti-export crowds allowing ships to leave port when civic or voluntary bodies adopted price-reduction measures, such as subsidizing staple items.[27] Again, protest was not a response to actual or apprehended shortage, per se; rather, it was a response to perceived breaches of a social contract and an attempt to assert moral entitlements. Thompson held that it was not possible to mobilize a crowd of ordinary citizens for a purpose that they did not themselves believe to be a moral one. People did not protest against a ‘visitation of god’, therefore, but against those individuals and human institutions they identified as acting immorally or as failing to fulfill their social responsibilities. The perception held by such protesting crowds that food scarcity was liable to be exacerbated by speculators receives support in the writings of the economist Amartya Sen, who has shown that famines tend to result from distribution bottlenecks, in which sections of the population are unable to assert their entitlement to adequate nourishment, rather than from an absolute shortage of food.[28]

Consequently, at the time of the Famine, there was a well-established repertoire of protest to regulate the food trade centered on four key locations—seaports, the inland waterways, roads and marketplaces. In the port town of Galway, grain exports had been obstructed in 1808, 1812, 1817, 1827 and 1831, and there were other mobilizations to reduce prices in 1829 and 1842.[29] The Claddagh fishing community usually played a leading part in such movements. Hence, in mid-November 1845, with ‘excitement among the working classes’ and with threats having been made to ‘sink the first ship laden with corn attempting to put to sea’, resident magistrate John Kernan calculated that the threats could not be given effect without the fishermen. Consequently, he visited the Dominican priory in Claddagh, whose friars had a long history of ministering to that community, and who, Kernan knew, had great influence in the area. The friars duly dissuaded the fishermen from involving themselves in any effort to obstruct the export of food.[30] There were similar interventions by Catholic clergy in other places.[31]

There were limits to the influence of clergymen and friars. Some days after the intervention of the Dominicans in the Claddagh, a crowded public meeting called at the behest of the ‘trades of the town’ heard a ringing endorsement for the assertion, derived from Scripture, that it was ‘better to die trying to keep the food at home than to die later of starvation’.[32] Anonymous notices posted around the town carried the same message: ‘It is better to die by the sword than to die of starvation’.[33] The authorities responded to the alarm of merchants and magistrates by sending an Admiralty steamer to Galway Bay and moving two additional regiments into the town, thereby ensuring that grain continued to leave the port. As in previous seasons of scarcity, the Galway crowd anticipated that prices would rise precipitously during the following spring and summer if food exports were allowed. In February 1846, Kernan reported that the town was peaceful because the ‘civil authorities now have sufficient force’, and that ‘the assembling of this force will have the effect of overawing the mob’.[34]

Notwithstanding the second failure of the potato in 1846, there was a new grain harvest for export. Sustained riotous protest in the streets of Galway in October led the authorities to once again deploy armed boats in order to 'protect the river between Claddagh and the shipping so as to prevent their crossing in the hookers . . . in case the Claddagh men should be persuaded to join the townspeople'.[35] Frustrated, the people placed blockades on the eastern side of the town to prevent provisions leaving by road, in the belief that their needs should be addressed before those of people in distant places. A merchant complained that the 'mob are administering oaths to the carmen that they will not even attempt to carry out flour or meal'.[36] The town commissioners, fearing that public order was on the point of collapse, borrowed £500 'on the security of the tolls' and purchased Indian meal, 'to be retailed to the poor in small quantities under cost price, and prevent, if possible a recurrence of violence and outrage'. This move, however, did not appease the crowd. Concerned that disorder was preventing relief provisions from reaching the people of the inland town of Tuam, a Catholic priest organized a vigilante escort. This escort met stiff resistance, and on 8 October, Bridget Kelly, one of a blockading crowd, was killed in a clash with the vigilantes.[37] A state of high excitement persisted, with Kernan reporting in January 1847:

> On my return to Galway on Friday, I found the town in a great state of excitement, the people enraged against the millers and corn factors were with the greatest management kept down and prevented from attacking the stores. The Claddagh fishermen who are now in the greatest state of destitution, were with great difficulty kept to their own locality by the [Dominican] clergy of the West Convent and promises from me of my endeavouring to get employment for them . . .[38]

Clearly indignant at the treatment of the poor, Kernan reported that 'the millers are so completely masters of this market that they charge what prices they like . . . and that their arrangements, one with the other, as to prices was such that no private interference can check their monopoly and extortion'.[39]

The Admiralty, which had been assisting in the importation of Indian meal, instructed the crews of its vessels to 'preserve their character and efficiency as men-of-war', and to remain ready to 'assist the civil powers in the case of outbreak'. Twelve men-of-war, including the *Stromboli*, which was based for a period in Galway, and five other Admiralty vessels were now deployed at strategic points along the coast.[40] The likelihood of arranging successful popular blockades to prevent food exports was consequently much less than it had been during previous periods of scarcity and public alarm. It is noteworthy, however, that the administration's focus on lawless Ireland during the crisis allowed communities affected by the potato crisis elsewhere in the United Kingdom to take effective action to protect their own food supply. In the east of Scotland, where there had not been any food riots for a generation, the absence of naval and military forces gave people relatively free rein in this regard. Eric Richards estimated that there were more than forty ‘locations of riot’ in a two-month period between January and March 1847, mostly involving fishing communities between Banffshire and Caithness. The export of grain from the entire region was completely stopped.[41]

However, there were some successful Irish efforts to prevent the removal of provisions by ship, most especially in small and medium size ports, where the military and naval presence was slight. For instance, in Westport, County Mayo, at 5 a.m. on 21 September 1846, a crowd of six to seven hundred people obstructed access to the quays, declaring that they wouldn’t ‘allow one grain of corn to leave the country as they were starving’, and forcing the return to the stores of a convoy of merchants’ carts. According to a police inspector ‘they did not offer the slightest violence’.[42] Similar scenes had been witnessed in Tarbert, in north Kerry, in April 1846, when a ‘mob’ gathered to prevent the *Vulcan* departing for nearby Ballybunion with a hundred barrels of Indian meal. There followed a stalemate, reported a magistrate, explaining his reluctance to use force on the grounds that ‘there has been no attempt at plunder but merely to prevent it being taken away’.[43] In the same month, in Dungarvan, where a merchant complained that he had been intimidated into ceasing grain exports, the resident magistrate requested military reinforcements so as to avert ‘disturbances about provisions’.[44] That autumn, the Dungarvan fishing community acted in a manner similar to the people of the Claddagh around the same time, and a few months later fishing communities in Scotland acted similarly. On 30 September and 1 October 1846, with several thousand people gathered on the outskirts of the town, the resident magistrate Howley reported that he had deployed soldiers ‘for the protection of these gentlemen who were shipping on yesterday’. The soldiers ‘cleared off the crowd who commenced stone throwing’, whereupon ‘workmen who were loading the vessel became so intimidated by the yells and threats that they struck work’. It was women who were making the threats. Fishermen who had blockaded the port with their boats during the previous days had taken advantage of favorable conditions to go fishing. In their absence, the grain merchants became emboldened, but the women of the community had come out and remained out, ‘bodies of them relieving each other at intervals’ through the night. Their demand at this point was for a supply of cheap meal, indicating that the purpose of the blockade had changed and that the grain was being held as security against future hunger or high prices rather than itself remaining the principal object of the protest. Although undertaking to allow loading to recommence when relief provisions arrived, the women refused to accept mere promises in this regard and remained in the streets. The police having been forced to withdraw, Howley called up a body of Hussars. They too were assailed with stones. Notwithstanding the seriousness of the matter at issue, the *Waterford Freeman* reported the outcome of the encounter in jocular fashion: 'This great triumph on the part of the women of Dungarvan over the British troops is every night since celebrated on the Quay amidst dancing, singing and shouting, which are all kept up with unabated and most edifying perseverance . . .'.[45] Although the disorder had presented challenges for Howley—and he had given the orders that resulted in a man's death—he was not without sympathy for the demonstrators. He advised his superiors that 'a few individuals have the entire command of the food and charge what prices they please'. He pleaded for the opening of a relief depot so as to 'check their monopoly'.[46]

Fifteen miles from Dungarvan, in Youghal, there were similar scenes, involving 'a large concourse' composed of townspeople and laborers from nearby rural places who had been attending a public meeting. When the meeting had broken up, the people remained for a time at the Mall, before advancing to the quays, boarding vessels that were loading grain and refusing to allow any of them to sail. Corn merchants' stores were blockaded, and all carloads of grain entering the town were 'driven out by force'. To the consternation of the authorities, the crowd took control of the portcullis bridge linking the Counties of Waterford and Cork, and raised it so as to hinder trade and to inconvenience the military. On 23 September, some hundreds of laborers from the Waterford side marched with their spades into Youghal, causing further alarm and stirring the local Relief Committee into action. The Committee put the men to work 'levelling a hill', and 'large placards stating this and announcing a reduction in the price of meal were conspicuously posted throughout the town'.[47]

Youghal is located at the mouth of the River Blackwater, along whose banks determined efforts were being made to prevent food exports during the same period. Requesting the assistance of a 'war steamer' early in October 1846, Baron Stuart de Decies emphasized that the corn trade 'between Lismore, Cappoquin and Youghal . . . was entirely suspended owing to the opposition made by the peasantry to the passage of corn'. The boatmen engaged did not recognize any of their attackers, 'and even if they did they would not prosecute'.[48] And there were efforts to disrupt the movement of grain in other districts along the river. Determined crowds assembled at several points, and even the deployment of two naval patrol vessels had not the desired effect. When Commander Fisher of the *Stromboli* found a barge owner who was willing to be escorted to Youghal, a hostile crowd followed all the way to that port.[49]

Commotion on the inland waterways was predictable. In previous periods of dearth, assemblies of the poor, anxious to prevent the removal of food to Dublin, had disrupted the potato and grain trade on the Royal and Grand Canals. Hence, in 1845 and 1846, the canal companies and civil authorities anticipated trouble, and took action to reduce its impact. Barges on the Grand Canal moved in convoys under escort and the number of soldiers stationed along its banks was greatly increased. Nonetheless, great difficulties were experienced in the efforts to convey the 1846 harvest to Dublin and other cities.[50] These difficulties included an intended blockade by 'the lower orders' on the Grand Canal between Ballinasloe and Shannon Harbour and an attack on a barge laden with provisions 'by an unknown number of persons' on the Newry Canal just outside Portadown.[51] In short, canal-side populations took measures similar to those they had taken during the crises of 1812 and 1817.[52] On the Fergus, Clarecastle, from where grain and flour from the Ennis area was shipped to the city of Limerick, had likewise been a flashpoint during previous periods of scarcity.[53] Now, on 5 October 1846, a crowd of between four and five hundred obstructed the loading of a boat with oats. A similarly sized crowd turned back cargoes at the same place on 10 November and again on 24 November. About twenty miles away at O'Briensbridge, on the Shannon, on 28 October, a crowd of 'several thousands' assembled, with a view to preventing the removal of food from Denniston's mill to the Limerick market. Notwithstanding a dozen-strong police escort, vessels carrying freshly milled oatmeal and flour were turned back at the first of the two locks on the short canal crossing a loop on the River Shannon. Popular price-fixing was apparent in the action of the same 'mob' in extracting a promise from the mill-owner to 'sell his meal at 2s 8d per stone' as long as he could buy oats at 1s 8d per stone. For their part, the leaders of the crowd assured him that they would 'persuade' the local farmers to supply him at that price.[54] Similar price-fixing was recorded in other places. At Scarriff, County Clare, an estimated five to six hundred people extracted a promise from a mill-owner that he wouldn't charge more than 2s 3d per stone for flour, and 2s for meal. When he protested that he would lose money at such prices, they promised that if the farmers would not sell 'at such a price as would enable him to keep himself safe, they would go and thresh every stock yard in the County and bring him the grain'. On discovering some people had earlier paid the mill-owner 2s 6d for meal, they forced the purchasers to go back to the mill and secure a refund of the difference.[55] In an attempt at price-fixing in Ballinasloe, a crowd prevented farmers from supplying a merchant, Mr. Horseman, with grain, instructing them to bring it instead to a Mr. Hood's stores. The latter evidently retailed 'small quantities at moderate prices, which the people alleged Horseman did not do'.[56]

On Saturday 7 November, at Timoleague in west Cork, four hundred people assembled at a mill with a view to obliging the owner to lower the price of his meal. The owner called the magistrates who remained with a force of police until nightfall, while the miller sold his meal to 'every person who requested it in small quantities at so reasonable a rate as he said he could afford'.[57] In Dunfanaghy, County Donegal, in May 1847, local people intervened at an auction for the insurers Lloyd's, when the cargoes of two recently wrecked ships were offered for sale. There are several accounts of the episode, including one in the memoir of Hugh Dorian, all of which confirm that the local people reached an accommodation with the authorities. According to one newspaper, the people 'declared that Providence had sent them the supply, and that when in great distress a wreck with provisions was sure to happen on their shore'.[58] The resident magistrate reported that the people showed 'a strong desire to prevent the sale of the Indian corn, except on terms regulated by themselves', and that the purchaser of an entire cargo, 'through a feeling of humanity, gave up his right, and Mr Forster [the auctioneer], with unwearied diligence continued to dispose of it in small quantities to every person in the neighbourhood who required it'.[59]

In May 1846, 'strangers' from Armagh and Monaghan bought carts of potatoes from farmers en route to the market of Aughnacloy, County Tyrone, with a view to selling the loads themselves at a higher price. They were attacked and beaten by the crowd. In a separate incident outside Aughnacloy later on the same day, two cartloads of potatoes were scattered all over the road.[60] In this instance, as with another in Kilmacthomas, County Waterford, where grain was 'scattered throughout the road,' it is not clear whether the scattering of the food was the accidental result of conflict, or a deliberate and punitive act on the part of the crowd, as frequently occurred in food riots in England. Certainly, a punitive destruction of oatmeal, by throwing it into the river, was threatened in the episode mentioned at O'Briensbridge in County Clare.[61]

Roads, meanwhile, were blocked in many places by crowds of people determined to prevent movement of food out of their area. In Killeagh, County Cork, in September 1846, 'the people' would not allow corn to be taken to the market and farmers found to have already sold grain were obliged by the crowd to pay a fine, presumably relieving them of 'unjust' profit. In the villages of Broadford and Hospital, County Limerick, the people were on alert to the extent that many farmers and merchants ceased trying to send their corn to market in Limerick.[62] In the parish of Grange, County Waterford, during the unrest of September–October 1846, five hundred men visited farms insisting that farmers not sell their grain, and promising that if landlords tried to force them, they would 'deal with the landlords'. In Birdhill, County Tipperary, 'a triumph to the people' was recorded in November 1846, when car drivers obeyed their instruction to cease conveying grain to Limerick for export.[63]

If crowds acted to prevent food from being taken from local communities, there were also groups, acting in the name of 'the people', who, disguised or under cover of darkness, tried to interrupt the food trade. Nocturnal enforcers of popular justice were especially active in the northwestern counties, from Roscommon to Donegal, where they frequently described themselves as Molly Maguires, and to a lesser extent in Clare, where the militants were usually known as Terry Alts. Likewise, on the eve of the Famine, the magistrates of County Longford wrote to the lord lieutenant to convey their apprehension about the spread of agrarian militancy from Leitrim, a county that they described as already 'actually in the possession of the peasantry, who have quite interrupted the ordinary course of business'.[64]

On several evenings during the latter half of September 1846, farmers in Ballycar, County Clare, were visited by up to ten 'armed men, dressed in women's clothing and with blackened faces', who warned them not to thresh any corn for market. Near Ballyshannon, County Donegal, the tail was cut off a cow to punish its owner for selling potatoes to the police, and in Glenties, in the same county, two cows were similarly injured to deter their owner from exporting potatoes.[65] At Ballykilty, County Clare, in November 1846, a notice was posted warning farmers not to send corn to market and 'not to charge more than 1s 6d per stone at home'. On the following evening, fourteen armed men, most of them with blackened faces, visited a number of farmers and beat them as punishment for selling corn, warning them not to repeat the offense. Another man was admonished for allowing his horse to be used to transport grain. In the previous month, two horses had been shot dead and one wounded 'on their way with corn to the market of Ennis'.[66] At Drumsilla and Ballyycalla, about fifteen miles apart in the south of the county, on the same night in September 1846, several horses were killed because their owners had brought grain to Limerick market on the previous day. A magistrate blamed 'a union of small farmers and labourers, who have joined together to intimidate rich farmers, preventing them from selling their corn outside of the county'.[67] Some of the nighttime interventions were of a milder character. Near Dunmore, County Galway, a large trench was cut in the road to prevent horses and cars with grain from passing in October 1846, and there was a similar incident on the road between Strokestown and Ballintubber, County Roscommon. Men hoping to get paid to carry out repairs were said to have dug the trench.[68]

APPROPRIATION OF FOOD

Eiríksson, in his survey of Famine-time food riots, draws a distinction between acts informed by a moral economy and straightforward acts of theft or plunder.[69] The distinction is not always clear-cut. Sometimes, individuals or groups took advantage of the shelter provided by a predominantly 'moral' crowd; sometimes, crowds angered by the authorities' response to a protest turned to looting; sometimes, the smell of fresh bread simply proved too tempting for people long deprived of food. And it was not unknown for bakers to preempt or to assuage gatherings outside their own premises by 'voluntarily' distributing bread. In some robberies of food, those involved displayed considerable restraint, perhaps indicating that they were reluctant thieves. Transport constraints may also have been a factor.

Although it is not always possible to draw firm conclusions about episodes where a small quantity of food was taken from a large consignment, there is some evidence of 'moral' restraint. In October and November 1846, for example, David Wakefield, who supplied the Ballinasloe Lunatic Asylum, reported that crowds that 'used no violence' had twice halted his drivers at Clonfert, County Galway. One bag was taken on the first occasion and seven on the second, with the drivers advised to cooperate, or they 'would take all of it'.[70] In November 1847, a man engaged in transporting flour between Birr, King's County, and Shannon Harbour reported that thirty men surrounded his convoy, while crying out, 'hunger, hunger'. Assuring the drivers that they wished them no harm, they said they would take just one sack from each car.[71]

There were instances too where food stolen in the heat of protest was returned to its owners, but it is not clear whether it was returned due to a desire to escape a punitive reaction or on account of some 'moral' factor. In September 1846, hundreds of men demanding employment in Killeagh, County Cork, removed several bags of flour from the village mill and bread from the bakeries. The flour was later 'returned uninjured'. In November 1846, in Castletownroche in the same county, the police were unable to prevent the removal of a ton of flour but, on the following day, it 'was returned or at least a part of it was'. Evidently, this protest achieved its object, for the owner of the flour announced he was ceasing to sell grain outside of the community.[72]

Police were on hand also in Ballybay, County Monaghan, when two hundred 'ragamuffins' assembled on the evening of 6 October 1846 in response to a notice calling a meeting of 'poor labourers' to discuss how their condition might be ameliorated. Afterwards, those attending called to the bakers' shops in the town, where they were given bread. The police did not 'interfere' because the bakers did not seek their help.[73] At O'Briensbridge, several hundred people who had been engaged in a negotiation with a mill-owner about the price of meal reassembled on a nearby hill, from where they marched and proceeded to break open and rob a bakery. At Listowel, County Kerry, a few days later, six hundred people who had been protesting outside the workhouse about inadequate pay on the public works went together to a bakery, where they were given £5 worth of bread, after offering the owner the choice of surrendering it voluntarily or having it taken forcibly. Protesting crowds in Cloyne and Youghal, County Cork, behaved in a very similar fashion in September 1846.[74] In Belfast and Armagh in December, there were negotiated appropriations at bakeries, with those involved citing desperate necessity in justification for their non-observance of the law.[75] In April 1847, a Youghal baker whose premises were being attacked protested to the five hundred-strong-crowd that he had 'always helped them in the past', to which the leader of the crowd responded, 'we cannot help it, we are starving'.[76] This justification echoes in *seanchas* (oral history) collected from the children of Famine survivors—it was 'no sin and you starving to steal whatever you could'—and in stories of priests forgiving theft: for instance, around Moycullen, County Galway, it was remembered that the 'people were told from the altar that they should always ask for food first but that in extreme cases they need not hesitate to take it in the event of a refusal'.[77]

Acts of piracy—a number of which were reported during 1847—bear comparison with theft from meal carts and bakeries, not least in terms of the sometimes semi-apologetic demeanor of the attackers. Raids on vessels at sea or taking shelter near the shore were particularly common and determined along the Mayo coast.[78] The county's singularity in this respect may be explained by the inability of much of the population in its northern half to access relief and by the incapacity of an over-stretched Admiralty (although there were arrests and at least one fatality). The largest raid was on 10 January 1847 when five vessels laden with food took shelter in Elly Bay, not far from Belmullet, an especially impoverished and neglected place. Three to four hundred people gathered on the beach, and numbers managed to board the ships. Reporting that he had never seen such 'objects of perfect misery', a seaman wrote that the people said that they 'had come to take away the cargo and that hunger and starvation had driven them to it'.[79] Three months later, at Black Rock, north of Achill, ten boats with fourteen men on each pulled alongside a schooner laden with wheat. According to the mate of the vessel, the raiders did not behave in a violent fashion, but 'merely said that they wanted the wheat to eat'. Conversely, *seanchas* from Mayo records that sympathetic crews 'would take pity on them and give them any amount of meal they wanted'.[80]

Of the many incidents of animal stealing, most took place at night, but sheep and cattle were occasionally 'distrained' by crowds in broad daylight, mimicking but subverting the legally sanctioned seizures for debt by landlords for rent and civic authorities for cess or rates. The purpose of these popular seizures of livestock was to oblige their owners to show more consideration toward the poor. Early in November 1846, several flocks of sheep were driven into East Cork from the 'the neighbouring county' (Waterford), those responsible announcing that they would not surrender them until a 'subscription had been entered into'. In May 1847, in the village of Carrigtwohill in the same area, people protesting against a reduction in the daily meal ration from the relief depot seized five sheep from each of four gentlemen farmers, and brought them to a point opposite the local Constabulary barracks. According to a police officer, the people did not intend 'to destroy these sheep but merely acted in the manner they did for the purpose of intimidating persons to comply with their demands'.[81] From Ferns, County Wexford, a magistrate reported that a crowd of three hundred men had called to his house, told him that they would 'take away sheep for food', but did not carry out the threat because of the consideration he had previously shown toward them. From a neighboring farm, however, a cow was taken and later sold back to the owner for £2, and there were also other similar incidents.[82] At Butlerstown, in West Cork, and at Bruree, County Limerick, cattle were taken but returned unharmed. At Skibbereen and Ballinspittle, County Cork, Dingle, County Kerry, Enniscorthy, County Wexford, and near Portumna, County Galway, crowds threatened to take away cattle if their demands for relief were not met. In the latter instance, three hundred people assembled at 'several gentlemen's houses' to deliver their demand for the provision of either employment or food.[83] The appropriation of food, then, seems to have been frequently negotiated.

'PROTOCOL OF RIOT'

A 'protocol of riot' has been discerned in contention about food in early nineteenth-century England, with offenders against popular morality first placed on notice to mend their ways, then becoming the focus of an orderly demonstration, and only being subjected to blockade, appropriation or another penalty if they remained recalcitrant.[84] Circumstances 'out of doors' often made it difficult to fully observe such a protocol, and this difficulty was particularly apparent during the Famine years when the bargaining position of the poor was limited by access to food and the state and committees of the well-to-do determined who would get employed on the public works and other relief schemes. A community might be denied sustenance in punishment for a collective protest or other act of 'outrage'.

Nonetheless, many venerable forms of protest were practiced in these years. One of the most salient, as mentioned above, was a single individual

Figure 1.1 A demonstration outside a bakery in Dungarvan, County Waterford

Source: Pictorial Times, 10 October 1846. A loaf of bread is raised on a stick to signify that there is food in the community, but high prices have pushed it beyond the reach of the poor.

carrying a loaf on a long pole marching at the head of a procession. This symbol, representing distress, had appeared in pre-Famine mobilizations, and, again, it featured in one of the most-widely reproduced images of the Famine, a sketch of the Dungarvan disturbances of October 1846, first published by the *Pictorial News* of London.[85] Indeed, it was used by demonstrators in all four provinces, notably at protests in Portumna, Ballinasloe and Tuam, County Galway,[86] in Parsonstown, King's County, in Ballinalee, County Longford, in Ballyconnell and Virginia, County Cavan, in Croom, County Limerick and in Cork city.[87] Ciarán Ó Murchadha has identified two variations: the foremost demonstrator of a group on the road between Doneraile and Mallow, County Cork, carried a diseased potato on a pole; a group of laborers at Skibbereen marched behind a man with a loaf fixed to his spade.[88] Again, the point made by the loaf was that there was food in the community, but high prices had pushed it beyond the people's reach. And it was not a specifically Irish symbol. The 'mourning loaf' sometimes surrounded by black crepe or even dipped in blood has been discussed by historians of English food protests.[89] The slogan 'bread or blood' was often associated with the mourning loaf in England. That slogan—which led to the East Anglian disturbances of 1816 being remembered as the 'Bread or Blood Riots'—was used in a threatening notice posted during anti-export protests in Galway as early as the spring of 1817, and in the course of the Great Famine it was heard in the cities of Limerick and Kilkenny, as well as in Listowel, County Kerry.[90]

ON THE PUBLIC WORKS

Seanchas from several parts of the country contains many allegations that 'officials, gangers, timekeepers, etc., got most of the money' allocated for public works. Hence, it is not surprising that these projects were the scenes of protest, demonstration and tumult.[91] Unlike Famine-time food protests, militancy on public works has received considerable attention in the historiography. However, similar mentalities informed both types of action. Surveying the midwest, Eiríksson argues that the earliest agitation on public work schemes was directed at overseers and stewards, with the objective of dissuading them from discharging workers, reducing wage rates or being too exacting. There was a spike in activity in late summer of 1846, when there were large-scale demonstrations, riots and even strikes in response to threatened reductions in wages. Fresh outbreaks occurred in opposition to piece-work in November 1846 and again in April and May 1847 when the authorities started to wind up the relief works.[92] In places, collective action had a positive effect on wage rates on relief works. Moreover, the achievement of higher wages by laborers in one area—such as the Clare laborers, described by Eiríksson—encouraged protest on relief works elsewhere. For instance, after two incidents in the Gort area of County Galway in November 1846, one involving five armed 'Terry Alts' and the other sixty-five laborers, a Board of Works inspector reported, that 'all along the borders of County Clare, men are in a state of insubordination, as they know that in Clare men get a shilling a day and they say they are dissatisfied with their own eight pence, and they will not undertake task work'.[93]

A sense of entitlement to employment in circumstances of great want informed many demonstrations. While the largest protests targeted relief committees and presentment sessions, some were directed at individuals. People gathered at the houses of landlords and well-to-do farmers in efforts to influence their conduct as grand jurors or members of boards of guardians or relief committees, or simply to appeal for work. In September 1846, near five hundred men and boys visited several 'gentlemen's houses' in the neighborhood of Omagh, County Tyrone, to demand employment. There was a similar report from Dunshaughlin, County Meath.[94] Sometimes, the demand for employment from landlords and large farmers was, at least in part, an attempt to press them into voting for relief works at special presentment sessions. For instance, in September 1846, when one hundred men, recently dismissed from public works around Arva, County Cavan, visited farmers and demanded work from them, it seems their real objective was to get public works restarted.[95]

Of all protests asserting an entitlement to employment, perhaps the most dramatic were in County Waterford. On the night of 13 September 1846, and on a number of subsequent nights, ahead of special presentment sessions for the Dungarvan area, the 'country was lighted as a far as eye could see with signal fires' and crowds were 'traversing the country, shouting and making the most hideous noises'. These demonstrations, which coincided with the vociferous anti-export and conacre protests in the same region, were intended to 'have an effect on the landed proprietors and cess-payers attending the sessions', specifically, the protesters hoped to get works commenced immediately and the wage rate set at a shilling a day. On the day of the sessions, four thousand people surrounded the Dungarvan courthouse, refusing to allow those attending to leave until they gave guarantees in relation to wage rates. There were similar scenes at sessions around the country. For instance, a siege of the courthouse at Newbliss, County Monaghan, was only lifted when commitments on wage rates were given by cess-payers.[96] Various other methods were used to press for 'fair' wages, including the holding of public meetings, the intimidating of officials and threatening laborers who worked under the 'fair' rate. Indeed, laborers in the parish of Donaghmore, County Tyrone, went on strike for higher wages in January 1847.[97]

Once works were established, there was intense competition to secure places on them, and there was trouble in the spring and summer of 1846 when relief committees issued more work tickets than there were positions.[98] In July 1846, when a relief committee in Tralee, County Kerry, restricted workers to a three-day week and started to pay them in Indian meal rather than cash, two to three hundred men went on strike, marching to other projects in the vicinity, 'compelling any there working to join them'.[99]

Intimidation and violence against 'strangers' were reported from many counties, including Longford and Roscommon.[100] A determined crowd, indignant at outsiders taking their jobs, caused the suspension of works near Castlebar in mid-August 1846. A threatening notice pithily expressed their grievance: 'We the lower part of the parishioners of Islandeady call on you who are at work on the Upper District—contrary to our wish and against our interest—to at once withdraw from said work, or else ye will mark the consequences with loss of life'.[101] In Ballymacelligot, County Kerry, in November 1846, seventy people working on the roads were assailed by some fifty others who 'pelted them with clods'. The attackers, who had been laid off the previous week, were given employment. Christine Kinealy has suggested that the robbery of wages was not common on work schemes, and some robberies and threatened robberies were merely claims of entitlement, that is, attempts to recover unpaid wages. For example, it was reported that two hundred men assembled on 8 December 1846 in Newcastle West, County Limerick, intending to rob a pay clerk. They did not succeed, and it transpired that these men had worked for a week without relief tickets and were merely attempting to get paid for the work they had done.[102]

Opposition to the introduction of task work, as James S. Donnelly, Jr. has pointed out, was sometimes prompted by its adverse impact on potential earnings, but more commonly by objections on the grounds of equity. Resistance to task work took many forms. For instance, in Westport, County Mayo, in late August 1846, three to four thousand protestors compelled workers to listen to 'inciting addresses' before dispersing at the urging of the local priest. Similarly, speakers at a rally of a thousand laborers carrying spades in Ballinspittle, County Cork, in November 1846, declared that they would 'supply themselves with food from the property of the neighbourhood' rather than consent to task work. On this occasion, three Catholic priests failed to disperse the protestors.[103]

CONCLUSION

Michael Davitt need not have been ashamed of his parents' generation. In late September and early October 1846, in particular, hundreds of thousands of people mobilized on docksides, canal quays and thoroughfares across Ireland to prevent the removal of provisions from their communities, and the authorities responded with extraordinary measures to protect the provisions trade. If collective action failed to close Irish ports, it at least diverted a portion of the grain destined for export to the domestic market. Moreover, as hunger and disease spread across the country, ordinary people acted together to render less humiliating the mechanisms by which limited state relief was offered to them. In often dehumanizing conditions, they had asserted not only their right of existence, but their own humanity. Such movements of protest and resistance arose during the initial stages of famines elsewhere, only to subside as conditions worsened.[104] In the case of the Great Famine, changes in the mechanisms of relief provision and in other circumstances would cause the established repertoire of protest to become redundant during 1847, but sporadic altercations at soup kitchens, insubordination in workhouses, and refusal of the terms under which outdoor relief was offered indicate that the impoverished people of Ireland did not become completely passive.[105] Further research will illuminate changing levels and patterns of popular political activity in the face of hunger and disease.

NOTES

1. In acknowledging the assistance of NUI Galway's College of Arts Summer Internship Scheme, I wish to express my gratitude to Florry O'Driscoll, Aibhlín O'Leary and Claire Smith for their contribution to the research for this article.
2. Michael Davitt, *Fall of Feudalism in Ireland; or, The Story of the Land League Revolution* (London and New York, 1904), 47. I am grateful to Laurence Marley for this reference.
3. *Irish Times*, 14 May 2012.
4. William Fraher, 'The Dungarvan Disturbances of 1846 and Sequels', and Des Cowman, 'Some Local Responses to the Famine, 1846–48', in Des Cowman and Donald Brady, eds., *The Famine in Waterford, 1845–50: Teacht na bPrátaí Dubha* (Dublin, 1995), 137–52, 239–62.
5. P.C. Howley to Under-Secretary, 3 October 1846, National Archives of Ireland (NAI), Outrage Papers, 1846/29/26911; hereafter Outrage Papers.
6. Police Sub-Inspector to Stuart de Decies, 26 September 1846, Outrage Papers, 1846/29/26359.
7. W. Slattery to Stuart de Decies, 2 October 1846; Thomas Fitzgerald to Stuart de Decies, 1 October 1846; 29/27091 Stuart de Decies to Under-Secretary, 7 October 1846, Outrage Papers, 1846/29/26761.
8. P.C. Howley to Under-Secretary, 3 October 1846, Outrage Papers, 1846/29/26911.
9. Thomas Fitzgerald to Stuart de Decies, 1 October 1846, Outrage Papers, 1846/29/26761.
10. Stuart de Decies to Henry Labouchere, 26 September 1846, Outrage Papers, 1846/29/26359.
11. *Poor Inquiry (Ireland), Supplement to Appendix D, Answers to Questions Circulated by the Commissioners Relative to the Position of Agricultural Labourers*, HC 1836 (36), xxxi, 1, 252, 254, 256.
12. Samuel Clark, *Social Origins of the Irish Land War* (Princeton, NJ, 1979), 36–38; James S. Donnelly, Jr., *The Land and People of Nineteenth-Century Cork: The Rural Economy and the Land Question* (London, 1975), 19–22.
13. Cited in K.T. Hoppen, *Elections, Politics, and Society in Ireland, 1832–1885* (Oxford, 1984), 95.
14. *Report of Her Majesty's Commissioners of Inquiry into the State of the Law and Practice in Respect to the Occupation of Land in Ireland, together with Minutes of Evidence, Part III*, HC 1845 (657), xxi, 1, 428, 445–46, 448; Clark, *Social Origins*, 29–30.

15. P. E. W. Roberts, ‘Caravats and Shanavests: Whiteboyism and Faction Fighting in East Munster, 1802–11’, in Samuel Clark and James S. Donnelly, Jr., eds., *Irish Peasants: Violence and Political Unrest, 1780–1914* (Dublin, 1983), 64–101; Brendan Kiely, *The Connerys: The Making of a Waterford Legend* (Dublin, 1994), 9–21.
16. *Waterford Mail,* 30 September 1846.
17. *Waterford Freeman,* 7 October 1846.
18. Ibid.
19. *Guardian*, 18 May 2012.
20. John B. Gracies to Under-Secretary, 22 September 1846, Outrage Papers, 1846/4/25311.
21. A recent example of the tendency to treat the subject of Famine-era protest cursorily is Crowley, Smith and Murphy, *Atlas of the Great Irish Famine* (Cork, 2012), in which popular protest takes up only two of almost seven hundred pages.
22. Andrés Eiríksson, ‘Food Supply and Food Riots’, in Cormac Ó Gráda, ed., *Famine 150: Commemorative Lecture Series* (Ballsbridge, 1997), 67–93. See also John Cunningham, *Galway, 1790–1914: A Town Tormented by the Sea* (Dublin, 2004), 125–61.
23. See ‘The Moral Economy of the English Crowd in the Eighteenth Century’, *Past and Present,* 50 (1971), 76–136, reprinted in his *Customs in Common* (London, 1991), 185–258, alongside ‘The Moral Economy Reviewed’, 259–351. Also see James C. Scott, *The Moral Economy of the Peasant: Rebellion and Subsistence in Southeast Asia* (New Haven, 1977).
24. Eoin Magennis, ‘Regulating the Market: Parliament, Corn and Bread in Eighteenth-Century Ireland’, in Michael Brown and Sean Patrick Donlon, eds., *The Law and Other Legalities of Ireland, 1689–1850* (Farnham, 2011), 209–30. Other studies dealing with the moral economy in the Irish context include Andrés Eiríksson, ‘Crime and Popular Protest in County Clare, 1815–52’ (PhD thesis, Trinity College Dublin, 1991); Michael Huggins, *Social Conflict in Pre-Famine Ireland: The Case of County Roscommon* (Dublin, 2007); Roger Wells, ‘The Irish Famine of 1790–1801: Market Culture, Moral Economies and Social Protest’, in Adrian Randall and Andrew Charlesworth, eds., *Markets, Market Culture and Popular Protest in Eighteenth-Century Britain and Ireland* (Liverpool, 1996), 163–93; Eoin Magennis, ‘In Search of the Moral Economy: Food Scarcity in 1756–57 and the Crowd’, in Peter Jupp and Eoin Magennis, eds., *Crowds in Ireland,* c. *1720–1920* (Basingstoke, 2000), 189–211; idem, ‘The Hearts of Steel and Agrarian Crowds in the Armagh/Down Borderlands in 1772’, in Allan Blackstock and Eoin Magennis, eds., *Politics and Political Culture in Britain and Ireland, 1750–1850* (Belfast, 2007), 242–61; John Cunningham, ‘Popular Protest and a “Moral Economy” in Provincial Ireland in the Early Nineteenth Century’, in Fintan Lane, Niamh Puirséil and Francis Devine, eds., *Essays in Irish Labour History: A Festschrift for John and Elizabeth Boyle* (Dublin, 2008), 26–48; John Cunningham, ‘“Compelled to Their Bad Acts by Hunger”: Three Irish Urban Crowds, 1817–45’, *Éire-Ireland*, 45, 1–2 (2010), 128–51.
25. Cunningham, *A Town Tormented by the Sea*, 86–87; Cunningham, ‘Three Irish Urban Crowds’, 128–29.
26. Lee, ‘Patterns of Rural Unrest’, 226.
27. See Cunningham, ‘Three Irish Urban Crowds’ and Eiríksson, ‘Popular Protest in County Clare’, 194–206.
28. Amartya Sen, *Poverty and Famine: An Essay on Entitlement and Deprivation* (Oxford, 1983), 1–8 and *passim.*
29. Cunningham, ‘Three Irish Urban Crowds’, 146–47.
30. Cunningham, *A Town Tormented by the Sea*, 126–27.

31. Enda Delaney, *The Curse of Reason: The Great Irish Famine* (Dublin, 2012), 133–34.
32. *Galway Vindicator,* 22 November 1846.
33. Cunningham, *A Town Tormented by the Sea*, 128. The biblical reference here is to Lamentations 4:9: 'Better are those slain with the sword than those slain with hunger'.
34. Ibid., 128.
35. Ibid., 134.
36. Rush and Palmer to T.N. Redington, 5 October 1846, Outrage Papers, 1846/11/26995.
37. *Galway Vindicator,* 7, 14 October 1846.
38. Ibid.
39. Ibid.
40. *Belfast Newsletter*, 6 October 1846.
41. See Eric Richards, *The Last Scottish Food Riots* (Oxford, 1982).
42. Sub-Inspector Denis Walshe, Report of Outrage, 21 September 1846, Outrage Papers, 1846/21/26029.
43. N. Keane to R. Pennefather, Coast Guard Office, 23 April 1846, Outrage Papers, 1846/12/10175.
44. Fraher, 'The Dungarvan Disturbances', 137–52; Cowman, 'Some Local Responses', 242–45.
45. *Waterford Freeman,* 3 October 1846.
46. P.C. Howley to Chief Secretary, 29 September 1846, Outrage Papers, 1846/29/26315; P.C. Howley to Chief Secretary, 3 October 1846, ibid., 1846/29/26959.
47. *Waterford Mail,* 26 September 1846.
48. Stuart de Decies to Henry Labouchere, 6 October 1846, Outrage Papers, 1846/29/26961; Sub-Inspector Slattery to Stuart de Decies, 4 October 1846, ibid., 1846/29/27299.
49. High Pigot to T.N. Redington, 26 September 1846, Outrage Papers, 1846/29/25987.
50. Ruth Delany, *The Grand Canal of Ireland* (Dublin, 1995), 163–64.
51. John Eyre to the Lord Lieutenant, 27 October 1846, Outrage Papers, 1846/11/29591; W. Miller to John Persse, 23 January 1847, ibid., 1847/2/53.
52. Cunningham, '"Moral Economy" in Provincial Ireland', 33, 41–42.
53. Ibid., 44, and Cunningham, 'Three Irish Urban Crowds', 142, 146.
54. John Ryan to Sub-Inspector Gallway, 29 October 1846, Outrage Papers, 1846/5/29929; —— to ——, 29 October 1846, 1846/5/30367; 'Limerick—Navigation History', *Inland Waterways News,* 28, 2 (2001).
55. T. Dailey to T. N. Redington, 30 October 1846, Outrage Papers, 1846/5/29941.
56. G. Fitzgerald to Constabulary Office, 14 October 1846, Outrage Papers, 1846/11/28027.
57. Thomas Lucas to Lord Bernard, 9 November 1846, Outrage Papers, 1846/6/31291.
58. Hugh Dorian, *The Outer Edge of Ulster: A Memoir of Social Life in Nineteenth-Century Donegal*, ed. Breandán Mac Suibhne and David Dickson (Dublin, 2000), 225–26, 224n.
59. B.H. Holmes to Under-Secretary, 15 May 1847, Outrage Papers, 1847/7/143.
60. R. Conlon to T.N. Redington, 15 May 1846, Outrage Papers, 1846/28/11819.
61. Robert Studdert and four others to Earl of Bessborough, 20 October 1846, Outrage Papers, 1846/29/29035, 5/29933; John Stevenson, *Popular Disturbances in England, 1700–1832* (2nd ed., London, 1992), 130, 318–20.
62. Quin Going to H. Labouchere, 12 October 1846, Outrage Papers, 1846/17/27705.

63. [Constabulary Sub-Inspector] to Stuart de Decies, 26 September 1846, Outrage Papers, 1846/29/26359; Illegible, Castleconnell, to T.N. Redington, 1 November 1846, 1846/17/29875.
64. Thomas Jessop and thirteen other Longford magistrates to Lord Lieutenant, 16 July 1845, Outrage Papers, 1845/19/15409.
65. Leyne to T.N. Redington, 24 September 1846, Outrage Papers, 1846/5/25309; B.H. Holmes to Under-Secretary, 15 September 1846, ibid., 1846/7/18917; B.H. Holmes to Under-Secretary, 18 June 1846, ibid., 1846/7/19319.
66. Leyne to T.N. Redington, 12 October 1846, Outrage Papers, 1846/5/27697; Leyne to T.N. Redington, 2 November 1846, ibid., 1846/5/31105.
67. Leyne to T.N. Redington, 22 September 1846, Outrage Papers, 1846/5/25629; Leyne to T.N. Redington, 23 September 1846, ibid., 1846/5/25631.
68. Thomas Blakeney, report of outrage, 6 July 1846, Outrage Papers, 1846/25/20051.
69. Eiríksson, 'Food Supply and Food Riots', 68.
70. David Wakefield to T.N. Redington, 24 October 1846, Outrage Papers, 1846/11/29375; Fitzgerald to T.N. Redington, 8 November 1846, ibid., 1846/11/30877.
71. John Supton to Thomas Hackett, 27 November 1847, Outrage Papers, 1847/15/[Not Numbered].
72. Illegible, JP, Killagh, County Cork, to Constabulary Office, 26 September 1846, ibid., 1846/6/25979; Arthur Grove Annesley to H. Labouchere, 2 November 1846, ibid., 1846/6/30457.
73. Arthur French to T.N. Redington, 6 October 1846, Outrage Papers, 1846/23/27157.
74. William Sands and four others to Lord Lieutenant, 29 October 1846, Outrage Papers, 1846/12/30085; Francis Rowland to W. Knaresborough, 23 September 1846, ibid., 1846/6/25897; Postmaster, Youghal, to illegible, 21 September 1846, ibid., 1846/6/25593.
75. M. Singleton to unnamed official, 17 December 1847, Outrage Papers, 1846/2/37127; Walter Moloney to Chief Secretary, 18 December 1846, ibid., 1846/1/35927; Christine Kinealy and Gerard Mac Atasney, *The Hidden Famine: Hunger, Poverty and Sectarianism in Belfast* (London, 2000), 62–63.
76. John Judge and John Duggan to Thomas John, JP, 7 April 1847, Outrage Papers, 1847/6/655.
77. Cathal Póirtéir, ed., *Famine Echoes* (Dublin, 1995), 74, 80.
78. Hugh Pigot to T.N. Redington, 10 January 1847, Outrage Papers, 1847/21/53; A. Bishop to Randolph Routh, 18 January 1847, ibid., 1847/21/66; W.J. Williams to Hugh Pigot, 16 April 1847, ibid., 1847/21/240; P. Coles to Hugh Pigot, 26 April 1847, ibid., 1847/21/270; A.R. Dunlop to Hugh Pigot, 25 April 1847, ibid., 1847/21/288; Fred Cary to the Inspector-General of the Coast Guard, 4 July 1847, ibid., 1847/21/397; Liverpool Marine Assurance Company to George Grey, 27 July 1847, ibid., 1847/21/405; J.L. Wood to T.N. Redington, 17 August 1847, ibid., 1847/21/441; Sub-Inspector Blake, report of outrage, 4 October 1847, ibid., 1847/21/473; Edwd Hickman, Crown Solicitor, to Under-Secretary, 7 September 1847, ibid., 1847/26/251.
79. J. Aylen to Hugh Pigot, n.d., Outrage Papers, 1847/21/53; Katrina Lavelle, 'The Famine in Belmullet, Co. Mayo, 1845–1849' (MA thesis, NUI Galway, 2011), 43–51.
80. W.J. Williams to Hugh Pigot, 16 April 1847, Outrage Papers, 1847/21/240; Póirtéir, ed., *Famine Echoes*, 77.
81. Arthur Grove Annesley to Henry Labouchere, 3 November 1846, Outrage Papers, 1846/6/30457; W. Knaresborough to T.N. Redington, 14 May 1847, ibid., 1847/6/786.

82. A.B. Manifold to OPW, 30 April 1847, NAI Outrage Papers, 1847/31/141.
83. Thomas Lucas, JP, and eight others to Lord Lieutenant, 19 February 1847, Outrage Papers, 1847/6/340; J. Johnstone to T.N. Redington, 21 October 1847, ibid., 1847/17/1725; Sub-Inspector, Bandon, report of outrage, 6 August 1846, ibid., 1846/6/22025; R. Pennefather to Chief Secretary and two others, 16 April 1846, ibid., 1846/27/9087; John Hickson to Chief Secretary, 22 November 1847, ibid., 1847/12/523, Carew to T.N. Redington, 30 April 1847, ibid., 1847/31/137.
84. John Bohstedt, *Riots and Community Politics in England and Wales, 1790–1810* (Cambridge, Mass., 1983), 3–7.
85. Cunningham, 'Three Irish Urban Crowds', 137–38; *Freeman's Journal,* 17 June 1840; *Pictorial Times,* 10 October 1846.
86. R. Pennefather to Chief Secretary, 16 April 1846, Outrage Papers, 1846/27/9087; G. Fitzgerald to T.N. Redington, March 1847, ibid., 1847/11/284; T. Stenson, 'Disease and Death in a Galway Town: How the Town of Tuam Responded to the Great Famine, 1845–50' (MA thesis, NUI Galway, 2010), 27.
87. John Warburton to T.N. Redington, 8 September 1846, Outrage Papers, 1846/15/23459; W. Markey to T.N. Redington, 4 October 1846, ibid., 1846/4/26803; *Anglo-Celt,* 18 September 1846; *The Times,* 22 September 1846; *Freeman's Journal*, 16 May 1846.
88. Ciarán Ó Murchadha, *The Great Famine: Ireland's Agony, 1845–1852* (London, 2011), 58.
89. Stevenson, *Popular Disturbances in England*, 129; Bohstedt, *Riots and Community Politics,* 7.
90. Graham Seal, 'Tradition and Agrarian Protest in Nineteenth-Century England and Wales', *Folklore*, 99, 2 (1988), 146–69; Cunningham, *A Town Tormented by the Sea,* 88; Tom Donovan, 'Bread or Blood', *Old Limerick Journal,* 32 (1995), 66; *The Times,* 11 December 1846; *The Nation*, 5 December 1846.
91. Póirtéir, *Famine Echoes*, 154, 157, 158.
92. Eiríksson, 'Food Supply and Food Riots', 78–80, 84–85.
93. John O'Flaherty to R. Trephook, 16 November 1846, Outrage Papers, 1846/11/31653.
94. R. Conlon to Henry Labouchere, 25 September 1846, Outrage Papers, 1846/28/25925; John Christie to T.N. Redington, 8 December 1847, ibid., 1847/22/316.
95. John B. [unclear but probably Gracie] to Under-Secretary, 1 September 1846, Outrage Papers, 1846/4/23597.
96. P.C. Howley to Under-Secretary, 14 September 1846, Outrage Papers, 1846/29/23895; P.C. Howley to Under-Secretary, 15 September 1846, ibid., 1846/29/24069; P.C. Howley to Under-Secretary, 18 September 1846, ibid., 1846/29/24081; Brian MacDonald, '"A Time of Desolation": Clones Poor Law Union, 1845–50', *Clogher Record,* 17 (2000), 39–40. For a siege in Kells, County Meath, see —— to T.N. Redington, 23 November 1846, Outrage Papers, 1846/22/34165.
97. Constable Cornsby to Board of Works, 20 February 1847, Outrage Papers, 1847/28/92.
98. Cunningham, *A Town Tormented by the Sea,* 130–31.
99. George Stokes to Lord Lieutenant, 10 July 1846, Outrage Papers, 1846/12/20521.
100. J. Mulrany to Board of Works, 9 July 1846, Outrage Papers, 1846/16/5173; Thomas Barton to Board of Works, 10 January 1846, ibid., 1846/25/1027.
101. M. Walker to T.N. Redington, 23 August 1846, Outrage Papers, 1846/21/22915.

102. Christine Kinealy, *This Great Calamity: The Irish Famine, 1845–52* (Dublin, 1994), 94; Capt. Dill, Royal Engineers, to Secretary, Board of Public Works, 8 December 1846, Outrage Papers, 1846/17/34619.
103. James S. Donnelly, Jr., *The Great Irish Potato Famine* (Stroud, 2001), 76; Kinealy, *This Great Calamity,* 94; Cuthbert, Kinsale, to Chief Secretary, 11 November 1846, Outrage Papers, 1846/6/31475.
104. Cormac Ó Gráda, *Famine: A Short History* (Princeton, NJ, 2009), 52–56.
105. Eiríksson, 'Food Supply and Food Riots', 84–88; Gerard Moran, ' "Disorderly Conduct": Riots and Insubordination in the Workhouses during the Great Famine', in John Cunningham and Niall Ó Ciosáin, eds., *Culture and Society in Ireland since 1750: Essays in Honour of Gearóid Ó Tuathaigh* (Dublin, 2015), 160–80; Cunningham, *A Town Tormented by the Sea,* 148.

2 'The Tottering, Fluttering, Palpitating Mass'

Power and Hunger in Nineteenth-Century Literary Responses to the Great Famine

Melissa Fegan

That literature and politics were intermeshed in nineteenth-century Ireland was evident in what were arguably the country's two most significant journals—the *Dublin University Magazine* (1833–77) and *The Nation* (1842–8; second series 1849–96). The *Dublin University Magazine*, 'the supreme archive of Irish Victorian experience',[1] was subtitled 'A Literary and Political Journal', and contributors frequently addressed the intersection of the two spheres. An article in March 1837, 'Past and Present State of Literature in Ireland', asserted that 'the literature of a nation, and of this nation in particular, is affected by its political state and influential upon it'.[2] The *Nation*'s ambition 'to create and foster public opinion, and make it racy of the soil' was underpinned by its literary contributions; the publication of *The Spirit of the Nation* (1843–5), and the fact that so many poets were involved in the 1848 rising, illustrates the symbiotic relationship of poetry and politics in the Young Ireland project. 'The art of nineteenth-century Ireland moves under the shadow of the political',[3] and the gloomiest shadow of all was cast by the Great Famine, which abruptly ended what had been 'a remarkable period of cultural and intellectual growth' in Ireland.[4] The consequences for the Irish publishing industry were catastrophic, with seventy-three publishers declared bankrupt between 1844 and 1848.[5] The notable survivor, James Duffy, warned the novelist William Carleton in 1855 that 'the people seldom think of buying books, because they are luxuries, which they can do without'.[6] Carleton had been proud that unlike Moore, John Banim, and other Irish writers, he had been able to build a successful career in Ireland, but now he too was forced to look to the London market, only to discover, as the Irish-born publisher John Maxwell informed him, 'the Irish are not able to buy' novels set in Ireland, while 'the English will not'.[7] In the last years of the Famine, the poets James Clarence Mangan, John Keegan, and John de Jean Frazer, suffered miserable deaths in their forties from malnutrition and disease. Mangan's final poems, written while he was dying in the Meath Hospital, Dublin, in 1849, were incinerated by a nurse. The poet and journalist Thomas D'Arcy McGee fled to the United

States following the 1848 Rising. John Mitchel and Kevin Izod O'Doherty were transported to Van Diemen's Land for treason-felony as a result of their articles in *The United Irishman* and *The Tribune*. O'Doherty's fiancée, Mary Kelly, who met him while he was imprisoned, was one of the most famous of the *Nation*'s poets, writing as 'Eva', and O'Doherty's transportation led to her eventual emigration, first to Paris, then to Australia. Richard D'Alton Williams, a poet and publisher of the *Irish Tribune*, was also tried for treason-felony and narrowly escaped conviction, but moved to America in 1851. The cultural consequences of mass mortality, emigration, and forced social change were profound, perhaps most notably in accelerating the decline of the Irish language in the post-Famine period, which all but silenced what Denvir describes as 'the public voice of the dispossessed, a discourse of rights and revolts from below',[8] poetry in Irish.

In the worst years of the crisis itself, the public voices of both Young Ireland and the dispossessed being censored or silenced, middle-class observers from both home and abroad proved crucial in drawing attention to the sufferings of the poor and attracting charitable donations and government relief. Letters from doctors, priests, and vicars were published in British newspapers, and narratives of journeys to hard-hit locales such as Skibbereen and Schull by Irish, British, and foreign—particularly American—travellers proliferated. Laurence M. Geary suggests that 'a degree of anthropological inquiry or even ghoulishness' may have given impetus to some of these journeys, but generally it was 'an overriding sympathy for and sense of duty to their fellow man' that prompted them.[9] Those who read these descriptions were usually geographically and experientially far removed from such scenes; the *Times* represented the typical metropolitan reader of Famine reports as a 'gentleman in a dressing-gown, with a devilled drumstick on his plate, and a game pie in reserve'.[10] Writers had to work hard to persuade such a reader of the reality and accuracy of their testimony. In his recollections of the Famine in north Donegal, Hugh Dorian, himself an intimate of the hungry, renders an Irish proverb, *Ní thuigeann an sách an seang*, as 'The satiated never understands the emaciated'.[11] The British government initially seemed inclined to agree with Dorian; Peter Gray notes that Peel made few efforts to promote charitable donations either within Great Britain or abroad, believing there was little sympathy for the starving.[12] Donations for famine relief arrived from other nations with a history of hunger, such as India, Jamaica, and Antigua; perhaps most memorably, the Choctaw tribe sent $710 in 1849.[13] However, the widespread observation of the National Day of Fast and Humiliation on Wednesday 24 March 1847, while emanating from and giving state sanction to a providentialist interpretation of the Famine as punishment for unspecified sin,[14] suggests a sincere (if short-lived) attempt by 'the satiated' to express sympathy for and solidarity with 'the emaciated', and may be some measure of the success of fictional and factual narratives in representing the plight of the Irish poor.

'HUNGER'S A CRUEL HEART'

William Carleton describes his desire to provoke sympathy for Famine victims as 'the paramount wish of the author's heart', and 'one of the purposes' for which his novel *The Black Prophet* (1847) was written. Such a novel, Carleton adds, published at such a time, 'when our countrymen are perishing in thousands for want of food, ought, one would imagine, to excite a strong interest in the breasts of all those who can sympathize with them under sufferings so desolating and frightful'.[15] Carleton invites readers who can to sympathize, but does not presume them capable of the imaginative leap necessary to empathize with those who are nevertheless 'our countrymen'. There are few first-person narratives from the perspective of Famine victims in prose fiction, perhaps suggesting an uneasy awareness of the ethical and aesthetic problems of appropriating or comprehending the voice of the victim. There are isolated examples, but even these involve a certain distance; for obvious reasons, the narrator is unlikely to die in the course of a novel or short story. Mary Anne Hoare's 'Little Mary: A Tale of the Black Year' is narrated by Sally, a maid in a Big House, whose parents and sister Mary die during the Famine. Randy O'Rollick, narrator of Carleton's *The Squanders of Castle Squander* (1852), is peasant-born, but as a servant of the Squanders is preserved from want during the Famine, and is forced to participate in the extermination of his former neighbors.

Those who wrote—or at least those who managed to get their writings into print, and whose work has survived—were not the starving, but usually middle-class witnesses who were often terrified, disgusted, and alienated by them. Dorian, who became a schoolteacher, had come out of the lower-class, and he later recalled that during the Famine 'the poor were treated and despised as if they were beings of quite a different creation'.[16] Even Carleton, who like Dorian was born into a smallholding family, describes in *The Black Prophet* 'wild and wolfish' crowds of 'famished maniacs' besieging the homes of the middle classes like demonic zombies: 'the fire of famine blazed so savagely in their hollow eyes, that many of them looked like creatures changed from their very humanity by some judicial plague that had been sent down from heaven to punish and desolate the land'.[17] The editor of the *Nation*, Charles Gavan Duffy, saw beggars on the streets of Galway in 1849 'more debased than the Yahoos of Swift—creatures having only a distant and hideous resemblance to human beings'.[18] Alexander M. Sullivan recalled scenes around the 'brutal public soup-boiler' where 'there daily moaned and shrieked and fought and scuffled crowds of gaunt, cadaverous creatures that once had been men and women made in the image of God'.[19] Ironically, Carleton, Duffy, and Sullivan had all dedicated their work to challenging stereotypes of the Irish as inferior, yet confronted by the effects of the Famine they characterize their stricken countrymen as degraded and subhuman. The tendency in both fiction and factual writing is to privilege the abject horror of the bystander struggling to comprehend and articulate the scale of the disaster, which David Lloyd has referred to as 'the much-theorized unrepresentability of the traumatic event, being registered as a shock suffered by observers who do not themselves undergo the perils of starvation'.[20] Sullivan's emotional response is a complex mix of pity, disgust, shame, fury, and powerlessness, foregrounding his own pain: 'I frequently stood and watched the scene till tears blinded me and I almost choked with grief and passion. It was heart-breaking, almost maddening to see; but help for it there was none'.[21] Similarly, Samuel Ferguson's poem 'Dublin' describes the city as a 'hell-on-earth' where the middle-class speaker is assaulted by 'the weakling infants' moans, / The mother's sobs, the maddened father's groans', and his health undermined by what he sees:

> Who, without shortened days, could daily pass
> The tottering, fluttering, palpitating mass,
> Who gaze and gloat around the guarded dole,
> That owned a heart of flesh, or human soul?[22]

His solution is to emigrate.

Ferguson's poem and other English-language verse of the Famine are products of 'well-intentioned middle-class reactions' rather than 'popular attitudes in areas where the famine was most intense'.[23] Still, as Chris Morash argues, these poems express the sincere 'attempt at understanding [. . .] that is at the basis [of] any movement towards an adequate response to atrocity'.[24] The immediacy and lyric sensibility of poetry seem to provide a license to employ the viewpoint of the dying not often afforded by prose fiction. The speakers are frequently plaintive, as in John Keegan's 'The Dying Mother's Lament', Elizabeth Willoughby Varian's 'The Irish Mother's Lament', John Walsh's 'Lament of the Ejected Irish Peasant', W. C. B.'s 'Lay of the Famine: The Irish Husband to his Wife', or T. C. D.'s 'The Last Appeal': 'By this bleak ditch-side must I fall unknown, / And none to raise my fever'd head, weak, famine-struck, alone?'[25] However, the anonymous 'The Song of the Famine', published in the *Dublin University Magazine* in July 1847, depicts the poor not as sentimental passive victims, but as internally riven, tormented individuals. The speaker is a mother who feels 'a strange, strange joy' at the death of her son, not just because his suffering has ended, but because it means more food for her: 'hunger's a cruel heart, / I shudder at my own'.[26] Famine releases 'horrid instincts', and the wealthy are warned to beware spurning the famishing, for fear their 'loathing madness' may turn to 'reeking crime'. If they cannot sympathize with the starving, perhaps self-interest will spur the rich to charity. Hunger also turns the poor against each other in the struggle for food:

> The strongest snatch it away from the weak,
> For hunger through walls of stone would break—
> It's a devil in the heart![27]

The speaker is haunted by 'hideous scenes / I cannot shut from my sight';[28] unlike the speaker of 'Dublin', she cannot emigrate to escape them. Remarkably, this intense and striking poem immediately precedes an article on 'Agricultural Resources of the Kingdom' which introduces squeamish scruples about whether the Famine can or should be written about at all:

> in a recent number we expressed at great length, and with much consideration, our views as to the extent of the calamity, the means for alleviating its pressure, and the duties and responsibilities of the state. Having thus done so, having so far discharged our duty, we can have no inducement to recur to it again. The subject is a painful, an intensely painful one, it is one upon which men must feel too deeply to write or to talk unnecessarily.[29]

The value of the *Dublin University Magazine*'s combination of the literary and political becomes clear in this conjunction of poem and article; 'The Song of the Famine' seems licensed to engage graphically and emotively with the social and psychological consequences of the Famine on the poor, while the author of the accompanying prose article feels duty-bound to avoid such 'painful' areas as much as possible, while providing important statistical evidence about the state of the country.

In their essay 'Recent Irish Poetry' in the *Dublin Review* in April 1865, John and Frances Cashel Hoey credit Lady Wilde with condensing memories of the Famine in her 1864 collection *Poems by Speranza*, containing many of the poems she wrote for the *Nation*:

> the corpses that were buried without coffins, and the men and women that walked the roads more like corpses than living creatures, spectres and skeletons at once; the little children out of whose sunken eyes the very tears were dried, and over whose bare little bones the hideous fur of famine had begun to grow; the cholera cart, with its load of helpless, huddled humanity, on its way to the hospital; the emigrant ship sending back its woeful wail of farewell from swarming poop to stern in the offing; and, far as the eye could search the land, the blackened potato-fields, filling all the air with fetid odours of decay.[30]

Wilde (then Jane Francesca Elgee), like many Irish writers, had not been seriously politically engaged until the Famine radicalized her. While Duffy was in jail, she wrote a seditious—suppressed—article for the *Nation*, 'Jacta Alea Est' ('The Die is Cast'), calling for rebellion. This new patriotic fervor was dashed by the failure of the 1848 Rising; like its leaders, Wilde failed to recognize the disjunction between her own outrage and the incapacity of Famine victims to physically act it out. 'I do not blame the leaders in the least', she wrote to Duffy, 'in Sicily or Belgium they would have been successful'.[31]

Despite her expectations of blood sacrifice by the poor, Wilde's poetry displays a sensitive engagement with their agony, often making powerful use of a dialogue between a baffled middle-class observer and a Famine victim. 'The Famine Year' offers a series of questions—'Weary men, what reap ye?', 'Pale mothers, wherefore weeping'—that allow the horrors of the crisis to emerge from the perspective of mothers, fathers, and children watching loved ones die: 'We left our infants playing with their dead mother's hand: / We left our maidens maddened by the fever's scorching brand'.[32] 'The Exodus', Wilde's response to the 1851 Census (documented, ironically, by her future husband), disrupts the calm, cold statistical reckoning of the million dead, the 'units [. . .] read by our statesmen sage', with a reminder that these were 'Men that were made in the image of God'.[33] As Matthew Campbell argues, she 'granted her famine victims indignation and eloquence in the face of their suffering',[34] but she also criticizes their passivity: 'What! Are there no MEN in your Fatherland[?]' asks the speaker in 'The Enigma', unable to understand why they have not rebelled:

> Are your right arms weak in that land of slaves,
> That ye stand by your murdered brothers' graves,
> Yet tremble like coward and crouching knaves,
> To strike for freedom and Fatherland?[35]

This would become a common trope in nationalist and republican writing on the Famine; Michael Davitt decried the 'measureless, unadulterated, sickening shame' of 'the complete surrender of all the ordinary attributes of manhood by almost a whole nation, in the face of an artificial famine'.[36] Few of Wilde's victims seem to have recourse to any option but death or rebellion; the call for immediate violence in 'The Enigma' is muted in 'The Exodus' and 'The Famine Year', which suggest this vengeance can take place only after death, when a 'ghastly, spectral army' will indict the guilty on Judgment Day. Even the speakers of 'The Itinerant Singing Girl' and 'The Voice of the Poor', who are granted a measure of agency in their ability to survive through work, long for release: 'Lord, grant us *Death*!'[37] Intriguingly, Morash suggests that the enduring popularity of Famine poetry like Wilde's depended on the fulfillment of this death wish: the obliteration of those she and others tried to give voice to, through death, emigration, and fewer and later marriage, the increased adoption of English, and the consolidation of the rural middle classes 'eased the disjunction between image and audience that had existed when the poems were first published'.[38]

HIERARCHIES OF SUFFERING

William Carleton hoped that the readers of *The Black Prophet* would include those who had the power to legislate to end the Famine. Carleton's novel, set during a previous famine in 1817, was published serially in the *Dublin University Magazine* from May 1846. Carleton added a dedication to Lord John Russell in the one-volume edition in early 1847, explaining:

> I cannot help thinking that the man who, in his ministerial capacity, must be looked upon as a public exponent of those principles of Government which have brought our country to her present calamitous condition, by a long course of illiberal legislations and unjustifiable neglect, ought to have his name placed before a story which details with truth the suffering which such legislation and neglect have entailed upon our people.[39]

The chief purpose of 'the first Tale of Irish Famine that ever was dedicated to an English Prime Minister' was to persuade him to 'put it out of the power of any succeeding author ever to write another'. Carleton follows the dedication with a polemical preface reinforcing his message that the government was responsible for the social and economic circumstances that allowed such famines to occur, and had the power and the obligation to assuage the suffering. There is no evidence that Russell read the novel, but Carleton's dedication was not politically naïve. Russell was himself a biographer and historian, and had published a novel, *The Nun of Arrouca* (1820), and a five-act play, *Don Carlos, or, Persecution* (1820), which was dedicated to the Whig politician Lord Holland. Russell had been a close friend of Thomas Moore, and edited Moore's *Memoirs, Journal, and Correspondence* (1853–6).[40] Another friend, Charles Dickens, was to dedicate *A Tale of Two Cities* to Russell in 1859. Like another future Prime Minister, Disraeli, who combined his political and literary careers, publishing influential novels such as *Coningsby* (1844), *Sybil* (1845), and *Tancred* (1847) while rising through the ranks of the Conservative party, Russell knew that literature and politics were not separate spheres, and literature had the potential to sway those who mattered in political life.

Like Carleton, Mary Anne Hoare presents her short stories (written during the Famine and published in several periodicals before collection in 1851) as pleas for immediate intervention by those in power: 'while I write, such things, and worse, if possible, are happening throughout our land'.[41] She praises 'the liberality of our English brethren', and in particular the work of the Society of Friends,[42] but she too draws attention to the failure of government: Carleton excoriates exportation during a famine, while Hoare exposes the inadequacy of the relief works. Both are also intent on portraying the poor as not wholly reliant on charity, but potentially resourceful. A repeated motif in Hoare's stories is the poor child rewarded for returning a valuable item to a wealthy person when her own family is starving. In 'The Knitted Collar', Mary, who 'alone of all the family tried *to do something*' to prevent her family perishing, uses the shilling she has earned knitting to buy bread, but returns money to the shop-boy who has given her too much change, drawing the attention of the kindly Miss Saville. Mary's honesty is contrasted with the dishonesty and meanness of Miss Saville's sister, Mrs. Elliot, who had bought Mary's knitted collar for much less than its value, and dismissed her description of the plight of her family as 'the old story'.[43] Charles Murphy in 'The Bog-Oak Shamrocks' finds and returns an antique coin and is rewarded with an education as an architect which lifts him and his family out of poverty. The eponymous Daniel Leary returns a gold pencil case dropped by Mr. Forrest, who is so impressed by his honesty he takes him to England as his servant; Daniel returns during the Famine to rescue his family, and Mr. Forrest gives them a cottage on his English estate. Those without wealthy patrons to rescue them must fend for themselves, like the Sullivans in 'A Sketch of Famine', who attempt to subsist on seaweed: 'Oh! if our English brethren could only have seen the famishing eagerness with which they devoured this wretched substitute for food, having obtained leave from a kind cottager to boil it on his fire, they would not wonder at the importunate cries for help which reach their ears from starving Ireland'.[44] Most of the family die horribly. In 'The Black Potatoes', Tade Mahoney, once an industrious laborer, is employed on the public works, earning eight pence a day—'poor wages, indeed, yet hailed by the perishing people as a blessed boon'[45]—absolutely inadequate for the support of Tade, his wife Jude, and their six children. Tade contracts typhus and dies; Jude chooses not to enter the workhouse, fearing the 'over-crowded pestilential precincts [. . .] where she would be separated from her children' (43–4). Failed by, or rejecting, state relief, the Mahoneys are dependent on their own resources, the help of family, and even of strangers. Tade's cousins Dennis and Jerry each take in one of the children. Jude and her other children are briefly sheltered by another poor family; the husband has worked on the Caherah road relief works for a week without wages, yet insists the Mahoneys share the family's only food—a pint of flour. Two of the children, and later Jude, die, and the remaining four children are rescued by Tade's brother James, who returns from America to seek them. The returned emigrant, or life-saving remittance, became the recurring *deus ex machina* of Famine literature, underlining the significance of self-reliance and family loyalty in the absence of adequate state support.[46]

In *The Black Prophet*, Carleton consistently blames government policy for creating famine conditions, and landlords and middlemen for exacerbating them. The landlord is an absentee drawing around £32,000 a year from the estate, yet sends only £100 for the relief of distress—which Carleton footnotes 'A recent fact'—and middlemen comprise 'one of the worst and most cruel systems that ever cursed either the country or the people'.[47] Yet he also excoriates two other groups in the rural community: forestallers—the 'vast number of strong farmers, with bursting granaries and immense haggards' who hold back their provisions until a year of scarcity when prices are high; and a 'still viler class', mealmongers—the 'hard-hearted and well-known misers' who 'prey upon the distress and destitution of the poor'.[48] However,

Carleton does not restrict his criticism to these objectionable figures; death and suffering are consequences of a wider failure of communal responsibility, in which the vulnerable are let down by their own families and neighbors, as well as those in power. Peggy Murtagh dies in Darby's shop, having been denied credit, but blame is not laid at his door with any certainty: whether she died 'from a broken heart, caused by sin, shame, and desertion, or from famine and the pressure of general destitution and distress, could never properly be ascertained'.[49] An unmarried mother, abandoned by her lover, rejected by her parents, Peggy has no refuge from starvation; the novel's enigmatic heroine Sarah M'Gowan prevents Peggy's lover from murdering Darby by persuading him: 'it wasn't he but yourself that starved her and her child. Who desarted her—who brought her to shame an' to sorrow in her own heart and in the eyes of the world?'[50]

The Black Prophet also demonstrates Cormac Ó Gráda's 'hierarchies of suffering',[51] differentiating between levels within the peasant 'class'. The Sullivans may be stinted, but they are wealthy enough to shelter Peggy, and later an orphan, and for Mave to donate meal to the Daltons. The fact that the formerly well-off Daltons are driven to begging is taken as a sure sign of the father's guilt of murder, as only God's displeasure could have brought them to such distress. The Black Prophet's wife Nelly spurns 'a poor famine-struck looking woman, with three or four children, the very pictures of starvation and misery', telling her: 'We're poor ourselves, and we can't help every one that comes to us. It's not for you now'. Nelly's refusal breaches the moral code of hospitality and charity among the poor, reflected in the many stories in the Famine folklore archive of the poor woman rewarded for sharing her meager supplies with someone worse off.[52] Sarah contradicts Nelly: 'You have it if you wish to give it. [. . .] If every one treated the poor that way, what would become of them?'[53] Famine novels frequently reveal the disparity between the relatively secure strong farmers and those with literally nothing, with all the gradations in between. In *Dick Massey* (1860), the narrator points out that 'Very few of those possessing even six or seven acres suffered want; it was the poor labourer and cottier who were doomed to starvation'.[54] In *The Hunger* (1910), stout Mrs. Meehan, the driver's wife, is ashamed when she meets her skeletal neighbors, while Mrs. Rafferty remarks that thanks to the kindness of the priest, the doctor, and the Quaker Goodbodys, 'it's in the height of luxury we are against manny places'.[55] In *Denis* (1896), Mrs. Cassidy says of the first year of the Famine: 'Troth, many were worse off nor us [. . .]. We kept off the Injy male anyway', while the Rooneys exemplify the worst fears of the charitable, using relief money to buy guns, dissembling poverty because 'the poor mouth's the mouth the praties 'll fall into, an' a poor mouth's the best mouth to make'.[56]

David Lloyd suggests that in *The Black Prophet* Carleton 'minimized the anger and resistance among the poor' and 'underplayed the rage that was often expressed in popular attempts to halt the daily export of foodstuffs from the country throughout the Famine years' in order not to antagonize his British readers.[57] Certainly, Carleton represents the initial response of the poor as 'timid' and 'furtive', stirred up by more well-off and mischievous characters such as Red Rody, who 'lead the misguided and thoughtless people into crime, and ultimately into punishment'.[58] But as the Famine progresses, the poor become infuriated, intercepting meal-carts on their way to market or exportation, and attacking mills: 'it was difficult to know where or how to prescribe bounds to the impetuous resentment with which they expressed themselves against those who held over large quantities of food, in order to procure high prices'.[59] They are degenerate and bestial—'There is no beast [. . .] in the deepest jungle of Africa itself, so wild, savage, and ferocious, as a human mob'; but if they have reverted to animals, their actions are instinctive and understandable: 'the most savage animals, as well as the most timid, will, when impelled by its ravenous clamours, alike forget every other appetite but that which is necessary for the sustainment of life'.[60] Carleton refuses to criticize them for it, stressing that the people are driven to their outrages by disease and misery: 'Indeed, if there be any violation of the law, that can or ought to be looked upon with the most lenient consideration and forbearance, by the executive authorities, it is that which takes place under the irresistible pressure of famine'.[61] When Darby's house is attacked, Sarah criticizes the people—particularly the women—not for taking the food, which they are badly in need of, but for wanton destruction, when 'there's many a starvin' mouth would be glad to have a little of what they're throwin' about so shamefully'.[62] In *Castle Squander*, Carleton defends those who emigrated without paying their arrears, as they were forced to do by the inequities of property rights. *Castle Squander* and *Red Hall; or the Baronet's Daughter*, both published in 1852, also refer explicitly to the most taboo of Famine survival strategies, cannibalism, emphasizing that it is performed not by ghouls, but by 'tender and affectionate' parents.[63] Frazer's 'The Three Angels', published in the *Cork Magazine* in August 1848, similarly suggests the lengths individuals could be driven to:

> Themselves and their kindred, thro' sheer despair,
> Some slew, in belief that *to slay* was *to spare*!—
> A cannibal fierceness but ill-suppressed
> In many—made some—we must veil the rest![64]

Horror is tempered with sympathy for what Carleton calls '*the insanity of desolation*'.[65]

CABIN SCENES: THE POWER OF PORTRAYAL

No encounter better exemplifies the mechanisms of power than that which takes place in a cabin, where those doomed to starve and those destined to survive come face to face. Sometimes this demonstrates the levelling or overturning of social hierarchies, when characters discover previously prosperous friends, neighbors, even family members in the throes of fever or starvation. In *Castle Cloyne*, Oonagh MacDermott, daughter of a strong farmer, who survives the Famine and prospers as a peddler, finds her cousin, once 'the beautiful Susie Burke, who, reared in comfort, had never known what pain or sorrow meant', now 'this wasted woman, prematurely aged, through whose yellow, shrivelled skin the sharp bones were working their way'.[66] In *Kingston's Revenge* (1917), a dying man discovered in a cabin with his two children asks merely for water and the door to be closed for fear of the dogs; he is recognized, by someone he often gave charity to, as Pat Mangan, once a 'comely, broad-built farmer'.[67] But the most potent examples are cabin scenes—both fictional and factual—which bring the gentry into direct contact, or even confrontation, with the starving.

In October 1849, four men entered a 'deserted' cabin in Kilkee, County Clare. One was the local inspector; two were prominent Anglo-Irishmen, the poet Aubrey de Vere of Curragh Chase, County Limerick, and William Monsell of Tervoe, who had been elected MP for County Limerick in 1847; and the last was an English Catholic, Henry Granville Fitzalan-Howard, Earl of Arundel and Surrey. The cabin was not in fact entirely deserted; inside they discovered a baby, its mother presumably having left it in search of food:

> On slightly moving the tattered coverlet of the cradle, a shiver ran over the whole body of the infant, and the next moment the dark, emaciated little face relapsed again into stillness. Probably the mother returned to find her child dead. Mr Monsell burst into a flood of tears. Nothing was said; but a few days later, on Lord Arundel's return to England, the inspector at Kilkee received a letter from him enclosing a cheque for two hundred pounds to be added to the local relief fund.[68]

What these four men saw could not have come as a surprise; the Kilrush Union was well-known to be one of the most distressed.[69] From July to December 1848, 6,090 people had been evicted in Kilrush Union, besides those who voluntarily surrendered holdings; Christine Kinealy adds that 'none of these people even possessed the means with which to emigrate'.[70] The men were clearly seeking such an encounter; they had passed the day, de Vere says, 'in roaming over famine-stricken moors and bogs in the neighborhood, then among the most severely tried districts in Ireland'.[71] De Vere and Monsell were heavily involved in famine relief efforts on their own estates; in October 1846 de Vere wrote to a friend of the desolate scenes he had witnessed 'in wilder parts of the country': 'In one day I have sat within nearly eighty mud hovels, without windows or chimneys—the roof so low that you could not (in some cases) stand upright, and within and around a mass of squalidness and filth'.[72] The Earl had come to Ireland, like many others, to see the impact of the Famine first-hand.[73]

Yet the reaction to the starving child suggests profound shock. De Vere stresses the emotional impact of the encounter for the men, which is both devastating and redemptive. De Vere links this scene not only with the Earl's donation, but with Monsell's letter to the Chief Secretary of Ireland, which de Vere suggests prompted 'Labouchere's letter', supplementing the Public Work Act by allowing reproductive works.[74] Matthew Potter emphasizes the profound public and personal transformations Monsell underwent in the 1840s and 1850s, from Anglican Tory to Catholic Liberal, a dual conversion greatly influenced by the Famine and the inadequate government response to it.[75] De Vere too converted to Catholicism in 1851, a year after Monsell; both were influenced in this much more by contact with Cardinals Manning and Newman than their own Catholic tenantry, but the Famine undoubtedly played a part in shifting the political, social, and religious affiliations of both men. In *English Misrule and Irish Misdeeds* (1848), de Vere traces an enhanced sense of his own national identity back to the imperial reaction to the unfolding crisis:

> There never was a time when I did not feel Ireland to be my country; and the stormy scorn with which for a year and more you have assailed her, trampling upon her in the hour of her sorest adversity, and embittering the flavour of the bread you gave, has pressed that sentiment around me with a closeness for which I thank you.[76]

The Earl of Arundel, then in his thirties, became a noted philanthropist. In 1851, he resigned his English seat and became MP for Limerick (Daniel O'Connell's son John retired in his favor).[77] One pertinent fact de Vere does not mention is that the Earl's father, the Duke of Norfolk, had been much mocked for his suggestion early in the Famine that 'in place of the potato the Irish should learn to consume curry powder, on which, mixed with water, he appeared to believe the population of India was nourished'.[78] So, in a sense, this visit and the Earl's reaction to it redeems his family's honor also.

Yet the men's silence, and the emphasis on their distress, elides the actual victims, the 'dark, emaciated' baby and its absent mother. De Vere does not even note what sex the child is; he twice refers to it as an 'infant', which is apt in that the word derives from the Latin *infans*, 'unable to speak'. Silent and still, rendering the men who view it speechless, the child still provides them with something to speak of, an experience enhancing their ability to persuade others to intervene. But they seem powerless to help this child. Their only effect on the child is to provoke a violent shiver. Presumably, they abandon it—they certainly do not take it with them, given the expectation the child will be dead when its mother returns, nor do they send for help, nor do they stay with it to keep it safe—and given many contemporary reports of dead bodies in cabins savaged by rats or dogs, it is possible the mother returned to find worse than a corpse.

In *English Misrule and Irish Misdeeds*, de Vere describes a very different entrance into a 'mud hovel', in which all is darkness apart from a single shaft of light:

> Right beneath that beam, there sat upon the earthen floor a little naked infant, an orphan, who laughed as if in scorn of the misery around him. In his hand he held a green hazel wand, moist with autumnal shoots, and, exulting in such strength as was his, lifted it with beautiful gesture and beat it with rapture against the ground, as if he possessed power to summon spirits out of the earth. It was probably the contrast between that fearless child and the haggard group around him that impressed me; and I have since thought that the outcast I then saw, so unprotected, yet so well protected, might be a symbol of his country.[79]

Of the hundreds of cabin scenes de Vere must have witnessed, he chooses to record these two contrasting depictions of infants: one dark, emaciated, silent, and still, the other bright, laughing, fearless, and strong. If the former encounter has Damascene overtones, despite the obvious predisposition of the men to sympathy and relief, the latter seems Epiphanic in its recognition of a Messiah-like symbol of renewal. One of the reasons for the difference may be that the pitiful scene was recollected five decades after the Famine, retrospectively acknowledging the immensity of the death and suffering, while the hopeful scene was written during the Famine (the text is dated November 1847), in the form of a defiant series of letters to an English MP, in which de Vere wishes to demonstrate and promote the possibility of recovery: 'Never was there more room for hope than now, if the two countries, wakened by so painful a shock, be capable of understanding themselves and their mutual relations'.[80]

These two cabin scenes also suggest a conscious shaping of experience to fit what Morash terms the 'intertextual archive' of Famine representation. Famine literature is part of 'a culturally specific semiotic web'[81] which includes specters, living skeletons, unroofed houses, trap coffins, bodies by the roadside, mouths stained with grass, cannibalism, desecration of the dead:

> the Famine as a textual event is composed of a group of images whose meaning does not derive from their strategic location within a narrative, but rather from the strangeness and horror of the images themselves, as dislocated, isolated emblems of suffering.[82]

This archive of emblematic images also includes the cabin scene; no travel book, no newspaper report from a distressed area, and no novel set during the Famine is complete without its cabin scene, and the encounter often emphasizes a huge disjunction of power, most obviously in the social chasm between observer and victim, but also in the observer's disturbing recognition of their own essential impotence. Most often, as Margaret Kelleher argues, the inhabitant of the cabin is poor and female, while the visitor is wealthy and male; the cabin scene is frequently combined with another recurring image from the Famine archive, 'the hunger-stricken mother, holding a child at her breast'.[83] Thomas Carlyle, travelling with Charles Gavan Duffy in Kerry in July 1849, records entering a hut 'under pretence of asking for a draught of water; dark, narrow; *two* women nursing [. . .]. No water; the poor young woman produces buttermilk; in real pity I give her a shilling. Duffy had done the like in the adjoining cottage'.[84] The breastfeeding mother is in several instances used to expose the failure of the public works scheme. An anonymous author who published an account of her experiences in 1846 and 1847 visits a poor woman with seven children; her husband works but does not earn enough to feed them all, so the woman breastfeeds her two-year-old. The child is ailing, the mother a bag of bones: 'Look at me, I'm a show!' she exclaims. Typically, the emphasis shifts to the distress of the observer:

> Believe me, it required no small effort to stand firmly on that wretched floor, and to talk firmly to that wretched mother; but if I had given way, and turned hysterical too, who was to do *my* duty? So I kept down all feeling; but that scene, and that voice, will haunt me in dreams.[85]

Hoare records in her short story 'The Brethren of the Pups' an incident she describes as 'a matter of fact' from the spring of 1847, when a 'benevolent visitor' enters the cabin of a starving family to find the mother breastfeeding her eighteen-year-old son, the only one of the family working on the roads and able to 'draw the wretched pittance which, when converted into Indian meal, scarcely afforded them enough to drag on existence'.[86] The mother is forced to choose between her youngest and eldest children, and sacrifices the infant in order to preserve the rest of the family. As Patricia Lysaght notes, the mother striving against almost overwhelming odds to feed her starving family is one of the most powerful images in Famine folklore,[87] and it sharply underlines both the inadequacy of relief works and the desperate resilience of these poor women.

These mothers, still capable of producing milk for their children, are wretched and pitiful; still more wretched are depictions of mothers incapable of breastfeeding at all. Starving mother and child represent the acme of vulnerability. Mary Kelly's 'A Scene for Ireland' opens in a cabin on a wild day in December; a mother whose 'hungry children stood aloof' tries to still her baby's cries, but 'She has no food to give it now / Save those hot tears outgushing'. The mother's plight is contrasted with a wealthy woman's luxury, seen to be in inverse relationship to, and dependent on, the suffering of the poor:

> Far, far away, with pearls and gold
>   My lady's hair is gleaming;

For every gem our eyes behold
  A crimson drop is streaming!—
For all the grace of silks and lace
  Some wretches naked shiver;
For every smile upon her face
  Some death-blue lips will quiver![88]

In Matthew Magrath's 'One of Many', an evicted mother stands with her baby at the door of a rich man, 'Motionless; waiting, not asking for food'; harshly rejected, both die on the pathway: 'Her infant lay close to her clay-cold breast; / In the world to come they are both at rest'.[89] Aubrey de Vere's 'The Year of Sorrow: Ireland—1849' depicts the land itself as a mother who has withdrawn food: 'Take back, O Earth, into thy breast, / The children whom thou wilt not feed'.[90] Kelleher suggests that 'the breakdown in the maternal relationship, such as a mother's inability to feed her child, or her rejection of her child, is used to spell the ultimate catastrophe, a collapse in the natural order'.[91] This collapse is further enhanced when either mother or baby is dead. Among various cabin scenes in *Frank O'Donnell* (1861), one is so disturbing that it can only be told second-hand, by Frank's sister Kate: 'It is only yesterday, Frank went into a cabin in the bog, where he was fowling; there he found a poor woman dead, and two children sucking her breast'.[92] In *The Love That Kills* (1867), the agent Clayton enters a dark, stinking cabin, and as 'like a dissolving view beginning to form, the scene took shape', he sees a dying mother attempting to suckle her dead baby.[93] Regarding the prevalence of this motif in oral tradition, Lysaght adds that the most horrific version shows the starving infant eating the dead mother's breast.[94]

The most compelling—and most analyzed—of these cabin scenes involving a female famine victim and a middle-class male observer occurs in Anthony Trollope's *Castle Richmond* (1860), in what Roy Foster describes as 'one of the bleakest chapters Trollope ever wrote'.[95] Trollope, who had lived in Ireland from 1841, and published his first novels there, saw *Castle Richmond* as his parting word to a country where he had, paradoxically, spent his happiest years, in the midst of that land's worst catastrophe. It is a novel he struggled to get published, 'a valedictory novel which he was determined to write in open opposition to a prevailing hostility to all things Irish'.[96] Indeed, Trollope opens the novel with this concern foremost: 'I wonder whether the novel-reading world [. . .] will be offended if I lay the plot of this story in Ireland!' he asks, adding that currently 'Irish stories are not popular with the booksellers'.[97] It is written reluctantly; he delayed writing his Famine novel for a decade, but now, leaving Ireland, feels obliged: 'If I do not say that word now it will never be said' (2).

The cabin scene takes place at a pivotal moment in the narrative; the protagonist, Herbert Fitzgerald, has been informed that his parents' marriage was bigamous, and in consequence has lost his name, his estate, and (as far as her mother is concerned) his fiancée, Clara Desmond. The day before he leaves to take up work in London, on his way to bid farewell to Clara, Herbert enters a cabin to shelter from the rain. Inside he discovers a woman and baby in 'loose rags', and the body of a dead child 'stripped of every vestige of clothing' (369, 371). Their lack of clothing is in marked contrast with Herbert, who has 'dressed himself with some care', with an eye to impressing Clara's mother; even his horse is 'well-groomed' (366). Indeed, he enters the cabin in order to prevent his clothes from being ruined, and brings his horse in with him. The disparity between the well-dressed man and the naked and nearly-naked female famine victims is continually referred to and explicitly gendered, particularly when Herbert, in touching the baby, causes the woman to try to conceal her own nakedness. Kelleher describes Herbert's touch and gaze as intrusive, even violent: 'Herbert's power to cause embarrassment in a woman previously described as almost dead is horrifically clear'.[98] Herbert's clothing and possessions are also deployed ostentatiously; the silver handle of his whip is used to move the straw from the body of the dead child, and his silk handkerchief becomes a makeshift shroud. Herbert's horror and pity are genuine, and salutary; 'this simple act of compassion' marks 'the transformation of Herbert into a responsible subject'.[99] Herbert can no longer consider himself to be unfortunate now he has witnessed true suffering, and he will go on to become a fine landlord and model chair of a relief committee. But the issue of responsibility for this woman's death, and the death of her children, remains; as Yvonne Siddle suggests: 'The silk handkerchief alerts the reader to resources at Herbert's disposal which were not employed to avert the death'.[100]

Herbert is 'quite extraordinarily ineffectual'.[101] He struggles even to communicate with the woman, and his questions are blundering and incompetent: 'You seem to be very poorly off here' (370), is his initial comment on a cabin that 'seemed to be empty of everything' (368). Finding the body of the dead child, his first question is 'Was she your own?' (371). He crassly asks the dying woman about her 'hopes for the future' (373). He asks of the baby 'Is she not cold?' (373), though as 'the damp and chill of the place struck through his bones' (370) he already knows the answer, and must know the woman has had no way to prevent it. This last question provokes a response that may suggest the woman's frustration at his ignorance: ' "Cowld," she muttered, with a vacant face and wondering tone of voice, as though she did not quite understand him. "I suppose she is cowld. Why wouldn't she be cowld? We're cowld enough, if that's all" ' (373). The woman's reticence is disturbing to Herbert: 'he had entered without eliciting a word from her', and while she does bid him welcome when he speaks to her, she doesn't show 'any of those symptoms of reverence which are habitual to the Irish when those of a higher rank enter their cabins' (370). When he discovers the body of the dead child, Herbert is initially speechless:

> For a minute or two he said nothing—hardly, indeed, knowing how to speak, and looking from the corpse-like woman back to the life-like corpse, and then from the corpse back to the woman, as though he

> expected that she would say something unasked. But she did not say a word, though she so turned her head that her eyes rested on him. (371)

Her look suggests that a response is due from him, yet Herbert seems incapable of acting without a direct request for help. Her failure to 'ask for alms when he pitied her in her misery' increases Herbert's dilemma: 'But what was he to do? He could not go and leave them without succour. The woman had made no plaint of her suffering, and had asked for nothing; but he felt that it would be impossible to abandon her without offering her relief' (373). Her silent gaze is more eloquent than any appeal; as Herbert lays out the dead body of her child, she 'looked on him the while, shaking her head slowly, as though asking him with all the voice that was left to her, whether it were not piteous; but of words she still uttered none' (373–4). Later, Herbert will be haunted by 'the eloquence of that silent, solitary, dying woman' (377), which made her strangely dignified amidst the squalor of her death. It also exposes Herbert, and those like him, as negligent; it is not the much-criticized passivity of the victim that is to blame, but the passivity of those who could relieve them.

The cabin is 'beyond the confines of [Herbert's] father's property' (367), absolving him of direct responsibility for the welfare of a tenant, but as a member of the relief committee for Kanturk, Herbert might be expected to know not only about the woman's existence, but how to assess her needs and offer help. The cabin is not out in the wilds, but on the road, 'built in an angle at a spot where the road made a turn, so that two sides of it stood close out in the wayside' (368), easy to find and enter, particularly given that 'people are more intimate with each other, and take greater liberties in Ireland' (368). But, as becomes clear, the woman and her daughters are failed not only by the mechanisms of relief, but by the decisions made by her husband, Mike. Crippled with rheumatism, Mike is unable to work on the roads; he manages to find work enough to feed himself, but not his wife and children, and 'this work to the last he would not abandon. Even this was better to him than the poor-house' (373). Mike's desperation to avoid the poor-house is passed over without further comment, a silent indictment of 'less eligibility'; but the decision has doomed his wife and children, for 'as long as a man found work out of the poor-house, his wife and children would not be admitted into it' (372). The narrator admits the injustice of this, adding 'Exceptions were of course made in such cases, if they were known: but then it was so hard to know them!' (372). The narrator's certainty that an exception would have been made for Mike's wife if only she had appealed is, however, unsupported and improbable. By the time Herbert finds them, it is too late to save the family, and his attempts to offer relief are worse than useless; he gives her 'a silver coin or two', though she has no way to spend them, and promises to send someone to take her to the workhouse, but his orders are not followed in time, because 'People then did not think much of a dying woman', and 'the mother and the two children never left the cabin till they left it together, wrapped in their workhouse shrouds' (374). As Kelleher suggests, 'Underlying these famine scenes is an anxiety which the female figure threatens to expose—the failure of a political system'.[102] It is also the failure of a social system that increased the vulnerability of women and children by making their fate dependent on the ability of their husbands and fathers to either work or access relief, where available, on their behalf. In 1847, Maria Edgeworth wrote to the Central Relief Committee about the importance of 'preserv[ing] some sense of self-respect' among the poor by enabling them to work where able, and in particular urging the need to provide work for women:

> A poor woman the other day in thanking our vicar for the assistance he gave in employing men and boys, regretted that when as much was done for men, nothing has been thought of for women or children, who are, as she said, also anxious for work; if they could be employed and paid, they would work to their utmost.[103]

What is remarkable about the Famine scenes in *Castle Richmond* is that the failure of the political system emerges almost against Trollope's intention. The narrator is at pains throughout to defend the decisions taken by government and the majority of the gentry and officials responsible for relief. In an authorial intrusion early in the novel, Trollope refers to his personal experience of the Famine: 'I was in the country travelling always through it, during the whole period, and I have to say [. . .] that in my opinion the measures of the government were prompt, wise, and beneficent; and I have to say also that the efforts of those who managed the poor were, as a rule, unremitting, honest, impartial, and successful' (69). Yet several times in the novel peasant characters emerge whose vocal—or as in the scene above, eloquently silent—protests undermine this view. While the main plot focuses on the loves and losses of the landlords, and presents the Famine as ultimately beneficial and providential, Trollope also manages 'to show the Famine from below',[104] through the eyes of those who suffered most.

In an earlier encounter, Herbert and Clara had been confronted by Bridget Sheehy and her five children, begging for 'a thrifle of money' for her 'wretched, naked brood' (190). Murty Brien, Bridget's husband, is working, but his four shillings a week won't feed a family of seven, so he has sent his wife and children back to her people—though Bridget denies he has deserted her. Herbert, a disciple of political economy, initially refuses to help them. He suggests the poor-house, but Bridget is no keener than Mike had been about that. He then suggests they can get a ticket for meal twice a week at Clady, but this is what the woman and her children have been living on for the past month, and its effects are devastatingly clear:

> It was a child nearly two years of age, but its little legs seemed to have withered away; its cheeks were wan, and yellow and sunken, and the

> two teeth which it had already cut were seen with terrible plainness through its emaciated lips. Its head and forehead were covered with sores; and then the mother, moving aside the rags, showed that its back and legs were in the same state. 'Look to that,' she said, almost with scorn. 'That's what the mail has done—my black curses be upon it, and the day that it first come nigh the country'. (191)

Bridget is forced to resort to stratagem to get what her children need; she provokes Herbert's jealousy of his cousin Owen, his rival in love, so that Herbert is shamed into giving her money to save face before Clara. These are not anonymous victims; the woman is given definition by being named and placed as one of the 'Desmond tinantry', and while Herbert does not recognize Bridget, she knows the intimate details of his life, and has the cunning and desperation to use them.

Trollope also uses encounters between the gentry and the poor at meal-shops and relief works to examine the resistance of the poor to unfair treatment. Clara and Herbert's sisters volunteer at a store distributing food; the narrator explains the meal initially had been given free, but it had been found better for 'the morals of the people' to sell it at its 'true price' to prevent hucksters making huge profits or those who did not require it selling it (84). Clara is aggressively challenged by a woman complaining that the meal she has received is unfit to eat when boiled. The narrator—and indeed other poor people waiting patiently in the store—express pity for 'delicate women' like Clara whose 'hardest burden [. . .] was the ingratitude of the poor for whom they worked' (86). The confrontation is reminiscent of the account by 'a Lady' who sells soup for a penny a quart; a stranger with two children, clamorous to get in, becomes impudent, to the lady's outrage: 'I could not hear more than "is this your charity!" but I did not think it proper that she should continue, so I told the door-keeper to send to the next police station, unless that woman was silent immediately'.[105] In *Castle Richmond*, however, the woman's complaint is seen to be justified; she has bought the meal with money she can ill afford and deserves better. Her protest epitomizes the injustice of expecting gratitude for harsh conditions, as the narrator acknowledges, gesturing toward other hardships:

> When they received bad meal which they could not cook, and even in their extreme hunger could hardly eat half-cooked; when they were desired to leave their cabins and gardens, and flock into the wretched barracks which were prepared for them; when they saw their children wasting away under a suddenly altered system of diet, it would have been unreasonable to expect that they should have been grateful. Grateful for what? (86)

The refusal to distribute food gratis drives those who cannot afford it to extravagant display of their wretchedness. In Hoare's 'Irish Beggars', mothers imploring 'a soup-ticket for the love of God' display sick, dying, or dead children to advertise their need, while the American William Balch described a fair-day in Carrickmacross where 'the lame, the halt, the blind, the sick, the decrepit, were there, begging of whom they could, and exhibiting their deformities to excite sympathy and secure a penny'.[106]

Herbert is also accosted by a gang of 'road-destroyers' employed by the Board of Works, who turn out to be his own tenants. Herbert's careless question, 'I hope the work suits you all', gets the response it deserves, and again the narrator is sympathetic: 'Men whose whole amount of worldly good consists in a bare allowance of nauseous food, just sufficient to keep body and soul together, must be excused if they wish to utter their complaints to ears that can hear them' (286). The men criticize the insufficiency of their wages for a family of six, the quality and cost of meal, and in particular its impact on the health of their children: 'Saving yer honer's presence, their bellies is gone away most to nothing' (286). This novel, written by a middle-class Englishman from the perspective of the Anglo-Irish gentry, thus grants a hearing, however brief, to voices of the dispossessed that sound strikingly similar to Peatsaí Ó Callanáin's *Na Fataí Bána*:

> *Is iomaí teach a bhfuil ochtar daoine ann,*
> *Is gan fear le saothrú ach aon duine amháin,*
> *Siúd pingin don duine acu, gan caint ar an tSaoire,*
> *Agus lá na díleann níl faic le fáil.*
>
> (It is many a household that contains eight people, and with only men working, that's a penny each, taking no account of Sunday, and on wet days there is no work.)[107]

Nobody has anything good to say about the public works; for Dorian, they were 'the great blow for slowly taking away human life, [. . .] by forcing the hungry and the half-clad men to stand out in the cold and in the sleet and rain from morn till night for the paltry reward of nine pennies per day'.[108] *Dick Massey* shows engineers getting paid more in one day than the workers do in a fortnight, and sitting down to beef and capon, while the men eat stirabout.[109] In *The Hunger*, men working on the roads starve to death because 'someone in the pay department had blundered'.[110] In *Castle Squander*, Carleton indicts Sir Charles Trevelyan for the callousness of the scheme:

> if he had witnessed their feeble limbs and emaciated features, he must have remembered that it was the throe of hunger and destitution which had brought them to that state, and that it would be as unreasonable for him to expect the same amount of labour from a sick man as from a man in health, as to expect a full day's labour from those unfortunate creatures, who were utterly prostrated by want and wretchedness, and

who had *nothing else* on which to subsist but the bare shilling a day for themselves, their wives, and their children, and that, too, in a year of famine.[111]

The famine roads become symbols of waste and senseless destruction; in *Castle Daly*, Connor, returning from exile, breaks down on a famine road.[112] In *Denis*, the road does not last twenty years.[113] Trollope underlines his awareness of the way the failure of relief had shaped resentment in post-Famine Ireland when in his final novel, *The Landleaguers* (1883), Florian Jones is shot from a vantage-point afforded by a cutting in the road commenced during the Famine, and never completed.[114]

CONCLUSION

Margaret Kelleher points out that the Famine, 'a crisis in authority, both economically and politically', was also 'a crisis in representation' for the writers who sought to mediate it.[115] The huge responsibility of authentically presenting the scale and impact of the disaster on the poor was onerous and often thankless, but many of the writers discussed here rose to the challenge of transcending the values and prejudices of their class by attempting to engage honestly and imaginatively with the experience of the poor. In doing so they disrupted stereotypes of the Irish peasant during the Famine as passive, feckless, violent, or ungrateful, offering a new perspective to their contemporary metropolitan readers—Irish as well as British. They also called to account a social system, and a government, that had failed the Irish people.

NOTES

1. W.J. McCormack, 'The Intellectual Revival (1830–50)', in Seamus Deane, Andrew Carpenter and Jonathan Williams, eds., *The Field Day Anthology of Irish Writing*, 3 vols. (Derry, 1991), vol. 1, 1176.
2. 'Past and Present State of Literature in Ireland', *Dublin University Magazine*, 9 (1837), 365. The editors of *The Field Day Anthology of Irish Writing* attribute the article to Isaac Butt (vol. 1, 1200), while the *Wellesley Index* argues for Samuel O'Sullivan; see *The Wellesley Index to Victorian Periodicals 1824–1900*, vol. 4, ed. Walter E. Houghton (Toronto and Buffalo, 1984), 231.
3. Terry Eagleton, *Heathcliff and the Great Hunger: Studies in Irish Culture* (London and New York, 1995), 227.
4. Matthew Campbell, 'Poetry in English, 1830–1890: From Catholic Emancipation to the Fall of Parnell', in Margaret Kelleher and Philip O'Leary, eds., *The Cambridge History of Irish Literature*, 2 vols. (Cambridge, 2006), vol. 1, 519.
5. Charles Benson, 'Printers and Booksellers in Dublin, 1800–1850', in Robin Myers and Michael Harris, eds., *Spreading the Word: The Distribution Networks of Print 1550–1850* (Winchester, 1990), 57.
6. D.J. O'Donoghue, *The Life of William Carleton: Being his Autobiography and Letters: and an Account of his Life and Writings, from the Point at which the Autobiography Breaks Off*, 2 vols. (London, 1896), vol. 2, 215.

7. Ibid., vol. 2, 176–77.
8. Gearóid Denvir, 'Literature in Irish, 1800–1890: From the Act of Union to the Gaelic League', in Kelleher and O'Leary, eds., *Cambridge History of Irish Literature*, vol. 1, 578.
9. Laurence M. Geary, 'The Great Famine in County Cork: A Socio-Medical Analysis', in Michael de Nie and Sean Farrell, eds., *Power and Popular Culture in Modern Ireland: Essays in Honour of James S. Donnelly, Jr.* (Dublin and Portland, 2010), 44.
10. *Times*, 1 December 1846.
11. Hugh Dorian, *The Outer Edge of Ulster: A Memoir of Social Life in Nineteenth-Century Donegal*, ed. Breandán Mac Suibhne and David Dickson (Dublin, 2000), 223.
12. Peter Gray, *Famine, Land and Politics: British Government and Irish Society 1843–50* (Dublin and Portland, 1999), 257.
13. Christine Kinealy, *This Great Calamity: The Irish Famine 1845–52* (Dublin, 1994), 163.
14. Gray, *Famine, Land and Politics*, 259.
15. William Carleton, *The Black Prophet: A Tale of Irish Famine* (1847) (Poole and Washington, 1996), v.
16. Dorian, *Outer Edge of Ulster*, 223.
17. Carleton, *Black Prophet*, 250–53.
18. *The Nation*, 8 September 1849; Duffy later reprinted the description in his *Conversations with Carlyle* (London, 1892).
19. A. M. Sullivan, *New Ireland: Political Sketches and Personal Reminiscences of Thirty Years of Irish Public Life* (Glasgow and London, 1877), 62.
20. David Lloyd, 'The Indigent Sublime: Specters of Irish Hunger', *Representations*, 92, 1 (2005), 156; reprinted in his *Irish Times: Temporalities of Modernity* (Dublin, 2008), 39–72.
21. Sullivan, *New Ireland*, 62. Louis J. Walsh uses Sullivan's account for his description of a public boiler in his novel of the Famine, *The Next Time: A Story of 'Forty-Eight* (Dublin, 1919): 'Around it there fought and shrieked and scuffled a crowd of gaunt, famished-looking creatures that had once been men and women. The young man almost choked with grief and passion at the sight' (156).
22. Samuel Ferguson, 'Dublin: A Poem in Imitation of the Third Satire of Juvenal', in Chris Morash, ed., *The Hungry Voice: The Poetry of the Irish Famine* (Dublin, 1989), 100–05, ll. 11, 13–14, 187–90.
23. Cormac Ó Gráda, *Black '47 and Beyond: The Great Irish Famine in History, Economy, and Memory* (Princeton, NJ, 1999), 215.
24. Morash, ed., *The Hungry Voice*, 37.
25. T.C.D., 'The Last Appeal', in Morash, ed., *The Hungry Voice*, 49–50, ll. 5–6.
26. 'The Song of the Famine', *Dublin University Magazine*, 30, 175 (1847), 103.
27. Ibid., 104.
28. Ibid.
29. 'Agricultural Resources of the Kingdom', *Dublin University Magazine*, 30, 175 (1847), 105.
30. Cited in Joy Melville, *Mother of Oscar: The Life of Jane Francesca Wilde* (London, 1994), 20. The attribution to J.C. Hoey and Frances C. Hoey is provided by the *Wellesley Index to Victorian Periodicals*, Vol. 2.
31. Melville, *Mother of Oscar*, 37.
32. Lady Wilde, 'The Famine Year (The Stricken Land)', in Morash, ed., *The Hungry Voice*, 221, ll. 21–22. Owen Dudley Edwards describes 'The Famine Year' as 'the Great Famine's first major poetic response' in 'Wilde, Jane Francesca Agnes ('Speranza')', in James McGuire and James Quinn, eds., *Dictionary of Irish Biography* (Cambridge, 2009), vol. 9, 927.

33. Wilde, 'The Exodus', in Morash, ed., *The Hungry Voice,* 219, ll. 2, 18.
34. Campbell, 'Poetry in English, 1830–1890', 533.
35. Wilde, 'The Enigma', in Morash, ed., *The Hungry Voice*, 218, ll. 42–45.
36. Michael Davitt, *The Fall of Feudalism in Ireland; or, The Story of the Land League Revolution* (London and New York, 1904), 47–48.
37. Wilde, 'The Itinerant Singing Girl' and 'The Voice of the Poor', in Morash, ed., *The Hungry Voice*, 80, l. 15; 231, l. 56.
38. Morash, ed., *The Hungry Voice*, 30.
39. Carleton, *Black Prophet*, iii.
40. John Prest, 'Russell, John, first Earl Russell (1792–1878)', *Oxford Dictionary of National Biography* (Oxford, 2004).
41. Mary Anne Hoare, 'A Sketch of Famine', *Shamrock Leaves; or, Tales and Sketches of Ireland* (Dublin and London, 1851), 206.
42. Hoare, 'A Sketch of Famine', 207.
43. Hoare, 'The Knitted Collar', *Shamrock Leaves*, 59–63.
44. Hoare, 'A Sketch of Famine', 211.
45. Hoare, 'The Black Potatoes', *Shamrock Leaves*, 37.
46. See, for instance, Margaret Brew's *The Chronicles of Castle Cloyne; or, Pictures of the Munster People*, 3 vols. (London, 1885), which describes the vast amount of money sent home by 'those poor exiles' (vol. 3, 41); Dick Considine's brother sends a cheque for £20 to get him to New Orleans, and Hyacinth Dillon strikes gold in California and returns to Ireland rich. Conversely, Louise Field's *Denis: A Study in Black and White* (London and New York, 1896) describes 'an enriched Irish-American [who] travelled once over a great extent of his native country seeking traces of his family and seeking them in vain, for the Black Forty-Seven had obliterated these traces with so many others' (213).
47. Carleton, *Black Prophet*, 280, 101.
48. Ibid., 213–14.
49. Ibid., 94.
50. Ibid., 265.
51. Cormac Ó Gráda, *Famine: A Short History* (Princeton, NJ, 2009), 90.
52. See, for example, the stories collected under 'Of Curses, Kindness and Miraculous Food' in Cathal Póirtéir's *Famine Echoes* (Dublin, 1995).
53. Carleton, *Black Prophet*, 131–32.
54. Thomas O'Neill Russell, *The Struggles of Dick Massey; or, The Battles of a Boy* (Dublin, 1860), 284.
55. Mildred Darby, *The Hunger, Being Realities of the Famine Years in Ireland 1845 to 1848* (London, 1910), 203, 219.
56. Field, *Denis*, 6, 388.
57. David Lloyd, *Irish Culture and Colonial Modernity, 1800–2000: The Transformation of Oral Space* (Cambridge, 2011), 52.
58. Carleton, *Black Prophet*, 262. See also W. G. Wills's *The Love That Kills*, 3 vols. (London, 1867) vol. 1, 75, where those who conspire to murder 'were all of the most respectable class of farmers, who had money, land, and characters to lose, instead of low desperate ruffians, such as he had expected to see'.
59. Carleton, *Black Prophet*, 249.
60. Ibid., 251.
61. Ibid., 247–48.
62. Ibid., 266.
63. William Carleton, *Red Hall: or, The Baronet's Daughter*, 3 vols. (London, 1852), vol. 2, 51.
64. John de Jean Frazer, 'The Three Angels', in Morash, ed., *The Hungry Voice*, 187, ll. 254–57.
65. Carleton, *Black Prophet*, 251.

66. Brew, *Castle Cloyne*, vol. 2, 280.
67. Elizabeth Hely Walshe, *Kingston's Revenge: A Story of Bravery and Single-Hearted Endeavour* (first published as *Golden Hills: A Tale of the Irish Famine* in 1865) (London, 1917), 291, 288.
68. Aubrey de Vere, *Recollections* (New York and London, 1897), 250.
69. Ignatius Murphy, *A Starving People: Life and Death in West Clare, 1845–1851* (Dublin and Portland, 1996), 68.
70. Kinealy, *This Great Calamity*, 235–36.
71. De Vere, *Recollections*, 250.
72. Quoted in Wilfrid Ward, *Aubrey De Vere: A Memoir Based on his Unpublished Diaries and Correspondence* (London, New York, and Bombay, 1904), 120–21.
73. See Melissa Fegan, *Literature and the Irish Famine 1845–1919* (Oxford, 2002), ch. 3.
74. As Labouchere's Letter is dated 5 October 1846, de Vere's recollection seems to be anachronistic.
75. Matthew Potter, *William Monsell of Tervoe 1812–1894: Catholic Unionist, Anglo-Irishman* (Dublin and Portland, 2009).
76. Aubrey de Vere, *English Misrule and Irish Misdeeds: Four Letters From Ireland* (London, 1848), 259.
77. Dermot Quinn, 'Henry Granville Fitzalan-Howard, fourteenth duke of Norfolk (1815–1860)', *Oxford Dictionary of National Biography* (Oxford, 2004).
78. Cecil Woodham-Smith, *The Great Hunger: Ireland 1845–9* (London, 1977), 43.
79. De Vere, *English Misrule and Irish Misdeeds*, 205.
80. Ibid., 264.
81. Christopher Morash, *Writing the Irish Famine* (Oxford, 1995), 5.
82. Chris Morash, 'Literature, Memory, Atrocity', in Chris Morash and Richard Hayes, eds., *Fearful Realities: New Perspectives on the Famine* (Dublin and Portland, 1996), 114.
83. Margaret Kelleher, *The Feminization of Famine: Expressions of the Inexpressible?* (Cork, 1997), 21–22.
84. Thomas Carlyle, *Reminiscences of My Irish Journey in 1849* (New York, 1882), 129.
85. *Christmas 1846 and the New Year 1847, in Ireland; Letters from a Lady*, ed. W. S. Gilly (Durham, 1847), 18. Proceeds were to be donated to a relief fund.
86. Hoare, 'The Brethren of the Pups: An Irish Sketch of the Olden Times', in *Shamrock Leaves*, 199.
87. Patricia Lysaght, 'Women and the Great Famine: Vignettes from the Irish Oral Tradition', in Arthur Gribben, ed., *The Great Famine and the Irish Diaspora in America* (Amherst, 1999), 34.
88. Mary Kelly, 'A Scene for Ireland', in Morash, ed., *The Hungry Voice*, 61–62, ll. 17–24. Kelly was herself from a relatively genteel family, and was educated at home by a governess.
89. Matthew Magrath, 'One of Many', in Morash, ed., *The Hungry Voice*, 62–64, ll. 26, 47–48. The poem was first published in *The Irishman* in June 1849.
90. Aubrey de Vere, 'The Year of Sorrow: Ireland—1849', in Morash, ed., *The Hungry Voice*, 92–98, ll. 49–52.
91. Kelleher, 'Woman as Famine Victim: The Figure of Woman in Irish Famine Narratives', in Ronit Lentin, ed., *Gender and Catastrophe* (London and New York, 1997), 250.
92. David Power Conyngham, *Frank O'Donnell: A Tale of Irish Life* (Dublin and London, 1861), 223; first published as *The Old House at Home* in 1859.
93. Wills, *The Love That Kills*, vol. 2, 278.

94. Lysaght, 'Women and the Great Famine', 36–37.
95. Roy Foster, *The Irish Story: Telling Tales and Making it Up in Ireland* (London, 2001), 135.
96. Yvonne Siddle, 'Anthony Trollope's Representation of the Great Famine', in Peter Gray, ed., *Victoria's Ireland?: Irishness and Britishness, 1837–1901* (Dublin and Portland, 2004), 143.
97. Anthony Trollope, *Castle Richmond* (1860), ed. Mary Hamer (Oxford, 1989), 1. Further references will be given in the body of the text.
98. Kelleher, *The Feminization of Famine*, 54.
99. Morash, *Writing the Irish Famine*, 44.
100. Siddle, 'Anthony Trollope's Representation of the Great Famine', 148.
101. Kelleher, *The Feminization of Famine*, 54.
102. Ibid., 56.
103. Maria Edgeworth, from 'Letter to Central Relief Committee (1847)', in Angela Bourke *et al.*, eds., *The Field Day Anthology of Irish Writing, IV–V* (Cork, 2002), vol. 5, 698.
104. Foster, *The Irish Story*, 134.
105. *Christmas 1846 and the New Year 1847, in Ireland*, 35.
106. Hoare, 'Irish Beggars', *Shamrock Leaves*, 51. William Balch, *Ireland, As I Saw It: The Character, Condition, and Prospects of the People* (New York and London, 1850), 411. See also James Mahony's famous *Illustrated London News* sketch (13 February 1847) 'Woman Begging at Clonakilty', in which a woman displays her dead child in order to get money to bury it.
107. Peatsaí Ó Callanáin, '*Na Fataí Bána*', cited in Ó Gráda, *Black '47 and Beyond*, 218.
108. Dorian, *Outer Edge of Ulster*, 216–17.
109. Russell, *Dick Massey*, 286–88.
110. Darby, *The Hunger*, 225.
111. Carleton, *Castle Squander*, vol. 2, 117–18.
112. Annie Keary, *Castle Daly: The Story of an Irish Home Thirty Years Ago*, 3 vols. (London, 1875), vol. 3, 342–43.
113. Field, *Denis*, 396.
114. Anthony Trollope, *The Landleaguers*, 3 vols. (London, 1883), vol. 2, 256–57.
115. Margaret Kelleher, 'Woman as Famine Victim', 247.

3 Soup and Providence

Varieties of Protestantism and the Great Famine

David W. Miller

In a volume on popular politics in the Great Irish Famine, the author of an essay primarily exploring the role of Protestant clergy must confront a contradiction in terms. 'Popular politics' is a term that entered the English language early in the French Revolution[1] to describe the politics of the 'people' in the sense of '[t]hose without special rank or position in society; the mass of the community as distinguished from the nobility or the ruling classes; the populace'.[2] The largest component of the Protestant clergy in the Atlantic Archipelago—those of the Church of England and Ireland—were simply incapable of engaging in 'popular politics'. They were, by definition, members of a ruling class, and if they were involved in protests or riots they were probably trying to minimize the harm that the populace might instigate. One might suppose that the ministers of the Church of Scotland were in the same category, but two years before the Great Irish Famine that institution had its own 'Great Disruption'. That event, together with the Famine, led directly to important popular politics on the part of the Presbyterian clergy in post-Famine Ireland. So, whereas most of the essays in this volume address popular politics *during* the Great Famine, in this essay the popular politics prompted by the Famine mostly occur *after* it. Although I do not emphasize the Roman Catholic clergy in my treatment of the Famine, I do suggest in my conclusion that the difference between their post-Famine popular politics and that of their Presbyterian counterparts can help us understand how the Great Famine contributed to the conversion of Irish politics from largely Anglicans versus non-Anglicans in 1798 to Protestants versus Catholics in 1886.

Throughout Europe, the appearance of 'popular politics' in the 1790s marks the division of the modern state that had arisen out of the late middle ages[3] into two stages that historians call the confessional state and the nation-state. We can grasp the meaning of that division in terms of Max Weber's well-known definition of the 'ideal type' of the state: 'a human community that (successfully) claims the *monopoly of the legitimate use of physical force* within a given territory'.[4] This sociological description, however, immediately poses one particular question to historians: 'Who does the legitimizing?' In much of Europe, events associated with the

Reformations and Wars of Religion had assigned the legitimizing role to the particular religious denomination—Catholic, Lutheran, Calvinist, Anglican or Orthodox—that won the favor of the successful claimant to a monopoly of force in a given territory (ordinarily the denomination with the strongest presence within that territory, but not in Ireland). Such confessional statehood was the norm until the French Revolution dismissed the Church from the legitimizing function and handed that role to *le peuple*, 'the nation'.[5] The transfer of the role of legitimizing physical force from the church (almost *any* church) to *le peuple* brought chills to the spines of governing classes throughout Europe, and especially in the Atlantic Archipelago. The political and social history of that archipelago in the long nineteenth century involves a process of transition from confessional state to nation-state(s).[6]

Daniel O'Connell, the unchallenged leader of the Catholic majority of Ireland prior to the Famine, was a nationalist but not a nation-statist. His stated objective was a return to a subordinate Irish parliament, albeit with Catholic members as well as Protestants, and, although glad to take advantage of British apprehension that his mass repeal movement might lead to violence comparable to that of the 1790s, he repeatedly denounced 'physical force'—the very phrase that Weber would incorporate into his definition of a state—on the part of his followers. In the summer of 1848, a year after O'Connell's death and while the country was still shattered by the effects of the Famine, the Young Ireland faction that had split from his movement attempted a rebellion that was easily crushed. From then on, however, 'physical force' was always a presence (albeit often an unspoken presence) in Irish nationalism. And a Young Ireland exile, John Mitchel, published an account of the Great Famine—*The Last Conquest of Ireland (Perhaps)*[7]—that would legitimize physical force for generations of Irish nation-statists. So the Great Famine was indeed a major component in Ireland's eventual transition from a confessional state to a nation-state (or arguably one nation-state and one protectorate of another nation-state).

I focus primarily on those Protestants who identified themselves as Evangelicals to clarify how the Famine contributed to this central development in Irish history in the long nineteenth century. I concentrate on two types of behavior ascribed to Protestant clergy of the Famine years. One of them, emphasized in recent academic work, is the involvement of evangelicals in the promotion of extreme *laissez-faire* economics—most especially by representing blight, hunger and disease as the work of divine providence—to such an extent that they bear significant responsibility for Famine fatality. The other arose in the nineteenth century when Catholic clergy and lay leaders accused Evangelicals (whom they usually described simply as 'Protestants') of using food intended to be distributed to the starving as a means of proselytizing. By implication, the victim was being given a choice between death by starvation or even worse, no doubt, in the mind of the devout Catholic: a choice between dying of starvation as a Catholic or living as a Protestant, but suffering eternal damnation (after a lifelong humiliation of being a 'souper'). By examining these two issues, providence and soup, and exploring relationships between them, this essay seeks to clarify how the Great Famine contributed to Ireland's transition from confessional state to nation-state.

PROVIDENCE

To understand any connection between Evangelical clerics and the teachings of political economy—what we now call 'economics'—we must grasp what 'Evangelicalism' meant during the mid-nineteenth century. It was not a religion, a church, a sect or a denomination. It was a movement. There were dozens of organizations that identified themselves as evangelical, but the movement itself had no center of authority comparable to that of a hierarchy of prelates or an assembly. Nor did it have a systematic theology or creed such as Calvin's *Institutes* or the Anglican *39 Articles*. Rather it had a certain style of Protestant religious behavior. Evangelicals themselves described that style with terms like 'serious religion', 'vital religion', and 'experimental religion'—an expression that meant what today we might call 'experiential religion', i.e., emphasis on a palpable experience from condemnation to absolution. An example of such conversion was the experience of Evangelicalism's founder John Wesley, who on 24 May 1738 felt his heart 'strangely warmed'.[8] Wesley's practice of itinerant preaching to excitable gatherings had initially reminded members of the governing class of the dreaded 'enthusiasm' of popular religious gatherings in times of political unrest in the previous century.[9] However, Wesley was careful to avoid class conflict, and the movement that he created attracted not only the humble, but also members of the élite. No doubt some members of the privileged class genuinely experienced conversions comparable to that of Wesley himself, but the appeal of Evangelicalism to members of the élite was also due to the movement's attention to the 'lower orders', for perhaps 'serious religion' would persuade *le peuple* to leave judgments about physical force to their clergy.

An ironic characteristic of this period of transition from church to nation as the legitimizer of physical force—and thereby matters of life and death—was the fact that nearly everyone agreed that what we today would call a 'natural' disaster was actually the result of God's anger.[10] Protestant observers might attribute the blight to the Almighty's anger over Popery, but in subsequent years when the potato disease spread to Scotland and other parts of Europe and had negative effects on the British economy it became necessary to widen the objects of providential fury. Perhaps the wisest theological spokesman was the Irish Presbyterian minister John Edgar, who regularly used the term 'mysterious Providence' when discussing the blight. When one of his peers scoffed at the pervasive providentialism with a joke about a neighbor who blamed the Famine on 'challenges given and accepted at farming dinners, respecting the produce of the land', he was careful to use a pseudonym in his letter to the press.[11]

Perhaps the most influential analysis of providential certainty during the Famine appears in a monumental study by Boyd Hilton, who argues that nineteenth century evangelical theologians adopted 'Christian economics', i.e., *laissez-faire* economic principles based on a belief that many of the problems for which government action is proposed actually reflect the work of divine providence.[12] Thomas Chalmers, the leader of evangelicalism in Scottish Presbyterianism, is the central figure in Hilton's argument. In the spring of 1847, the most dismal phase of the Famine, Chalmers published an article entitled 'The Political Economy of a Famine' that his recent biographer, Stewart J. Brown, interprets as a reversal of his theology of economics—a claim that Hilton strongly rejects.[13] Since Chalmers died only a few weeks after the publication of the article, this disagreement is probably insoluble, but he made clear in the first paragraph of the article that his goal was to remove human fatality from the toolbox of the economist: 'the preservation of human life is a far higher object than any which comes within the range or contemplation of Political Economy'.[14] Hilton extends his criticism of Brown's analysis by dismissing the latter's use of the term 'godly commonwealth'—an expression based on Scottish covenanter and English puritan discourse—to characterize Chalmers's career.[15]

To understand this disagreement, we must return to the structure of Evangelicalism. Although Evangelicalism was a *movement* in the context of the whole United Kingdom, it was often a *party* within a particular denomination. In the Church of England, the Evangelical party had replaced the eighteenth-century Low Church (as opposed to the High Church and Broad Church parties). In the Church of Scotland, from about the turn of the century until 1843, the Evangelicals were the successors of the Popular Party (as opposed to the Moderate party).[16] There was a tendency among Evangelicals to fold into their version of Evangelicalism certain cherished traditions of their respective denominations—a tendency that still exists throughout Evangelicalism.[17] In the case of Scotland, the primary such tradition was that of the Covenanters. Although warfare within the United Kingdom was no longer an option on the part of the Scottish Evangelicals, some covenanting doctrines of the seventeenth century had been kept alive by the Popular Party throughout the eighteenth century and were carried into the nineteenth despite the change of its name to 'Evangelical'. Those tenets centered upon opposition to erastianism: the principle that an established church was essentially the religion department of the government. The Scottish refusal to accept the central rule of the Church of England's erastian model—ecclesiastical governance by bishops appointed by the secular government—was respected from the Settlement of 1689 forward. However, several years after the 1707 Act of Union, Westminster imposed upon the Church of Scotland the Church of England's erastian practice of having local members of the civil polity—the landed élite—appoint the parish clergy rather than allowing the congregation to elect its minister. This practice—known as 'lay patronage'—was bitterly unpopular in Scotland, but the secession of a number of congregations in protest did help the Moderate Party to maintain a majority over the Popular Party for most of the eighteenth century. In the early nineteenth century the Popular Party, under its new name of 'Evangelical', continued to despise lay patronage, which was increasingly complicated by the difficulties of developing spiritual ministry for people moving from the countryside to rapidly growing industrial cities and creating dense populations unanticipated by the existing parish system.[18] It was such an urban ministerial initiative that first brought Chalmers to public notice. In 1843, the lay patronage issue triggered the 'Great Disruption', in which over a third of the ministers of the Church of Scotland forfeited their incomes, their manses and their church buildings to form the Free Church of Scotland under Chalmers's leadership. It also had a dramatic impact upon Irish Presbyterians during the Famine, as we shall see. Hilton's dismissal of Chalmers's emphasis on the priority of human life and of Brown's usage of 'godly commonwealth' to characterize Chalmers's objectives probably result from his concentration on intellectual history to the neglect of social and political history. The fact that Chalmers was engaged in two very different vocations—academic theologian and ecclesiastical politician—must be considered in order for one to understand his mind in the multiple crises of the 1840s.

In 1847, the worst year of the Famine, the Queen—on the advice of her government—called for two 'humiliation days', during which her subjects were to attend religious services and to fast in recognition of their own shortcomings that might have angered the Almighty into the punishment that He had visited upon her realm. Peter Gray identifies three groups of Protestant clerical opinion concerning the humiliation days: ultras, moderates and liberals. The ultras attributed God's anger primarily to Catholic Ireland, while the liberals saw the Famine as a 'providentially inspired imperative of promoting the social and moral transformation of Ireland'. The moderates avoided anti-Catholic explanations and called upon the English to look for providential anger not only upon the Irish but upon themselves as well. Their sermons called for a 'shared "national" responsibility' for Ireland within the nation of the United Kingdom. The collection of some £171,533 on the first day of humiliation, in March, suggests success on the part of the moderates. By the time of the second event, in October, however, what we today call 'compassion fatigue' had emerged and only about £27,000 was collected.[19]

Gray's classification of Protestant opinion into three categories is useful, provided that we understand that individual clerics might well construct their judgments from more than one category. For example, in its May 1847 issue, *The Evangelical Magazine and Missionary Chronicle* published a contemplation of the humiliation day by a contributor who identified himself as 'T. W.'. After a poem entitled 'our fast day in 1847—national trials', T. W.

offers a homily emphasizing special considerations, special humiliation and special prayer in response to Divine Providence. He then describes the effects of the economic depression upon both rich and poor in Britain—created by 'the almost universal failure of the potato crop throughout the world'. This calamity 'had gone forth *from the Lord*, and that on which multitudes principally relied, was smitten, and *smitten by him*. . . . Let us, then, "humble ourselves under the mighty hand of God," and instead of complaining, offer the prayer, "When thy judgments are abroad in the earth, may its inhabitants learn righteousness" '. Having spent nearly five columns of his eight-column article on Britain and the wider world, T. W. turns to Ireland—'the sister-country'. In this section he relies almost entirely on eyewitness accounts of appalling conditions and the efforts of Christians to alleviate misery. He quotes verbatim the conclusion of an account by Rev. Alexander King, a Congregationalist minister in Cork, as the climax of his own article:

> May God pity Ireland! May God alleviate the woes of Ireland! May our heavenly Father soon come to her deliverance! Still, Ireland must learn many *valuable lessons*, from past and present calamities. The ignorance and superstition of multitudes of the lower class there must be checked. Improvident marriages must be guarded against. Periodical, instead of *continuous* labour, must be discountenanced. The soil must be well cultured; and *wheat*, instead of potatoes, must be *depended* on. An efficient poor-law must be introduced. There must be a better and happier understanding between landlord and tenant, and the curse of absenteeism must be removed. Then we should anticipate a brighter day for ill-fated Ireland: and, especially, when we found that the simple, benevolent, expansive, and ennobling institutions of Protestantism were generally received and observed, instead of the superstitious, meretricious, unscriptural, and pernicious of popery being regarded.[20]

T. W.'s article is a narrative in five scenes. First, the narrator places himself and his audience (in this case the readers of *The Evangelical Magazine*) among those who have angered the Almighty, by 'our coldness, infidelity, rebellion, and frequent departure from God'. Second, he extends the population upon whom God is infuriated beyond evangelicals to include the general public in the country of his audience and even—perhaps just for emphasis—all parts of the world where potatoes are grown. Third, he celebrates the efforts to minimize mortality. Fourth, he lists practical changes in educational, demographic, economic, agrarian and legal arrangements. Fifth, he anticipates the eventual conversion of Irish Catholics to Protestantism. Certainly the reference to 'improvident marriages' indicates awareness of Malthusian reasoning that is attributed to 'Christian economy'. However, it would be a mistake to interpret the call for an 'efficient poor-law' as simply a commitment to the extreme 'less eligibility' plan for poor relief as proposed by political economy. That plan had been adopted for Ireland in 1838, and an observer like Rev. King in County Cork nine years later would be intensely aware that that plan had proved to be an appalling failure. In general, T. W. demonstrates, I suggest, that an evangelical could find himself in more than one of Gray's three categories. Indeed, T. W.'s perspective reminds us that, among British evangelicals, a believer's reflections on divine chastisement of what today we call 'the other' could well entail similar reflection on the believer himself.

In the 1840s, Evangelical clergy were probably no more committed to unwavering providentialism than most other British or Irish ecclesiastics. It would be another decade before the appearance of *On the Origin of Species* and *Essays and Reviews* would seriously challenge that belief among religious professionals. However, Hilton's more serious error is his dismissal of Chalmers's categorization of life above economics as well as his commitment to a godly commonwealth. The importance of these conceptions on the development of popular politics in the post-Famine Ireland will emerge as we examine the proselytizers and their theological opponents.

SOUP

In popular Catholic memory, proselytizing the starving during the Famine is called 'souperism', from the term 'souper' that was applied to a starving Catholic who was converted to Protestantism.[21] Apparently the word 'souper' was not widely used during the Famine itself. The *Oxford English Dictionary*'s earliest quotation of it is from *The Tablet* in 1854. Interestingly, we learn from a book written a few months *before* the 1845 potato crop failure that a somewhat successful effort to convert a few Catholics to the Church of Ireland in and around Dingle in County Kerry since the early 1830s had led to 'souper' as one of the local 'appellations' applied to converts.[22] A conjecture that 'souper' was at that time a term confined to the Dingle vicinity is consistent with the fact that the New England evangelical Asenath Nicholson, in her account of her 1844–45 excursion in Ireland, mentions the term 'souper' only in her visit to Dingle.[23]

This conjecture is corroborated by a search for uses of the word 'souper' in the electronic file of the *Freeman's Journal*, the most prominent Catholic/Nationalist newspaper in nineteenth-century Dublin. Sixty-nine usages of 'souper'[24] in the three decades of 1830 to 1859 were found. The first appearance is in the spring of 1845 (well before the harvest failure) in an unclear reference in an item from another paper.[25] Significantly, the second appearance, in September of 1849, recounted a confrontation in Dingle between attendants of a funeral of a local Catholic priest and a group of former Catholics who had been converted in the two decades of missionary activity in that vicinity.[26] As can be seen in Figure 3.1, from that time forward, 'souper' ceased to be a mere local jargon in Dingle and became a term continually used throughout Ireland to describe and humiliate converts from

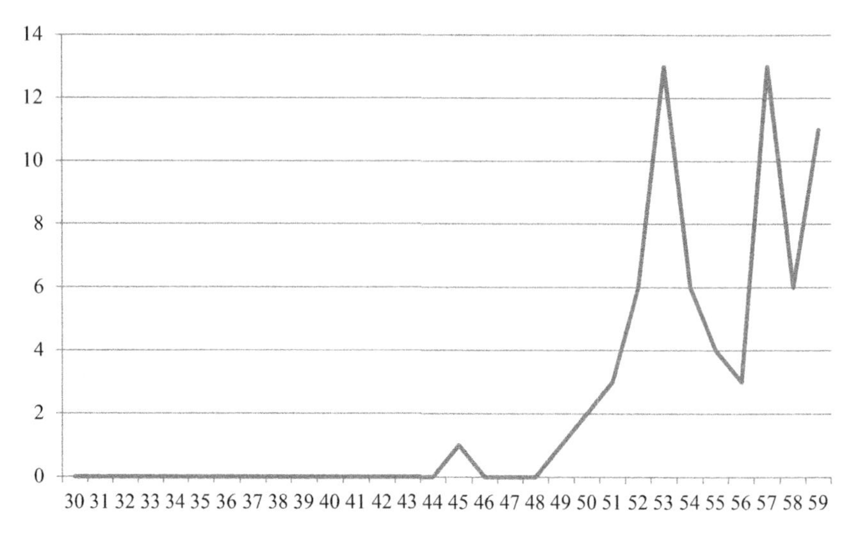

Figure 3.1 Articles mentioning 'souper' in *Freeman's Journal*, 1830–59

Catholicism to Protestantism. So the term 'souper' was coined more than a decade before the Great Famine, but only after the Famine did it become a nationwide term of defamation to describe a former Catholic who had converted to Protestantism for temporal advantage. It was the role of soup kettles in the public memory of the Famine that inserted 'souperism' into that memory.

To understand the events that caused the souper phenomenon, we must return to evangelicalism, this time with attention to the countryside rather than the academy and the élite political world. By the end of Wesley's long and active career in 1791, he had produced an army of travelling preachers in both the Atlantic Archipelago and North America. In Ireland, his followers, the Methodists, were not a separate denomination but saw themselves as a movement within the Church of Ireland until the late 1810s, when they divided into what would be called the Primitive Wesleyan Methodist Society (whose members continued to take communion in the Church of Ireland) and the Methodist Church.[27] No doubt occasionally a Catholic had heard an outdoor sermon of one of the movement's travelling preachers, but in general their main objective was to make lackadaisical Protestants into vital Christians. The most important influence of Methodists in the late eighteenth and early nineteenth century was to gradually convince Church of Ireland ministers that evangelicalism was an effective method for strengthening the religious commitment of their own congregations.

In the 1820s, this growth of evangelicals in the Church of Ireland met the growing demand for Catholic Emancipation, which, in the minds of many Anglicans, meant an eventual end to the confessional state. Such concern was exhibited by William Magee, the new Archbishop of Dublin, in his first charge to his clergy in 1822:

> We, my Reverend Brethren, are placed in a station, in which we are hemmed in by two opposite descriptions of professing Christians: the one, possessing a Church, without what *we* can properly call a Religion [i.e. Catholics]; and the other, possessing a Religion, without what we can properly call a Church [i.e. Presbyterians]: the one so blindly enslaved to a supposed infallible Ecclesiastical authority as not to seek in the Word of God a reason for the faith they profess; the other so confident in the infallibility of their individual judgment as to the reasons of their faith, that they deem it their duty to resist all authority in matters of religion.[28]

Magee was a high churchman, not an evangelical. Most Anglican evangelicals sought cooperation with fellow proponents of vital religion in other Protestant denominations and would avoid any such an insult as Magee's comparison of Presbyterians with Catholics. However, he seems to have been quite content to encourage evangelicals in what came to be labeled the 'new reformation' or 'second reformation'.[29]

Several prominent evangelical landlords, including Lord Farnham in County Cavan, the Earl of Roden in County Down, Lord Mandeville (later Duke of Manchester) in County Armagh and Viscount Lorton in Roscommon, were actively engaged in efforts to convert Catholics in their estates through various means, such as schools emphasizing Bible teaching and 'moral agents' whose duties included being sure that tenants took advantage of their landlord's educational initiatives. A brief success in the mid-1820s in converting some Catholics in the Farnham estate in County Cavan led to the claim that a 'new reformation' or 'second reformation' was taking place, but efforts by a deputation of Catholic bishops discouraged potential converts and accusations of bribery to gain conversions worried the promoters of the movement. By the late 1820s, the 'reformation' seemed to have failed.[30]

However, the Catholic Church's ability to prevent proselytizing was not uniform throughout the country. In 1835, the report of a royal commission charged to determine the population of the three major religious denominations was published. For obvious political reasons, contemporaries were very interested in the commission's overall estimate of the population of Ireland's three principal religions in 1834 (Church of Ireland 11 percent, Roman Catholics 81 percent, Presbyterians 8 percent),[31] but paid little attention to the estimates of average Sunday attendance that they collected for nearly every place of worship in Ireland. We now know that south Leinster, where in some chapels (as Catholic church buildings were identified) more than 80 percent of the Catholics attended mass each Sunday, was very different from west Connacht, where often fewer than 20 percent attended.[32] In general, the factors that accompanied low mass attendance were scarcity of priests, long walking distances to the nearest chapel, poverty of the laity and the absence of a market town in the vicinity of the chapel.[33] In west Connacht, many localities had exactly these attributes, but it took more than a decade for the major advocates of a 'second reformation' to realize that west Connacht was their best bet.

However, in 1831, a young individual Church of Ireland clergyman from a family with both Protestant and Catholic connections, Edward Nangle, who had been influenced by the Cavan initiative and was seeking a mission of his own, did stumble upon a very promising west Connacht location while supplying food to peasants of the island of Achill in County Mayo during a local famine. With the cooperation of the landlord, he not only converted probably about 300 Catholics but also created an attractive village where his converts and others formed a community in which life was considerably more comfortable than in the surrounding locale. Among the establishments in the village was a print shop that enabled Nangle to publish a monthly journal, *The Achill Missionary Herald and Western Witness*, and distribute some 2,000 copies to potential contributors to his project.[34] Although no further comparable program was started elsewhere in west Connacht prior to the Great Famine, Nangle had demonstrated and broadcasted two important findings: (1) it was actually possible to convert Catholics and keep them converted at least for a few years if you did it in west Connacht, and (2) if you undertook such a project, you could get lots of money to fulfill it from wealthy English evangelicals. The most important figure who seems to have benefited, at least indirectly, from the Achill experience, Alexander R.C. Dallas, learned the second of Nangle's findings first.

Dallas, the rector of Wonstan in Hampshire, had a strong aversion to Tractarianism: a High Church movement that urged Anglicans to return to various liturgical and theological traditions and whose most prominent spokesman, John Henry Newman, had become a Roman Catholic in 1845. His anti-Catholic tendency led him to an interest in missionary work in Ireland. He found a like-minded, wealthy businessman, Enoch Durant, to support his project. However, his first Irish initiative was a fiasco: he arranged for several Protestants who happened to be distributing a government publication throughout Ireland to collect addresses of 'Romanists of the respectable and middle class', and in January of 1846 he mailed twenty thousand copies of two of his tracts against Catholicism to these addresses. Needless to say, this was not an effective undertaking. However, during the next several months his benefactor directed him toward more practical and business-like initiatives, on one occasion showing him the 1841 census map of literacy and pointing to an area west of Galway where few could read; he also observed that Catholic priests were scarce in that area. By the end of 1846, Dallas had started a mission in Castelkerke, County Galway.[35]

As the Great Famine was becoming more appalling, however, Dallas was doing more than just establishing his own mission. In December, a committee of himself, the evangelical Rev. Edward Bickersteth and 22 other English Protestants appealed for contributions to a 'Special Fund for the Spiritual Exigencies of Ireland'.[36] This initiative to add to the various efforts to collect money for 'temporal exigencies' (e.g., urgent needs for food) by soliciting cash for 'spiritual exigencies' (e.g., urgent needs for salvation—i.e., conversion to Protestantism) is the principal undertaking that was criticized as proselytizing during the Famine and made 'souper' a widespread term of affront in post-Famine Irish Catholicism. The project received immediate condemnation in O'Connell's Conciliation Hall in Dublin and more contemplative disapproval by the Protestant Archbishop of Dublin, Richard Whately.[37] The committee succeeded in developing several missions in west Connacht, and at the end of the Famine the project was renamed the Society for Irish Church Missions to the Roman Catholics (ICM).

How did the Church of Ireland clergy respond to the Spiritual Exigencies Fund? This proselytizing initiative seems to have been almost entirely an initiative of English, not Irish, evangelicals. In his memoir of the ICM, Dallas mentions the difficulty of persuading the 'Irish clergy' to support such a project.[38] Some analysis of Church of Ireland clerics' messages to British evangelicals may help to explain that difficulty. In late April of 1847, the committee published in the evangelical London newspaper, the *Record*, a second appeal for contributions and included statements by recipients of funding. Seventeen of these statements were from individual clergymen,[39] and, as anyone who has written a grant proposal would expect, they generally applauded the objectives of the Fund and alluded to prospects of possible conversions of Catholics in their vicinities.

Another perspective of Church of Ireland clerical outlook appears in letters and other messages that were published in the *Record* between January and mid-May 1847 from sources *other than* the Special Fund committee. In that period, I have identified 33 such clergymen (ten of them having written more than one letter and four unidentified by name). Typically the letters describe the appalling situation in the writer's parish. Rev. William Fisher of Crookhaven, County Cork, writes, 'We can scarcely sit down to our meals, without having two or three hungry faces thrust in at our low little windows, craving something, for "God's sake" '.[40] Rev. James Anderson of Ballinrobe reports, 'I was actually obliged to give food to the gravediggers, from thence to enable them to perform their task!'[41] Rev. J. Cather of Spiddal expresses despair that 'Our aim can now only be to save a few out of many who we fear must fall'.[42] Rev. Giles Eyre near Westport writes, 'Thank God! oh, thank God, from my heart, you see not what I see today, at this moment. Crying, starving before my face, and not able to help, for want of food. O Lord, send some one to the Central Committee, and tell them to send food! food! food'.[43] Rev. R. B. Townsend, near Skibbereen, ends his description of the local situation with a condemnation of what David Nally[44] calls biopolitics: ‘God knows, nothing but a stern sense of duty detains me here; for we cannot, with all we get, do more than give a taste—we have not enough to feed the creatures—victims of a most mistaken national policy, on whom the principles of political economy have been carried out in practice to a murderous extent’.[45]

Among the 33 writers of these unsolicited letters, only seven, in my judgment, mention taking advantage of the Famine to convert Catholics. For example, Rev. Robert Potter of Louisburgh, County Mayo, after mentioning discord between himself and the Catholic priests in the local Relief Committee, writes:

> It may be well here to remark that the poor Roman Catholics themselves are almost universally well affected towards the Protestant clergyman, being convinced of the importance of his exertions for their benefit. And very many of them would gladly conform to Protestantism were any opening or *protection* afforded them. Should the funds permit, the clergyman [i.e. Potter] is determined to take a small farm in which to sow flax, corn, &c., to be cultivated by persons thus disposed.[46]

According to George Read, curate at Ballina, County Mayo,

> The awful visitation under which we suffer is so far beneficial that our Roman Catholic peasantry acknowledge the hand of God, and turn to Him that smites. A great door and effectual is opened unto us, though there are many adversaries. Some have renounced the errors of the Church of Rome, and I now purpose to provide, with God’s help, a little clothing for their children, and to send them to our Infant School, where a little bread shall be given them daily. Thus the parents shall be so far relieved, and the children benefited in a temporal and spiritual point of view.[47]

Rev. James Freke of Kilcoe, County Cork, is less specific: ‘The victims are almost all members of the Roman Catholic Church, but I do believe that the Lord is bringing good out of evil and overruling this dispensation to give us access to the hearts and affections on the poor benighted people’.[48] In a letter to a lady who apparently forwarded it to the *Record*, Robert Oliver, curate of Myross, County Cork, asks her for money ‘first to alleviate the appalling misery of my fellow-creatures, by affording them some sustenance; and secondly, that I may be able to speak to them occasionally on spiritual matters, for I have many opportunities now that I never had before of laying the Gospel before them in its beautiful simplicity’. An anonymous superintending clergyman in County Leitrim, where ‘crowds of children’ are now attending his school, where they receive a nourishing meal and ‘that truth that makes wise unto salvation’, sees ‘an opening now for scriptural instruction, such as never existed before in Ireland’.[49] The other two unsolicited letter-writers that seem to have adopted the Special Fund's plan of using the Famine as an opportunity to convert Catholics are Henry de L. Willis, Incumbent of Portadown, and James Disney, Curate of Charlemont.[50] Both of these parishes are in the northern part of County Armagh, an area that is distinguished by three relevant characteristics. First, it was one of the few predominantly Protestant Armagh locales where Churchmen outnumbered Dissenters; second, it was one of the few mainly Protestant districts in Ireland that experienced severe adversity in the Great Famine; and third, it has arguably the country's most malevolent history of conflict between Protestants and Catholics. Any well-informed evangelical would require an exceptionally solid confidence of providential intervention to take seriously the plans of Reverends Willis and Disney.

So there were certainly some Church of Ireland clergy who responded enthusiastically to the assumptions of the Special Fund for the Spiritual Exigencies of Ireland. At least seventeen of the approximately 2,000 Anglican clerics in Ireland applied for grants from the fund during its first four months. However, of the 33 Church of Ireland clergymen whose unsolicited letters appeared in the *Record* in about the first four months of 1847, only seven seemed to be particularly concerned about converting Catholics under the situation. The other 26 seem to have been much more concerned about 'temporal exigencies'—how to keep the starving alive.

Perhaps the most conspicuous effort by Church of Ireland clergy to distance themselves from the extreme evangelicals of the Church of England occurred in Belfast. Shortly after the appeal for the Special Fund for the Spiritual Exigencies of Ireland, a committee of Belfast Anglicans announced a 'Fund for the *Temporal* Relief of the Suffering Poor of Ireland'.[51] In one of their appeals they write, 'Calumniated as the religion of Protestants has been to our Roman Catholic fellow-countrymen, it is surely a matter of the utmost moment that we should exhibit a practical refutation of such slanders and demonstrate to all, now in the period of Ireland's dire emergency, that ours is a "faith which worketh by love," even to enemies'. Their aging bishop, Richard Mant, one of the few high churchmen still in the Church of Ireland hierarchy, seems not to have participated in the project. Nevertheless he must have been pleased by this disparagement of the fanatics among the low churchmen that he had encountered during his career.

But the differences between Irish and English Anglicans involved more than the respective theological opinions of church parties. Although only a small minority around 1800, by the 1840s probably a majority of Church of Ireland clergy would have identified themselves as evangelicals (though it was only after the 1869 disestablishment that that majority became 'overwhelming').[52] However, nearly all of them were probably Irish (as opposed to English) Protestants. A typical Church of Ireland minister was the son—presumably often the second or later son—of an Irish clerical or gentry family or perhaps an upper middle class family in an Irish city. He had entered a career that offered social status and income appropriate to his background, although a year of distress might make that income uncertain (an anxiety that was somewhat, but not absolutely, resolved by the Tithe Rentcharge Act of 1838). If from a landed family he—the brother who went into the morality business—might have inherited a sense of responsibility—something like what today we call 'moral economy'—for members of the 'lower orders' in his keeping during times of distress. Even if he was not so inclined, ordinary economic considerations might well prompt him to avoid projects that might anger the Catholic majority of his parish.

So there was a significant difference between the typical Church of Ireland clergymen and the Church of England members who conceived the Spiritual Exigencies Fund. Edward Nangle, who was a recipient of support from the Fund, exhibited his Irish ancestry when he wrote that during the Famine many Catholics in his mission had requested to join the Church of Ireland,

> and they have, without a single exception, been refused. Now is the season for instruction, and not proselytism. The answer to all such applications is this:—'Whatever religion you profess, we will give you all the help in our power; and if you desire instruction for yourselves and your children, you shall have that too; and when the famine is over, and no reasonable ground exists for doubting your sincerity we will admit you into our Church, if you desire it, but not sooner'.[53]

Another difference between established churchmen in Ireland and England concerned the role of the Catholic Church in the two kingdoms. Although Church of Ireland clergymen had a realistic concern that the government might disestablish their institution, they had no fear that any of their own colleagues were clandestine Catholics somehow plotting to hand over the Church of Ireland to the Holy See. The situation was different in England. Since the mid-1830s, the tractarian movement had gradually convinced some evangelical English churchmen that members of the High Church party were conspiring to return the Church of England to Rome. These evangelicals became a faction within the Evangelical Party that was eventually given a name, the 'Recordites' (from the title of the *Record* newspaper) in 1853 by William Conybeare, who called it 'the extreme section of the Evangelical party' in the Church of England.[54] It is now conceived by historians as a faction of 'extreme' evangelicals spanning about three decades beginning in 1828 when the *Record* began publication.[55]

The Spiritual Exigencies Fund was a Recordite project. Six of its 24 committee members appear among the 43 Recordites mentioned in John Wolffe's article on Recordites in the *Oxford Dictionary of National Biography*.[56] *ODNA* contains full biographies of 24 of the Recordites mentioned by Wolffe (including four of the Spiritual Exigencies committee members). Among those 24 prominent Recordites, eight were born in Ireland, including four who were ordained as Anglican clerics and pursued anti-Catholic careers in England: perhaps yet another indication that the Church of Ireland was not overwhelmingly welcome to extreme enemies of their neighbors.

The Recordite who apparently managed the Spiritual Exigencies project was the committee's secretary, Rev. Edward Bickersteth, rector of a parish close enough to London to enable him to be active in ecclesiastical politics and who also was a productive author of both professional and popular religious material. Perhaps the best way to describe the Recordites of the mid-nineteenth century to twenty-first century readers is to explain its connection to the late-nineteenth century American movement that we call Fundamentalism.[57] Conybeare stresses the Recordites' insistence on 'the sole supremacy of Scripture' and 'Verbal Inspiration', leading to 'the most arbitrary and unscrupulous misinterpretations, either violently wresting Scripture to make it accord with facts, or denying facts which they cannot reconcile with Scripture'. No doubt such extreme literal approaches to the Bible contributed such topics to their sermons as 'the approaching restoration of the Jews' and 'the date of the Millennium'.[58] Indeed millenarianism was the topic of two of Brickersteth's recent publications when he took charge of the Spiritual Exigencies fund. In 1843, he published *The Divine Warning to the Church, at this Time of our Enemies, Dangers, and Duties, and as to our Future Prospects; with Information Respecting the Diffusion of Infidelity, Lawlessness, and Popery,* and in 1845, *The Signs of the Times in the East; a Warning to the West: being a Practical View of our Duties in the Light of the Prophecies which Illustrate the Present and Future State of the Church and of the World.*[59] Though not esteemed in the theological profession like Bickersteth, his friend Alexander Dallas, another committee member, was also a millennialist, and between 1841 and 1851 he published at least eleven items on the topic.[60]

Why should we care about the eschatology of the Rev. Bickersteth and his Recordite colleagues? The answer to that question is *not* that they were worried lest the Catholics, even if they should survive the Famine, might miss their last chance for salvation prior to the end of the world. In order to grasp the meaning of their eschatology, we must understand that Christian millennialism in the nineteenth century came in two flavors: premillennial and postmillennial. Recordites were premillennialists. Premillennialists believe that Christ's second coming will be the *beginning* of the thousand years mentioned in Revelation 20:1–6. Postmillennialists believe that it will mark the *end* of the thousand years (often understood to be metaphorical). This means that postmillennialists might well believe that it is their duty to engage in good works in this world to hasten the day when God's kingdom shall come to earth as it is in heaven.

At the time of the Famine, the keepers of a postmillennialist tradition in Irish Protestantism were Presbyterians. In two brilliant essays, Andrew Holmes has recounted the blossoming of postmillennialism among Ulster Presbyterian clergy from Thomas Ledlie Birch, a colorful supporter of the United Irishmen, until the late nineteenth century when some well-educated

Protestants were beginning to stop trying to make literal sense of apocalyptic texts.[61] From the 1790s to the mid-nineteenth century, Presbyterian ministers often supported worthy actions, from slavery emancipation to the establishment of missionary projects in India, as steps toward the kingdom of God on earth. During the Famine, however, there was one Ulster Presbyterian *pre*millennialist, and he is probably the most frequently mentioned Presbyterian minister in Irish historical literature: Rev. Henry Cooke.[62]

Cooke seemed to outsiders to be the unchallenged leader of mainstream Irish Presbyterianism after 1829, when he drove the Unitarians out of the General Synod of Ulster. He developed relationships with conservative politicians and Anglican churchmen in the hope of gaining for the Irish Presbyterians equal privilege with members of the Church of Ireland. However, he lost his leadership dramatically when he tried to use his relationship with Peel to avoid the Great Disruption and failed dismally. The Irish Presbyterian General Assembly (a merger since 1840 of the General Synod and the Seceding Synod) then humiliated him by a resolution to seek Presbyterian candidates for the House of Commons (as opposed to Cooke's Anglican landlord friends), and Cooke refused to attend the General Assembly again until the resolution was rescinded, which it was four years later, in 1847. By that time the Assembly had developed new leadership, and Cooke would live another two decades, bitterly denouncing its liberal dominance. In the aftermath of the Famine, farmers initiated a movement for 'tenant right', i.e., legislation to grant any tenant farmer a claim to certain legally enforceable property rights to his farm as were reflected in existing, but merely customary, practices in much of Ulster and some other parts of Ireland by which, when land was rented to a new tenant, the outgoing tenant was entitled to collect a certain payment from his successor. The General Assembly strongly supported tenant right and despite the fact that Cooke accused ministers who advocated tenant right of communism,[63] many Presbyterian ministers appeared on the platforms of tenant right demonstrations, (sometimes side by side with Catholic priests) in what Holmes has labeled 'covenanter politics'.[64] In other words, Ulster Presbyterian clergy had recovered from their seventeenth century tradition the concept of a 'godly commonwealth' in which the church's duty is not an erastian responsibility to legitimize whatever the governing class wants, but a calling to proclaim to the state what we now call 'social justice'.

THE FAMINE AS A PATH TO POPULAR POLITICS

So how did the three ethno-religious communities of Ireland respond to the transformation from confessional state to nation-state in the wake of the Great Famine? The Church of Ireland's clergy and laity continued to hope that somehow their confessional state could survive. The fact that English Recordites had insisted on coming to their rescue by trying to make more

Anglicans out of starving Catholics did not help to sustain the confessional state, but that debacle was generally not the fault of the existing Irish Anglicans. It was clear that sooner or later the Church of Ireland was going to be disestablished; it happened in 1869. Having lost their confessional state, a very few Irish Anglicans—notably Isaac Butt, the initiator of the Home Rule movement, and Charles Stewart Parnell, who succeeded him as leader of it—lost trust in the United Kingdom of Great Britain and Ireland as their nation-state, but for most of their coreligionists, disestablishment probably strengthened their UK nation-statist commitment.

In the three decades following the Famine, the Irish Catholic Church was dominated by one individual—Archbishop (Cardinal from 1866) Paul Cullen—an Irish priest who had spent the first half of his career in Rome. Cullen's perspective on matters of state remained situated in the Holy See, where nationalism was anathema and the United Kingdom was a world power whose global interests were of greater concern to the papacy than were any bothersome issues in Ireland. After Cullen's death in 1878, the Irish hierarchy resumed their usual pattern of thinking like Irishmen, not like the ecclesiastical variety of world statesmen. As a genuine nationalist party emerged in the House of Commons under the leadership of Parnell, the hierarchy came to terms with Irish nationalism in what the late Emmet Larkin has described as an 'informal concordat': an agreement in 1884 to support the Irish Parliamentary Party in return for the Party's support of the Church's interests.[65] This understanding, however, was a commitment to nationalism, not legitimization of physical force within the territory of the nation in question. The hierarchy did not begin to come to terms with an Irish nation-state until the aftermath of Easter week of 1916. Although there is no such thing as a concordat between a church and a political party, Larkin used the term to remind the reader of the church-state relations in the southern Irish state during the period prior to Vatican II that many observers now describe as a 'confessional state'.[66]

The Famine occurred while Presbyterians were in the process of rejecting Henry Cooke's dream of gaining for them the status of an established church alongside the Churches of England, Scotland and Ireland in the UK confessional state. They were not seeking a nation-state. (Would anyone die for the Ulster nation?) They were seeking a godly commonwealth: i.e., a confessional state that would listen to a church that proposed social justice rather than protecting the interests of the wealthy and powerful. It was the Famine that seemed to make that project practical. Moreover, in informal alliance with the Catholic electorate, they succeeded by 1881 in obtaining land legislation that eventually made possible ownership of farms by the farmers through the Land Purchase Act of 1903. Thereafter, 'landlords', if not extinct, were at least an endangered species.

The Famine prompted both Catholic and Presbyterian clergy to engage in popular politics. In the language of today, the Catholic politics focused on ethnicity and the Presbyterian politics on social class. Both churches opposed the use of physical force but, in the nation-state of *le peuple*, European democracy had granted to a majority ethnic group a claim to control of that force. Protestants—both Presbyterians and Anglicans—united, lest they be treated in a Home Rule Ireland as their descendants eventually treated the Catholics in the six-County province.

In his recent *Human Encumbrance*, Nally proposes an intriguing revision of how we should assess the blame for the hundreds of thousands of deaths during the Great Irish Famine that might have been avoided given different government policies. His argument rests upon Michel Foucault's assertion that sovereigns in emerging European states claimed the privilege of *patria potestas* (the right of a Roman father to 'dispose' of the lives of his children and slaves) over their subjects. During medieval and early modern times, that privilege was gradually limited to forcing subjects to risk their lives in warfare to defend the state. In the nineteenth century, however, Nally argues that sovereign power introduced 'biopolitics': the allowance of non-combat risks of death in the interest of the state's security and the progress to sustain it. Nally identifies starvation of those whose culture deviates from that of capitalist modernity as one of those risks.[67]

Nally's decision to address the Famine's consequences by examining the development of acquiescence to death is brilliant, and I especially welcome his rejection of genocidal interpretations of the event.[68] However, I suggest that that conclusion can be better understood if we conceive of the eventual outcome of *patria potestas* not only through the perspective of the social theorist, but also that of the social scientist. Weber's grasp of the centrality of 'legitimate' physical force in the modern descendant of the *patria potestas*—the state—is the key to understanding the relationship—for better or for worse—between politics and morality. In this essay I have not attempted to turn that key, but I hope that it will be turned.

NOTES

1. A search for 'popular politics' in the scanned texts of two relevant databases of English books, 'Eighteenth Century Collections Online' and 'The Making of the Modern World' (1460–1914), yields 21 books in ECCO, of which the earliest was published in 1792, and 14 books in MMW, beginning in 1791.
2. people, n. II. 3. a. OED Online. September 2012. Oxford University Press. (accessed September 24, 2012).
3. Joseph R. Strayer, *On the Medieval Origins of the Modern State* (Princeton, NJ, 1970).
4. Max Weber, Hans Heinrich Gerth, and C. Wright Mills, *From Max Weber: Essays in Sociology* (London, 1991), 78 (italics omitted).
5. For an argument that the twentieth-century state relied on the nation for legitimizing, see Rupert Emerson, *From Empire to Nation; the Rise to Self-Assertion of Asian and African Peoples* (Cambridge, 1960), 95–96.
6. Arguably the transition within Ireland (south and/or north) might be understood as continuing for much if not all of the twentieth century. Since that would take us well into the uncertainty of the future of the nation-state in Europe, the historian has little to say about it yet.

7. John Mitchel, *The Last Conquest of Ireland (Perhaps)*, ed. Patrick Maume (Dublin, 2005). See vii-xxx for history of the book, which was originally serialized in Mitchel's newspaper the *Southern Citizen* (Knoxville, TN) in 1858–59. Mitchel's father, the Presbyterian minister in Newry, was expelled in 1829 from the Synod of Ulster in Henry Cooke's first major step toward his goal of gaining for the Presbyterian Church equal status with the Church of Ireland in the confessional state. As a Unitarian, however, the Rev. Mitchel's theological disagreement with Cooke in 1829 should not be confused with the much broader opposition among Presbyterian clergy toward Cooke in the 1840s and thereafter.
8. John Wesley, *The Heart of John Wesley's Journal* (New York, 1903), 43.
9. R. A. Knox, *Enthusiasm: A Chapter in the History of Religion* (Oxford, 1950). Susie I. Tucker, *Enthusiasm: A Study in Semantic Change* (Cambridge, 1972).
10. Cathal Póirtéir, ed., *Famine Echoes* (Dublin, 1995). For an eyewitness of the providential thought of peasants, see Hugh Dorian, *The Outer Edge of Ulster: A Memoir of Social Life in Nineteenth-Century Donegal*, ed. Breandán Mac Suibhne and David Dickson (Dublin, 2000), 172–73, 224.
11. David W. Miller, 'Irish Presbyterians and the Great Famine', in Jacqueline Hill and Colm Lennon, eds., *Luxury and Austerity* (Dublin, 1999), 174–75. *Banner of Ulster*, 23 March 1847. A strong belief in providentialism was not confined to Ireland. For an excellent account, see Stewart J. Brown, *Providence and Empire: Religion, Politics and Society in the United Kingdom, 1815–1914* (Harlow and New York, 2008).
12. Boyd Hilton, *The Age of Atonement: The Influence of Evangelicalism on Social and Economic Thought, 1785–1865* (Oxford, 1988).
13. Thomas Chalmers, 'The Political Economy of a Famine', *North British Review*, 7 (May 1847), 247–90; Stewart J. Brown, *Thomas Chalmers and the Godly Commonwealth in Scotland* (Oxford, 1982), 367–69; Boyd Hilton, *Age of Atonement*, 110.
14. Chalmers, 'Political Economy', 247–48.
15. Hilton, *Age of Atonement*, 87–88.
16. John R. McIntosh, *Church and Theology in Enlightenment Scotland: The Popular Party, 1740–1800* (East Linton, 1998), 176–232.
17. Michael A. G. Haykin and Kenneth J. Stewart, eds., *The Advent of Evangelicalism: Exploring Historical Continuities* (Nashville, 2008), a recent volume of critiques of David Bebbington, *Evangelicalism in Modern Britain: A History from the 1730s to the 1980s* (London, 1989).
18. Stewart J. Brown, 'The Ten Year's Conflict and the Disruption of 1843', in Stewart J. Brown and Michael Fry, eds., *Scotland in the Age of the Disruption* (Edinburgh, 1993), 1–27.
19. Peter Gray, 'National Humiliation and the Great Hunger: Fast and Famine in 1847', *Irish Historical Studies* 32, 126 (2000), 193–216.
20. T. W., 'Pictures from Life. No. III', *Evangelical Magazine and Missionary Chronicle*, new series 25 (May, 1847), 229–32. For details re: Rev. King: *Slater's National Commercial Directory of Ireland* (Manchester and London, 1846), 188 and 221 of section following Dublin.
21. In some cases, the word 'souper' was also applied to the proselytizer. *Oxford English Dictionary*, sub 'souper'.
22. Mrs. D. P. Thompson, *A Brief Account of the Rise and Progress of the Change in Religious Opinion now Taking Place in Dingle, and the West of the County of Kerry, Ireland* (London, 1845), 47. On iii–iv, a letter from the author to a gentleman in London, apparently in hopes that he will find a publisher for her manuscript, is dated '*Dingle, Feb.* 10, 1845'.
23. Asenath Nicholson, *Ireland's Welcome to the Stranger, or, An Excursion through Ireland, in 1844 & 1845, for the Purpose of Personally Investigating the Condition of the Poor* (New York, 1847), 367–69.

24. Uses of the French word 'souper' and the surname 'Souper' were discarded.
25. *Freeman's Journal*, 26 April 1845.
26. Ibid., 25 September 1849.
27. Dudley Livistone Cooney, *The Methodists in Ireland: A Short History* (Blackrock, 2001), 58–66.
28. William Magee, *A Charge Delivered at his Primary Visitation, in St. Patrick's Cathedral, Dublin, on Thursday the 24th of October, 1822* (2nd edition, London, 1822), 25.
29. Peter Nockles, 'Church or Protestant Sect? The Church of Ireland, High Churchmanship, and the Oxford Movement, 1822–1869', *The Historical Journal*, 41, 2 (1998), 462; Irene Whelan, *The Bible War in Ireland: The 'Second Reformation' and the Polarization of Protestant-Catholic Relations, 1800–1840* (Madison, Wisc., 2005), 157.
30. Irene Whelan, *The Bible War*, 152–91. Stewart J. Brown, 'The New Reformation Movement in the Church of Ireland, 1801–29', in Stewart J. Brown and David W. Miller, eds., *Piety and Power in Ireland, 1760–1960: Essays in Honour of Emmet Larkin* (Belfast and Notre Dame, 2000), 180–208. J.R. Wright, 'Evangelical Landlords and Moral Agents in Nineteenth-Century Ulster, with Special Reference to the Manchester Estates in County Armagh', *Moirae: Journal of the School of Philosophy, Politics and History*, 8 (1984), 37–64.
31. *First Report of the Commissioners of Public Instruction, Ireland*, HC 1835 (45, 46), xxxiii, Appendix, 74.
32. David W. Miller, 'Mass Attendance in Ireland in 1834', in Brown and Miller, eds., *Piety and Power*, 158–79.
33. David W. Miller, 'Landscape and Religious Practice: A Study of Mass Attendance in Pre-Famine Ireland', *Éire-Ireland*, 40, 1–2 (2005), 90–106. (Table 2 on 95 of the article contains several errors. The following numbers are correct: Clergy, col. D: 0.2675; Market town, col. D: 0.3224; P-value of Moran's I, col. A: 0.8198. The following two coefficients are significant at the 0.05 level: Walking distance, col. D and Underclass, col. C. All other coefficients are significant at the 0.001 level.)
34. Mealla Ní Ghiobúin, *Dugort, Achill Island, 1831–1861: The Rise and Fall of a Missionary Community* (Dublin, 2001).
35. Alexander R.C. Dallas, *The Story of the Irish Church Missions: Part One: An Account of the Providential Preparation which Led to the Establishment of the Society for Irish Church Missions to the Roman Catholics in 1849* (London, 1867), 52–59, 103–07. Miriam Moffitt, *The Society for Irish Church Missions to the Roman Catholics, 1849–1950* (Manchester, 2010), 51–53.
36. Miriam Moffitt, 'The Society for Irish Church Missions to Roman Catholics: Philanthropy or Bribery?', *International Bulletin of Missionary Research*, 30, 1 (2006), 32.
37. Richard Whately, *Address to the Clergy and Other Members of the Established Church of the Use and Abuse of the Present Occasion for the Exercise of Beneficence by the Archbishop of Dublin* (Dublin, 1847).
38. Dallas, *Story of the Irish Church Missions*, 105–109.
39. *Record*, 22 April 1847. There were also statements from societies and individual scripture readers.
40. *Record*, 4 January 1847.
41. *Record*, 1 March 1847.
42. *Record*, 1 March 1847.
43. *Record*, 1 February 1847. By 'the Central Committee' he means the government's 'Central Relief Commission'.
44. David P. Nally, *Human Encumbrances: Political Violence and the Great Irish Famine* (Notre Dame, 2011).
45. *Record*, 11 May 1847.

46. *Record*, 15 March 1847.
47. *Record*, 25 February 1847.
48. *Record*, 11 January 1847.
49. *Record*, 25 February 1847.
50. *Record*, 11 January and 22 February 1847.
51. *Belfast News Letter*, 8 January 1847. Italics added.
52. Donald Harman Akenson, *The Church of Ireland: Ecclesiastical Reform and Revolution, 1800–1885* (New Haven and London, 1971), 132.
53. *Record*, 22 April 1847. Curiously, Nangle is the only one of the recipients whose name is published in this set of solicited letters. Perhaps this was a way of suggesting that Nangle's practice which, given his admiration, could hardly be suppressed, was not the policy of the Spiritual Exigencies committee.
54. William John Conybeare, *Essays, Ecclesiastical and Social: Reprinted with Additions from the Edinburgh Review* (London, 1855), 58. Preface to 'Church Parties', which was originally published in *Edinburgh Review* in 1853.
55. John Wolffe, 'Recordites (act. 1828–*c.*1860)', in *The Oxford Dictionary of National Biography*.
56. These 43 Recordites include 24 for whom there are full biographies in *ODNB*, including four of the six who were members of the Spiritual Exigencies Fund committee. When I refer to 'prominent' Recordites, I mean the 24.
57. For a study of the relationship of British millenarianism and American Fundamentalism, see Ernest R. Sandeen, *The Roots of Fundamentalism: British and American Millenarianism, 1800–1930* (Chicago and London, 1970), 3–41.
58. Conybeare, *Essays*, 75, 81, 82, and 91.
59. Edward Bickersteth, *The Divine Warning to the Church* (London, 1843); idem, *The Signs of the Times in the East* (London, 1845).
60. Moffitt, *Society for Irish Church Missions* (2010), 47–48 n. 11 and 90.
61. Andrew Holmes, 'Millennialism and the Interpretation of Prophecy in Ulster Presbyterianism, 1790–1850', in Crawford Gribben and Timothy C. F. Stunt, eds., *Prisoners of Hope? Aspects of Evangelical Millennialism in Britain and Ireland, 1800–1880* (Carlisle, 2004), 150–76; idem, 'The Uses and Interpretation of Prophecy in Irish Presbyterianism, 1850–1930', in Crawford Gribben and Andrew Holmes, eds., *Protestant Millennialism, Evangelicalism and Irish Society, 1790–2005* (New York, 2006), 144–73.
62. Patrick Maume's endnote 112 in William McComb, *The Repealer Repulsed*, ed. Patrick Maume (Dublin, 2003), 297. Cooke is the only Irish Presbyterian (and one of among only two Presbyterians from any location) in Wolffe's list of Recordites.
63. *Londonderry Standard*, 5 May 1850.
64. Andrew Holmes, 'Covenanter Politics: Evangelicalism, Political Liberalism and Ulster Presbyterians, 1798–1914', *English Historical Review*, 125 (2010), 340–69.
65. Emmet J. Larkin, *The Historical Dimensions of Irish Catholicism* (Washington, DC, 1984), 111–12, 120.
66. E.g., Lawrence John McCaffrey, review of Louise Fuller, *Irish Catholicism since 1950: The Undoing of a Culture* in *New Hibernia Review*, 7, 2 (Summer 2003), 154–57.
67. Nally, *Human Encumbrances*, 15–16.
68. Ibid., 228.

4 Walking Backward to Heaven?

Edmond Ronayne's Pilgrimage in Famine Ireland and Gilded Age America

Kerby A. Miller and Ellen Skerrett, with Bridget Kelly[1]

> We advance to the truth by experience of error; we succeed through failures. We know not how to do right except by having done wrong. . . . We know what is right, not positively, but negatively—we do not see the truth at once and make towards it, but we fall upon and try error, and find it is not the truth. We grope about by touch, not by sight, and so by a miserable experience exhaust the possible modes of acting until naught is left, but truth, remaining. Such is the process by which we succeed; we walk to heaven backward.
>
> —John Henry Cardinal Newman, *Parochial and Plain Sermons*

> Strange, indeed, that you should not have suspected that your universe and its contents were only dreams, visions, fiction! Strange, because they are so frankly and hysterically insane—like all dreams. . . . Dream other dreams, and better.
>
> —Mark Twain, *The Mysterious Stranger*

The Great Famine of 1845–52 was the most important and traumatic event in modern Irish history: it resulted in more than one million deaths and by 1855 over two million emigrants; it transformed the structures of Irish and Irish-American societies; and it strengthened and intensified both Irish nationalism and Anglo-Protestant supremacism on each side of the Atlantic. Collectively and often personally, Irish Catholic fugitives from *An Gorta Mór* interpreted their experience in traditional terms of 'exile', forced by British and landlord oppression, and they did so in the alienating contexts of the poverty and hostility that most Famine emigrants experienced in their adopted countries. By contrast, Irish Protestants generally believed, as their transatlantic spokesmen assured them, that their adherence to the Reformed faith and their loyalty to the Crown virtually guaranteed their economic success or, at least their social respectability, overseas as well as at home.

But what, then, of poor or unsuccessful Irish Protestant emigrants? Unlike Irish Catholics, they were fully exposed to the hegemonic myths of Anglo-American capitalism and evangelicalism, and thus lacked collective cultural and political resources that could 'explain' exploitation and dispossession in Ireland, or 'failure' and poverty abroad, in ways that mitigated feelings of personal accountability and guilt. As a result, Irish Protestant modes of 'adjustment' to objectively negative circumstances could be mundanely conformist and yet, paradoxically, highly individualistic, even eccentric. Conformist, because in general capitalist and evangelical belief systems were mutually reinforcing in stressing individual responsibility for material and spiritual success; and because American Protestant culture, like its Irish counterpart, was suffused with missionary zeal, providential beliefs, and millennial expectations. And yet, under stress, those same religious impulses could generate singular and 'extreme' (if logically consistent) beliefs that qualified or even challenged at least some aspects of the 'established order' and often led their adherents into the spiritual and political margins of American society.[2]

In general, then, it is arguable that Irish Protestant emigrants' incorporation into bourgeois American society and culture was usually more thorough and 'successful' than that of most Irish Catholics, who even in the early 1900s remained, as their critics charged, astride the socio-cultural 'hyphen'. On the other hand, the pilgrimage of one Irish Protestant, Edmond Ronayne, provides examples of the many kinds of emigrant 'adaptation'—of the multiple, mutable varieties of Irish identity—which scholars often now posit in contrast to the traditional image of the homesick, anglophobic Irish Catholic 'exile'. Indeed, one further complication is that Ronayne was not born and raised an Irish Protestant, but rather he converted from Catholicism before he left Ireland. And yet, despite his convert's zeal, several episodes in Ronayne's long career suggest that some traditionally 'Irish' and even 'Irish Catholic' continuities can still be discerned among what otherwise appear to be the disconnected shards of a life shattered by the trauma of Black '47 and by his post-Famine conversion.

In addition, Ronayne's life story may posit several broad qualifications of the emigrant adaptation model. Most nineteenth-century emigrants unavoidably adapted to capitalist societies that were more 'modern' or 'advanced' than the ones they left. Before their departures, however, emigrants, such as Ronayne, already had undergone the profound socioeconomic and cultural changes that launched their migrations and destabilized their customary social relationships, cultural assumptions, and individual personalities. An Irish person born in the early 1800s, for example, experienced severe economic depression, rural deindustrialization, intense social, political, and sectarian conflict, and the rapid erosion of traditional beliefs and customs wrought by Anglicization, 'devotional revolution' Catholicism, and capitalist relationships—all of which were then accelerated and intensified by the Great Famine. Nevertheless, most emigrants, however 'modernized' before their departures, exhibited a mixture of 'traditional' (pre-capitalist) and 'modern' behavioral, cultural, and psychological patterns, as even traumas like the Famine or initial encounters with American slums could reinforce as well as disrupt customary relationships and attitudes. As a result, an emigrant's adaptation or assimilation was not necessarily linear: it could proceed or revert—go 'backward', as it were—during his or her lifetime, depending on a host of environmental as well as personal factors.

Finally, the adaptability thesis—driven by assumptions about the benign inevitability of 'modernization' and perhaps also by beliefs in 'American exceptionalism'—may underestimate the negative and even destructive *quality* of many of the environmental factors to which emigrants to the United States perforce adapted. The great majority of Irish (and other) emigrants were obliged to 'adjust' to—and, at least to a degree, internalize the values of—an urban-industrial America that was characterized, as Irish emigrants and native reformers alike lamented, by brutal exploitation and ruthless competition. The adaptation model generally discounts or ignores this 'future shock'—the personal pain and confusion, so poignantly described in Oscar Handlin's *The Uprooted*[3]—which emigrants often experienced as they tried to jettison or reconcile imported communal beliefs with the exigencies of individual 'success' or family survival in Gilded Age America.

In response, of course, many emigrants created and relied on 'ethnic' networks for practical assistance and imagined continuities and solace. In that respect, late nineteenth-century Irish Catholic emigrants—with their panoply of Irish-American institutions, united by religion and a collective 'exile' self-image—may have been greatly advantaged, although alienation from capitalist America still pervaded many of their letters. As noted, however, Irish Protestant emigrants generally lacked such ethnic buffers and thus were obliged to construct their own means of social aid and spiritual salvation out of 'mainstream' American institutions and belief systems, which mystified as much as they 'explained' social realities. For Edmond Ronayne, who spent his long life trying to 'make sense' of his Famine experience, the results were ambiguous, contradictory, problematic. Despite their religious differences, Cardinal Newman might have interpreted Ronayne's resolutions of his 'miserable experience' as ultimately redemptive. Yet for a radical skeptic like his contemporary Mark Twain, they would surely have seemed as 'hysterically insane' as the 'dreams' on which they were based.

•

The principal source for this essay is *Ronayne's Reminiscences*, a unique memoir by an Irish-speaking Famine survivor, which was published in 1900 by the Free Methodist Publishing House in Chicago.[4] Its author, Edmond Ronayne, was born on 5 November 1832, in the coastal 'hamlet' of Gurtrue (now Gortaroo), near the port of Youghal, in Clonpriest parish and Imokilly barony in southeast County Cork. During Ronayne's youth, East Cork was in such rapid and profound transition that it might be described as an almost schizophrenic society. Generally, it was one of southern Ireland's most prosperous areas, based on commercial farming for the Cork City and British markets, but its society was extremely inequitable, marked by sharp contrasts between affluent 'strong farmers', struggling smallholders, and a large mass of chronically underemployed, impoverished, and exploited cottiers and farm laborers. Likewise, whereas local Catholic society was in the forefront of the Catholic Church's modernizing 'devotional revolution', closely tied to continental Catholicism, and also of urban-centered republican and O'Connellite politics, in 1843 the Catholic diocese of Cloyne provided only one priest per 3,118 parishioners (the worst ratio in pre-Famine Ireland), and Imokilly barony remained predominantly Irish-speaking, with a long tradition of literary production in Irish, and a peasantry steeped in folk customs and beliefs. As a result, intense religious devotion, both modern and customary, and anti-Protestant animosities flourished alongside popular anticlerical traditions extant since the late 1700s. And despite Church condemnation, faction fighting and traditional forms of political and lower-class social protest—the Whiteboys and other secret agrarian societies—still competed vigorously with modern expressions of political alienation sanctioned and led by Catholic traders, strong farmers, and priests.[5]

Edmond Ronayne's family came from the very bottom of East Cork society. His parents, John and Elizabeth Ronayne, were impoverished, illiterate, monolingual Irish-speaking farm laborers, and he was raised in a series of one- and two-room thatched cottages on a 2,000-acre estate owned by Sir Arthur Brooke, an absentee English landlord. Save on rare occasions, Ronayne's and his family's sole food was potatoes. According to Ronayne, his family members and neighbors were 'ardent, zealous Catholics', but their faith blended formal devotion to the Church with traditional peasant 'superstitions'; they believed, for instance, that priests had magical faith-healing powers, and Ronayne himself was allegedly cured of a childhood eye disease by a local priest's 'miraculous' ministrations.[6]

Ronayne was an 'only child' because in early 1834, when he was about fifteen months old, his mother died from overwork in the fields. Subsequently, he was raised by his father and his two unmarried aunts, Margaret and Mary Ronayne, also farm laborers on the Brooke estate. In March 1837, when Ronayne was four years old, his father and his uncle William Ronayne contracted typhus fever while attending Mass, and despite 'the generous help of kind and willing neighbours', both soon died—'I have never forgotten that night', Ronayne testified—and were waked and keened in traditional fashion and interred in Clonpriest's burial ground. Soon after, his aunts took Ronayne to live in the small town of Killeagh (population 800 in 1841) in nearby Killeagh parish.[7]

In 1841, at age nine, Ronayne began attending Killeagh's National School. He learned English quickly and was an exceptional student, especially in geometry. Despite his family's lowly status, he also became a great favorite of Killeagh's Catholic curate, Fr. Henry Power, a French-trained Holy Ghost father who, because of his epilepsy, was credited with magical healing powers, and whose brother, Fr. Maurice Power, was the parish priest. Fr. Henry personally supervised Ronayne's religious instruction (which in Killeagh and in Cloyne diocese, generally, was still conducted primarily in Irish) and apparently viewed him as a budding candidate for

Figure 4.1 Edmond Ronayne wearing his full Masonic regalia

Source: an advertisement for Ronayne's anti-Masonic lectures in *The Free Methodist* (Chicago), 8 March 1876, Free Methodist Church Library, Marston Historical Center, Indianapolis, IN.

the priesthood. After Ronayne's first communion—which gave his aunts 'boundless pleasure'—and confirmation, Fr. Henry recruited him to serve as an altar boy during Mass—'one of the highest marks of honor that [could] be conferred upon a Catholic boy', as Ronayne later remembered.[8]

Very shortly, however, 'the famine was upon us': in late summer 1845, the 'blight' appeared in East Cork and brutally terminated Ronayne's 'merry, careless boyhood'. The blight destroyed much of that year's potato crop,

Figure 4.2 Killeagh, County Cork, c. 1900, where Ronayne lived in 1836–49 and where his aunts died of typhus in Black '47

inaugurated the Great Famine, and, as Ronayne lamented, 'caused great suffering, especially among the poorer classes'. 'Everything now appeared to be at an end', Ronayne testified, and 'I have no recollection whatever as to how much I attended school during that terrible year of 1846, or whether I attended at all'. Nevertheless, Ronayne's aunts enjoyed fairly steady employment, his family survived late 1845 and 1846 without great hardship, and Ronayne himself remained 'quite regular' in his 'attendance on the altar, both on Sundays and during the week'. However, Ronayne remembered that local relief measures were stingy and capricious, and he witnessed at least one major food riot in Killeagh, when migrants from the countryside, 'maddened by hunger', tried vainly to stop local farmers and merchants from shipping grain out of the district; only Fr. Henry's intervention restored order, but his promise of future aid proved hollow when, the next day, the people found 'every shop in the town closed and the street lined with horse dragoons from one end to the other'.[9]

In early 1847, widespread malnutrition hastened the spread of typhus, which, Ronayne recalled, brought 'awful misery . . . and widespread desolation'. In April, both of Ronayne's beloved aunts died of 'Black Fever' and were buried beside his parents in Clonpriest; most members of his uncle John Cunningham's family perished as well. Thus, when Ronayne was merely fifteen years old, 'all who were near and dear on earth to [him] were gone'. Then Ronayne himself contracted typhus and lay in his cabin, virtually alone, for six weeks; only Fr. Henry Power's daily visits and care kept him alive.[10]

Between 1841 and 1851, the population of Killeagh town and parish fell nearly 30 percent, from 2,815 to 1,996, and the numbers of the parish's illiterate inhabitants and fourth-class (one-room) houses—rough indicators of Killeagh's most impoverished inhabitants—declined by nearly 40 and 80 percent, respectively.[11] When Ronayne recovered from typhus, he discovered that all the poor families that had lived on his street had either died or emigrated. Ronayne's was the only cabin still standing, and now his landlord demanded that he leave as well. For eight months after his eviction, Ronayne lived with his uncle David Cunningham, a carpenter in adjacent Ballymacoda (*alias* Kilmacdonogh) parish, who survived the Famine by building coffins and fever sheds for the Poor Law authorities. Then in November 1847, with the help of his uncle and Killeagh's priests, Ronayne secured an apprentice clerkship in a tavern and distillery owned by James Hayes, on Killeagh's main street, at a salary of £5 per year plus board. 'It had been my ambition to be a clerk', Ronayne remembered, 'and now my cherished desire was being more than gratified'. In 1849, however, Ronayne quit Hayes's employ, because, he later claimed, sixteen months 'engaged in the profession of . . . multiplying crime and pauperism', amid dire 'temptations' and scenes of 'blasphemy . . . and drunken folly', had given him a lasting hatred of alcohol. In September 1849, Ronayne left Killeagh forever, allegedly to pursue his ambition to become a schoolmaster: first in Midleton, then at Youghal, and for six months in Britway, County Cork, where he served as a substitute National School teacher, before he began wandering through South Tipperary.[12]

In summer 1850, Ronayne arrived in the small town of Cappamore (population 579 in 1851), in east County Limerick near the Tipperary border, in what was sometimes called the district of Doon.[13] Cappamore straddled two parishes, Tuogh and Doon, which had suffered intensely during the Famine—between 1841 and 1851, their populations declined by 22.0 and 39.5 percent, respectively—and mass evictions and high mortality remained common; indeed, in August 1853, Doon's parish priest declared that 614 local families had been 'exterminated' since 1847.[14] Also, as Ronayne later wrote, he 'could not have found a place more unsettled or disorderly than Cappamore and the neighbouring villages, and none in which the *Sasanach* and the *Sasanach*'s religion were more thoroughly detested'. Indeed, since the late 1700s, the region had been wracked by secret agrarian society violence, faction fighting, and sectarian strife, the latter especially during the Tithe War of the early 1830s.[15]

After 1845, religious conflict intensified when the Doon district became a 'mission station' of the Irish Society for the Education of the Native Irish through the Medium of their Own Language. The Irish Society, as it was generally known, had been founded in 1818 as one of numerous educational and missionary agencies, created and funded to spearhead what Irish and British Protestants heralded as the 'New' or 'Second Reformation' of Ireland. As the 'flagship' of the evangelical movement, which from

Figure 4.3 Outdoor meeting of Protestant missionaries and converts, at the Church of Ireland glebe house, Doon parish, County Limerick, c. 1850

Source: Edmond Ronayne, *Ronayne's Reminiscences* (1900), 183.

the 1820s dominated the Church of Ireland, the Irish Society's ultimate mission—like that of its sister organizations—was to proselytize and convert Irish Catholics to Protestantism and thereby make them both 'civilized' and loyal to the Crown. Almost uniquely, however, the Irish Society made scriptural education in the Irish language central to its efforts; nearly all other proselytizing agencies despised Irish and taught only in English. As a result, the Society attracted many Irish-speaking schoolmasters and rural literati to its employ, but it remained deeply controversial. In the 1820s, the Society's labors in South Ulster helped spark the so-called 'Bible War' between Ireland's Protestant and Catholic churches, and during the Famine its missionaries were accused of 'souperism'—of using food (soup) to entice starving Catholics to abandon their faith.[16] For whatever reason, the Irish Society's mission station in the Doon district enjoyed considerable success. In 1834, the district's three parishes of Doon, Tuogh, and Grean contained only 118 Protestants, but by 1851 they reportedly boasted 762, most of whom lived in discrete 'colonies', huddled together under their ministers' supervision, in defense against the hostility of the region's Catholic priests and parishioners.[17]

At first, Ronayne's career in Cappamore was conventional. He befriended Fr. Patrick Ryan, the priest of Tuogh parish, and with the latter's patronage he started a private school for the children of Catholic strong farmers and shopkeepers. He even joined Fr. Ryan and other Catholics in persecuting local Protestant missionaries and converts. Soon, however, by chance or, as he later saw it, by 'God's providence', Ronayne came under the influence of Thomas McMahon, a Gaelic scholar, Protestant convert, and one of the Irish Society's 'Scripture readers'. During the winter of 1850–51, McMahon convinced Ronayne, through 'reason' and biblical scholarship, that 'Romanism' was 'Satan's lie', that the Mass was a travesty of Christ's sacrifice, that saints and relics were mere 'image worship', and that the Catholic Church was a 'spiritual despotism', which forbade its followers access to the Bible in order to keep them in ignorance and 'slavery' to 'priestcraft' and superstition.[18]

Now persuaded that Catholic teachings were 'absurd and nonsensical', on Easter Sunday, 1851, Ronayne attended the Church of Ireland service, in the Tuogh parish schoolhouse, and thereby publicly announced his rejection of 'Popery'. As a result, he later wrote, '[t]he vials of the fierce wrath of the poor priest-ridden Romanists were poured forth in deadly earnest': he was denounced from the Catholic altar, his pupils vanished, and he was ostracized and physically assaulted. Ronayne joined the local Protestant colony and, after 'a special course of study' under Rev. William Fitzpatrick, the Irish Society's chief missionary in Doon, in late summer 1851 he passed the entrance examinations for the Society's teacher-training college at Kildare Place in Dublin. In February 1852, he graduated, returned to Cappamore, married Margaret Lynch, daughter of a local convert family, and began teaching in the Society's mission schools.[19]

Between 1852 and 1856, Ronayne taught successively in several Protestant schools in Counties Limerick and Clare, often facing fierce opposition.[20] At Ronayne's last school, on the Vandeleur estate at Ralahine, County Clare, the local priest cursed him during Mass and imposed a boycott on his family and school; as a result, during his nineteen months in the parish, he had no pupils and spent most of his time in the Vandeleurs' well-stocked school library, where his reading of *Uncle Tom's Cabin* made him an abolitionist and, later, a supporter of full equality for America's former slaves. As in the Doon district, Ronayne noted that, although Ralahine's poor Irish-speaking small farmers and laborers were willing to send him their children for instruction, the formidable alliance between their employers and creditors (the Catholic strong farmers and shopkeepers) and the priests prevented them from doing so. Thus, although Ronayne successfully championed Vandeleur's smallholders against the 'brutal and . . . oppressive conduct' of 'Paddy' Frawley, the estate's Catholic bailiff, the hostility of the local priest—Frawley's ally in 'espionage' on the tenants, Ronayne charged—only increased after the bailiff's dismissal.[21]

By spring 1856, Ronayne was ready to emigrate, in part, he later wrote, because he was 'thoroughly tired of fighting Mother Church'. However,

Ronayne had also become disenchanted with the Church of Ireland—partly because he found many Anglican rituals and doctrines, such as infant baptism, too similar to those of Catholicism. His greatest disillusionment came in 1854, however, while teaching school in Ballybrood parish, County Limerick, after he pressed charges and testified against another Protestant convert, a member of the Irish Constabulary named John Leary (or O'Leary), who had raped Ronayne's servant girl, a poor twelve-year-old Catholic orphan named Jennie Donavan. Ronayne's 'class treason' outraged local Protestants, especially the Anglican clergyman, Rev. Michael Lloyd Apjohn, who punished Ronayne by evicting him from his school and home.[22] With the aid of Rev. Fitzpatrick, his former mentor in Cappamore, Ronayne quickly found another school. But by 1856, many members of Doon's Protestant colony, including his own wife's family, had already emigrated, with funds from the Irish Society, to North America and Australia, or had 'reverted' to Catholicism. Consequently, between 1851 and 1861, the number of Protestants in Doon district declined nearly 40 percent.[23]

On 13 June 1856, Ronayne, his wife, and their two young sons landed in Quebec City, but if Ronayne had hoped to escape 'priestly domination', he was soon disappointed.[24] In 1861, nearly 60 percent of Quebec City's 51,109 inhabitants were French-speaking Catholics. Also, thanks to heavy Irish settlement (mostly from Munster) during and after the Famine, the local Irish population (28 percent of the city's total) was over three-fourths Catholic. Between 1842 and 1861, the proportion of Protestants among Quebec's Irish-born inhabitants fell from about one-third to less than one-fifth, and their numbers declined even in absolute terms. One reason was economic: mid-century Quebec City's economy was relatively stagnant, and many Protestant traders and skilled workers migrated to Montreal and elsewhere. Another reason was increased feelings of insecurity, which were due partly to the mid-century surge in Irish Catholic immigration but also since 1840 to a vigorous Catholic revival led by ultramontane French bishops and imported French clergy. Ordinary Quebec Protestants also felt politically isolated, as the province's dominant party, the so-called *bleus*, was allied closely with the Catholic Church. As in Ireland, Quebec's Protestants had a 'siege mentality', but they were too few to create powerful and belligerent Orange Lodges, like those in Ulster and Ontario, to challenge local Irish or French 'Catholic aggression'.

Most of Quebec City's Irish (and British) Protestants were members of the middle and working classes, but their affluent coreligionists dominated the upper echelons of the city's commercial, manufacturing, and professional sectors. As a result, Quebec's Protestants overall were greatly superior in wealth and status to Irish and French Catholics, most of whom were concentrated in semi- and unskilled labor, the Irish especially in loading and unloading the thousands of timber ships that annually visited Quebec port; likewise, most Irish Catholic women in the city's workforce were domestic servants. The city's geography reflected this economic disparity, as the

Protestant upper and middle classes congregated primarily in Upper Town, whereas Irish Catholic dockworkers and other laborers were concentrated disproportionately in Lower Town's waterfront wards, which were notorious for poor housing, epidemic disease, and high mortality rates. Nevertheless, although relations with their French neighbors were often strained, as a part of Quebec's large Catholic majority, Irish Catholics did not face effective Anglo-Protestant job discrimination. As a result, their upward mobility was much less restricted than in Orange-controlled Toronto; their dockworkers' union was perhaps the strongest in North America; and by the 1860s, Quebec City's Irish Catholics outnumbered Irish Protestants in Upper as well as Lower Town. Likewise, the high rates of intermarriage between working-class Irish Catholics and Protestants also signified the latter's collective vulnerability.[25]

Thus, in 1856, Edmond Ronayne, with his superior education, was a welcome recruit to Quebec's Protestant—especially Irish Protestant—society, and very quickly he found sponsors among the local mercantile and professional élite. Ronayne's only marketable skill was teaching, but in the 1850s and 1860s Quebec's educational system—strictly segregated by religion—expanded greatly: in the entire province the number of pupils nearly doubled, and in 1852–61 the number of schoolmasters among Quebec City's household heads rose from 14 to 43. Between 1852 and 1865, Ronayne taught in several of Quebec's most prestigious Protestant academies, and at the end of his local career he was master of his own school in Upper Town. His longest employment was as principal of the élite British and Canadian Model School, also in Upper Town. Ronayne obtained this and other well-paid positions through the patronage of Jeffrey Hale, Quebec's most prominent Anglican evangelical and philanthropist. Ronayne's family attended Rev. Edmund Sewell's Trinity Chapel, the most evangelical of the city's Anglican churches. Under Trinity's auspices, Ronayne delivered a series of what were called 'controversial' (that is, anti-Catholic) lectures, and he also taught a night school for young Protestants.[26]

It was in Quebec that Ronayne, expanding on those contacts, began his career as an inveterate 'joiner' of secret fraternal societies. In spring 1858, he joined a local lodge of the Loyal Orange Order—the anti-Catholic, ultra-loyalist organization that had emerged out of mid-Ulster's Peep o' Day gangs in 1795 and been brought to Canada by Irish emigrants and British soldiers in the early 1800s. In the early 1850s, the Canadian Orange Order expanded greatly, especially in Toronto, partly in reaction against the Famine influx of poor Catholic migrants. Compared with its presence and power in Ontario and the Maritimes, however, Orangeism remained weak in Quebec City and province: in the 1850s–60s, the city hosted only three lodges, which rarely dared celebrate publicly the 12 July anniversary of King William's victory at the Boyne in 1690. Nevertheless, Ronayne became an enthusiastic Orangeman: he rapidly 'took all the degrees of Orangeism', and in December 1858 he became Master of his lodge.[27]

Soon, however, Ronayne became disillusioned, mostly as a result of his and other local Orangemen's involvement in what historian Richard Vaudry calls the 'Synodical Controversy' of 1857–59 in Quebec's Anglican Diocese. This was a heated and sometimes violent power struggle between Quebec's Anglican evangelicals, led by Jeffrey Hale and Ronayne's pastor, Rev. Sewell, and the High Church Anglicans, led by Bishop George J. Mountain. The evangelicals strongly condemned the allegedly 'Romanizing' influences of the Tractarian or Oxford Movement—what Ronayne called 'Puseyism'—on Anglican doctrines and rituals. However, the controversy also had social and political implications: although evangelical leaders were as affluent and 'respectable' as their High Church opponents, the former denounced Bishop Mountain for his autocratic leadership and 'aristocratic' political views, while the Bishop's supporters branded his foes as 'ignorant' 'Irish rabble', charged them with 'republicanism' and disloyalty to the Crown, and accused them of favoring Canada's annexation to the United States.[28]

Defeated locally, in 1859 Ronayne and Quebec's Orangemen took their case to the Grand Lodge meeting at Ottawa, where they called on Canada's Orange Order to denounce 'popish ritualism' in the Anglican Church. Having assumed, he wrote, that 'Orangeism was organized' to support 'pure Protestantism' and 'to oppose Romanism' in all its guises, Ronayne was 'disgusted' when Ontario's Orange delegates rejected his resolution and when the Order's Grand Master, John Hillyard Cameron, threatened to expel Ronayne and his associates from the meeting.[29] After this 'betrayal', Ronayne abandoned Anglicanism and began to question 'what the Orange Society was good for'. Eventually, he decided that the Orangemen's rituals were as absurd as those of the Catholic Church; that Canada's Orange Order, controlled by wealthy Anglicans, was indifferent to its plebeian members' 'true Protestant' sensibilities; and, finally, that most Orangemen preferred to persecute and 'crack the heads' of poor Irish Catholics than to bear witness against the errors of Rome. In fact, Ronayne concluded that the history of Orangeism—in Canada and Ireland alike—was no more than 'a record of bigotry, brutality, and bloodshed'.[30]

In 1860, Ronayne quietly disengaged from his Orange brethren and joined Quebec's equally loyal but more high-toned Masonic Order, which, like Orangeism, also experienced explosive growth in mid-nineteenth-century Canada. Eager to learn the Freemasons' 'great and wonderful secret[s]', Ronayne joined Harrington Lodge, No. 49, and soon was initiated into 'the sublime degree of a Master Mason' and later into higher degrees and 'mysteries'. Again, however, Ronayne quickly became disenchanted. For example, he felt duped and cheated when he learned that he had paid $30 in initiation fees (over $600 in today's currency) to learn so-called 'Masonic secrets', which in fact were not 'secrets' at all, but merely bizarre and 'degrading' initiation rites—the details of which were already published in books readily available for a few pennies in local bookstores. In addition, so he later claimed, Ronayne became convinced that the Masons' oaths of brotherhood—allegedly unbreakable under penalty of death—contradicted the principles of equal citizenship and often were employed to subvert the course of justice. Thus, in his memoir, Ronayne wrote that he had ceased active participation in Masonry by early summer 1865, when he decided—quite abruptly and allegedly for economic reasons—to relinquish his school, leave Quebec City, and migrate to the United States, albeit with no promise of employment there.[31]

Around 1 July 1865, Ronayne and his family arrived at Stevens Point, Wisconsin, where his wife's parents and siblings had settled eleven years earlier. Ronayne's in-laws were only poor laborers, however, and Stevens Point, a rough lumber town of 1,700 inhabitants, offered few prospects for schoolmasters.[32] Leaving his wife and two children with her relations, Ronayne travelled to Chicago to find work, arriving in mid-August with only $20 and a letter of introduction to an Irish commission merchant named Mullally. Mullally was helpful, but, without prior business experience, Ronayne could not find the clerical post he desired. While job-searching, he boarded with the family of a poor Irish sailor, Dennis Heany (or Heaney), in a heavily Irish, working-class district north of the Chicago River called Kilgubbin—also known as Goose Island and, later, as Little Hell. Located on Chicago's Near North Side, Kilgubbin was a vaguely defined neighborhood of wooden shanties, boarding houses, brothels, and saloons—and what Ronayne described as 'one of the [city's] most undesirable localities'. Indeed, most of Kilgubbin's denizens were squatters on sufferance, until industrialists or real estate developers, backed by Chicago's police, periodically forced them to move further north or west.[33]

Economically, socially, and environmentally, Chicago in 1865 was the antithesis of both rural Cork and relatively staid Quebec City. On one hand, Chicago's economic vitality and demographic growth were extraordinary, the former based on spectacular increases since mid-century in the city's railroad network, food processing, timber trade, commerce, manufacturing, and property speculation. Between 1850 and 1860, the city's population had soared from less than 30,000 to over 109,000, and by 1870, Chicago would be the nation's fourth largest city, with almost 300,000 inhabitants. Roughly half the city's residents in 1860–70 were foreign-born; over one-fifth of them (nearly 40,000 in 1860, 60,000 in 1870) were Irish-born; and three-fourths of the latter were manual workers, half of them unskilled. In 1870, the mean total wealth of Irish immigrant families was less than 14 percent of that of native-American households; in the same year, the Irish comprised over half of the 14,000 Chicagoans on outdoor relief, although they made up only 13.4 percent of the city's population.

Chicago in 1865 also had over 200 churches, but that was misleading. The city was a capitalist 'free-fire zone': its ruling class was notorious for naked, unregulated greed and shameless displays of wealth, flaunted alongside degrees of poverty, filth, pollution, crime, violence, and vice that shocked genteel visitors from the eastern states and abroad. When Ronayne arrived,

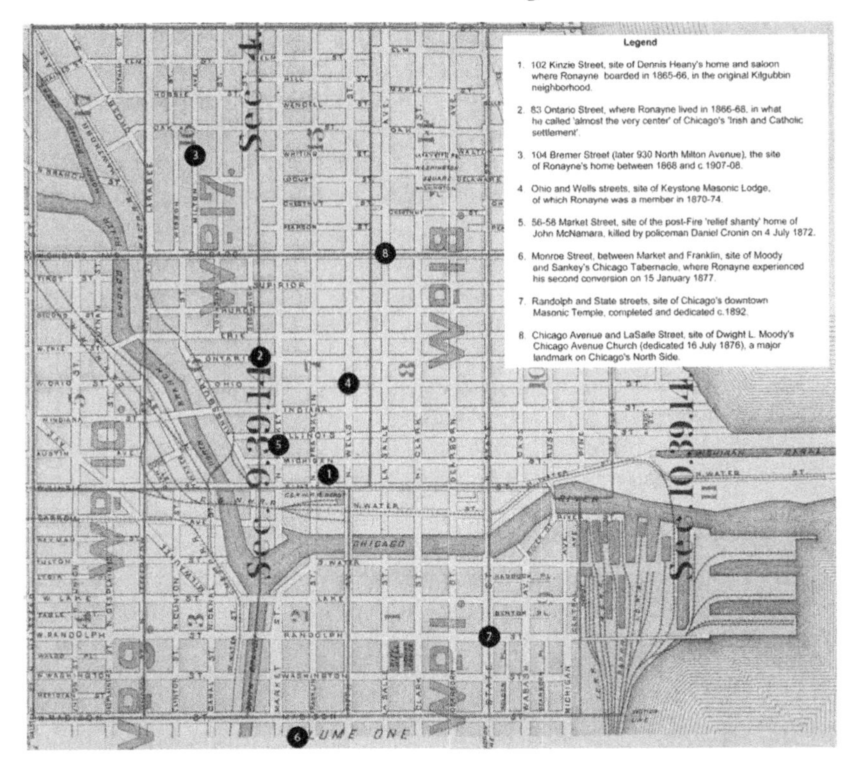

Map 4.1 Chicago, showing important sites in Edmond Ronayne's life there, 1865–1907

Source: Robinson's Atlas, vol. 5 [1886], Chicago History Museum, iCHI-68201.

the wealthiest tenth of Chicago's inhabitants owned between two-thirds and four-fifths of the city's real property, while the poorest half of the population owned less than 1 percent; some 200,000 Chicagoans lived in flimsy wooden houses, on unpaved streets without sidewalks or sewers, alongside 2,000 saloons, brothels, and gambling dens. The city government (like the state's) was notoriously corrupt, regardless of which party held power. Both politicians and police profited from graft, bribery, election fraud, and illegal gambling and prostitution, but arguably their principal function was to support capital, by law and brute force, in its relentless exploitation of local labor.[34]

In short, postwar Chicago was a 'shock city' of predators, 'suckers', and strangers, and in summer 1865 it hosted thousands of recently demobilized Civil War veterans, many of whom, like Ronayne, searched vainly for work. Lonely, anxious, hungry, and unemployed, Ronayne quickly exhausted the money he had brought from Wisconsin. Although he sold his coat and watch to pay for his lodgings, soon he was two weeks in arrears. Seeking aid in finding work, he visited Chicago's Episcopalian bishop and the YMCA's employment bureau, but, to his disgust, all he got was a pious religious tract, which he 'tore . . . into shreds' with fury. Finally, Ronayne found a job shoveling dirt out of a cellar, and Mrs. Heany, his Irish landlady, loaned him money to buy work-clothes, tools, and a wheelbarrow. Unaccustomed to hard manual labor, however, in a week Ronayne was crippled with muscular rheumatism and dysentery, unable to leave his bed. A doctor visited and told him that, unless he went to hospital at once, he would die, but Ronayne could not walk and had no money.[35]

Desperate, Ronayne asked a fellow boarder to locate three 'respectable Freemasons' and request they visit him. When they came, Ronayne begged them to relieve 'a poor brother Master Mason in distress'. However, they questioned whether Ronayne was *really* a Mason; when he showed them his Masonic documents, they accused him of having stolen them. Finally, after Ronayne proved that he was indeed a Master Mason, they told him it would take weeks before Masonic officials could authorize and provide him aid—by which time, Ronayne knew, he would be dead. Fortunately, Mullally, Ronayne's initial Irish contact in Chicago, now discovered his plight. He rushed Ronayne to Chicago's Sisters of Mercy Hospital and paid $35 for five weeks' treatment. The 'good nuns', as Ronayne fondly remembered them, nursed him back to health and even insisted he remain in hospital for two additional weeks, without charge, so he would not suffer a relapse.[36]

Ronayne left hospital in early February 1866, fully recovered but with only 50 cents in his pocket. However, this was on the eve of the major Fenian invasions of Canada—the attempts by Irish American nationalists, many of them Civil War veterans, to conquer British North America as a prelude to liberating Ireland from British rule. Ronayne invested his 50 cents in penny-postcard pictures of the Fenian leader in New York City, John O'Mahony, and peddled them in Chicago's Irish saloons. With his profits, he purchased more pictures and other items to peddle. Within a few weeks, Ronayne had saved $100 and was finally able to send for his wife and children. Before their arrival, he rented new lodgings at 83 Ontario Street, in what Ronayne described as 'almost the very center' of the city's 'Irish and Catholic settlement'.[37]

After a year of peddling goods and night-clerking at the Merchants' Exchange, Ronayne had saved over $1,000 and was ready to resume school teaching. In late 1867, he purchased from William B. Ogden, the Near North Side's principal landlord and developer, a lot at 104 Bremer Street (later North Milton Avenue) for $300 down, and hired a carpenter to construct a substantial frame house. In spring 1868 and likely on the ground floor of his new home, Ronayne opened a private school, which, he claimed, soon became prosperous and 'one of the largest of its kind in the city'. Then, on the opposite side of Bremer Street, he bought two more lots and built houses, which he rented out for extra income. Thus, at age 37, Ronayne had re-achieved at least a modicum of financial stability: the 1870 census recorded him as owning real estate and personal property valued at $3,000 and $200, respectively; in addition, his two sons, William (age 17) and John

(15), brought home their wages as printers in the city. In retrospect, however, Ronayne was scarcely on a path of 'upward mobility', and 1870 likely represented his pinnacle of economic success. His new home remained on the edge of Kilgubbin, in the 'tough, downscale' 18th Ward (the 17th in 1880), and his neighbors were mostly skilled and unskilled laborers of Irish and other foreign birth. Indeed, Ronayne lived on the same street for the next forty years, never joining the middle-class migration to Chicago's new neighborhoods along the Lakefront and Northside boulevards.[38]

Perhaps it was to fortify his precariously 'respectable' status that Ronayne now began to join American fraternal societies, as did millions of lower middle-class males in the late 1800s—the 'Golden Age of Fraternity' in the United States. After a brief flirtation with the Good Templars, a temperance organization (whose rituals he later described as 'utter nonsense'), Ronayne returned to Freemasonry, despite his earlier disappointments in Quebec City and at Heany's boarding house in Kilgubbin. He was scarcely unique: in the 1840s, American Masonry began to recover from the devastating effects of the anti-Masonic crusade of the 1820s; between 1850 and 1860 membership soared from 66,000 to 221,000. By 1870, Masons numbered nearly a half-million—mostly native-born Protestant small businessmen and low-level white-collar workers, such as clerks, salesmen, and accountants; in 1866, Illinois alone boasted some 430 Masonic lodges with 25,000 members. According to its historians, Freemasonry's popularity was rooted in its incorporation and seeming transcendence of the tensions and contradictions

Figure 4.4 North Milton Avenue and Oak Street, Chicago, 1911

Source: Chicago Daily News, 15 March 1911, Chicago History Museum, DN-0056708. Ronayne lived on North Milton Avenue (formerly Bremer Street) from 1867 to *c.* 1907–08. When this picture was taken, the intersection of Milton and Oak was dubbed 'Death Corner' because of the great number of unsolved murders attributed to the secret Italian 'Black Hand' society.

in American bourgeois culture. On one hand, for example, Masons claimed to promote the individual virtues—industry, piety, honesty, sobriety—that were the 'self-made man's' alleged keys to material success in capitalist America; and yet Freemasonry, like the nation's burgeoning corporations, was hierarchical as well as class, race, and gender exclusive; it was also 'big business', garnering millions of dollars in members' fees and in costs of Masonic regalia. On the other hand, however, Freemasonry exalted egalitarian, noncompetitive, and precapitalist values such as brotherhood, community, and charity. Indeed, Masonic lodges were touted as masculine asylums from the world of commerce, although in that respect they competed with the bourgeois, home-centered myths of domesticity, separate spheres, and women's moral superiority.

Similarly, American Freemasonry's relationship to religion was 'highly malleable'. In its eighteenth-century Enlightenment and Deistic origins, the Order was an 'alternative religion' to Christian dogmas and disputes. That spirit survived in some Masonic rituals, but in self-defense against Protestant assaults in the 1820s–1830s, most Masons now claimed that the Order was merely the 'handmaiden of religion'—supporting, not competing with, the 'truths' of Christianity. Indeed, the social and occupational characteristics of Chicago's Freemasons were virtually identical to those of converts in local Protestant revivals; and some Masons, especially in the South, even claimed that Freemasonry buttressed *fundamentalist* Christianity, with its belief in biblical inerrancy. It was therefore ironic that Masonry's 'ersatz mysticism'—its rituals, ceremonies, vestments, paraphernalia—bore much more resemblance to Catholic than to evangelical Protestant church services. However, late nineteenth-century Freemasonry was strongly anti-Catholic, which no doubt appealed to Ronayne, as perhaps did Masonry's character of a 'fictive family' that might compensate for the one he had lost in Ireland and for any domestic unhappiness he felt in America. He may also have been attracted to Freemasonry's exposition of the 'secret meanings of geometry'—Ronayne's favorite school subject—to reveal the hidden plans and purpose of 'the Great Architect of the Universe'.[39]

Thus, in fall 1869, Ronayne began to frequent Chicago's many Masonic lodges, and in early 1870, he formally joined Keystone Lodge, No. 639—located at the corner of Ohio and North Wells streets, just a few blocks from his home—primarily, he alleged, to accommodate his friends and to enjoy the sociability and 'relaxation' of the lodge-room. Ronayne quickly rose to the position of lodge secretary, with responsibility for memorizing and teaching new members all the 'Masonic secrets', rules, oaths, and initiation rites. In 1871, he even started an informal 'Masonic school' to instruct new members in the Order's rituals. Ronayne's class met every Sunday morning at 10:00, because, he admitted, 'we were not [good] Christians in Keystone Lodge'.[40]

On Sunday morning, 8 September 1871, Ronayne's Masonic school assembled for its weekly meeting. That evening, the Great Chicago Fire broke out, allegedly in the O'Leary family's barn, on De Koven Street, on the city's Near West Side. The Fire consumed most of Chicago's business district, made homeless about a third of the city's inhabitants, destroyed $22 million in property, and killed nearly three hundred people. In some respects, however, the Fire's aftermath was worse than the conflagration itself: Chicago's wealthiest citizens bypassed the city's elected officials, secured Federal troops to impose martial law, and privatized public relief in the hands of their own Chicago Relief and Aid Society, which discriminated between 'deserving' (native-born, middle-class Protestant) and 'undeserving' (working-class, foreign-born, especially Irish Catholic) aid recipients. They also launched a public relations campaign in the local press to exculpate their own responsibility for the disaster and shift public blame and fear onto the city's 'lower orders', including the O'Learys. Ironically, a few weeks after the Fire, while engaged in relief work, Ronayne visited De Koven Street and, by speaking to its inhabitants in the Irish language, he gained their trust and learned what he claimed was the 'true story' behind the Fire's origins—a story that belied the media propaganda and exonerated the much-maligned O'Learys.[41]

The Fire destroyed most of Chicago's Near North Side, including the original Kilgubbin neighborhood and Ronayne's three houses on Bremer Street. Insurance covered only part of his losses, but he managed to rebuild his home and recommence his school fairly quickly. Although unable to save his own possessions from the flames, Ronayne had fulfilled his fraternal 'duty' by rescuing all of Keystone Lodge's Masonic paraphernalia. Also, immediately

Figure 4.5 Downtown during the Great Chicago Fire of 8–10 October 1871

Source: Rudolf Doehn, 'Chicago in Schutt und Aldje', *Illustrirte Zeitung*, 1481, 18 November 1871.

following the Fire, he had helped create and lead an ad hoc Chicago Masonic relief committee, which, after five days of 'excellent service' to 'poor, distressed' Masons, was superseded by the state's formal Masonic Relief Board. In gratitude, in December 1871 Keystone's members unanimously elected Ronayne as Senior Warden, the lodge's second highest honor.[42]

Shortly after the Fire, however, Ronayne again became disenchanted with Freemasonry, for at least two reasons. First, Ronayne accused Keystone's Masons of 'conspiracy' to pervert justice on behalf of a fellow lodge-member, a Chicago policeman named Daniel Cronin (or Cronan), who on 4 July 1872, shot and killed an unarmed Irish laborer, John McNamara, for causing a drunken 'disturbance' in his own shanty at 56–58 Market Street. According to Ronayne, the coroner at the inquest into McNamara's death was a Mason, as were the members of the coroner's jury, who rendered a verdict of '"justifiable homicide"—on the grounds of self-defense'. Ronayne was particularly incensed that most of Keystone's members excused Cronin's actions because he was a 'brother' Mason, whereas McNamara was merely a poor Irish Catholic 'foreigner'. By contrast, Ronayne assisted McNamara's widow, and, at the next Keystone Lodge meeting, denounced Cronin as a murderer.[43]

Despite this incident, in December 1872, Keystone's Masons elected Ronayne as their Grand Master, the Lodge's highest office. During 1873, however, Ronayne publicly accused city and state Masonic officials of misappropriating two-thirds of the $91,000 that Freemasons elsewhere in the

Figure 4.6 Home of Catherine and Patrick O'Leary on DeKoven Street, shortly after the Chicago Fire

Source: Chicago Public Library, Special Collections and Preservation Division, GP Smith 891. Local journalists quickly pinned blame for the Great Conflagration on Mrs. O'Leary and her cow, demonizing the respected member of Holy Family parish as 'Our Lady of the Lamp'.

United States had donated 'for the relief of [Chicago's] distressed and homeless brethren'. Most of the money, he charged, was spent to rebuild Masonic lodges and purchase 'lodge trumpery', whereas needy Masons, their widows, and their children were 'degraded to the condition of mendicants'. To Ronayne, this was reminiscent of Irish Famine relief, especially when what he called 'aristocratic' Masonic officials discriminated against their poorer brethren. Indeed, he charged that one of the state's Grand Masters, Harmon Reynolds of Springfield, personally stole $800 from the Masonic Relief fund, but, despite Ronayne's efforts, the Grand Lodge's other officers refused to expel or prosecute him.[44]

In late 1873, Ronayne refused reelection as Keystone's Grand Master and was determined to withdraw altogether from Freemasonry, for he was now convinced (he later claimed) that 'the whole system [was] the most vile, the most corrupting, and [had] the worst influence of any organization in the country, not alone on its own members, but . . . on the entire community'. Yet, Ronayne hoped to withdraw gradually and unobtrusively in order not to alienate friends or jeopardize his school's financial situation. On 31 May 1874, Ronayne published in the *Chicago Times* a letter denouncing Freemasonry as a 'grand humbug': 'there does not exist in the world a more useless or a more good-for-nothing society than Freemasonry', Ronayne wrote, 'nor one that is built upon a more rotten foundation! It is neither benevolent nor charitable nor religious, but is an asylum for deadheads, for scalawags, for hypocrites and for bummers of every kind . . .'. However, Ronayne signed his letter, 'A FREEMASON'; he did *not* reveal himself as its author. 'Prudence suggested', Ronayne remembered, 'that I drop the institution quietly'. In late 1874, however, one of his personal enemies and a friend of Cronin, the policeman whom Ronayne had denounced two years earlier, exposed Ronayne's *true* opinions of Freemasonry to Keystone's other members. Ronayne could no longer dissimulate, and, in response, he delivered impromptu what he called 'my first anti-masonic lecture', and then he bid the Order 'good-bye forever'.[45]

However, Ronayne never *really* abandoned Freemasonry, for his animosity to it was now as profound and obsessive as his hostility to the Catholic Church. Soon he became one of the nation's most prominent anti-Masonic writers and lecturers, and the demand for his message was so great, he claimed, that he closed his school to devote himself full-time to his crusade. In his lectures and books, Ronayne employed his intimate knowledge of Masonic rituals to reveal the Order's most closely-guarded and 'sacred' secrets, hoping through exposure and ridicule to demonstrate, as he put it, that 'Freemasonry belongs to the barbarous ages of paganism, . . . not to the civilization and Christianity of the nineteenth century, and hence ought to have no place under our system of government'.[46]

In his memoir, Ronayne stated that, in the years before he quit Freemasonry, he had had 'no fellowship with Christian people' and 'care[d] . . . little for churches'. Yet, Ronayne claimed that what now gave him moral strength for his crusade, in the face of sometimes violent Masonic hostility, was his nightly attendance, in the winter of 1876–77, at the great 'gospel meetings' held by America's leading evangelists, Dwight L. Moody (1837–99) and Ira D. Sankey (1840–1908), at the Chicago Tabernacle on Monroe Street. Moody's and Sankey's 'Great Western Revival' had been ongoing since early October 1876, but it was not until the evening of 15 January 1877, the day before the revival concluded, that Ronayne had a second religious conversion—one much more personal, dramatic, and permanent than his more intellectual experience in Cappamore twenty-five years earlier. As in Moody's own second conversion five years earlier, Ronayne now moved from mere 'belief to faith'. Now he realized that 'Jesus [had] died for *me*. . . . [I]t is through his death—and his death alone—that all my sins are put away'. 'From that time forward', Ronayne relied totally on the Scriptures and his new personal relationship with Jesus. These sustained him, he said, as no religious or secular institutions and rituals had ever done before.[47]

Ronayne's 'new birth' was very important: now his anti-Masonry was fortified by the conviction that, since 'Christ [w]as man's only Savior', Freemasonry's claim to religiosity was not only fraudulent but literally Satanic. Ronayne may also have been influenced by Moody's apocalyptic worldview. Despite the evangelist's basic and (critics charged) shallow optimism, Moody was a fundamentalist who preached a pre-millennial interpretation of Christ's Second Coming, which demanded not social and political reform, which Moody scorned, but rather a sharp separation of the 'saved' from the sinful to prepare for the 'end times'. In Ronayne's youth, pre-millennialism (usually accompanied by virulent anti-Catholicism) had permeated Irish evangelicalism, due in part to the influence of John Nelson Darby (1800–82), an Anglo-Irish theologian, former Anglican clergyman, and founder of the Plymouth Brethren. Thus, Ronayne's own pre-millennial views, which pervaded his memoir, may have been attributable less to Moody—whose strengths were preaching and fundraising, not theology—than to earlier Irish Protestant influences.

Also, it appears that Ronayne was more deeply affected by Sankey's pathetic songs about orphans and other 'lost sheep'—such as the latter's most famous hymn, 'The Ninety and Nine', which Ronayne quoted in his memoir—than by Moody's 'business-' or 'salesman-like' evangelical style. Indeed, it may be that Moody's mass revivals, financed by wealthy capitalists to combat rising discontent in the terrible depression of 1873–77, were too conventional or 'mainstream' for Ronayne's tastes. Moody mirrored the class and ideological sympathies of the overwhelming majority of Chicago's Protestant (and Catholic) clergy. Unlike Ronayne, for example, he avoided controversy and fully supported the socioeconomic order and its rulers' interests; and although Moody denounced liquor, Catholicism, evolution, and Biblical criticism, he never criticized Freemasonry or other secret societies, much less Gilded Age capitalism or the era's rampant racism, segregation, and denial of African-American civil rights.[48]

Figure 4.7 Dwight L. Moody preaching at the Royal Agricultural Hall in Islington, London, in March 1875, to a crowd estimated at 16,000

Source: The Graphic [London], 20 March 1875. Moody and Ira D. Sankey achieved transatlantic recognition during their two-year mission abroad, just prior to their triumphant 'Great Western Revival' in winter 1876–77 in the Chicago Tabernacle.

Thus, Ronayne's conversion was not the only key to his subsequent career. For his anti-Masonic crusade, especially, Ronayne garnered his principal intellectual, emotional, and practical support from much more marginal and 'extreme' Protestant groups—particularly the National Christian Association (or NCA), a radical Protestant organization headquartered in Chicago

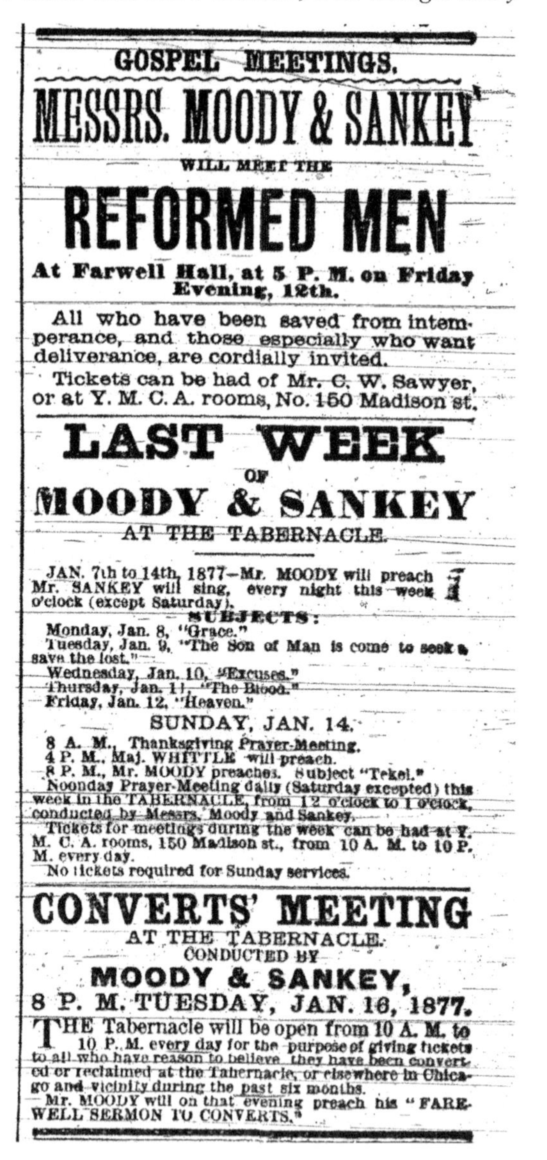

GOSPEL MEETINGS.

MESSRS. MOODY & SANKEY

WILL MEET THE

REFORMED MEN

At Farwell Hall, at 5 P. M. on Friday Evening, 12th.

All who have been saved from intemperance, and those especially who want deliverance, are cordially invited.

Tickets can be had of Mr. C. W. Sawyer, or at Y. M. C. A. rooms, No. 150 Madison st.

LAST WEEK

OF

MOODY & SANKEY

AT THE TABERNACLE.

JAN. 7th to 14th, 1877—Mr. MOODY will preach Mr. SANKEY will sing, every night this week o'clock (except Saturday).

SUBJECTS:

Monday, Jan. 8, "Grace."

Tuesday, Jan. 9, "The Son of Man is come to seek a save the lost."

Wednesday, Jan. 10, "Excuses."

Thursday, Jan. 11, "The Blood."

Friday, Jan. 12, "Heaven."

SUNDAY, JAN. 14.

8 A. M., Thanksgiving Prayer-Meeting.

4 P. M., Maj. WHITTLE will preach.

8 P. M., Mr. MOODY preaches. Subject "Tekel."

Noonday Prayer-Meeting daily (Saturday excepted) this week in the TABERNACLE, from 12 o'clock to 1 o'clock, conducted by Messrs. Moody and Sankey.

Tickets for meetings during the week can be had at Y. M. C. A. rooms, 150 Madison st., from 10 A. M. to 10 P. M. every day.

No tickets required for Sunday services.

CONVERTS' MEETING

AT THE TABERNACLE.

CONDUCTED BY

MOODY & SANKEY,

8 P. M. TUESDAY, JAN. 16, 1877.

THE Tabernacle will be open from 10 A. M. to 10 P. M. every day for the purpose of giving tickets to all who have reason to believe they have been converted or reclaimed at the Tabernacle, or elsewhere in Chicago and vicinity during the past six months.

Mr. MOODY will on that evening preach his "FAREWELL SERMON TO CONVERTS."

Figure 4.8 Newspaper advertisement for the last week of Moody's and Sankey's 'Great Western Revival'

Source: Chicago Times, 12 January 1877. Ronayne experienced his second conversion at this event on 15 January 1877.

and founded in 1868 to mobilize Christian opposition to Freemasonry and other secret societies. The NCA's leader was Rev. Jonathan Blanchard (1811–92), a Congregational clergyman and founder of Wheaton College, some twenty-five miles west of Chicago. By Gilded Age standards, Blanchard was a radical social as well as religious reformer: he advocated the eight-hour day for workers, justice to Native Americans, and equal rights for both women and African Americans, and he opposed monopoly capitalism as well as liquor, Sabbath-breaking, Catholicism, and Freemasonry. Blanchard and the NCA also sponsored the American Party, which, although dismally unsuccessful at the polls, ran presidential candidates in the late 1870s and 1880s. One of Ronayne's critics accused him of being a mere huckster for Blanchard's party, and although Ronayne claimed that he was 'never employed' to give anti-Masonic lectures, his first major public performance was on 21–22 June 1876 at the NCA's eighth national convention in Chicago. Thus, in the NCA Ronayne acquired a new 'support system' or 'fictive family' shortly after he left Keystone Lodge and six months *before* his conversion in Moody's revival. Also, given the financial implications of his resignation from school teaching, it is likely that, in the 1870s–80s, Ronayne was employed as one of the NCA's thirty or so anti-Masonic circuit lecturers.[49]

Simultaneously, Ronayne also associated with the Free Methodist Church, one of many small 'fringe' denominations that opposed secret societies and supported the NCA's work. The Free Methodists had originated in the late 1850s, in a schism from the Methodist Episcopal Church, under the leadership of Rev. B.T. Roberts (1823–93). Like the NCA, Free Methodism was rooted in the antebellum abolitionist and anti-Masonic crusades, and, although fundamentalist in religion, Roberts was even more 'progressive' than Blanchard on social and political issues; for example, Roberts supported public ownership of banks and railroads, advocated direct election of US senators and the abolition of the electoral college, and was a leading figure in the early Farmers' Alliance and Populist movements. No records survive to document a formal affiliation between Ronayne and the Free Methodists—indeed, he claimed 'membership in the mystic body of Christ only'—but in the late 1870s, their periodical, *The Free Methodist*, advertised his anti-Masonic lectures, and in 1900, their official publisher printed his *Reminiscences*, for which Burton R. Jones, a Free Methodist bishop, wrote the introduction.[50]

Thus, from the late 1870s, Ronayne published anti-Masonic literature and gave anti-Masonic lectures at what he called 'mighty gatherings' throughout the midwestern and eastern United States, and in Canada. Commonly, he spoke before audiences associated with the NCA or with small, radical, and egalitarian Protestant denominations, such as the United Brethren and the Covenanting (or Reformed) Presbyterians, as well as the Free Methodists. As a result of his efforts, he claimed, 'Churches having a rule against secret societies were greatly encouraged . . . [and] Christians were awakened to greater zeal' against the 'work of darkness'.[51]

Judging from his memoir, however, by the early 1880s, Ronayne's crusade had flagged, and in the winter of 1883–84, he was reduced to marching silently through downtown Chicago, bearing aloft banners inscribed with Gospel messages, such as 'He that believeth not shall be condemned'. By the 1890s, Ronayne lamented, all his anti-Masonic comrades had died or abandoned their posts, and from the mid-1880s through the mid-1890s, his own public performances apparently focused less on anti-Masonry than on 'witnessing' for Christ in conventional lay-preaching, especially in the upper midwest and Ontario. But Ronayne was no Moody or Sankey: his labors for the Lord produced few material rewards, and at least one reason why he wrote his memoir was to make money sufficient to pay off the mortgage on the three-story frame house he had built, nearly thirty years earlier, after the Chicago Fire.[52]

By the late 1890s, when he wrote his memoir, Ronayne was convinced that 'there is not to-day throughout all Christendom any denomination into whose creed and discipline even a single one of the Epistles would fit'. His principal consolation was the pre-millennial belief that he was now living in the 'end times' or 'last days'—'at the close of this gospel age'—when Christ would finally return to separate the wheat from the tares. Certainly, Ronayne's conviction that the world was literally 'going to hell' as the Second Coming approached would have been reinforced by contemporary developments. His inspirations, Blanchard and Roberts, were dead; the former's NCA was moribund and the latter's Free Methodist Church had merely 34,000 members. Moreover, despite all their and Ronayne's efforts, Freemasonry and other secret societies were flourishing: between 1880 and 1900, the number of Masons in the United States soared from 537,000 to over 1.3 million, and in 1890, Chicago's Freemasons began construction of a downtown temple, which, at twenty-two stories, was then the world's tallest and, Masons claimed, most expensive building.[53]

Nor was Ronayne's urban environment any less 'wicked' than before the Chicago Fire. To be sure, Chicago was no longer an overgrown frontier town; it was now a metropolis, the nation's second largest city, and the site of the 1893 World's Fair. Between 1875 and 1900, the city's population quadrupled from 400,500 to nearly 1.7 million inhabitants, of whom nearly 80 percent were immigrants and their children; almost 237,500 Chicagoans were Irish immigrants and Irish-Americans, of whom between 72 percent (males) and 62 percent (females) were still manual workers. Despite Moody's and others' frequent revivals, the number of Irish and other Catholics in Chicago was now two-and-one-half times larger than all members of the city's seven leading Protestant denominations combined. Since 1875, the number of Chicago policemen had increased more than six-fold, but Chicago remained, as one mayor proudly proclaimed, a 'wide-open' city, rife with saloons, gambling, prostitution, and political and police corruption—in all of which Ronayne's countrymen, although now merely one-seventh of the city's inhabitants, were notoriously prominent. Late nineteenth-century Chicago also remained 'first in violence', as reformer Lincoln Steffens declared in 1903, as well as 'deepest in dirt': violent conflicts between capital (and its political servants) and organized labor were frequent, while Chicago led all American cities, outside the deep south, in homicides. To be sure, since

Figure 4.9 The Masonic Temple, designed by Daniel H. Burnham and John W. Root

Source: 'View on State Street', *Picturesque Chicago and Guide to the World's Fair* [1892], Chicago History Museum, iCHI-68200. Widely regarded as an 'architectural marvel', it was the tallest skyscraper in Chicago when it was completed in 1892.

1875, the number of Chicago's schoolteachers (many of them Irish women) had also risen by nearly 800 percent, but the impressive expansion of Chicago's public and parochial education would only have threatened Ronayne's apparent attempt to resume private school teaching.[54]

Thus, Ronayne concluded, '[t]he night grows darker as we approach the dawn'. In fact, however, in 1900, Ronayne's life was far from over, and two developments, at which he hinted in his memoir's closing chapter, launched a remarkable finale to his career. First, in the 1890s, Ronayne experienced a dramatic change in his domestic circumstances. On 14 April 1893, his younger son, John, died at age 38 and in 'circumstances . . . so peculiarly painful' that his mother, according to Ronayne, 'never entirely recovered from the shock' and also soon died. In fact, however, Margaret Lynch Ronayne did not die of heart disease until 3 April 1897, at age 68, and later that same year Ronayne married Ellena Darwood, aged only 30 or 31 (34 or 35 years younger than Ronayne, then aged 65), whom he had met and converted twelve years earlier (when she was merely 18 or 19), in Milton Junction, Wisconsin, during one of his evangelical tours. During their marriage, Ronayne and his new wife had three children: the first died in infancy before 1900; and the other two, Ruth and Rachel, were born in Chicago in 1901 and 1902, respectively. Thus, in his late sixties, Ronayne acquired a new, young family—and the responsibilities thereof.[55]

Second, Ronayne rejuvenated his anti-Masonic crusade when, on 23 May 1897, he lectured before 3,000 people at the Sunday morning service of Dr. John Alexander Dowie, at the latter's Zion Tabernacle in Chicago. Dowie was one of the most extraordinary figures in American religious history. Born in Scotland in 1847, Dowie emigrated with his parents to Australia, where he became in turn a Congregational minister, a popular faith-healer, and leader of a personal cult with thousands of adherents. Fleeing legal troubles, in 1888, Dowie moved to the United States and settled in Chicago, where in 1893 he established his tabernacle just outside the World's Fair entrance, as well as many 'healing homes', and amassed another large, devoted following. In 1896, Dowie founded the Christian Catholic Church, and in 1899, he established, on 6,000 acres purchased with funds from zealous donors, a utopian, semi-socialist, and racially integrated religious community, Zion City, forty miles north of Chicago. Soon nearly ten thousand followers settled in Dowie's prosperous but absolute theocracy—centered on his enormous Shiloh Tabernacle—in which drinking, smoking, theatres, dance halls, doctors' surgeries, and secret societies, like Freemasonry, were strictly forbidden. In 1901, Dowie declared himself to be 'Elijah the Restorer' and the 'Messenger of the Covenant', sent by God in the 'end times' to restore the spiritual gifts (such as faith-healing) and apostolic offices of the early Christian church, and thus prepare His chosen few for the Second Coming. In September 1904, Dowie, dressed in Old Testament prophet's robes, announced that he was 'the First Apostle of the Lord Jesus Christ' and renamed his denomination the Christian Catholic Apostolic Church: 'Clothed by God with Apostolic and Prophetic authority', he declared, 'I have now the right to speak as the instructor of the nations'.[56]

Apparently, Ronayne never moved from his Chicago home to Zion City, but in 1901, attracted by its 'spirit of brotherhood and sharing', he was ordained a deacon in Dowie's church. Despite his past rejections of 'priestly' authority and 'trumpery', Ronayne's obituary described him as one of Dowie's 'most influential followers', who, like the Prophet, was 'clad in the showy vestments of his office'. But that was in 'the palmy days of Dowieism', and in 1906, disgruntled followers deposed Dowie for reasons that included the Prophet's illness, growing megalomania, personal extravagance, and financial mismanagement. After a brief, vicious power struggle, what remained of Zion City fell under the more efficient but equally autocratic and less personable sway of Wilbur Glenn Voliva, one of Dowie's former lieutenants, who in the 1920s–1930s turned the town into a mini-police state and became a fanatical exponent of 'flat-earth theory'. In early 1907, Dowie died in Zion City, while ironically the fragmentation of his quasi-socialist utopia helped spawn the modern and politically reactionary Pentecostal movement.[57]

It is impossible to determine whether Ronayne himself became disillusioned with Dowie, or whether he was one of the 1,500 or so Dowie loyalists who departed after the latter's downfall. What is known, however, is that c. 1907–08, after more than forty years in Chicago, Ronayne and his second family relocated to the outskirts of Boulder, Colorado, a small city of less than 10,000 inhabitants, where he took out a mortgage on a one-acre 'chicken ranch'. There, in the foothills of the Rocky Mountains, Ronayne lived a reclusive existence, selling eggs and chickens, and still writing about religion and Freemasonry until he died, at age 79, on 21 January 1911. Fittingly, both Ronayne and his wife, who died on 30 March 1918 from a cerebral hemorrhage, were buried side-by-side in Boulder's racially integrated 'charity' graveyard, probably not for lack of means, but rather on principle and because the town's 'respectable' cemetery was also a Masonic one.[58]

•

It is difficult to connect and analyze the fragments of Ronayne's long life, which, as related in his memoir, arguably unfolded in four fairly discrete stages. First was the period between 1832, when he was born in Gurtrue, and 1841, when his aunts moved to Killeagh; before 1841, Ronayne was the illiterate Irish-speaking child of poor farm laborers, immersed in peasant folk culture. Second was the period between 1841, when he began attending Killeagh's National School, and 1849–50, when he left Killeagh and journeyed to Cappamore; between those dates, Ronayne became literate in English and an insatiable scholar; he embraced modern 'devotional revolution' Catholicism (and perhaps was on course for the priesthood); and, most important, in Black '47 he lost his family, his home, many neighbors, and nearly his own life. Third was the longest and most complex period, between 1850 and 1875–76, which began in Cappamore with his initial, intellectual conversion to Protestantism, continued through his successive school teaching positions in Munster, Quebec City, and Chicago, and was marked by deep involvement in the Masonic Order. Finally, the last stage, between 1875–76 and his death in 1911, began with Ronayne's break from Freemasonry and his second and more profound conversion to evangelical Protestantism, which in turn launched his last career as an anti-Masonic agitator and lay-preacher.

How can we discern links and continuities among the disparate phases of Ronayne's life? How did he do so in his memoir? Arguably, memoir writing itself promotes self-invention, as do also immigration and the individualistic and transient character of American life, generally. So, how much of Ronayne's memoir is literally true? How much is fabricated or omitted? How can we disentangle the 'facts' of Ronayne's life—that is, his actual experiences and how he understood them *at the time*—from the controlling, interpretive frameworks, which he later imposed in his memoir?

Ronayne's interpretations of his entire life were grounded in Protestant beliefs and prejudices, which he adopted in Cappamore, and, especially, in the radical evangelical worldview that he espoused after his 'new birth' in Moody's revival. To be sure, his critical attitudes toward many aspects of traditional Irish society and culture were no doubt shaped initially by 'devotional revolution' Catholicism, but his opinions of the latter were profoundly altered by Protestant evangelicalism, as represented initially by the Irish Society's missionaries. From the mid-1870s, his negative opinions of Freemasonry were formalized and broadened by the teachings of American Protestant clergymen such as Blanchard and Roberts, but his overall worldview was molded by the pre-millennialism of figures such as Darby and Moody, whose 'dispensational' theology of the 'end times' before Christ's Second Coming, as well as their intense anti-Catholicism, linked radical Protestantism across the Atlantic.[59]

Consequently, Ronayne's most important interpretive framework was Christian 'providentialism'—the belief that his life was the unfolding of God's plan to lead him to personal salvation in anticipation of Christ's imminent return.[60] Ironically, providentialism was a key British and Irish Protestant interpretation of the Great Famine—as a heaven-sent opportunity to 'reform', restructure, and anglicize Irish society. Likewise, many of Chicago's Protestant clergy and laymen saw the Great Fire as a providential stroke to cleanse their city of wickedness. However, Ronayne did not apply providentialism consistently. He did not so interpret the Chicago Fire, for example. More important, although in retrospect he interpreted the Famine as God's intervention to save Ireland from 'popish tyranny', he did not adopt the conventional British evangelical view that God sent the Famine to punish Irish Catholics for their sins, for that would have implied that his beloved aunts and generous neighbors deserved God's wrath and were themselves responsible for their terrible sufferings.[61] In fact, as will be seen below, Ronayne must have embraced (at least temporarily) a very different, highly politicized, and very traditionally 'Irish' explanation for the 'Great Hunger'.

Stemming from Ronayne's twin conversions were his obsessive prejudices against Catholicism and Freemasonry, linked by Ronayne's belief that both were 'un-Christian', 'pagan', and literally diabolical in their spirit and rituals. Paradoxically, they also were linked by the Catholic Church's own longstanding opposition to Freemasonry and other secret societies—although that was a coincidence that Ronayne never mentioned.[62] Of course, for long periods of his life, Ronayne was either a devout Catholic or an enthusiastic Mason. Hence, it is difficult to tell whether Ronayne's *early* encounters with Catholicism and Freemasonry were marked by growing doubts, as claimed in his memoir, or whether his hostility evolved much later and was imposed retrospectively. Ronayne's anti-Catholic diatribes, which filled much of his memoir, were quite conventional—stock arguments recycled to suit evangelical readers' prejudiced expectations—and in fact his actual memories, when he allowed them to surface, often contradicted his anti-Catholic formulae. For instance, Ronayne's account of his father's death gave him an opportunity to launch a conventional anti-Catholic attack on priestly avarice and 'extortion' from the poor. However, Ronayne admitted that the priest, who gave his father the Last Rites and officiated at his burial, charged no fees for doing so. Likewise, his father's death enabled Ronayne to describe and denounce the Irish wake for the dead as a prime example of 'popish superstition'; but, again, Ronayne admitted that he was too young to attend and observe the ceremony.[63] Overall, Ronayne seemed confused—although perhaps no more so than most Irish evangelicals—about the precise nature of the Catholic Church's and its priests' culpability for Irish 'barbarism': sometimes, he argued, their false teachings, tyranny, and greed were the direct *causes* of Irish 'ignorance'; elsewhere, however, he implied that it was the Church's alleged *neglect* of its duties to the Irish poor that allowed them to remain uncivilized.[64] Ironically, of course, Ronayne himself was in 1841–1850 a beneficiary and product of the Church's own efforts to 'modernise' Irish religious and secular beliefs, and to eradicate the traditional customs of which he now disapproved.

Why, then, *did* Ronayne reject Catholicism and convert to Protestantism?—an action that usually implied rejection of 'Irish' identity, as traditionally understood. The mystery is deepened by several factors. First, despite his early poverty, Ronayne's personal memories of Killeagh and East Cork—of his childhood, his family, and the kindness of his neighbors and parish priests—were unambiguously positive. Ronayne's memoir describes no personal conflicts with, or abuse by, Irish Catholic clergy or relatives that might have alienated him from his religious and social background.

Second, Ronayne did not comport with most missionaries' ideal of an Irish Protestant convert—ashamed of his origins, eager to appear 'British', and reflexively loyal to his social superiors. Likewise, Ronayne never expressed disdain for what he called his 'pure, poetic' native language, and he often employed it in America, especially when he was in trouble or danger.[65] Moreover, Ronayne's frequent confrontations with Protestant (as well as Catholic) authority figures in Ireland, Quebec, and Chicago demonstrated that his political and social attitudes were democratic and egalitarian. Unlike most Anglican clergymen in both Ireland and Canada, Ronayne rejected hierarchy, aristocracy, and, eventually, monarchy. And, unlike most middle-class Protestants in Gilded Age America, Ronayne showed little deference to either the rich or the 'respectable', especially when their actions contradicted his religious beliefs or sense of justice. Finally, even though Ronayne wrote for an anglophile audience, he criticized Irish landlords (especially absentees), Ireland's 'abhorrent tithe system', and Britain's 'incessant' imperialist wars, and his only, occasionally stated objection to Irish nationalism was the conventional apprehension that its success might result in 'Rome Rule'.[66]

Many years ago, the lead author of this essay wrote that: 'As for thousands of his countrymen, the Famine had severed Ronayne from his family [and] community, [and he] spent the rest of his life wandering spiritually as well as physically through Ireland and North America, searching for something irretrievably lost in the shambles of his and his people's past'.[67] In general, that explanation for Ronayne's conversion and subsequent travails may still hold true. Arguably, the Famine shattered Ronayne's cosmology, and for the next sixty years he searched for alternative forms of 'family', 'fraternity', and 'community' to replace those he had lost—or, as an orphaned only child, had never fully enjoyed. Arguably, also, he sought 'answers' or 'explanations' for the crisis that had destroyed his and his people's entire way of life. Indeed, it may be that, even before the Famine, Ronayne was a 'cultural orphan' or exile, already stripped of his peasant heritage by anglicizing education and modernizing Catholicism. If so, then arguably it may have been the 'failure' of Ronayne's new belief system to prevent or alleviate the Famine—or, perhaps, to enable him to become a priest—that weakened his ties to the Church.[68] In this sense, it may be revealing that Ronayne's most heartfelt objection to Catholicism was its doctrine of Purgatory, which reflected, he believed, the Church's teaching, as expressed by Killeagh's priests, that God was 'an angry Being . . . ever ready . . . to hurl the poor guilty sinner into the gloomy regions of everlasting torment', rather than what he believed was the evangelicals' 'gentle, kind and loving father'. Although Ronayne formalized his critique of Purgatory in conventional anti-Catholic terms, it seems clear that his objection was deeply personal: he could not bear the thought that his parents and aunts would suffer eons of hellfire to expiate their sins. Instead, he took great consolation in the belief that, at the Second Coming's imminent and 'glorious morning', his kinsmen and -women in their graves at Clonpriest, 'beside the moaning waves of the Atlantic . . ., shall hear His voice and come forth' to rejoin him at Christ's right hand.[69]

More broadly, perhaps one of Ronayne's initial attractions to both Protestantism and Freemasonry was his quest to discover the 'secrets'—previously 'hidden' away from him in the Protestant Bible or in Masonic rituals—that might dispel life's 'mysteries' and enable him to understand what had happened to his world in Black '47. Indeed, one common thread in all of Ronayne's post-conversion associations is that they promised either a secular or a supernatural 'restoration' of a past 'golden age' of brotherhood or apostolic purity.[70] Inevitably, of course, Ronayne was bitterly disappointed. He could never recover what he had lost. Instead, he was self-condemned to repeat a tragic, personal cycle, which the Famine (or perhaps his father's death in 1837) had begun: crisis, followed by a search for new 'community' and 'meaning', culminating in disillusion and 'betrayal', rebellion and persecution, and finally a recommencement of his quest. Arguably, Ronayne's second conversion in 1877 provided a lasting resolution of his pilgrimage, but the end of his memoir—and, in Colorado, of his life—suggests instead spiritual isolation and recourse to apocalyptic visions. Likewise, it is ironic that Ronayne's rejection of Catholic, then Orange, and finally Masonic authority and rituals should culminate in Dowieism, which was perhaps the most autocratic and 'priestly' institutional and belief system—replete with 'gaudy vestments' and 'gorgeous processions'—that Ronayne ever embraced; indeed, in his acceptance of Dowie's claim to faith-healing powers, Ronayne re-engaged with traditional beliefs that had marked his own early childhood.[71]

Ironically also, and despite his religious conversions, in many respects Ronayne remained intransigently 'Irish'. As noted, his actual memories of Ireland were both deep and positive, and—unlike his eldest son, William, who pretended that he and his parents had been born in Canada or Illinois—Ronayne never denied his Irish origins.[72] Also, at key points in his American life—particularly when he was sick and broke in Chicago—it was his Irish Catholic associations that rescued and comforted him. Equally singular are the many instances when Ronayne himself defended or championed poor Irish Catholics, who were victims of élite and usually Protestant oppression or scorn—the tenants on the Vandeleur estate, for example; the Irish victims of Orange violence in Canada; Jennie Donavan, the rape victim in Ballybrood; John McNamara, the immigrant laborer shot by a Chicago policeman; even the O'Leary family on the city's Near West Side—and often did so at great risk to his livelihood or 'respectable' standing in bourgeois-Protestant society.

Despite his abhorrence of Catholicism, Ronayne was very proud of those 'Irish' episodes in his life. Indeed, Ronayne's republican sentiments, his hatred of injustice and hypocrisy, and his penchant for self-sacrifice and even martyrdom for 'truth' appear strangely reminiscent of the writings of radical Irish and Irish-American nationalists, especially of another devoted 'fanatic': Ronayne's fellow Corkman, Irish-speaker, and Famine sufferer, Jeremiah O'Donovan Rossa (1831–1915), one of the leaders of the Fenian movement in Ireland and, after his 1871 exile to New York, a lifelong conspirator for Irish revolution.[73] Might Ronayne have made a good Fenian, at least temperamentally? Given Ronayne's anti-Catholicism, and despite the Church's own condemnation of Fenianism, that would seem a dubious analogy. And yet, sometime before mid-1865, when he lived in Quebec City, Ronayne joined the Fenian Brotherhood and subscribed to the *Irish People*, the Fenians' revolutionary-republican newspaper, which was published in Dublin and edited by O'Donovan Rossa himself. The Dublin police did not find Ronayne's name on the paper's subscription list until they raided the *Irish People's* offices in September 1865. It is highly likely, however, that an earlier, local discovery of Ronayne's membership in what was, in Canada, a treasonous and illegal organization, comprised the real reason why he lost his élite Protestant school and patronage, and left Quebec City so suddenly and almost penniless in June 1865.[74]

Astonishingly, then, Ronayne in Quebec was simultaneously—or at least sequentially—an evangelical Protestant, a member of the Loyal Orange and Masonic orders, *and* a member of a secret revolutionary organization that was dedicated to the violent overthrow of all the institutions and symbols that Orangemen, Masons, and Anglo-Protestants most revered. How can Ronayne's Fenian affiliation be understood in conjunction with the other aspects of his life and beliefs that are revealed, or concealed, in his autobiography?

First, it is important that Ronayne not only wrote his memoir for money. He also wrote it to glorify God and, as he acknowledged, under the guidance of his second and staunchly evangelical wife, Ellena Darwood.[75] Ellena's influence may explain why Ronayne's memoir scarcely mentioned his first wife, Margaret, or their children, although another reason may be that in November 1877 their younger son, John, married a Catholic, Della (or Delia) Quigley, the daughter of an Irish immigrant laborer, in Chicago's Holy Name Cathedral, which almost certainly means that he reverted to Catholicism. Likewise, it is possible that Margaret herself rejoined the Church—as did her parents and siblings in Wisconsin—which surely would have caused a rift with her husband.[76]

More important, Ellena's influence (or censorship?) may be responsible for the contradictions between Ronayne's personal 'Irish' memories and his rhetorical anti-Catholicism, and also for the flimsy explanations that he provided for crucial transitions in his life. On the one hand, there is no evidence that Ellena or her husband fabricated his life story: its most controversial episodes, such as the rape of Jenny Donavan and the killing of John McNamara, are fully documented. On the other hand, for pious or pecuniary reasons, they omitted or obscured key moments in Ronayne's life, such as his membership in the Fenian Brotherhood, that would have revealed his Irish nationalist activities and sympathies, and which were thereby likely to alienate middle-class, evangelical Protestant, and Anglo-American publishers, readers, and reviewers. As Mimi Cowan and other scholars have shown, in the late nineteenth century such Americans were deeply fearful of 'subversive' and 'revolutionary' threats to private property and the capitalist order, and they increasingly associated such threats with Irish and Irish-American nationalism—especially with Fenian 'terrorism'.[77] This may explain why Ronayne and his new wife omitted from his memoir the real reason for his precipitous departure from Quebec.

In turn, that deletion raises the possibility that they also omitted a similar reason for Ronayne's earlier, equally sudden, and also weakly explained departure in September 1849 from Killeagh and East Cork. According to his memoir, Ronayne left Killeagh to pursue educational goals. But why would he abandon his clerkship, his remaining kinsmen, and especially his priests, Frs. Henry and Maurice Power, whose care and patronage had rescued him from poverty, illiteracy, and typhus fever? Perhaps it was no accident that Ronayne's departure occurred almost simultaneously with Young Ireland's so-called 'second rising' of mid-September 1849, centered only a few miles from Killeagh in South Tipperary and East Waterford. Like its better-known 1848 predecessor, the 1849 rebellion, planned primarily by the agrarian revolutionary James Fintan Lalor, ended quickly and ignominiously; yet its leaders had sworn and mobilized some 2,000 men, and the authorities responded with wholesale arrests throughout the region.[78] Of course, the conjuncture of this event and Ronayne's departure from Killeagh may be purely coincidental. Yet, why did Ronayne write that, when he left East Cork, he was confident that his ability to speak fluent Irish would 'guarantee' his 'safety wherever [he] went'?[79] That phrase—which presumably escaped Ellena's scrutiny—raises an obvious question: why would Ronayne—still at this point a Catholic—have worried for his 'safety' unless, for some reason, he was 'on the run' and needed to hide himself in the Irish-speaking 'underworld' of the South Tipperary peasantry?

In short, the authors suspect that in 1848 or 1849 Ronayne had joined one of County Cork's thirty-three local Confederate or Felon clubs—as existed in nearby Youghal and Midleton, for example—and was involved in some kind of treasonous activity. It is even possible that, if he was 'sworn', it was in his employer James Hayes's tavern, which in the mid-1860s became a center of East Cork Fenianism.[80] If so, then Ronayne's involvement or sympathies with revolutionary Irish republicanism may have triggered his alienation from Killeagh's priests and from the Catholic Church, generally, and may have led to his first conversion to Protestantism. East Cork's priests, including Frs. Maurice and Henry Power, idolized Daniel O'Connell and supported enthusiastically his legal, nonviolent movement to repeal the Act of Union. More broadly, they associated Irish national identity and aspirations exclusively with Catholicism and the Church. Indeed, according to Ronayne, Fr. Henry Power had drawn 'as black a picture of Protestants as he possibly could', to convince his young acolyte that ' "Protestants always had dealings with the devil" '.[81] However, Young Ireland temporarily shattered those traditional associations and prejudices, for Thomas Davis's, Smith O'Brien's, and John Mitchel's brand of Irish nationalism was both ecumenical and Protestant-led. Also, despite their earlier approbation and militant rhetoric, in summer 1848, Munster's Catholic clergy denounced Young Ireland and dissuaded their parishioners from joining its rebellion. As a result, Young Ireland's leaders and sympathizers bitterly charged the bishops and priests with 'betrayal'.[82]

Moreover, and despite his unusual advantages (not least his literacy), Ronayne was a child of East Munster's poorest inhabitants, and so there may have been at least a vague 'class' basis for his alienation and subsequent conversion. Interdenominational and social relations in the region had always been much more complex and ambiguous than either Catholic or Protestant mythologies allowed. On the one hand, both sectarian and nationalist sentiments ran strongly and deeply among the region's Catholics, and instances of Catholic suffering and Protestant persecution, especially of the clergy, were remembered bitterly. Although Munster's Catholics and Protestants shared similar millenarian outlooks, they looked for dramatically different results from God's expected intervention in Irish affairs. On the other hand, however, the area's Protestant gentry had recognized since the late 1700s that Catholic bishops and priests provided what historian David Dickson calls 'a vital instrument of social control', preaching obedience, resignation, and submission to the laws; and many peasants themselves deeply resented what they regarded as the clergy's often arrogant attitudes and avaricious behavior toward the poor—a resentment that erupted dramatically in the so-called Rightboy movement of 1785–88, but which endured long after its suppression. Other fissures in Catholic solidarity also became evident: in the late 1700s, several noted Gaelic schoolmasters and poets converted to Protestantism, as did the former priest who in 1775 became Church of Ireland vicar of Killeagh. Observers commented frequently on the eagerness of the Catholic poor to secure education for their children, even in Protestant schools, and the Irish Society and other missionary bodies were active in Youghal and surrounding towns. Likewise, in 1843, Youghal's parish priest complained that some 'infatuated' Catholics were defying the Church and joining the town's Masonic lodge. And in the same year, Fr. James Maher of Carlow, writing about southern Ireland generally, observed 'with pain' that 'the relative position of the people and Clergy has been greatly changed', as the former had become 'much poorer' while the latter 'have adopted a more expensive style of living'. As late as 1866, the local bishop of Cloyne admitted that 'it was said over and over again' by the rural poor, that ' "the priests don't care about us any longer" ', but only for their strong farmer and shopkeeper allies, and he warned that such sentiments generated mass support for Fenianism, despite clerical condemnations.[83]

Also, both in East Cork, where Ronayne was raised, and in East Limerick, where he converted, Whiteboyism—that is, violent class conflicts between Catholic strong farmers and poor, Irish-speaking subtenants and laborers—was endemic, as were faction fighting and (during the Famine) food riots. And, almost invariably, the Catholic clergy were allied with the Catholic middle classes in their condemnations of the poor for engaging in such activities. In pre-Famine Killeagh, for example, young Ronayne had been horrified by Fr. Maurice Power's harsh excommunication of local sheep stealers. Likewise, Ronayne recorded how, during the Famine, Fr. Henry Power had helped Killeagh's strong farmers and merchants to suppress a food riot by the starving poor. In Cappamore, meanwhile, Fr. John Ryan's relationships with his parishioners were so 'stormy' that he feared assassination. And in neighboring Doon, Fr. Patrick Hickey, a strong farmer who before the Tithe War had dined and hunted foxes with the local gentry, in the depths of the Famine successfully dunned his parishioners for £2,400—'a massive amount of money to extract from a people already on their knees'—to build a large new church, and in 1864 he would die 'a very wealthy man' with railroad stock alone worth over £2 million in today's currency.[84]

To be sure, Young Ireland itself was a bourgeois movement that offered little to Munster's lower classes. Nevertheless, in its challenge to the established order, in the agrarian radicalism of Lalor's essays, and, especially, in its 'explanation' for the Famine (as caused by British and landlord tyranny), Young Ireland may have offered more than enough to enable someone like Ronayne to reshape the ideological structure of his shattered world. Moreover, it had generally been the Irish-speaking rural poor, people from Ronayne's own background, whom both priests and middle-class Catholics scorned as 'vile rabble', who were most likely to 'take the soup' and convert to Protestantism before as well as during the Great Famine.[85]

In short, there may have been threads of continuity, of political and social alienation, that connected Ronayne's flight from Killeagh to both his first conversion to Protestantism and his later membership in a Fenian Brotherhood, which in the 1860s would enjoy strong support in the East Cork region that may have nurtured Ronayne's own democratic and anti-clerical convictions. Indeed, many of the young men who were 'out' in East Munster in 1848–49 became prominent Fenian leaders in the 1860s, including Protestants such as Thomas Clarke Luby and John O'Leary, as well as John O'Mahony, whose pictures Ronayne later peddled in Chicago's Irish saloons. Thus, Edmond Ronayne may provide an exceptional example of what historian Irene Whelan has called 'the tangled genealogy of Irish Nationalism'.[86] And yet, Ronayne's memoir also reveals how the exigencies of immigrant adaptation and bourgeois acculturation clashed with an ethical code shaped both by Irish republicanism and by evangelical Protestantism's radical tendencies. Likewise, his memoir reveals the social and political limitations of both those ideologies.

Clearly, during most of his life in North America, Ronayne was torn between his democratic and egalitarian sympathies, and his need to advance his personal prospects by joining the Masonic Order and other bourgeois social and religious institutions. Although Young Ireland and Fenianism *theoretically* reconciled Irish republicanism and evangelical Protestantism, Ronayne's 1865 career debacle in Quebec proved that the practical, if not the ideological, conflicts between them were insuperable. Perhaps it was little wonder, then, that when describing his life after 1866, Ronayne never mentioned the nationalist agitations that were so popular among Chicago's Irish in the late 1800s. Instead, Ronayne described (or invented?) an event that allegedly happened to him on Chicago's Ontario Street in summer 1866—a physical assault by an Irish Catholic neighbor, who had discovered his religious apostasy—that became Ronayne's literary device to explain his quick transition from Kilgubbin's Irish milieu back to the bourgeois-Protestant security, respectability, and Freemasonry that he had forfeited in Quebec.[87] Indeed, it is possible that this assault masked something more sinister, for in 1866–67, Ronayne found a clerkship with a Captain James Fitzgerald of Chicago's Pinkerton Detective Agency, which the Canadian government employed to spy on the Fenian Brotherhood on both sides of the border.[88] Thus, it may be that the physical attack on Ronayne was indeed an assassination attempt, as he characterized it, but one that was politically rather than religiously motivated.

If Ronayne did inform on his former Fenian comrades, he was continuing a pattern—of 'exposing' organizations to which he had belonged but which he later decided fell short of his ideals—that had begun in Ireland with his repudiations, first of his inherited folkways and second of 'devotional revolution' Catholicism, and that would culminate in Chicago with his final rejection of Freemasonry. Conversely, the assault on Ronayne, if it actually occurred, may have preceded and merely spurred his work for Fitzgerald, whatever its nature, and it may have been no more than a local stimulus or excuse for a final disengagement from Irish nationalism. After all, in mid-1866 and early 1867, the Fenians' calamitous military failures in Canada and Ireland alike; in late 1867, their violent prison rescue attempts in Manchester and London, England; and in April 1868, their assassination in Montreal of Thomas D'Arcy McGee, Canada's leading Irish loyalist politician, all made Fenianism (now labeled 'terrorism' by an anglophile press) deeply embarrassing to many Irish Americans—and perhaps especially to an ethnically marginal figure like Ronayne.[89]

Nevertheless, even after he achieved home ownership, recommenced school teaching, and rejoined the Masons, Ronayne still defended poor Irish Catholics, such as the O'Learys and John McNamara, against established authority and Protestant prejudice. Thus, it may be that only his second conversion in early 1877 completed his full transition from 'Irishness'—as well as from Freemasonry—to a wholesale immersion in evangelical American Protestantism. And yet, again, Ronayne's chosen brands of Protestantism were on the radical-republican or 'Christian commonwealth' fringes of American Christianity: doctrinally extreme as well as ultra-democratic, radically egalitarian in the abolitionist tradition, and, under Dowie, reminiscent of early Christian or Owenite socialism. Thus, in both a spiritual and a political sense, Ronayne remained a committed rebel against many middle-class conventions.

Yet, it is therefore surprising that Ronayne's autobiography never mentioned Chicago's titanic conflicts between capital and labor: the workers' eight-hour day crusade of 1865–67, the violent railroad strikes of 1877, the Haymarket bombing of 1886, or the great Pullman strike of 1894.[90] Of course, it is possible that Ronayne was involved in one or more of these controversies, but that he and Ellena decided that those stories, too, had best be excluded from his memoir. Yet, Ronayne rarely even mentioned Chicago's labor unions, and, when he did so, he characterized them as anti-individualistic 'secret societies'—akin to Freemasonry—which he (like Blanchard and Roberts) condemned indiscriminately, regardless of their purposes. Therefore, it is more likely that Ronayne's omission of those cataclysmic events reveals that neither his Irish republicanism nor his Protestant evangelicalism—both of which were resolutely bourgeois in emphasizing *individual* (not collective) rights—could engage coherently with the new forms of corporate capitalism and working-class resistance that clashed so explosively in Gilded Age America.[91]

Moreover, it is probable that, after Ronayne's second conversion in 1877, he became preoccupied not only with anti-Masonry but also with Biblical prophecy, divine providence, and personal salvation. Indeed, Ronayne's pre-millennial worldview was profoundly ahistorical as well as deeply pessimistic: injustice, corruption, and catastrophes were to be expected, even welcomed, as harbingers of the 'last days' before the Second Coming. Hence, and despite Blanchard's, Roberts's, and even Dowie's radical reformism (which their successors generally repudiated), by the late 1890s Ronayne may have viewed secular solutions to earthly problems, whether in rural Ireland or in working-class Chicago, as no longer feasible, desirable, or even relevant. In his radical separatism, indeed, Ronayne became so apolitical that he never even completed the naturalization process to become a US citizen.[92]

Yet, despite the apocalyptic note that pervaded the last pages of Ronayne's memoir, perhaps his life still had a 'happy ending'. Perhaps through his second conversion he had finally exorcized the Famine's demons, and it may be revealing that the Free Methodist bishop who wrote the introduction to Ronayne's autobiography did not mention the latter's Famine experience. After all, in 1900, when he published his memoir, Ronayne was married to a young woman less than half his age, and by 1902, when he was seventy years old, he had two infant daughters. In addition, either the sales of his memoir or his association with Dowie may have resolved Ronayne's financial problems, finally enabling him to leave Chicago's Near North Side and move to Colorado's more salubrious clime. Geographically and spiritually, Ronayne had come a long way from Killeagh and the horrors of Black '47, and so it is feasible that he ended his pilgrimage on some kind of 'Rocky Mountain high', rather than as one of the homesick, anglophobic Irish 'exiles' about whom this essay's lead author has often written. Certainly, Ronayne did not fear death. Instead, he rejoiced that, 'when we see the Lord Jesus . . ., we shall often talk of all these things, the conflicts, trials and triumphs of our pilgrim journey'—and only then, and not through the mediation of churches, clergymen, or secret societies, 'we shall fully understand why every event had transpired as it did'. At last, he believed, the 'answers' to all the 'secrets' would be revealed.[93]

So, perhaps Ronayne in the end was one of Cardinal Newman's ultimately triumphant Christians, having meandered 'backward', by trial and error, toward 'truth' and heaven. Realistically, however, the Famine had plunged Ronayne into an existential abyss from which he could not emerge unscarred. Haunted by both the 'ghosts' of his past and of alternative futures that the Famine had forever precluded, Ronayne's life after Black '47 was filled with disappointments, as he floundered in what his contemporary, Mark Twain, darkly called the 'puerile insanities' of American culture—'the silly creations of an imagination . . . not conscious of its freaks'.[94] Despite his moments of moral heroism, Ronayne was at length overwhelmed, physically and ideologically, by transatlantic capitalism's predatory forces and by the hegemonic belief systems that promoted, 'explained', and obscured their operations and consequences in Ireland and America alike. As a result, poor Ronayne's achievements rarely approached his ambitions, efforts, and ideals; and in his own 'last days' he eked out a bare living on a plot of land scarcely bigger than his aunts' potato garden in Killeagh.

And yet, when Ronayne finally died in 1911, perhaps his last reveries were in Irish—and perhaps, in the language of his childhood, he 'dream[ed] other dreams and better' than the ones that had obsessed him for so long. Perhaps, in his dying imagination, he sat with his father and aunts at the hearthside of their cottage. Or perhaps he even marched with a Fenian host, down the slopes of Slievenamon, to battle the forces that had destroyed his world.

NOTES

1. In spring semester 2012, Bridget Kelly wrote a senior honors thesis, 'An Examination of the Nineteenth-Century Irish Immigrant Experience through *Ronayne's Reminiscences*', under Kerby Miller's direction at the University of Missouri-Columbia, and her insights and research discoveries fully merit her inclusion as co-author.

The authors express their gratitude to Professor Patricia Kelleher of the Kutztown University of Pennsylvania, Professor Liam Kennedy of the University of Ulster, and Professor David A. Wilson of the University of Toronto, for especially invaluable assistance: Kelleher for advice and research concerning Ronayne and his contemporaries in late nineteenth-century Chicago; Kennedy for extraordinary research in the Archbishop Slattery Papers in the National Library of Ireland; and Wilson for his crucial discovery of Ronayne's Fenian affiliation in Quebec City.

In addition, we are deeply indebted as well to the following Irish, American, and Canadian scholars, archivists, and librarians for their generous advice and assistance; listed alphabetically, they include: Fr. Robert Altman, Marti Anderson, Fr. Steven Avella, Richard D. Barrett, Peter Beirne, Martin Blais, Christina Brophy, Pádraig de Brún, David J. Butler, Mimi Cowan, Maura Cronin, Kay Cullen, Barbara Dobschuetz, Jim Donnelly, Cathy Fortner, Larry Geary, Brian Gurrin, Jim Herlihy, Eugene Hynes, Simon Jolivet, Ann Durkin Keating, Ted Koditschek, Mona Lambrecht, Bill Lowe, Barbara McCormack, Tim McMahon, Breandán Mac Suibhne, Elizabeth Malcolm, Martin Millerick, Miriam Moffitt, Tim Morse, Willie Nolan, Ciarán Ó Murchadha, Garry Owens, Elodie Peyrol, Liam Ronayne, Howard Snyder, Richard Vaudry, and Irene Whelan; in many instances, their specific contributions are detailed in the following notes. Also, for their indefatigable efforts to track down obscure sources, we thank Delores Fisher, Debbie Melvin, and the other staff of the University of Missouri's interlibrary borrowing service.

Early versions of this essay were presented by Kerby Miller at the Ohio Valley History Conference (Murray, Kentucky, October 2011); Glucksman Ireland House, New York University (April 2012); the Canadian Association for Irish Studies (Ottawa, June 2012); York University (Toronto, October 2012); and Radboud University (Nijmegen, Netherlands, March 2013); and we thank those who hosted and commented on these presentations.

2. On the Great Famine and the Irish Catholic interpretation of emigration as 'exile', see Kerby A. Miller, *Ireland and Irish America: Culture, Class, and Transatlantic Migration* (Dublin, 2008), chs. 1–5; and on the development of

Irish Protestant political culture, especially with regard to emigration and the Famine, see ibid., chs. 8–10.

3. Oscar Handlin, *The Uprooted: The Epic Story of the Great Migrations that Made the American People* (1951; Boston, 1973 revised edition).
4. The full title is *Ronayne's Reminiscences: A History of his Life and Renunciation of Romanism and Freemasonry*. In 1999, the book was republished electronically in an online Adobe pdf version, with an introduction by Thomas Ronayne of Detroit, Michigan; we were unable to locate this on the internet, but we thank Liam Ronayne, Cork City Librarian, for emailing us his copy.
5. Ronayne, *Ronayne's Reminiscences* (*RR* hereafter), 13–15. On pre-Famine East Cork's economy, society, culture, and politics, generally, see: David Dickson, *Old World Colony: Cork and South Munster, 1630–1830* (Madison, Wisc., 2005), 225, 249, 260–64, 272–74, 284–85, 297–98, 311–12, 316, 389–95, 441, 464–73, 480–90; James S. Donnelly, Jr., *The Land and the People of Nineteenth-Century Cork: The Rural Economy and the Land Question* (London, 1975), 33, 41–44; K. Theodore Hoppen, *Elections, Politics, and Society in Ireland, 1832–1885* (Oxford, 1984), 90–102, 311; Anon., *The Ancient and Present State of Youghall . . .* (Youghal, 1784); John B. O'Brien, 'Agricultural Prices and Living Costs in Pre-Famine Cork', *Journal of the Cork Historical and Archaeological Society* (*JCHAS* hereafter), 82, 235 (1997), 1–10.

   On religion, literary, and popular culture in the region, see: Cornelius G. Buttimer, 'Gaelic Literature and Contemporary Life in Cork, 1700–1840', in Patrick O'Flanagan and Buttimer, eds., *Cork: History and Society* (Dublin, 1993), 633; Vincent Morley, 'The Penal Laws in Irish Vernacular Literature', in John Bergin, Eoin Magennis, and Lesa Ní Mhungaile, eds., *New Perspectives on the Penal Laws* (Dublin, 2011), 188–90; Seán Ó Coindealbháin, 'Uí Macaille: Its Anglo-Irish and English Schools', *JCHAS*, 50, 172 (1945), 125–35; Brian Ó Cuív, 'Irish Language and Literature, 1691–1845', in T.W. Moody and W.E. Vaughan, eds., *A New History of Ireland, VI: Eighteenth-Century Ireland, 1691–1800* (Oxford, 1989), 404, 410–12; Seán Ó Súilleabháin, 'Some Folklore Traditions of Imokilly', *JCHAS*, 50, 172 (1945), 71–82; Rev. W. Rice, *Memoir of Rev. Peter O'Neil, P.P., Ballymacoda, Co. Cork: The Exiled Priest of '98* (Cork, 1900); Nicholas M. Wolf, 'The Irish-Speaking Clergy in the Nineteenth Century: Education, Trends, and Timing', *New Hibernia Review*, 12, 4 (2008), 69, 82; and on the priest-Catholic ratio in Cloyne diocese, see Donal A. Kerr, *Peel, Priests and Politics: Sir Robert Peel's Administration and the Roman Catholic Church in Ireland, 1841–1846* (Oxford, 1982), 33. Also valuable are Bishop Michael Collins's Visitation Record, Cloyne Diocese, 1828–30, and the Diary of Rev. Richard Canon Smiddy of Youghal, 1840–75, both in the Cloyne Diocesan Archive in Cobh, County Cork; we thank Martin Millerick, a graduate student at the National University of Ireland at Maynooth (NUIM hereafter), for transcripts of these documents, as well as for his unpublished paper, 'A Historical Geography of the Catholic Communities of Cloyne Diocese, County Cork, 1700–1830' (2011).

   On secret societies, sectarian conflict, and popular anti-clericalism in Youghal and Imokilly barony, see: Ann Barry and K.T. Hoppen, 'Borough Politics in O'Connellite Ireland: The Youghal Poll Books of 1835 and 1837', *JCHAS*, 83, 238 (1978), 106–46, and 84, 239 (1979), 15–43; Maurice J. Bric, 'Priests, Parsons and Politics: The Rightboy Protest in County Cork, 1785–1788', *Past and Present*, 100 (1983), 100–23; R.E. Burns, 'Parsons, Priests, and the People: The Rise of Irish Anti-Clericalism, 1785–89', *Church History*, 31, 2 (1962), 151–63; Ian d'Alton, *Protestant Society and Politics in Cork, 1812–1844* (Cork, 1980), 105–06, 163–65, 171–72, 213–14; James

S. Donnelly, Jr., *Captain Rock: The Irish Agrarian Rebellion of 1821–24* (Madison, Wisc., 2009), esp. 200 and 419, n. 132; 'The Rightboy Movement, 1785–8', *Studia Hibernica*, 17–18 (1977), 120–202; and 'The Whiteboy Movement, 1761–5', *Irish Historical Studies*, 21, 81 (1978), 20–54.

6. *RR*, 13–17, 35, 53–54; Elizabeth Ronayne's maiden name was Cunningham. On the Brooke estate, see: *Land Owners in Ireland: Return of Owners of Land of One Acre and Upwards . . . in Ireland* (Dublin, 1876), 118. On Irish peasants' belief in priests' 'magical' healing powers, see: Seán Ó Súilleabháin, *Irish Folk Custom and Belief* (Dublin, n.d.), 38.
7. *RR*, 13–15, 19–26, 34–35, 53–54. On Killeagh town and parish, see: Killeagh-Inch Historical Group, *Killeagh Parish through the Ages* (Killeagh, County Cork, 2011), esp. 73–94, 104–05; Samuel Lewis, *A Topographical Dictionary of Ireland*, 2 vols. (London, 1837), vol. 2, 134–35; and the 1841 Irish Census, *British Parliamentary Papers*, HC, 1843, 24, 294–95. Our thanks to Kay Cullen of Ballymacoda, County Cork, who located and photographed the Ronayne family gravestones still 'facing the Atlantic' (*RR*, 90–91) in the Clonpriest burial ground. Ronayne's childhood home had an extraordinarily evocative setting, for Killeagh town was on the verge of Glenbower Wood—one of Ireland's few remaining ancient oak forests.
8. *RR*, 38–51, 56–62. Ronayne's first National Schoolmaster was Dan Sullivan from Kerry, and, after the latter's abrupt dismissal, Patrick Heffernan. On Fr. Maurice Power (1791–1877) and Fr. Henry Power (1800–68), see: Killeagh-Inch Historical Group, *Killeagh Parish through the Ages*, esp. 98, 105, 231–36, 247; and Buttimer, 'Gaelic Literature and Contemporary Life . . . ', 629.
9. *RR*, 72, 75–85. During the Famine, there were major food riots in Killeagh town (on 26 September 1846 and on 7–8 May 1847) as well as in Ballinacurra, Carrigtwohill, Castlemartyr, Midleton, Youghal, and other nearby towns. On the Famine and food riots in Killeagh and East Cork, generally, see: Catherine Mary Cotter, 'From Prosperity to Pauperism: The Poor Law Union of Middleton during the Great Famine' (MPhil thesis, University College Cork, 1999); Michael Duggan, 'The Great Famine in East Cork' (MA thesis, University College Cork, 2010); T. Fitzgerald, *An A-Z of Youghal* (Youghal, 2008), 38–39; and P. Ó Loingsigh, ed., *The Book of Cloyne* (Middleton, 1994 [1977]), 263–68; the authors are grateful to Martin Millerick and Dr. Laurence Geary of University College Cork for providing copies of the MA theses by Cotter and Duggan.
10. *RR*, 86–95.
11. In 1841–51, the inhabitants of Killeagh town fell from 789 to 663 or by 16 percent; and the population of Imokilly barony declined from 62,170 to 53,570 or nearly 14 percent. 1841 Irish Census, 295–96; 1851 Irish Census, *British Parliamentary Papers*, HC, pt. 1, vol. 2 (Munster), 1852–53, 41, 243–44.
12. *RR*, 102–12. James Hayes, Ronayne's employer, was one of Killeagh's wealthiest Catholic entrepreneurs, although his wife, Mary, whom Ronayne described as a hopeless alcoholic, died in 1853, aged merely 33. Hayes's tavern, 'The Old Thatch', still stands and prospers in Killeagh today, although his adjacent grain store is in ruins. On Hayes, see: R. Henchion, 'The Gravestone Inscriptions of Co. Cork—IX: Killeagh Burial Ground', *JCHAS*, 77, 226 (1972), and 89, 227 (1973), 53, 63; Killeagh-Inch Historical Group, *Killeagh Parish through the Ages*, 285; and information from Kay Cullen of Ballymacoda. Ronayne's annual salary of £5.00, not including food and lodging, was worth roughly $600–$800 in today's purchasing value.

13. Cappamore town straddled the boundary between the parishes of Tuogh (alias Cappamore) and Doon, part of which was in County Tipperary. What Irish Society missionaries referred to as Doon district included those two parishes plus Grean (or Pallasgrean). On Cappamore town and these parishes in the mid-1830s, see Lewis, *Topographical Dictionary of Ireland*, vols. 1–2.
14. 1841 Irish Census, 212–16, and 1851 Irish Census, 298–302. Fr. Patrick Hickey, Doon, to Archbishop Michael Slattery, Cashel, County Tipperary, 27 August 1853, in Archbishop Michael Slattery Papers, Cashel Archdiocesan Archives, on microfilm at the National Library of Ireland, Dublin (NLI hereafter); originals at the Archbishop's House, Thurles. The authors thank Professor Liam Kennedy of the University of Ulster for his research in the Slattery Papers.
15. *RR*, 113–14. For Cappamore town's population, see 1851 Irish Census, 302. On Tuogh (Cappamore) and Doon parishes, and pre-Famine social, sectarian, and political conflicts, see: Ellis Duggan et al., *Cappamore: A Parish History* (Cappamore, County Limerick, 1992), esp. 135, 231–33; W. Crowe, 'Faction Fighting in the 19th Century', *Ceapach Mhór: Journal of the Cappamore Historical Society* (December 1999), 127–29; Seamus Fitzgerald, comp., *Cappawhite and Doon* (Newtown, Pallasgrean, County Limerick, 1983?); Noreen Higgins, *Tipperary's Tithe War, 1830–1838* (Tipperary, 2002), 129–35, and 'Tithe Troubles in the 1830s', *Dún Bleisce: Journal of the Dún Bleisce Historical and Literary Society* (2003), 132–35; W. R. Le Fanu, *Seventy Years of Irish Life* (New York, 1894), 33–35, 44–45, 58, 67–71; Anon., 'Population Trends during the Nineteenth Century', *Ceapach Mhór* (2009), 53; 'The Religious Struggle in Doon in the 19th Century', 'The Tithe War', and 'Tithes', on the Dún Bleisce Historical and Literary Society website http://doonbleisce.com/Historical?Articles.htm (accessed 11 November 2011); Patrick J. O'Connor, *Exploring Limerick's Past: An Historical Geography of Urban Development in County and City* (Coolanoran, Newcastle West, County Limerick, 1987), 96–102, 114–115, 137, 141; and Ruán O'Donnell, 'The United Irishmen in Limerick, 1791–8', in Liam Irwin, Gearóid Ó Tuathaigh, and Matthew Potter, eds., *Limerick: History and Society* (Dublin, 2009), 201, 206–07. The authors thank Martin Millerick and Dr. Miriam Moffitt of NUIM for providing access to the *Ceapach Mhór* and Dún Bleisce articles.
16. On the Irish Society and the New Reformation, see: Donald Harman Akenson, *The Church of Ireland: Ecclesiastical Reform and Revolution, 1800–1885* (New Haven, 1971), esp. 133–36, 204–05; Desmond Bowen, *Souperism: Myth or Reality! A Study of Catholics and Protestants during the Great Famine* (Cork, 1970), 79–81, 109–10, and *The Protestant Crusade in Ireland, 1800–70: A Study of Protestant-Catholic Relations between the Act of Union and Disestablishment* (Dublin, 1978), esp. 185–86 and 206 on the Doon area; Stewart J. Brown, *Providence and Empire: Religion, Politics and Society in the United Kingdom, 1815–1914* (Harlow, 2008), 155–56, *The National Churches of England, Ireland, and Scotland, 1801–1846* (Oxford, 2001), 93–167, and 'The New Reformation Movement in the Church of Ireland, 1801–29', in Brown and David W. Miller, eds., *Piety and Power in Ireland, 1760–1960: Essays in Honour of Emmet Larkin* (Belfast, 2000), 180–208; Janice Holmes, 'Irish Evangelicals and the British Evangelical Community, 1820s–1870s', in James H. Murphy, ed., *Evangelicals and Catholics in Nineteenth-Century Ireland* (Dublin, 2005), 209–22; Miriam Moffitt, *The Society for Irish Church Missions to the Roman Catholics, 1849–1950* (Manchester, 2010), 27–107; Mealla C. Ní Ghiobúin, *Dugort, Achill Island, 1831–61: A Study of the Rise and Fall of a Missionary Community* (Dublin,

2001); Thomas O'Neill, 'Sidelights on Souperism', *Irish Ecclesiastical Record*, 71 (1949), 50–64; Irene Whelan, 'The Bible Gentry: Evangelical Religion, Aristocracy, and the New Moral Order in the Early Nineteenth Century', in Crawford Gribben and Andrew R. Holmes, eds., *Protestant Millennialism, Evangelicalism, and Irish Society, 1790–2005* (Houndsmills, 2006), 52–82, and especially *The Bible War in Ireland: The 'Second Reformation' and the Polarization of Protestant-Catholic Relations, 1800–1840* (Madison, Wisc., 2005), esp. 65, 85, 114–23, and 169–73 on the Irish Society; and Nigel Yates, *The Religious Condition of Ireland, 1770–1850* (Oxford, 2006), esp. 252–78. Pre-Famine missionary work in County Limerick is also detailed in Richard Sinclair Brooke, *Recollections of the Irish Church* (London, 1877), 52–53; and Rev. Dawson Massy, *Footprints of a Faithful Shepherd: A Memoir of the Rev. Godfrey Massy . . .* (London, 1855).

17. 1831–34 Irish Religious Censuses, in the *First Report of the Commission of Public Instruction, Ireland*, HC 1835 (45, 46), xxxiii, 33, 330; Rev. Edward A. Stopford, *The Income and Requirements of the Irish Church; being a Reply to Sergeant Shee . . .* (Dublin, 1853), 74. According to Stopford, between 1841 and 1851, the Protestant inhabitants of Doon, Grean, and Tuogh parishes rose from 84 to 342, from 103 to 269, and from 17 to 151, respectively. Yet in their late 1853 reports to Archbishop Slattery, the local priests enumerated only 49 'apostates' or 'perverts' in Doon, 78 in Grean, and 56 in Tuogh; by late 1853, however, the district's Protestants were already depleted by emigration and reconversion, and its priests, deeply embarrassed by reports to Rome of wholesale conversions, had strong motives to minimize defections; see the letters of Fr. Patrick Hickey, Doon, 27 August 1853; Fr. James Ryan, Pallas Grean, 12 October 1853; and Fr. Patrick Ryan, Cappamore, 12 October 1853, in the Archbishop Michael Slattery Papers, cited fully in n. 14. For inquiries from Rome, see Mark Tierney, ed., 'A Short-Title Calendar of the Papers of Archbishop Michael Slattery in Archbishop's House, Thurles', *Collectanea Hibernica*, Part 4 (1847), in 34/35 (1993), 158; and Part 5 (1848), in 36/37 (1994/1995), 264–65.

    On the Doon mission, also see: Philip Fitzgerald, 'Aspects of Souperism in Cappamore and Doon', *Ceapach Mhór* (2000), 25–27 (2001), 179–19, and (2002), 43–45; and Irish Society, *Brief Account of the Work of the Society during the Past Fifty Years* (Dublin, 1868), 9, 12, which counted 1,300 total converts in the district since the late 1840s; we thank Dr. Brian Gurrin, then of the University of Limerick, for locating this rare source in the NLI. Most Doon/Cappamore converts were concentrated in Gortavalla (or Gurtavalla) townland, which Fr. John O'Dwer, Doon's curate, called 'the land of the perverts'; see 'The Religious Struggle in Doon in the 19th Century.' The Doon area's converts were supported financially and eventually aided to emigrate by Rev. Robert Daly, the Protestant Archbishop of Cashel and an ardent evangelical; see *RR*, 176–77, and Mrs. Hamilton Madden, *Memoirs of the Late Right Rev. Robert Daly, Lord Bishop of Cashel* (London, 1875), 291–96; as well as Akenson, *Church of Ireland*, 133; Bowen, *Protestant Crusade in Ireland*, 206; and Whelan, *Bible War in Ireland*, 112.

18. *RR*, 113–64. On Thomas MacMahon (or M'Mahon) see: Pádraig de Brún, *Scriptural Instruction in the Vernacular: The Irish Society and its Teachers, 1818–1827* (Dublin, 2009), 40–42, 92, n. 2; we thank Dr. Breandán Mac Suibhne, of Centenary College of New Jersey, for alerting us to this extraordinary work. The religious journal, *Irish Intelligence: The Progress of the Irish Society of London* (London, 1850–53), provides much information about the Doon district's missionaries and converts, including Thomas McMahon's obituary

in the 1852 issue, 37–39, which mentions Edmond Ronayne; our thanks to Dr. Miriam Moffitt and Pádraig de Brún for providing these and other data from *Irish Intelligence*, located in the NLI. For an excellent summary of contemporary, transatlantic Protestant (and especially Irish evangelical) criticisms of Catholicism, which mirror Ronayne's objections precisely, see: J. R. Miller, 'Anti-Catholicism in Canada: From the British Conquest to the Great War', in Terence Murphy and Gerard Stortz, eds., *Creed and Culture: The Place of English-Speaking Catholics in Canadian Society, 1750–1930* (Montreal and Kingston, 1993), 31–38.

On the sociology of Catholic-Protestant conversions in Ireland and generally, see: the editors' 'Introduction: Converts and Conversion in Ireland, 1650–1850', in Michael Brown, Charles Ivar McGrath, and Thomas P. Power, eds., *Converts and Conversion in Ireland, 1650–1850* (Dublin, 2005), 11–34, as well as Brown, 'Conversion Narratives in Eighteenth-Century Ireland', 237–74, and Power, 'The Theology and Liturgy of Conversion from Catholicism to Anglicanism', 60–78, in the same volume; and John Wolffe, 'Anti-Catholicism and Evangelical Identity in Britain and the United States, 1830–1860', in Mark A. Noll, David W. Bebbington, and George A. Rawlyk, eds., *Evangelicalism: Comparative Studies of Popular Protestantism in North America, the British Isles, and Beyond, 1700–1990* (New York, 1994), 180–92. On the conversion of one of Ronayne's more famous contemporaries, a Quebec priest, see: Richard Lougheed, *The Controversial Conversion of Charles Chiniquy* (Toronto, 2008).

19. *RR*, 165–94. Margaret Lynch Ronayne was born in Cappamore in 1829; her parents were William (1785–1865) and Bridget Lynch (1792–1889); William Lynch and his wife, son, and daughter converted to Protestantism in 1848, according to Fr. Patrick Ryan's report from Cappamore to Archbishop Slattery, 12 October 1853; see ns. 14 and 17. For vital statistics, see the Lynch Family genealogy <http://home.comcast.net/~dvictor06/genealogy/lynch.html>, which does not mention William and his family's defection from Catholicism; our thanks to Dr. Miriam Moffitt for bringing this source to our attention; unfortunately, the relevant marriage and other parish records for Tuogh/Cappamore and Doon were destroyed in the Four Courts fire of 1922. On the Irish Society's Dublin school, see Susan M. Parkes, *Kildare Place: The History of the Church of Ireland Training College, 1811–1969* (Dublin, 1984). We also wish to thank Dr. Moffitt for allowing us to see her typescript of the Rev. Edmund Dawe Wickham's Journal Letters during a Tour in Ireland in August 1852, which includes a fascinating description of the Doon mission, which, Wickham claimed, then contained 'about 800 converts'.
20. Ronayne taught successively in Irish Society schools in Doon, Oola, and Ballybrood parishes in County Limerick, and near Newmarket-on-Fergus in County Clare.
21. *RR*, 208–12. Ronayne described Frawley as 'a low, cringing, scheming hypocrite, . . . who was never so well satisfied as when exercizing some petty tyranny over the poor people . . . '; *RR*, 210. Our thanks to Peter Beirne of the Clare County Library, Ennis, County Clare, to Ciarán Ó Murchadha of St. Flannan's College, Ennis, and to the latter's informants, Canon Reuben Butler and Máire Ní Ghruagáin, for information about the Vandeleur family and sectarian conflict on the Ralahine estate and its environs.
22. *RR*, 198–208, 213. John Leary or O'Leary was appointed to the Irish Constabulary in June 1853, assigned to County Limerick in November, and promoted to Sub-Constable First Class on 1 January 1854; he was convicted of rape at the Limerick assizes on 25 September 1854 and sentenced to

transportation for life on 19 July 1855, although according to *RR*, 212–13, he died en route to Australia; see extract 17,157 in the Royal Irish Constabulary Register, Public Record Office, Richmond, Surrey, England; and 'County Criminal Court—This Day', *Limerick Reporter*, 17 July 1855; our thanks to Jim Herlihy and Martin Millerick for providing this information. The *Limerick Reporter* article names Leary's victim as 'Mary Maloney'; we are inclined to trust Ronayne's 'extraordinary memory' (*RR*, 190), but it is possible that Ronayne was protecting Maloney (or avoiding a potential libel suit) by disguising her name. On the Rev. Michael John Apjohn, Precentor of Emly Diocese in 1851–71, see Rev. St. John D. Seymour, *The Succession of Parochial Clergy in the United Dioceses of Cashel and Emly* (Dublin, 1908), 49, 63; we thank Dr. Brian Gurrin for this reference.

23. *RR*, 208, 213; it was through Rev. Fitzpatrick's influence that Ronayne moved from Ballybritt to the school on the Ralahine estate in County Clare (see above). Ronayne's Lynch in-laws emigrated in early spring 1854 and settled in Stevens Point, Wisconsin; *RR*, 203, and Lynch Family genealogy, for which see n. 19. Between 1851 and 1861, the number of Protestants in Doon, Grean, and Tuogh parishes fell from 762 to 474; see Stopford, *Income . . . of the Irish Church*, 74; and the 1861 Irish Census, *British Parliamentary Papers*, HC, pt. 4: Reports relating to the Religious Professions, Education, and Occupations of the People, vol. 1, 1863, 294, 301, 310, and 322.

    On reconversions and emigration of Protestant converts from Doon and other mission centers, see: Madden, *Memoirs of . . . Rev. Robert Daly*, 291–96; Moffitt, *Society for Irish Church Missions*, 97–130; 'The Religious Struggle in Doon in the 19th Century'; and the relevant clerical correspondence in Tierney, ed., 'Short-Title Calendar of the Papers of Archbishop Michael Slattery', in Part 6 (1849–52) in 44–45 (2002/2003), 241–45, and Part 7 (1853–56) in 48 (2006), 167–93; on 15–16 August 1855 (193), Fr. Patrick Ryan of Cappamore rejoiced that 'there is scarcely a vestige of apostasy left in the village . . . '. As a result of the post-Famine labors of imported Redemptorist missionaries, Christian Brothers, and teaching nuns, by 1903 'A Country Curate' [Rev. Joseph Guinan] could describe Doon's Catholics as characterized by 'simple, childlike faith, purity of domestic life, devotion to their religion', and absolute obedience to 'the judgments on all manner of questions' of their 'Soggarth Aroon' [beloved priest]; in *Scenes and Sketches in an Irish Parish, or, Priest and People in Doon* (2nd edition, Dublin, 1903), iv–3.

24. *RR*, 208–09, 213.
25. On Quebec City (and province), see: Gérald Bernier and Daniel Salée, *The Shaping of Quebec Politics and Society: Colonialism, Power, and the Transition to Capitalism in the 19th Century* (New York, 1992), esp. 130–43; Robert Bothwell, *Canada and Quebec: One Country, Two Histories* (Vancouver, 1995), esp. 68–69; J.M. Bumsted, *The Peoples of Canada: A Pre-Confederation History* (Toronto, 1992), esp. 184–86, 342, 363–65; John Dickinson and Brian Young, *A Short History of Quebec* (Montreal and Kingston, 2008 edition), 110–93; Serge Gagnon, *Quebec and its Historians, 1840 to 1920* (Montreal, 1982); Fernand Ouellet, *Economic and Social History of Quebec, 1760–1850* (Ottawa, 1980 edition); and Susan Mann Trofimenkoff, *The Dream of a Nation: A Social and Intellectual History of Quebec* (Toronto, 1982), 90–128.

    On Quebec's Protestants or English-speakers (including all the Irish), see: Louisa Blair, *The Anglos: The Hidden Face of Quebec City*, 2 vols. (Quebec, 2005); Ronald Rudin, *The Forgotten Quebecers: A History of English-Speaking Quebec, 1759–1980* (Quebec, 1985); and Garth Stevenson, *Community Besieged: The Anglophone Minority and the Politics of Quebec* (Montreal and Kingston, 1999), esp. 24–44.

On the Irish in Quebec city and province, see: Robert J. Grace, 'A Demographic and Social Profile of Quebec City's Irish Populations, 1842–1861', *Journal of American Ethnic History*, 23, 1 (Fall 2003), 55–84, 'Irish Immigration and Settlement in a Catholic City: Quebec, 1842–61', *Canadian Historical Review*, 84, 2 (June 2003), 217–51, and 'The Irish in Mid-Nineteenth-Century Canada and the Case of Quebec: Immigration and Settlement in a Catholic City' (PhD dissertation, Laval University, 1999); Fernand Harvey et al., *The Irish in Quebec: An Introduction to the Historiography* (Quebec, 1993); Cecil J. Houston and William J. Smyth, *Irish Emigration and Canadian Settlement: Patterns, Links, and Letters* (Toronto, 1990), esp. 211, 227–29; Marianna O'Gallagher, 'The Irish in Quebec', in Robert O'Driscoll and Lorna Reynolds, eds., *The Untold Story: The Irish in Canada*, 2 vols. (Toronto, 1988), vol. 1, 253–61. Also useful is John Francis Maguire, *The Irish in America* (London, 1868), 91–94, 99, which emphasizes upward mobility among Quebec's Irish.

On ultramontane Catholicism in mid-century Quebec, see: Roberto Perin, 'Elaborating a Public Culture: The Catholic Church in Nineteenth-Century Quebec', in Marguerite Van Die, ed., *Religion and Public Life in Canada: Historical and Comparative Perspectives* (Toronto, 2001), 87–105, and 'French-Speaking Canada from 1840', in Terrence Murphy and Perin, eds., *A Concise History of Christianity in Canada* (Toronto, 1996), 190–259; and Preston Jones, 'Protestants, Catholics and the Bible in Late Nineteenth-Century Quebec', *Fides et Historia*, 33, 2 (Summer/Fall 2001), 31–38. Also useful on Quebec Catholic-Protestant competition for political status is: Ian Radforth, *Royal Spectacle: The 1860 Visit of the Prince of Wales to Canada and the United States* (Toronto, 2004), 101–04, 132–34.

26. *RR*, 215–26, 271–73. On education in mid-nineteenth-century Quebec, see: Jean-Pierre Charland, *L'Enterprise Educative au Québec, 1840–1900* (Quebec, 2000), 40, 83–99, and the authors wish to thank Dr. Elodie Peyrol, then a graduate student at Paris VIII University, for translating portions of this work for us; Dickinson and Young, *Short History of Quebec*, 174; Roger Magnuson, *A Brief History of Quebec Education* (Montreal, 1980), 27–39; and Nathan H. Mair, *Quest for Quality in the Protestant Public Schools of Quebec* (Quebec, 1980), 19–21, 29. On Jeffery Hale, see n. 28 below.
27. *RR*, 227; Ronayne joined Quebec City's Aughrim Lodge No. 535, under the sponsorship of J.J. Larmouth, 'one of our wealthy manufacturers'. On the Orange Order in Canada, see: Michael Cottrell, 'Green and Orange in Mid-Nineteenth-Century Toronto: The Guy Fawkes Episode of 1864', *Canadian Journal of Irish Studies*, 19, 1 (July 1993), 12–21; Cecil J. Houston and William J. Smyth, *The Sash Canada Wore: A Historical Geography of the Orange Order in Canada* (Toronto, 1980), esp. 16, 49–56 on the Order in Quebec; Hereward Senior, 'The Genesis of Canadian Orangeism', *Ontario History*, 60 (1968), 109–29; David A. Wilson, ed., *The Orange Order in Canada* (Dublin, 2007); and especially Simon Jolivet, 'Orange, Vert et Bleu: Les Orangistes au Quebec depuis 1849', *Bulletin d'Histoire Politique*, 18, 3 (Spring 2010), 67–84, which contains data on Quebec lodge and membership numbers; we are grateful to Dr. Jolivet of the University of Ottawa for sending us a copy of his essay and for advice and research assistance.
28. *RR*, 226–27. On the Synodical Controversy, see Richard W. Vaudry, *Anglicans and the Atlantic World: High Churchmen, Evangelicals, and the Quebec Connection* (Montreal and Kingston, 2003), especially 172, 178, 186, and 222, for High Church attacks on the evangelicals as 'Irish', 'scum', ultra-democrats, etc.; and on Jeffrey Hale, 17, 146–52; for additional information, we are grateful to Professor Vaudry of King's University College, Edmonton, Alberta. Also on Hale, see: Blair, *The Anglos*, vol. 1, 65–67, 72; vol. 2, 28, 33–34. On the

Anglican Church in Canada, including Tractarianism and its evangelical critics, see: Terence Murphy, 'The English-Speaking Colonies to 1854', and Brian Clarke, 'English-Speaking Canada from 1854', in Murphy and Perin, eds., *Concise History of Christianity in Canada*, 108–89 and 322–23, respectively; William Westfall, 'Constructing Public Religions at Private Sites: The Anglican Church in the Shadow of Disestablishment', in Van Die, ed., *Religion and Public Life in Canada*, 23–49. 'Puseyism' referred to the Anglican divine and Oxford professor, Edward Bouverie Pusey, one of the principal authors (along with John Keble and John Henry Newman, the future Catholic convert) of *Tracts for the Times* (1833–41), the manifesto of the Tractarian or Oxford movement.

29. *RR*, 228. Neither Vaudry's *Anglicans and the Atlantic World* nor the works on Canadian Orangeism (cited in n. 27) refer to this episode, although the tensions and near-schism in the late 1850s between Quebec's ultra-Protestant Orangemen and the Ontario Order's more 'moderate' leaders, such as Cameron, are noted in Houston and Smyth, *The Sash Canada Wore*, 56. The background of this intra-Orange confrontation was that Ontario's middle-class Orange leaders made pragmatic alliances with French and Irish Catholic politicians, and even with Catholic (as well as Anglican) bishops, in support of John A. Macdonald's Liberal-Conservative Party, which in turn was allied with Quebec's *bleus* and their ultramontane clerical supporters. By contrast, Quebec's lodges opposed all compromises with 'papists', as did most plebeian Orangemen in Ontario itself, and the latter usually voted for George Brown's populist and fiercely anti-Catholic Reform (or 'Clear Grits') Party in opposition to the Liberal-Conservatives. Excellent analyses of these complex and fluid political configurations are found in: David A. Wilson, *Thomas D'Arcy McGee; Vol. 2: The Extreme Moderate, 1857–1868* (Montreal and Kingston, 2011), 44–45, 150–52; and '"Orange Influences of the Right Kind": Thomas D'Arcy McGee, the Orange Order, and the New Nationality', in Wilson, ed., *Orange Order in Canada*, 89–108; on politics, also see: Dickinson and Young, *Short History of Quebec*, 182–93; and Trofimenkoff, *Dream of a Nation*, 98–105.
30. *RR*, 228–41. Of course, Ronayne's strictures were written in the late 1890s, but it is likely they reflected his contemporary reactions to Orange mob violence and murders of Irish Catholics in Toronto in 1858 and 1864 as well as in Belfast during August of the latter year; see Cottrell, 'Green and Orange in Mid-Nineteenth-Century Toronto', 14–16; and Wilson, '"Orange Influences of the Right Kind"', 97–98.
31. *RR*, 243–77. On the Masonic Order in Canada, see: Jessica L. Harland-Jacobs, *Builders of Empire: Freemasons and British Imperialism, 1717–1927* (Chapel Hill, North Carolina, 2007), esp. 35, 53–55, 76, 133–76, 183–84; and Bumsted, *Peoples of Canada*, 367–68. In his memoir (110–11), Ronayne claimed that he first heard of Freemasonry while teaching in Britway, County Cork, in 1849–50; however, there were Masonic Lodges in Youghal, County Cork, since 1695, and at least one of them was still active when Ronayne lived in Killeagh, only five miles distant. In the late 1700s and early 1800s, Irish Masonic membership, generally, was ecumenical, and in the 1790s, many lodges had been associated with the United Irishmen. After the 1798 Rebellion, the Irish Order perforce embraced loyalism, but in 1800–29, it supported Catholic Emancipation, despite the Order's condemnation by the Vatican (which in 1837 forced Daniel O'Connell to disavow his membership) and its steady infiltration and eventual domination by Orangemen; on Irish Freemasonry, see: Harland-Jacobs, *Builders of Empire*, 122–31, 151–59; John Heron Lepper and Philip Crossle, *History of the Grand Lodge of Free and Accepted*

Masons of Ireland (Dublin, 1925), vol. 1, 98–99, 137, 423, 427; and David J. Butler, *Three Hundred Years of Freemasonry in Youghal* (Cork, 2010); we are grateful to Dr. Butler and to Martin Millerick for enabling us to secure a copy of this work.

32. On Stevens Point and the Lynch family, see: Edward McGlachlin et al., eds., *A Standard History of Portage County, Wisconsin* (Chicago, 1919), vol. 1, 80–81; Maurice Perret, *Portage County: Of Place and Time. A Historical Geography of Portage County, Wisconsin* (Stevens Point, 1992), esp. 2–10, 24–25, 47–53; Malcolm Rosholt, *Our Country, Our Story: Portage County, Wisconsin* (Stevens Point, 1959), 74–78, 87–90, 141, 495–98, and *Pioneers of the Pinery* (Rosholt, Wisc., 1979); and the Lynch Family genealogy (see n. 19), which includes relevant extracts from the US Census schedules of 1860, 1870, and 1880 for the Stevens Point area. For the town's 1865 population, see: Riley Moffat, *Population History of Eastern U.S. Cities and Towns, 1790–1870* (Metuchen, NJ, 1992), 226.
33. *RR*, 278–81. Mullaly was probably James Mullally, listed in *Edwards' Annual Directory* (Chicago, 1866), 391 and 684, as a salesman for Fairbank, Peck & Co., lard and oil manufacturers. City directories for 1865 and 1867 confirm that Dennis Heaney operated a saloon at 102 Kinzie Street, just west of Wells Street, which, according to Ronayne, provided lodging for boarders. On the Kilgubbin, Goose Island, and Little Hell neighborhoods on Chicago's Near North Side, see: Perry R. Duis, *Challenging Chicago: Coping with Everyday Life, 1837–1920* (Urbana, Ill., 1998), 93–95; Michael F. Funchion, *Chicago's Irish Nationalists, 1881–1890* (New York, 1976), 11–13; 'Little Hell: The Plague-Spot of the North Division', *Chicago Daily Tribune*, 27 November 1875, and 'Invading "Little Hell"', *Chicago Tribune*, 10 October 1890 (articles located by Ellen Skerrett); Dominic A. Pacyga and Ellen Skerrett, *Chicago: City of Neighborhoods. Histories and Tours* (Chicago, 1986), 37–42; Ann Durkin Keating, *Chicago Neighborhoods and Suburbs: A Historical Guide* (Chicago, 2008), 223–25; Amanda Seligman, 'Goose Island', in James Grossman, Ann Keating, and Janice Reiff, eds., *The Encyclopedia of Chicago* (Chicago, 2004), 348; and Charles S. Winslow, 'Historic Goose Island' (1938), a typescript at the Chicago Historical Society (notes provided by Professor Patricia Kelleher).
34. On Chicago in the 1860s and early 1870s, see: Edward Bubnys, 'Nativity and the Distribution of Wealth: Chicago 1870', *Explorations of Economic History*, 19 (1982), 105; William Cronon, *Nature's Metropolis: Chicago and the Great West* (New York, 1991); Duis, *Challenging Chicago*; Robin L. Einhorn, *Property Rules: Political Economy in Chicago, 1833–1872* (Chicago, 1991), 238 and *passim*; John B. Jentz and Richard Schneirov, *Chicago in the Age of Capital: Class, Politics, and Democracy during the Civil War and Reconstruction* (Urbana, Ill., 2012); Theodore J. Karamanski, *Rally 'Round the Flag: Chicago and the Civil War* (Chicago, 1993), 227–32, 241–43, 248; Harold M. Mayer and Richard C. Wade, *Chicago: Growth of a Metropolis* (Chicago, 1969), 42–54; Donald L. Miller, *City of the Century: The Epic of Chicago and the Making of America* (New York, 1997), 135–40; Moffatt, *Population History*, 22; Dominic A. Pacyga, *Chicago: A Biography* (Chicago, 2009), 71–72; Bessie Louise Pierce, *A History of Chicago, Vol. II: From Town to City, 1848–1871* (Chicago, 1940), 289–302, 354, 378, 481–82; Harold L. Platt, *Shock Cities: The Environmental Transformation and Reform of Manchester and Chicago* (Chicago, 2005); and Karen Sawislak, *Smoldering City: Chicagoans and the Great Fire, 1871–1874* (Chicago, 1995), 13. On political and police corruption, see: Richard C. Lindberg, *To Serve and Collect: Chicago Politics and Police Corruption from the Lager Beer Riot to the Summerdale*

Scandal (New York, 1991), 40 and *passim*; and James L. Merriner, *Grafters and Goo Goos: Corruption and Reform in Chicago, 1833–2003* (Carbondale, Ill., 2004), 43 and *passim*.

On Irish Catholics in Chicago, see: Bubnys, 'Nativity and the Distribution of Wealth', 105; Mimi Cowan, 'Ducking for Cover: Chicago's Irish Nationalists in the Haymarket Era', *Labor: Studies in Working-Class History of the Americas*, 9, 1 (2012), esp. 56–57; Michael F. Funchion, 'Irish Chicago: Church, Homeland, Politics, and Class—the Shaping of an Ethnic Group, 1870–1900', in Melvin G. Holli and Peter d'A. Jones, eds., *Ethnic Chicago* (Grand Rapids, Mich., 1984 revised edition), esp. 15–16 and 32–35; Funchion, *Chicago's Irish Nationalists*, 9–15; Lawrence J. McCaffrey et al., *The Irish in Chicago* (Urbana, Ill., 1987); Jentz and Schneirov, *Chicago in the Age of Capital*, 125–30 and *passim*; Patricia Kelleher, 'Young Irish Workers: Class Implications of Men's and Women's Experiences in Gilded Age Chicago', *Éire-Ireland*, 36, 1–2 (Spring/Summer 2001), 141–66; Charles Shanabruch, *Chicago's Catholics: The Evolution of an American Identity* (Notre Dame, Ind., 1980), esp. 234–36; and Ellen Skerrett, *Born in Chicago: A History of Chicago's Jesuit University* (Chicago, 2008), and 'Chicago's Irish and "Brick and Mortar Catholicism": A Reappraisal', *U.S. Catholic Historian*, 14, 2 (Spring 1996), 53–71.

35. Platt, *Shock Cities*; Karamanski, *Rally 'Round the Flag*, 227–29, 241; *RR*, 280–91.
36. *RR*, 289–93. The Sisters of Mercy, an Irish order, arrived in the United States in 1843 and in Chicago in 1846, led by their superior, Agatha O'Brien from County Carlow, who died in 1854 while nursing cholera victims. In early 1851, the Sisters took over and renamed Illinois General Hospital; in 1863, they moved it to 26th Street and Calumet, then out 'in the country', where in 1865 they nursed Ronayne back to health. See: Suellen Hoy, *Good Hearts: Catholic Sisters in Chicago's Past* (Urbana, Ill., 2006), 35–38; and Wallace Best, 'Mercy Hospital', in Grossman et al., *Encyclopedia of Chicago*, 522. Mullally's generosity was extraordinary: the $35 he paid the Sisters for Ronayne's treatment is worth nearly $500 in today's currency.
37. *RR*, 292–97. Ronayne's new residence was owned by John Philbin, one of Chicago's earliest Irish Catholic settlers; Philbin emigrated from County Mayo c. 1842 and settled in Chicago c. 1847; his Jesuit-educated son, John, Jr., became a prominent public official, businessman, Democratic politician, and Catholic layman; see Charles Ffrench, ed., *Biographical History of the American Irish in Chicago* (Chicago, 1897), 104–06. Ronayne's characterization of Ontario Street as at 'the very center' of Chicago's Irish Catholic community is problematic, since by 1866 both Holy Family parish, on the West Side, and Bridgeport had emerged as major Irish settlements.

The Irish Republican or Fenian Brotherhood was established in Ireland and New York in March 1858. In the mid-1860s, Chicago was a major Fenian center: in March 1864, Chicago's Fenian Fair garnered over $54,000; and the city became a principal mobilization point for the Fenian army, commanded by General Thomas Sweeny, which invaded Ontario on 31 May 1866. Ironically, in autumn and winter 1865–66, a few months after Ronayne peddled his pictures, John O'Mahony was deposed as Fenian leader by William R. Roberts and Sweeny, who later launched the Ontario invasion. In April 1866, O'Mahony's wing of the movement also initiated an attack on New Brunswick, but it was even less successful than its successor. Both invasions were thwarted principally by the duplicity of the US government, which earlier had connived with Fenian leaders, even selling them arms and ammunition, to pressure Britain in diplomatic negotiations, but then intervened militarily to intercept the invading forces. See: William D'Arcy, *The Fenian Movement in the United States, 1858–1886* (Washington, DC, 1947); Cowan, 'Ducking for Cover', 58–61; Brian Griffin, '"Scallions, Pikes, and Bog Oak Ornaments": The Irish Republican Brotherhood Fenian Fair', *Studia Hibernica*, 29 (1995), 85–97; Jentz and Schneirov, *Chicago in the Age of Capital*, 73–74, and 'Chicago's Fenian Fair of 1864', *Labor's Heritage*, 6 (Winter 1995), 4–19; Jack Morgan, *Through American and Irish Wars: The Life and Times of General Thomas W. Sweeny, 1820–1892* (Dublin, 2006); and W. S. Neidhardt, *Fenianism in North America* (University Park, Pa., 1975).

38. *RR*, 299–306. William B. Ogden was mid-century Chicago's leading entrepreneur; financed by New York capital, he was largely responsible for the Near North Side's commercial, industrial, and real estate development—and for evicting the area's poor squatters; see *A Biography of William B. Ogden: The Railroad Tycoon Who Built Chicago* (Carbondale, Ill., 2009) by Jack Harpster, who acknowledges that Ogden was 'seriously flawed' and only 'mostly honest' (xii, 255). Ellen Skerrett and Professor Patricia Kelleher traced Ronayne's house, family, and neighbors in the 1870 and later US Census schedules and city directories, and provided his neighborhood's socioeconomic profile. Bremer Street was later renamed Milton Avenue, by Ronayne himself, in honor of the Wisconsin town, Milton Junction, where in 1884–85 he first met and converted his future second wife, whom he married in 1897. Ronayne's second house, rebuilt after the 1871 Fire, was a three-story frame building that stood until 1941; its address in 1910 was 930 North Milton Avenue (later North Cleveland Avenue). We thank Lesley Martin of the Chicago History Museum Research Center for her help locating the demolition permit for 930 North Cleveland Avenue as part of land clearance for the Frances Cabrini row houses, public housing for war workers' families. On Chicago housing, generally, see: Joseph C. Bigott, *From Cottage to Bungalow: Houses and the Working Class in Metropolitan Chicago, 1869–1929* (Chicago, 2001); and Margaret Garb, *City of American Dreams: A History of Home Ownership and Housing Reform in Chicago, 1871–1919* (Chicago, 2005); and on the twentieth-century demolition of Ronayne's neighborhood, see: Lawrence J. Vale, *Purging the Poorest: Public Housing and the Design Politics of Twice-Cleared Communities* (Chicago, 2013).

39. On American Freemasonry and fraternalism, generally, see: Steven C. Bullock, *Revolutionary Brotherhood: Freemasonry and the Transformation of the American Social Order, 1730–1840* (Chapel Hill, 1996), 316–17; Mark Carnes, *Secret Ritual and Manhood in Victorian America* (New Haven, 1989), 1–9; Mary Ann Clawson, *Constructing Brotherhood: Class, Gender, and Fraternalism* (Princeton, NJ, 1989), 95, 211–13; Lynn Dumenil, *Freemasonry and American Culture, 1880–1930* (Princeton, NJ, 1984), esp. 12–14, 70–75, 91–103, 225, and 'Religion and Freemasonry in Late 19th-Century America', in William R. Weisberger, Wallace McLeod, and S. Brent Morris, eds., *Freemasonry on Both Sides of the Atlantic* (Boulder, 2002), 605–20; and Harland-Jacobs, *Builders of Empire*, 17–18, 131. On Masons in Chicago and Illinois, see: David M. Fahey, 'Fraternal Clubs', in Grossman et al., *Encyclopedia of Chicago*, 179; and Fergus MacDonald, *The Catholic Church and the Secret Societies in the United States* (New York, 1946), 70.

Ronayne's few references in his memoir to his family are at best ambivalent; e.g., after his denunciation of officer Cronin, he wrote that, '[T]here was no use in seeking counsel at home', which suggests at least an emotional detachment from his wife and perhaps also from his sons (*RR*, 339).

40. *RR*, 309–16.
41. *RR*, 316–21. As to the Fire's origin, according to Ronayne: 'The family occupying the second house from O'Leary's was having a party that Sunday night in honor of a relative recently arrived from Ireland, and their supply of milk running short it was suggested that one of the young women should milk Mrs. O'Leary's cow, while a young man of the party volunteered to accompany her and hold the lamp. Arriving at the barn, the lamp was placed on the floor, and the two engaging in some frolic it was overturned in their scuffling and the barn set on fire. Of course the guilty parties escaped at once, and fearing the consequences kept their own counsel' (320); it requires little imagination to suspect that either Ronayne or his informants censored the account of 'frolic' and 'scuffling'.

    On the Chicago Fire and its aftermath, including relief efforts, see especially: Sawislak, *Smoldering City*, 27–29 and *passim*; and also, Lisa Krissoff Boehm, *Popular Culture and the Enduring Myth of Chicago, 1871–1968* (New York, 2004), 1–27; Stephen Longstreet, *Chicago, 1860–1919* (New York, 1973), 135; Rose Miller, *American Apocalypse: The Great Fire and the Myth of Chicago* (Chicago, 1990); Pacyga, *Chicago: A Biography*, 79, 100; Christine Meisner Rosen, *The Limits of Power: Great Fires and the Process of City Growth in America* (Cambridge, 1986), 92–176; and Carl Smith, *Urban Disorder and the Shape of Belief: The Great Chicago Fire, the Haymarket Bomb, and the Model Town of Pullman* (Chicago, 2007 2nd edition), 19–98. On the O'Leary family and the Fire, see: Richard F. Bales, *The Great Chicago Fire and the Myth of Mrs. O'Leary's Cow* (Jefferson, North Carolina, 2002); Robert Cromie, *The Great Chicago Fire* (New York, 1958), 273–79; Jean M. Henry, 'Mrs. O'Leary's Cow: The Rhetorical Folklore and History surrounding the Great Fire of Chicago', *Midwestern Folklore*, 25 (Fall 1999), 54–99; Tom McNamee, '119 Years after the Fire, O'Leary's hurt smolders', *Chicago Sun Times*, 7 October 1990; and Skerrett, *Born in Chicago*, 33.
42. *RR*, 322–29; Ronayne rebuilt his home in February 1872, but he was forced to sell his two lots on the other side of Bremer Street for about half their pre-Fire value (329); on Ronayne's new house, a three-story frame building, see n. 38 above. The Fire caused a wave of failures among insurance companies, especially those locally based, with the result that property-owners, like Ronayne, overall lost two-thirds of their insured investments; see Alfred Theodore Andreas, *History of Chicago: From the Earliest Period to the Present Time, Vol. II* (New York, 1975 reprint edition; orig. 1885), 191. Ronayne's service on Chicago's temporary Masonic relief agency is described in Andreas, *History of Chicago, Vol. II*, 659–61, as co-author Bridget Kelly discovered.
43. *RR*, 330–44. McNamara's home at 56–58 Market Street (later the 400 block of North Orleans Street) was a 'relief shanty' built for poor Chicagoans in burned-out areas. The confrontation between Cronin and McNamara, the testimony at the coroner's inquests, and the latter's verdicts are described and commented upon in reports and editorials in: *Chicago Evening Journal*, 5, 6 and 8 July 1872; *Chicago Inter Ocean*, 5, 6 and 8 July 1872; *Chicago Times*, 5 and 6 July 1872; and *Chicago Tribune*, 5 and 6 July 1872. There were two coroner's inquests: the first jury deadlocked at 11–1 for Cronin's acquittal, perhaps because it contained one member who was an Irish immigrant grocer named Peter Conlan; the second jury, which contained no jurors with obviously 'Irish Catholic' names, voted unanimously for acquittal. Judging from their names and occupations (clerk, publisher, bookkeeper, grocer, lawyer, etc.), nearly all members of the two coroner's juries were native- or German-born white-collar workers; based on research by Ellen Skerrett in the above newspapers and in the 1871 *Merchants' Chicago Census Report*.

Most newspaper coverage and editorial comments were highly prejudiced against McNamara and the city's Irish lower classes, generally, and equally supportive of Cronin and 'law and order'; thus, 'Shot Dead: A Policeman Does His Duty', 'Resisting Police Officers', and 'The Shooting Done in Self-Defense' were typical headlines in the *Chicago Evening Journal* and the notoriously (but not uniquely) anti-Irish *Chicago Tribune* (all on 5 July 1872).

The newspaper reports of the testimony given at the coroner's inquiries were confused and contradictory. Our best judgment is that Ronayne's characterization of the fatal incident as a 'murder' was not over-stated. McNamara was drunk but, according to the bulk of the testimony, he was only damaging his own property and not threatening his family or neighbors. To be sure, there was a fight between McNamara and officer Cronin, who tried to arrest McNamara and drag him out of his home; also involved was an Irish neighbor, Dennis Kelly, who, reportedly armed with an axe, assisted McNamara, and whom Cronin also shot. However, McNamara himself had no weapon, Kelly did not strike Cronin with the axe, and the officer appears to have been in no physical danger when he shot the two Irishmen. Instead, it appears that McNamara and Kelly had succeeded in forcibly expelling Cronin, battered but essentially unhurt, from the house and in shutting the front door, when Cronin reopened the door and, standing on the front steps outside the house, fired into it, killing McNamara and wounding Kelly. Indeed, at one point in their struggle inside the house, Cronin succeeded in putting McNamara in primitive handcuffs called 'come-alongs', although it is unclear whether the latter was still wearing them when he was shot. The authors thank Richard D. Barrett, a historian of Chicago's police, for information about 'come-alongs'.

The newspapers describe McNamara only as an Irish 'river laborer' and provide no information on his background. However, McNamara (*Mac Conmara* in Irish) is a Munster name, usually associated with County Clare, which witnessed exceptionally high numbers of evictions in the late 1840s and early 1850s; that history may help explain McNamara's refusal to leave his home and his statement to Cronin that 'he would die first'; see his wife's testimony at the first coroner's inquest in *Chicago Inter Ocean*, 6 July 1872. Given his background, it is also likely that McNamara and his neighbors were mono- or bilingual Irish-speakers, which meant that Ronayne was probably the only middle-class observer who could speak to them in their principal language.

Ironically, only a few months after McNamara's killing, on 19 October 1875 near Stevens Point, Wisconsin, where Ronayne's in-laws lived, a mob led by prominent and 'respectable' Freemasons (lawyers, businessmen, public officials) lynched two brothers, small farmers and sawmill operators, for having killed Portage County's sheriff while resisting eviction; although their identities were well-known, no mob members were ever charged; Ronayne did not mention this incident in his memoir but, if he learned about it from his wife's family, it no doubt strengthened his anti-Masonic convictions; see Rosholt, *Pioneers of the Pinery*, 100–37; on Masonic lodges in the Stevens Point region, see: McGlachlin et al., *Standard History of Portage County*, vol. 1, 195–97.

44. *RR*, 324–28, 332–34, 346–50, 353–55; by summer 1872, Ronayne was so disillusioned with the failures of 'Masonic charity' that he briefly joined Home Lodge No. 416, of the Masons' greatest rival, the International Order of Odd Fellows, because of the latter's more equitable distribution of Fire relief (341–42). In his *History of Chicago, Vol. II*, Andreas, almost certainly a Mason himself, extolled Masonic relief efforts and made no reference to the misappropriations, which Ronayne alleged.
45. *RR*, 358–73; Ronayne's letter to the *Chicago Times* was occasioned by his outrage that Federal and local officials allowed the city's Freemasons to play

a prominent role in the laying of the cornerstone of the new Chicago customhouse and post office, which took place on 24 June 1874; nevertheless, on the occasion Ronayne marched with his lodge, wearing full Masonic regalia and trying, he admitted, 'to appear as proud and consequential as possible' (365).

46. *RR*, 381–93. Ronayne authored at least three anti-Masonic books, which he revised and republished throughout his life. In order of initial publication, they are: *Handbook of Free Masonry* (Chicago, 1876; rev. and enlarged ed., Chicago, 1902); *The Master's Carpet; or Masonry and Baal-Worship Identical* (Chicago, 1879; reissued 1887); and *Masonic Oaths Null and Void* (Chicago, 1880; reissued 1919). Also, published after his death was Ronayne's *Chapter Masonry: Being the Opening, Closing, Secret Work and Lectures of the Mark Master, Past Master, Most Excellent Master and Royal Arch Degrees* (Chicago, 1924). In 1917–43, these works were reprinted by E.A. Cook of Chicago.

   In the 1880 census schedule, Ronayne was not listed as a schoolteacher but rather as a 'publisher/lecturer' (or 'public lecturer'—the handwriting is nearly indecipherable), and his sons were no longer living at home; we thank Professor Patricia Kelleher for these results of her census research.

47. *RR*, 339, 349–50, and 370 on Ronayne's lack of religious inspiration and affiliation before his second conversion. On Masonic opposition to Ronayne's lectures, see: *RR*, 387–88, 391, 401, 416; and the hostile account in 'Secret Societies: The Wanderings of Ronayne in the Rural Districts', *Chicago Daily Tribune*, 30 July 1876, located by Ellen Skerrett; interestingly, one Masonic critic charged that Ronayne was an Irish priest, sent by the Jesuits to infiltrate and defame American Freemasonry (*RR*, 401).

   Moody's and Sankey's Chicago revival took place in the specially constructed (and élite-financed) Chicago Tabernacle, located on Monroe Street between Market and Franklin, from 1 October 1876 to 16 January 1877; however, Ronayne did not begin attending the meetings until shortly after Christmas 1876 and waited until nearly the last day to experience conversion. On Ronayne's attendance and conversion, see *RR*, 393–99.

48. *RR*, 395–96, 402. On Moody and his revivals, see: Edward J. Blum, 'Gilded Crosses: Postbellum Revivalism and the Reforging of American Nationalism', *Journal of Presbyterian History*, 79 (Winter 2001), 177–92; Barbara Dobschuetz, 'Fundamentalism and American Urban Culture: Community in Religious Identity in Dwight L. Moody's Chicago, 1864–1914' (PhD dissertation, University of Illinois-Chicago, 2002; we thank Dr. Dobschuetz allowing us to read her dissertation); Bruce J. Evensen, *God's Man for the Gilded Age: D.L. Moody and the Rise of Modern Mass Evangelism* (New York, 2003), esp. 123–63; James F. Findlay, Jr., *Dwight L. Moody: American Evangelist, 1837–1899* (Chicago, 1969), esp. 198–300; Thekla Ellen Joiner, *Sin in the City: Chicago and Revivalism, 1880–1920* (Columbia, Mo., 2007), esp. 10–53; Jentz and Schneirov, *Chicago in the Age of Capital*, 190–91; William G. McLoughlin, Jr., *Modern Revivalism: Charles Grandison Finney to Billy Graham* (New York, 1959), 166–281; Sandra S. Sizer, 'Politics and Apolitical Religion: The Great Urban Revivals of the Late Nineteenth Century', *Church History*, 48, 1 (March 1979), 81–98; and Bernard A. Weisberger, *They Gathered at the River: The Story of the Great Revivalists and their Impact upon Religion in America* (Chicago, 1958), 175–219.

   In his noncriticism of Freemasonry and secret societies, Moody mirrored the behavior of mainstream Protestant clergymen, many of whom, to Ronayne's disgust, were themselves Masons; thus, *Our Country* (New York, 1885), a best-selling denunciation of America's ills by Josiah Strong, a Congregational minister, attacked immigration, 'Romanism', Mormonism, intemperance, socialism, 'luxury', and 'the City', but never mentioned Freemasonry or other secret societies. On the ideological and class alliance between Chicago's clergy and wealthy capitalists, see: Heath W. Carter, 'Scab Ministers, Striking Saints: Christianity and Class Conflict in 1894 Chicago', *American Nineteenth Century History*, 11, 3 (September 2010), 321–49.

On John Nelson Darby, the Plymouth Brethren, and Darby's contemptuous but influential relationship with Moody, see: Robert H. Baylis, *My People: The Story of those Christians Sometimes Called Plymouth Brethren* (Wheaton, Ill., 1995), esp. 61–65; F. Roy Coad, *A History of the Brethren Movement* (Grand Rapids, Mich., 1968), esp. 188; [John Nelson Darby], *Letters of J.N.D.* (London, n.d.), vol. 2, 257; Findlay, *Dwight L. Moody*, 249–61; William Kelly, ed., *The Collected Writings of J.N. Darby* (Sunbury, Pa., 1972 reprint), vol. 31, 371; W.G. Turner, *John Nelson Darby* (London, 1944); and Max S. Weremchuk, *John Nelson Darby: A Biography* (Neptune, NJ, 1993), 143–44.

On Darby and pre-millennialism in Ireland's 'Second Reformation', see: Crawford Gribben, 'Antichrist in Ireland', and Timothy C.F. Stunt, 'John Nelson Darby: Contexts and Preconceptions', in Gribben and Holmes, eds., *Protestant Millennialism, Evangelicalism and Irish Society*, 1–30 and 83–98, respectively; Janice Holmes, 'Irish Evangelicals and the British Evangelical Community', in Murphy, ed., *Evangelicals and Catholics in Nineteenth-Century Ireland*, 215, 221; T.F.C. Stunt, 'Influences in the Early Development of J.N. Darby', and Gary L. Nebeker, '"The Ecstasy of Perfected Love": The Eschatological Mysticism of J.N. Darby', in Crawford Gribben and Stunt, eds., *Prisoners of Hope? Aspects of Evangelical Millenarianism in Scotland and Ireland, 1800–1880* (Carlisle, England, 2005), 44–68 and 63–95, respectively. Intriguingly, Darby spent much time preaching in County Limerick, and may have directly influenced the Anglican clergymen who converted Ronayne; see Weremchuk, *John Nelson Darby*, 51–54, 109. Darby's detractors noted that he developed his radical 'dispensationalist' theology only after he suffered severe head injuries in a horse-riding accident.

49. *RR*, 399–401. For newspaper reports of Ronayne's anti-Masonic lectures at the June 1876 NCA convention, see: 'Anti-Secret Societies' and 'Evening Session: The First Degree', *Chicago Daily Tribune*, 21 and 22 June 1876, located by Ellen Skerrett. On the National Christian Association and Jonathan Blanchard, see: Carnes, *Secret Ritual and Manhood in Victorian America*, 71–75, 88–89, 199 ns. 109 and 111; Clyde S. Kilby, *Minority of One: The Biography of Jonathan Blanchard* (Grand Rapids, Mich., 1959), 167–84, 198–200; MacDonald, *Catholic Church and the Secret Societies*, 70–72; George M. Marsden, *Fundamentalism and American Culture* (New York, 2nd revised edition 2006), 28–35; and Howard A. Snyder, *Populist Saints: B.T. and Ellen Roberts and the First Free Methodists* (Grand Rapids, Mich., 2006), 730–36.
50. On Rev. B.T. Roberts and the Free Methodist Church, see: Bishop Wilson T. Hogue, *History of the Free Methodist Church of North America* (Chicago, 1915), vol. 1, 24–28; Leslie R. Marston, *From Age to Age a Living Witness: A Historical Interpretation of Free Methodism's First Century* (Winona Lake, Ind., 1960), esp. 133–69, 392–98; John Wilkins Sigsworth, *The Battle Was the Lord's: A History of the Free Methodist Church in Canada* (Oshawa, Ont., 1960), 15, 61–66; Timothy L. Smith, *Revivalism and Social Reform: American Protestantism on the Eve of the Civil War* (New York, 1957), 129–34; and Snyder, *Populist Saints*, esp. 744–88. *RR*, 426–27. One of Ronayne's advertisements appeared in *The Free Methodist* on 8 March 1876; for this and also

for information about Bishop Burton, we thank Cathy Fortner, Free Methodist Church Librarian, at the Marston Historical Center, Indianapolis, Ind.

51. *RR*, 411–22. Additional churches that sponsored Ronayne's anti-Masonic lectures included the Wesleyan Methodists, United Presbyterians, Quakers, Seventh Day Baptists, Seventh Day Adventists, Mennonites, German Baptists, 'and perhaps a dozen other denominations'.
52. *RR*, 426–37. The gospel message quoted is from Mark 16:16.
53. *RR*, 423–24; Snyder, *Populist Saints*, 924; Carnes, *Secret Ritual and Manhood*, 1, 88–89, 199 ns. 109 and 111; and Dumenil, *Freemasonry and American Culture*, 16–19, 225. The new Masonic Temple, designed by the architectural firm of Burnham and Root, was located at Randolph and State streets.
54. On late nineteenth-century Chicago, generally, see: Bessie Louise Pierce, *A History of Chicago, Vol. III: The Rise of a Modern City, 1871–1893* (New York, 1957); and on the city's Irish and Catholics, see: Cowan, 'Ducking for Cover', 56–57; Funcheon, 'Irish Chicago', 16, 35; Joiner, *Sin in the City*, 32; and Shanabruch, *Chicago's Catholics*, 234–36. On labor strife, see: Eric L. Hirsch, *Urban Revolt: Ethnic Politics in the Nineteenth-Century Labor Movement* (Berkeley, 1990); Pacyga, *Chicago*, 71, 143–47; and Richard Schneirov, *Labor and Urban Politics: Class Conflict and the Origins of Modern Liberalism in Chicago, 1864–97* (Urbana, Ill., 1998). On drinking, corruption, homicides (also disproportionately Irish), and education, see: Perry L. Duis, *The Saloon: Public Drinking in Chicago and Boston, 1880–1920* (Urbana, Ill., 1983); Lindberg, *To Serve and Collect*, 16; Merriner, *Grafters and Goo Goos*, 43; Jeffrey S. Adler, *First in Violence, Deepest in Dirt: Homicide in Chicago, 1875–1920* (Cambridge, Mass., 2006), 1, 9–10, 15; and Janet Nolan, *Servants of the Poor: Teachers and Mobility in Ireland and Irish America* (Notre Dame, Ind., 2004), esp. 81–102.

    According to the 1900 US Census schedule, Ronayne had resumed school teaching, although that year's *Lakeside Directory* lists his occupation as 'evangelist' (1617); also, in 1904, Ronayne spoke at a local school board meeting in opposition to the construction of a new public school in his neighborhood, on the grounds that it was a political boondoggle and that a nearby parochial school made it unnecessary; see: 'Asks Right of Speaking', *Chicago Daily Tribune*, 8 April 1904; census, directory, and newspaper citations located by Professor Patricia Kelleher and by Ellen Skerrett.
55. *RR*, 424, 433–35. On John and Margaret Ronayne's deaths, see: Lynch Family genealogy (n. 19); and their Chicago death certificates, located by Ellen Skerrett; the listed cause of John Ronayne's death, after a two weeks' illness, was 'Lumbar Pneumonia', which often was an official euphemism for the effects of alcoholism. On William Ronayne, see n. 72 below.

    Ellena Darwood (sometimes Dorwood) was born July 1866 or 1867 in Otisco, New York, the daughter of James Darwood, an 'Allopathic Physician & Surgeon' in 1870, and his wife Esther; in 1880, Esther Darwood, either widowed or separated from her husband, was living with her two daughters, Ellena (age 13) and Phebe (age 10), in Fort Gratiot, St. Clair, Michigan; in 1900, Esther Darwood was a patient at the Eastern Michigan Asylum for the Insane in Pontiac City, Michigan. In the 1900 Chicago census, Ellena Ronayne was listed as living with Edmond in his old home at 104 Milton Avenue (formerly Bremer Street), and as the mother of one child, deceased. Again, these census records were located by Ellen Skerrett and Professor Patricia Kelleher. On Ruth and Rachel Ronayne, see: the 1910 US Census schedule for Boulder, Colorado; and the data posted by 'TRONA' (Thomas Ronayne) on http://boards.ancestry.myfamily.com/localities.northam.usa.states.colorado.counties.boulder/1726/mb.ashx; for the information from the 1910 US Census, we thank Mona Lambrecht of the Boulder Genealogical Society as well as Professor Kelleher.

56. *RR*, 435; a full report of Ronayne's 23 May 1897 lecture is 'Zion's Onward Movement', in *Leaves of Healing* (Dowie's religious periodical), 3 (1896–97), 500–14; our thanks to Tim Morse, secretary of the Zion Historical Society, Zion, Ill., for a copy of this account. On Dowie, Dowieism, and Zion City, see: Edith L. Blumhofer, *Assemblies of God: A Chapter in the Story of American Pentecostalism*, vol. 1 (Springfield, Mo., 1989), 31–34, 114–16; Philip L. Cook, *Zion City, Illinois: Twentieth-Century Utopia* (Syracuse, N.Y., 1996); 'Eddyism and Dowieism', *The Independent,* 53, 2735 (2 May 1901), 1443; Jean Finot, *Modern Saints and Sinners*, trans. Evan Marrett (London, 1920), 51–56; Harlan Rolvix, *John Alexander Dowie and the Christian Catholic Apostolic Church in Zion* (Evansville, Wisc., 1906); Gordon Lindsay, *The Life of John Alexander Dowie* (Shreveport, La., 1951), 235 and *passim*; 'The Dissolution of Dowie's Zion', *Literary Digest*, 32, 16 (21 April 1906), 603; Reinhold Willman, *The Errors of Mind Healing . . .* (St. Joseph, Mo., 1909), 111–12; and 'Zion City at a Crisis', *New York Times* (20 May 1907).
57. Ronayne's ordination as deacon is cited in *Leaves of Healing*, 9, 6 (24 May 1901), 182; we thank Tim Morse of the Zion Historical Society for this and other information. Ronayne's only obituary is 'Obscure and Alone Masonic Renegade Dies', *Rocky Mountain News* (Denver), probably 9 April 1911, in the *Boulder Daily Camera* clipping file at the Carnegie Branch Library for Local History, Boulder, Col.; we thank Marti Anderson, archivist at the Carnegie Branch Library, for this and other information. On Dowie's fall, Wilbur's reign, and Dowieism's links to modern Pentecostalism, see Blumhofer, *Assemblies of God*, vol. 1, 20–21, 31–34, 114–16; Cook, *Zion City, Illinois*, 200–23; and Lindsay, *Life of John Alexander Dowie*, 236–67.
58. It is unknown why Ronayne chose Colorado as his final home, but he may have found it spiritually and political congenial; from c. 1900 until World War I, advocates of 'Christian citizenship', which linked moral and Progressive reformism, flourished in the state; see R. Todd Laugen, *The Gospel of Progressivism: Moral Reform and Labor War in Colorado, 1900–1930* (Boulder, 2010). Also, in the early 1900s Boulder hosted a Free Methodist congregation; information from Cathy Fortner of the Marston Historical Center, Indianapolis.

    For Ronayne and his second family in Boulder, see the 1910 US Census schedule, Precinct 37 (South Boulder); and the *Boulder City Directories* of 1905–18; for these references and for information about Ronayne's 'ranch', Ellena Ronayne's death, and her and her husband's burials in Boulder's Valmont Cemetery, we thank Marti Anderson and Hope Arculin of Boulder's Carnegie Branch Library for Local History. On Boulder in the early 1900s, see: Riley Moffat, *Population History of Western U.S. Cities and Towns, 1850–1990* (Lanham, Md., 1996), 67; and Phyllis Smith, *A Look at Boulder: From Settlement to City* (Boulder, 1981); and on the city's Masons and their cemetery, see J. B. Schoolland, *Boulder in Perspective—From Search for Gold to the Gold of Research* (Boulder, 1980), 270–71, 313. Edmond and Ellena Ronayne's daughters, Rachel and Ruth, became teachers like their father, never married, died in 1929 and 1986, respectively, and were buried in the same grave in Scranton, Pennsylvania; see the website cited in n. 55 above.
59. On Darby and pre-millennialism, see the sources cited in n. 48 above. Unlike Moody, Blanchard and Roberts were post-millennialists, like the Abolitionists; they crusaded for social and political, as well as individual, reforms to 'perfect' American society to prepare for Christ's Second Coming. The line between post- and pre-millennial beliefs was thin and vague, however, and Blanchard's

own successors adopted the latter, pessimistic worldview. Although his memoir is suffused with pre-millennialism, Ronayne's own efforts to secure earthly 'reform' and 'justice' indicated that, especially in his early career, he shared post-millennial hopes, and he may have fully embraced pre-millennialism only near the end of his life, perhaps out of disillusionment with the growth of Freemasonry and the general crisis of the 1890s. As late as 1897, however, Ronayne was involved in a political effort, in his ward, to reform Chicago's boss-ridden Republican Party, in alliance with the city's new Civic Federation; see: 'Aid the Civic Party', *Chicago Record*, 23 June 1897, which includes a short, public letter from Ronayne to Republican reformers; on Republican Party corruption and violence against reformers, see: 'Old 12:45 Club in Peril', 'Riot in Twenty-Third [Ward]', and 'Renominating Objectionable Aldermen', *Chicago Daily Tribune*, 22 January, 23 February, and 28 February 1897, respectively; Ellen Skerrett located these articles. On Chicago's Civic Federation and efforts to reform the city's Republican Party, see: Laura M. Westhoff, *A Fatal Drifting Apart: Democratic Social Knowledge and Chicago Reform* (Columbus, Ohio, 2007).

60. E.g., *RR*, 18, 28, 166–71. As suggested in the preceding note, 'providentialism' could have either post- or pre-millennial connotations.
61. *RR*, 77–78. On providentialist interpretations of the Famine, see: Peter Gray, *Famine, Land and Politics: British Government and Irish Society, 1843–50* (Dublin, 1999); and of the Chicago Fire, see: Pacyga, *Chicago: A Biography*, 79, and Smith, *Urban Disorder and the Shape of Belief*, 35.
62. *RR*, 120. On Catholic opposition to Freemasonry in the United States, see: MacDonald, *Catholic Church and the Secret Societies*, 72 and *passim*.
63. *RR*, 19–26. For background, see: Gearóid Ó Crualaoich, 'The 'Merry Wake', in James S. Donnelly, Jr., and Kerby A. Miller, eds., *Irish Popular Culture, 1650–1850* (Dublin, 1998), 173–200.
64. E.g., *RR*, 36–38.
65. *RR*, 68–69.
66. E.g., *RR*, 69, 76–78, 188.
67. Kerby A. Miller, *Emigrants and Exiles: Ireland and the Irish Exodus to North America* (New York, 1985), 300.
68. Emmet Larkin, *The Historical Dimensions of Irish Catholicism* (Washington, DC, 1984 2nd edition), 82–83. By the late 1840s, the Famine had virtually bankrupted the Catholic Church, especially its southern and western dioceses, which sharply reduced the bishops' ability to finance clerical students at St. Patrick's College, Maynooth, and other seminaries; it is not known whether Ronayne aspired to the priesthood, although it appears likely that that was Fr. Henry Power's ambition for him, but, if so, the Famine's effects on Church finances radically reduced his opportunities; see: Donal A. Kerr, *'A Nation of Beggars'? Priests, People, and Politics in Famine Ireland, 1846–1852* (Oxford, 1994), 171–72, 178, 187.
69. *RR*, 90–92. In his memoir (91), Ronayne wrote that, when remembering the Famine or when feeling lonely and alienated, he gained comfort from Revelation 21:4, which promised that, at the Resurrection, 'He will wipe away every tear . . . ', and 'There will be no more death, or mourning, or crying, or pain, for the old order of things has passed away'.

    Maurice and Henry Power were both educated in French seminaries, and the latter taught in one for many years before returning to Ireland and joining his brother in Killeagh. It is likely that their sermons and teachings reflected the 'French rigorism', based on Jansenist beliefs, that were common among Ireland's French- and Maynooth-trained priests, and which emphasized divine wrath and human depravity and powerlessness; see Larkin, *Historical Dimensions of Irish Catholicism*, 102.

70. On religious restorationism, see: Blumhofer, *Assemblies of God*, vol. 1, 13–24. Arguably, both Freemasonry and Fenianism were also restorationist, as the former promised to recreate a milieu of pre-capitalist, artisanal 'brotherhood', while the latter aspired to 'restore' Irish independence and reverse the Famine's social effects.
71. *RR*, 187.
72. In the 1900 and 1915 US and New York state censuses, William Ronayne, printer, living in Brooklyn, N.Y., with his wife, Ada, listed his and his parents' birthplaces as Canada. In the 1920 US Census, William, still in Brooklyn, gave his birthplace as Canada and his parents' as Illinois; records located by Ellen Skerrett.
73. Jeremiah O'Donovan Rossa's writings include two memoirs: *O'Donovan Rossa's Prison Life* (New York, 1874); and *Rossa's Recollections, 1838 to 1898* (Mariner's Harbor, N.Y., 1898).
74. Ronayne's name is on the 'List of the Irish People [subscribers in Canada], up to July 14 [1865]', which is located in the Fenian Briefs, 1865–69, Carton 5, Envelope 18: 'Business Papers, 1865–69', in the National Archives of Ireland, Dublin; we are very grateful to Professor David A. Wilson of the University of Toronto for providing this reference. Ronayne is listed as a teacher, living at the Esplanade in Quebec's Upper Town; he is second on the list of sixteen subscribers, below only Francis Gallagher, a post office employee who in 1865 was Quebec City's most important Fenian leader. On the list, Ronayne's first name is given as 'Edward', but that was a very common mistake in both Canada and the United States, because he always wrote his name as 'Ed. Ronayne'; even the Free Methodist bishop, who wrote the glowing introduction to *Ronayne's Reminiscences*, misnamed him 'Edward'; see *RR*, vii-ix.

    Unfortunately, a search of Quebec City's Anglo-Protestant press in the months prior to July 1865 failed to uncover any specific incident that might have precipitated Ronayne's 'outing' and flight from Canada. However, two additional pieces of circumstantial evidence suggest that was the case: first, in Chicago, Ronayne did not—presumably because he could not—employ the glowing references from Jeffrey Hale and other leading Protestants that he had used to find superior teaching posts in Quebec City, which suggests that he left the city in disgrace among his former patrons; second, while starving, sick, and unemployed in Chicago, Ronayne received a letter 'alluding to the past' from his wife at Stevens Point, which caused him 'intense agony'—probably because it upbraided him for the actions which had caused his family's quick descent from Canadian prosperity and respectability to American poverty and dependence on his wife's poor relatives. The authors thank Martin Blais, a graduate student at Laval University, Quebec, for research in Quebec newspapers.

    See *RR*, 271–74, for Ronayne's references from Hale and other leading Quebec City Protestants; and 284 on his wife's distressing letter. On Fenianism in Quebec City and in Canada, generally, see: Desmond Bowen, 'Ultramontanism in Quebec and the Irish Connection', in O'Driscoll and Reynolds, eds., *The Untold Story*, vol. 1, 295–305; Hereward Senior, 'Quebec and the Fenians', *Canadian Historical Review*, 48, 1 (March 1967), 26–44; Grace, 'Irish in Mid-Nineteenth-Century Canada . . . ', 612–31; David A. Wilson, 'The Narcissim of Nationalism: Irish Images of Quebec, 1847–1866', *Canadian Journal of Irish Studies*, 33, 1 (2007), 13–21, and *Thomas D'Arcy McGee, Vol.* 2, 151–53, 222–23 and *passim*. Fenianism was denounced by Quebec's French Catholic bishops and by Quebec City's Irish priests, as well as by Chicago's Irish-born Bishop James Duggan; such condemnations discouraged many Irish Catholics from joining the Fenian Brotherhood but likely would have encouraged Ronayne to do so.

75. Regarding his second wife, whom he wed in 1897, Ronayne wrote that, 'it is entirely due to her intelligence, care and counsel in the preparation of my manuscript that I am able to present these Reminiscences in their present form'; *RR*, 435. By contrast, Ronayne's memoir contains not a word of praise for his first wife, Margaret, despite their marriage of over forty years!
76. In his memoir, Ronayne rarely mentions, and never by name, Margaret or their sons. The marriage on 27 November 1877 of John Ronayne, age 23, and Della Quigley, 18, is recorded in their Illinois marriage certificate and in the Holy Name marriage register, both sources located by Ellen Skerrett. The 1870 US Census schedule lists Delia, age 9, as one of five resident daughters of Samuel Quigley, an Irish-born day laborer, and his wife, Maria, also born in Ireland, living at the rear of 57 Wesson Street (later 859 North Cambridge Avenue) in Chicago's ninth ward. According to Ellen Skerrett's findings in the 1880 Census schedule and the 1880–81 *Lakeside Directories*, Maria Quigley was a widow and grocer, still at the same address; and according to the 1883 Directory, John and Della lived nearby at 45 Wesson (later 847 North Cambridge Avenue). According to the Lynch Family genealogy (see n. 19), Margaret Ronayne's mother and siblings in Stevens Point were buried or married in the local Catholic church, St. Stephen's; this is corroborated by the latter's parish records, for research in which we thank Fr. Robert Altman, Archivist of the Diocese of La Crosse, La Crosse, Wisc., and Steven Avella of Marquette University, Milwaukee. However, according to her 1897 death certificate, located by Ellen Skerrett, Margaret Ronayne was buried in Rose Hill, 'a fashionable North Side cemetery favoured by Protestants', although that may have reflected her husband's wishes rather than her own. On Catholicism and Irish immigrants in Stevens Point and Portage County, Wisc., see: McGlachlin, et al., eds., *Standard History of Portage County*, vol. 1, 183–85; Perrett, *Portage County*, 49–50; and Rosholt, *Our County, Our Story*, 74–78, 87–90, 141, 169, and which notes (89–90) that many Famine settlers were Irish-speakers and mentions William Lynch, Margaret's father, in 1863 (309).
77. Cowan, 'Ducking for Cover', 53, 66–69; and M.J. Sewell, 'Rebels or Revolutionaries? Irish-American Nationalism and American Diplomacy, 1865–1885', *The Historical Journal*, 29, 3 (September 1986), 723–33. On the impact of the Irish and European revolutions of 1848 on the political culture of the United States, see: John Higham, *From Boundlessness to Consolidation: The Transformation of American Culture, 1848–1860* (Ann Arbor, Mich., 1969); and Timothy M. Roberts, '"Now the Enemy Is Within Our Borders": The Impact of European Revolutions on American Perceptions of Violence before the Civil War', *American Transcendental Quarterly*, 17, 3 (September 2003), 197–214.
78. On Young Ireland, generally, and in Munster, see: David N. Buckley, *James Fintan Lalor: Radical* (Cork, 1990), esp. 82–88; Maura Cronin, 'Young Ireland in Cork, 1840–49', in Tom Dunne and Laurence M. Geary, eds., *History and the Public Sphere: Essays in Honour of John A. Murphy* (Cork, 2005), 114–26; Richard Davis, *The Young Ireland Movement* (Dublin, 1987); Laurence Fenton, 'Young Ireland in Limerick, 1848', *Journal of the Old Limerick Society*, 43 (Summer 2009), 34–41; Georgina Flynn, 'The Young Ireland Movement in Waterford', *Decies: The Journal of the County Waterford Historical and Archaeological Society*, 18 (September 1981), 41–49, and 19 (January 1982), 53–60; Denis Gwynn, *Young Ireland and 1848* (Cork, 1949); T.P. O'Neill, *James Fintan Lalor* (Wexford, 2003); Gary Owens, 'Popular Mobilization and the Rising of 1848: The Clubs of the Irish Confederation', in Laurence M. Geary, ed., *Rebellion and Remembrance in Modern Ireland* (Dublin, 2001), 51–63; and Robert Sloan, *William Smith O'Brien and the Young Ireland Rebellion of 1848* (Dublin, 2000).

On the 1849 rising, see: Anthony M. Breen, *The Cappoquin Rebellion 1849* (Gorey, County Wexford, 1998); Buckley, *James Fintan Lalor*, 24; Davis, *Young Ireland Movement*, 166; Sir Charles Gavan Duffy, *Four Years of Irish History, 1845–1849* (New York, 1883), 766; Breandan Kiely, *The Waterford Rebels of 1849* (Dublin, 1999); John O'Leary, *Recollections of Fenians and Fenianism*, vol. 1 (London, 1896), 22–23, 30–35; and T.P. O'Neill, 'Fintan Lalor and the 1849 Movement', *An Cosantoír*, 10, 4 (April 1950), 173–79.

79. *RR*, 112.
80. Owens, 'Popular Mobilization and the Rising of 1848', 56–58; we thank Professor Gary Owens of the University of Western Ontario (ret.) for sharing his list of the County Cork towns with Confederation or Felon clubs; it is intriguing that Ronayne visited several of those towns (Youghal, Cork, Midleton, Fermoy) very shortly before or after he left Killeagh. On Hayes's tavern and its association with Fenianism in the mid-1860s, see: Henchion, 'Gravestone Inscriptions of Co. Cork—IX: Killeagh [pt. 2]', (1973), 63; and Killeagh-Inch Historical Group, *Killeagh Parish through the Ages*, 285.
81. On Frs. Maurice and Henry Power's support for O'Connell and Repeal, see *RR*, 67. In early 1844, the former was scheduled to attend the Repeal Association ceremony in Cork City, welcoming O'Connell on his release from prison; see *Freeman's Journal* (Dublin), 27 March 1844; and for the week ending 3 February 1845, both priests subscribed £2 to O'Connell's 'Repeal Rent'; see *The Nation* (Dublin), 8 February 1845; we thank Dr. Brian Gurrin and Barbara McCormack, Russell Library archivist at NUIM, for locating and facilitating access to these articles. On Fr. Henry's anti-Protestant teachings, see *RR*, 43; and also 27–28, where Ronayne credited his aunts with 'spar[ing] no pains . . . to plant in my young mind an especial reverence and love for the Virgin Mary, and a corresponding hatred of Protestants, and the religion of Luther and Calvin, as they termed Protestantism'.
82. On the Catholic clergy and Young Ireland, see especially: Kerr, *'A Nation of Beggars'?*, 34–36, 86, 139–53. No records survive of Frs. Maurice and Henry Power's words and actions concerning Young Ireland in 1848–49; however, in the mid-1860s, the former opposed the Fenians: in 1867, he prevented them from waking one of their leaders, Peter O'Neill Crowley, in his Killeagh church, and earlier he had even confiscated the parish band's musical instruments, so they could not be used in pro-Fenian demonstrations; see: Henchion, 'Gravestone Inscriptions of Co. Cork—IX: Killeagh', pt. 2 (1973), 62; and R. Henchion, 'The Gravestone Inscriptions of Co. Cork—X: Dangandonovan Burial Ground', *JCHAS*, 29, 229 (1974), 51–52.
83. Dickson, *Old World Colony*, 272, 481–83, 490; Burns, 'Parsons, Priests, and the People', 161 and *passim*; Donnelly, 'The Rightboy Movement', 125 and *passim*; Hoppen, *Elections, Politics, and Society in Ireland*, 96; Buttimer, 'Gaelic Literature and Contemporary Life in Cork', 633; Ó Coindealbháin, 'Uí Macaille: Its Anglo-Irish and English Schools', 134; de Brún, *Scriptural Instruction in the Vernacular*, 41, 46–48, 101, 550; Diary of Rev. Richard Canon Smiddy [of Youghal], 1840–75 (ms. in the Cloyne Diocesan Archive, Cobh; transcript courtesy of Martin Millerick); Larkin, *Historical Dimension of Irish Catholicism*, 20, for the lament of Fr. Maher; and Emmet Larkin, *The Consolidation of the Roman Catholic Church in Ireland, 1860–1870* (Dublin, 1987), 415–16 for the statement by the bishop of Cloyne.
84. On the alienation of many poor Catholics from their priests, see: Kerr, *'A Nation of Beggars'?*, 79, 86, 152–53. See *RR*, 70–71, on Fr. Maurice Power's excommunication of sheep-stealers. On Fr. John Ryan, parish priest of Tuogh (Cappamore) in 1833–49 (when he was succeeded by Fr. Patrick Ryan, who patronized Ronayne before the latter's conversion), see: Duggan, *Cappamore: A Parish History*, 216; and on Fr. Hickey of Doon, see: Gerry Carew-Hynes,

'The Famine in Doon: Food or Faith', on the Dún Bleisce Historical and Literary Society website (see n. 15); and Higgins, *Tipperary's Tithe War*, 131. On class conflict, faction fighting, and anti-clericalism, see Whelan, *Bible War in Ireland*, 184–86; and Paul E.W. Roberts, 'Caravats and Shanavests: Whiteboyism and Faction Fighting in East Munster, 1802–11', in Samuel Clark and James S. Donnelly, Jr., eds., *Irish Peasants: Violence and Political Unrest, 1780–1914* (Madison, Wisc., 1983), 64–101.

85. Examples of Catholic priests' characterizations of converts in Doon, Cappamore, and elsewhere, as 'vile rabble', 'poor, starving, ragged, sick, and lame wretches', and of 'criminal', 'depraved', and 'defamed character', etc., appear in: Brown, *National Churches of England, Ireland, and Scotland*, 124; Duggan, *Cappamore: A Parish History*, 208; Fitzgerald, 'Aspects of Souperism in Cappamore and Doon' [pt. 1: 2000], 43; Anon., 'The Religious Struggle in Doon in the 19th Century', on the Dún Bleisce Historical and Literary Society website (see n. 15); Tierney, 'Short-Title Calendar of the Papers of Archbishop Michael Slattery', part 6 (1849–52), *Collectanea Hibernica*, 44/45 (2002/2003), 243.

    It is revealing that in Cappamore in 1850, when he first taught at an all-Catholic school under Fr. Ryan's patronage, Ronayne lodged with the family of Michael Cunningham, a strong farmer whose 35+ acres and house were valued at more than £30. After his conversion, however, Ronayne boarded with his future father-in-law, William Lynch, who occupied a house and small garden worth merely 30s. See Griffith's Valuation, Tuogh parish, County Limerick, December 1850; in http://askaboutireland.ie/griffith-valuation/index.xml.

    The Lysaght family of Cappamore provides a prime example of lower-class Catholics who were faction-fight stalwarts, estranged from the strong farmers and Catholic clergy before the Famine, allies of the local Anglican clergy in the Tithe War of the early 1830s, and converts to Protestantism during the Famine; see Fitzgerald, 'Aspects of Souperism in Cappamore and Doon' [pt. 1: 2000], 26; and LeFanu, *Seventy Years of Irish Life*, 33–35, 67–70.

86. On Fenianism in East Cork, see: Anon., *Historical Remains of Ballymacoda and Ladysbridge*, 52–62. On Fenian anti-clericalism, see: Amy E. Martin, 'Nationalism as Blasphemy: Negotiating Belief and Institutionality in the Genre of Fenian Recollections', in Murphy, ed., *Evangelicals and Catholics in Nineteenth-Century Ireland*, 123–35. Whelan, *Bible War in Ireland*, 117.

87. *RR*, 297–98.

88. *RR*, 301–02; unfortunately, Ronayne is vague about the dates of the physical assault and his employment by the Pinkertons. On Captain James Fitzgerald, see: *Edwards Annual Director to the Inhabitants . . . in the City of Chicago* (Chicago, 1866), 403; Fitzgerald's and the Pinkerton Agency's office was located at 92–94 Washington in downtown Chicago; research by Ellen Skerrett. The authors thank Professor David A. Wilson for information about the Canadian government's use of Pinkerton detectives to spy on the Fenians. It is also possible that the Chicago Pinkertons' main task in 1866–67 was to spy on the eight-hour day movement among the city's Irish and other workers; see Jentz and Schneirov, *Chicago in the Age of Capital*, 88–116.

89. The Fenian events in the United States and Canada are detailed in Neidhardt, *Fenianism in North America*, esp. 42–52, 57–75, 85–92, 118–22; in Ireland and England in Leon Ó Broin, *Fenian Fever: An Anglo-American Dilemma* (New York, 1971); and in Montreal in Wilson, *Thomas D'Arcy McGee*, vol. 2.

90. On Chicago's conflicts between capital and labor, see the sources by Hirsch, Pacyga, and Schneirov, cited in n. 54 above, as well as Smith, *Urban Disorder and the Shape of Belief*.

91. *RR*, 303, 429. Also see Snyder, *Populist Saints*, 727, 731–32.
92. On Ronayne's anticipation of the 'end times', see *RR*, e.g., 188–89, 423–24. During and after his first conversion by 'reason', Ronayne immersed himself in church history and scholarly commentaries on Christian doctrine and practice, but after his second conversion he studied the Scriptures only, intensely, and incessantly; *RR*, 160–64, 398. Ronayne's 1870 US Census return suggested that he had begun the naturalization process, but his 1900 return indicated that he never became an American citizen; for research in these census records, we again thank Professor Patricia Kelleher.
93. *RR*, 438.
94. David Lloyd, 'The Indigent Sublime: Specters of Irish Hunger', *Representations*, 92 (2005), 156, reprinted in his *Irish Times: Temporalities of Modernity* (Dublin, 2008), 39–72, 72; Mark Twain, 'The Mysterious Stranger', in Bernard De Voto, ed., *The Portable Mark Twain* (New York, 1946 edition), 743–44. We thank Professor Ted Koditschek, of the University of Missouri, for his intellectual contributions to these closing paragraphs.

5 The Great Famine, Land and the Making of the Graziers

David S. Jones

Graziers were extensive commercial farmers who reared large herds of cattle and flocks of sheep on large and sometimes multiple holdings, often comprising well over 100 acres. Some graziers, mainly in the western counties, concentrated on rearing young cattle (stores) as well as sheep, and then sold the cattle after six–eighteen months to another type of grazier, mainly found in north Leinster, who specialized in fattening them for six–twelve months in preparation for slaughter or export to England. Store graziers themselves also exported directly to the English market. Graziers existed well before the Famine. Arthur Young referred on his travels in the later part of the eighteenth century to them and the large herds of cattle they reared. This was echoed in various travelogues and surveys of the early nineteenth century. Despite the switch to tillage during the Napoleonic Wars, graziers became thereafter an increasingly significant element in Irish agriculture.[1] This trend was greatly accelerated by the Famine.

Coincident with the expansion of grazing, the first half of the nineteenth century saw the strengthening of certain sections of the commercial and professional classes in cities and towns. Their occupations included banking, accounting, insurance, legal services, estate management, land surveying, construction, retailing, supply distribution and freight forwarding. Also important were small-scale craft-based manufacturing and agricultural processing such as the production of leather goods and flour milling. Such was their wealth that a number from these classes, following the Famine, acquired ownership of estates which were encumbered.

This essay examines how the Famine increased the availability of land for commercial farming and provided opportunities for the graziers to expand their enterprises or establish new ones, thereby becoming a central part of the economy and society of rural Ireland. These opportunities will be attributed to a shift to a more hardheaded and commercially oriented approach to the management of estates, involving both existing estate owners who retained their land and those in the business and professional classes who acquired ownership of estates after the Famine.

LAND TENURE AND LAND HOLDING PRIOR TO THE FAMINE

Land tenure in pre-Famine Ireland was a complex pyramid of interests and rights, both formal and informal. At the apex were the landed proprietors. Their estates could range from less than a hundred acres to many thousands spread across several counties. There were several gradations of proprietary interest. At the highest level were the holders of the fee simple (or occasionally fee entail). As such, they could exercise all rights or interests of tenure indefinitely.[2] However, under the common law, as it evolved in Ireland, these rights were often granted by the fee simple owner to another party. These included the fee farm grantee, who was a second tier proprietor subject to various covenants and reservations, and an obligation to pay a head rent each year to the fee simple owner (in some cases this was not an inconsiderable amount in view of the value of the estate).[3] Alternatively, proprietary rights could be vested in a leaseholder with a perpetual or very long-term lease, the most common being a lease for lives renewable forever, or a lease for any long period of which 60 years of the lease remain, often ranging from 99 years to perpetuity. Like the fee farm grantee, the owner of any such lease was subject to covenants and reservations, and required to pay a head rent to the fee simple owner. In the case of a lease for lives renewable forever, a further payment (fine) was required for the renewal of the lease on the change of lives.[4] Such perpetual or very long-term leaseholders, as well as fee farm grantees, were referred to in certain later statutes as 'limited owners', holding an inferior interest relative to the holders of the fee simple who were the 'absolute owners'.[5]

At the lower end of the pyramid were the much more numerous holders of yearly leases, known commonly as yearly tenants. While the term of their lease was one year, the tenancy was automatically renewed in the absence of a notice to quit (in contrast to a leaseholder whose lease formally terminated and had to be renewed). The interests of yearly tenants were restricted, but they could cultivate or graze the land as they wished, make improvements and bequeath the tenancy to their heirs, but outside Ulster were often denied a saleable interest. The tenure was highly insecure since the landlord could evict the tenant on a notice to quit after one year.[6] Closely related to the yearly tenants were tenants-at-will, whose tenure was not defined in terms of a set period, and therefore could be evicted at any time.[7] A study of Bohola, County Mayo, during and after the Famine indicated that most tenants lacking tenancies for a specific period were in effect tenants-at-will.[8] Often the yearly tenancy and tenancy-at-will were regarded as almost the same, given the lack of security of tenure and other tenurial rights.

Both types of tenant were, in the main, small farmers with 3–20 acres of land, who earned a little income from the land, but often remained barely above subsistence. This was exacerbated by the practice of multi-geniture, which involved dividing the land at the death of the tenant among all or some of the heirs. The result was ever-shrinking plots of land less capable of supporting a household by the produce of the soil, and the creation of a class of landholding paupers.[9] It should be noted that rent rolls and lists of tenants kept by land agents often show joint tenancies, with from two to ten or more tenants sharing a holding. This was especially so in the so-called rundale settlements common in the far west, where occupiers held intermixed fragments or strips of land sometimes combined with a common tenure of the bogland and rough pasture (the commonage) outside the infields of the settlement. Such settlements were based on communal arrangements characterized by mutual aid, cooperation and the sharing of resources.[10]

Many landholders were subtenants, who rented land from terminable leaseholders or even yearly tenants, known as middlemen. Often middlemen were commercial famers and graziers in their own right, who sublet most or part of their land.[11] In some instances, the subtenants, if their holdings were substantial enough, further sublet the land, so constituting an additional tier(s) of middlemen.[12] The tenure of the subtenant was insecure, usually that of a tenancy-at-will. The extent to which middlemen controlled large estates is well illustrated on the estate of George Henry Moore in County Mayo on the eve of the Famine. In the Ballintubber electoral division, three middlemen with medium-term terminable leases (one had a lease for four lives) controlled nine out of sixteen townlands, comprising 75 percent of this part of the estate. The markup on the rent was considerable, with the tenants paying twice the rent paid by the middlemen to the estate owner himself.[13] Likewise, on the Hartland/Mahon Crown estate near Strokestown, most of the holdings covering 27 townlands were controlled by middlemen before the Famine, the tenants paying 45 percent more than the amount the leading middlemen paid to the owner (who was actually a leaseholder under the Crown).[14]

Even lower down the social scale were cotters or cottiers. They were laborers who rented a cabin and a small patch of land usually as a tenant-at-will; most were subtenants under a middleman. Typically cottiers worked wholly or in part for their middleman landlord if the latter cultivated some of his land, and their labor paid the rent and provided a subsistence wage.[15]

Before the Famine, it was normal for the landholders, laborers and also townspeople to obtain the right to use additional land for a season. The tenure was akin to that of a license rather than a tenancy, since the taker could only use the land for a specific purpose extending for less than one year; other interests were not allowed (including the rights of improvement, bequest and exclusive occupation).[16] One of the main types of license was seasonal lettings for grazing, commonly called agistment. Such lettings could range from a few acres to several hundred (as discussed below).[17] The seasonal lettings for cultivation were known as conacre and the predominant use was potato growing. Many small tenants and cottiers hired these patches of land in order to support their subsistence, but their entitlement to the crop was only valid after the rent had been paid, either in labor or money.[18] The rate at which land was let as agistment (usually by landowners) or conacre was usually higher than the rents from leases and tenancies.

There was considerable variation in how far letting arrangements were formalized. Substantial leases were normally incorporated into written contracts. Short-term leases and yearly tenancies were recognized in formal rent registers detailing the terms of tenure, kept by the land agent of the estate. Names of those holding tenancies-at-will were simply listed for each townland of the estate in order to facilitate rent collection and to record payments and arrears. Seasonal grass lettings on large holdings were normally based on written agreements and listed in the rent books of the property, but some conacre lettings may have been arranged simply by verbal agreement, although on the larger properties where accounts were kept the income received was recorded.

THE IMPACT OF THE FAMINE ON THE TENANTRY

The Famine left a good deal of land vacant and unlet as a result of death, surrender of land and eviction. This prompted the author of the preface of the 1850 agricultural returns to refer to 'immense alteration in the numbers and wealth of different classes of farmers'.[19] Many tenants, subtenants and cottiers simply abandoned the land as the effects of the repeated failure of the potato crop left them with no choice but to seek relief in the workhouse, from food handouts at the corn storage depots or on public works schemes where a small daily wage could be earned.[20] The surrender of land was made all the more necessary by the so-called 'Gregory clause' of the Poor Law Extension Act of 1847, which stipulated that relief could not be given to those occupying more than a quarter acre of ground, either within or without the workhouse.[21] In Westport, according to the poor law inspector, 'small farmers who held from 3 to 4 acres have nearly all been obliged to give up their holdings and seek relief'.[22] Holdings were also left vacant in consequence of high mortality in households suffering from disease and chronic under-nourishment.[23]

Other small tenants, subtenants and cottiers gave up their land in order to emigrate as an alternative to dependence on poor relief, confinement to a poor house and continued destitution. A number of landlords were forthcoming in providing financial assistance, as were relatives who had already emigrated and sent back remittances to pay for the sea passage. Among those who emigrated were also commercial leaseholders and tenants who grew cash crops on medium-sized holdings. In 1849, according to one estate owner in County Limerick, Aubrey de Vere, 'farmers, occupying considerable tracts of ground, have relinquished their farms and abandoned the country'.[24] This outcome was the result of the sharp downturn in the income of commercial farmers arising from the 50 percent fall in cereal prices during 1846–51, combined with the poor harvests in the last three years of the Famine (yield per acre dropped by 30 percent or more).[25] They, therefore, like the small holders, struggled to make ends meet and pay their rents and so looked to emigration as the way out of their predicament.

Land fell vacant, as well, as a result of eviction during the Famine years. Numerous tenants, subtenants and cottiers were turned out of their holdings and plots under eviction orders, and in most cases their houses were leveled. In some areas of the west, entire townlands were left without habitation.[26] As the *Tuam Herald* put it in 1848, 'every post, every day, every hour brings us accounts of evictions'.[27] An informative record of testimonies of the actions of landlords in West Mayo with respect to evictions and rents during the Famine and the post-Famine period was compiled by parish priests in 1880 on behalf of the Land League to enlist support in the United States for its cause. The record covers townlands in the parishes of Aghagower, Ballyovey, Islandeady, Kilcolman, Kilgeever. Kilmaclasser and Kilmeena.[28] It was possible to check the reports of group evictions in 32 townlands which were mentioned by referring to Griffith's Valuation. This in nearly all cases corroborated the evidence that a clearance had occurred. Confirmation that the townlands were well populated before the Famine was provided by the census townland returns for 1841.[29]

While the landowners and their agents were responsible for the bulk of evictions, middlemen too cleared entire townlands of subtenants. This was exemplified on the Hartland/Mahon Strokestown estate, where, according to Scally, the middlemen of Denis Mahon, the then landowner under the Crown, carried out in 1847 'wholesale evictions in his name'.[30] Other middlemen of the estate in a similar predicament simply abandoned their leases and left the estate, leaving Mahon to undertake the evictions and pay the poor rates.[31]

The extent of the dispossession is difficult to quantify during the years of the Famine, since for most of the period no figures on actual evictions were published. The main source of data are the ejectment figures furnished by the courts, which show that the number of ejectments served on tenant households increased substantially during the Famine, from 19,704 in 1846 to 69,899 in 1848.[32] However, many of the ejectment writs or decrees obtained by landlords did not result in an eviction, since tenants, once they were served, often paid up their rent and were allowed to stay.[33] In light of this, assessments of the actual number of evictions from 1846 to 1848 have varied: some scholars have provided conservative estimates, and others much higher ones. Ó Gráda has reviewed the estimates of eight scholars and notes that they vary from 17,000 to 38,000 families evicted for the period 1846–48.[34] Only in one of the Famine years (1849) were figures of actual evictions published (by the Constabulary). In this year, 13,384 families (72,065 persons) were turned out of their holdings and not readmitted.[35]

An appreciation of the scale of the evictions in the western counties can too be gained from two enumerations for the Kilrush Union of County

Clare. One was furnished by Arthur Kennedy, a poor law inspector, which covered the period from July 1848 to June 1849. It listed 9,261 persons evicted occupying 1,694 holdings (including about 200 cottier plots). Nearly all were under five acres, with the average area between two and a half and three acres. The amount of land that became vacant in the Kilrush Union as a result was just under 5,000 acres.[36] Kennedy's figures included tenants-at-will and subtenants, who had no formal tenancy and whose eviction did not involve a formal legal process.[37] The other return was provided by Francis Coffee, a civil engineer and land valuator for the Kilrush Board of Guardians. He reported that 14,364 persons were evicted (2,359 families) in the Kilrush Union, but his return covered a longer period than Kennedy's (November 1847 to July 1850).[38] Such a scale of eviction led the *Tuam Herald* to refer to 'the all but consummated destruction of the rural population of the Kilrush Union'.[39] The Kilrush Union was by no means atypical of other areas in the west which experienced mass evictions.

The distinction between an eviction and a voluntary surrender was blurred, as many evictions occurred under the guise of voluntary surrender. Tenants were prevailed upon by their landlords to give up possession, under the threat of eviction but with the inducement of a small cash hand-out and the waiver of rent arrears. In some cases the threat was little short of intimidation. Although not strictly speaking evicted, they often had little choice but to leave when faced with a landlord who had made up his mind to take the land and who was prepared to offer financial incentives to induce them to leave. This option was favored by landowners and agents because it involved the minimum of fuss and expense. They were spared the necessity of engaging in the bothersome litigation of the ejectment process, and were able to avoid court and solicitor's fees, which could easily exceed any handout to the outgoing tenant. With voluntary surrender, confrontations with resistant occupiers were less likely, and unwelcome publicity was avoided. For the tenants facing destitution and starvation, even the offer of a few shillings could not be refused. For example, in the Kilrush Union, the vice-guardians reported in October 1848 that tenants were giving up land, having been allowed 'a small sum' and promised 'a discharge from all claims of rent on the house being thrown down and possession given up'.[40]

One cause of mass evictions in the Famine years was nonpayment of rent. This was already a serious issue on the eve of the Famine, with arrears of rent having accumulated on many estates over several years. Evidence of arrears was provided by a wide spectrum of testimonies to the Devon Commission. In Scally's research on the Crown's estates at Ballykilcline in County Roscommon, none of the tenants in 1846 owed less than 9½ years rent, and 'some had paid nothing for twelve years'. Even the tenants of the larger holdings were in arrears.[41] During the Famine the situation became so much worse, as rental income from one estate to another in the western counties all but collapsed, despite the efforts of land agents at the insistence of landowners to collect rents.[42] As their rental income dried up, landowners, often struggling with rising debts and increasing poor rates, responded by turning the tenants out. The pressure to do this was particularly felt by limited owners (long-term and perpetual leaseholders and fee farm grantees) who were required to pay substantial head rents, as well as poor rates. Middlemen were in a similar position, with obligations to pay rents and poor rates as well, and so acted likewise.

Not all tenants evicted were in default in rent payments. The record of Famine evictions in the western parishes of Mayo compiled for the Land League in 1880 refers to quite a number of tenants who were not in default.[43] Although this is possibly an exaggeration (as the record was compiled to enlist American support for the Land League), it is certain that some tenants were turned out despite having kept up their rent payments. For instance, the *Tuam Herald* in 1848 reported that a farming family in Killoscully, near Newport, 'in comfortable circumstances, able to pay rents . . . and willing to afford security for the ensuing year's rent have been recently turned out by the landlord'.[44]

Such exceptions notwithstanding, the rapid decline of rental income at this time was serious and due to various reasons. The failure of the potato crop on the small holdings of the tenants and subtenants denied them not only a means of nutritional subsistence but also a small cash return from the surplus left over that could be used to pay the rent. It also reduced the rental income earned from conacre lettings. To make matters worse, the commercial farmers who grew cereals suffered from a sharp downturn in prices and poor grain harvests in 1848 and 1850, and so too struggled to pay their rents, as noted above. Furthermore, in certain unions in the west, tenants with holdings valued at £4 and above were impaired in paying their rents by steeply increasing poor rates, which siphoned off some of their much needed cash. In addition, cottiers found agricultural work more difficult to come by, and thus were unable to pay their rent. This was compounded in some families by the inability to work due to disease and lack of sustenance.

In response to the struggle of tenants to keep up with rent payments, landlords in some cases offered rent reductions or waived payments on a temporary basis. The *Freeman's Journal* in 1847 referred to 'good landlords' in Roscommon who did not claim rent payments in the second gale of 1847 or allowed reductions in rents of 20 percent or higher. Two years later it returned to the subject, citing 'occasional accounts of rent reductions'. It stated that 'in those cases where rent reductions have been made, the amount is for the most part apparently fair and equitable'. But to qualify this point, the same report recognized that in view of the drop in prices, 'the deduction falls considerably below the amount the landlords should concede'. It continued by contending that 'a reduction between fifteen and twenty five percent is manifestly inadequate' given that 'prices have fallen from forty to fifty percent'.[45] It appears that the main focus of the *Freeman's Journal* were the commercial leaseholders and yearly tenants earning a money income, rather than the impoverished small tenants, subtenants and cottiers. Further references were made to reductions in rent during the Famine years, when estates were subsequently advertised for sale in the Encumbered Estates Court.

The exemption from the poor rate granted to tenants with holdings below £4 under the poor law legislation also contributed to evictions. For these holdings, the landlords were required to pay the full poor rate. Most affected by this, of course, were landlords in the western areas, whose tenants were preponderantly small holders with farms under £4 valuation (in some poor law unions comprising more than 30 percent of the rateable land).[46] The rate burden of western landlords was felt all the more acutely since such land yielded little or no rent. To resolve their predicament, the option was to remove tenants with holdings under £4 valuation and relet the land in enlarged units.[47]

Finally, perhaps the greatest reason for clearing tenants was the conclusion by certain landowners, land agents and middlemen that the only way to make an estate commercially viable was to adopt a different system of farming based on new arrangements for letting land. The precarious system of semi-subsistence farming by small tenants and subtenants (including cottiers) occupying a few acres of land, which had come to prevail in the west, was incompatible with the system of regular money rents on which estates depended. The requirement was to abandon the old practices of subletting, subdivision and multi-geniture, and to replace small holdings and plots of land, even those occupied by solvent tenants, with much larger commercial holdings. This inevitably necessitated that numerous small tenants, subtenants and cottiers relinquish their land either by surrender or eviction.

THE ISSUE OF THE ENCUMBERED ESTATES

The Famine exposed and exacerbated the chronic indebtedness of estate owners. The upkeep of large residential properties, the pursuit of a leisured life style, continued high levels of conspicuous consumption and involvement in such activities as hunting and gambling were all a drain on estate finances and were thus paid for in part by borrowing.[48] This was facilitated by the willingness of professional money lenders and other landowners before the Famine to lend money at low rates of interest. A further burden on estate finances were costly family settlements, such as payments of a yearly income (jointure) to the landowner's wife or widowed mother and annuities to other family members, which were met out of the income of the estate.[49] Further obligations to be discharged included substantial head rent, tithe rent and poor rate payments.

Such liabilities could have been managed if estates remained commercially viable. However, the decline of rental revenue from the tenantry (for many estate owners the main source of income) in the 1840s and the eventual collapse of rent payments in the districts most affected by the Famine left estate owners in a perilous situation. They could not repay the principal of their loans or pay the interest from year to year, nor could they maintain the annual payments of jointures, annuities, rents and poor rates.[50] One option was to borrow ever more, so adding to the mountain of debt.

Lane has highlighted the plight of leading landowning families in Connacht, who were trapped by mounting debt with multiple charges against their properties, and who had thus become insolvent or near insolvent (one indicator was the number of estates in receivership in the Court of Chancery). In addition, the network of debt was ever widening, as the charge holders themselves, including personal creditors and recipients of annuities and jointures, when denied the payments that were due, were also compelled to borrow against the charges they held. Of particular note, which Lane drew attention to, were the reduced circumstances of the recipients of annuities and jointures, mainly members of the family circle of the landowner, whose payments were in arrears. Moreover, there was no guarantee that they could redeem the principal of the jointure or annuity out of the proceeds from any future sale of the estate given the prior claims of other charge holders.[51]

As a measure of the indebtedness of Irish estate owners, the Encumbered Estates Court had received by August 1850, less than twelve months after it was set up, 1,085 petitions seeking to recover a debt of £12.4 million (consisting of the outstanding principal of loans, arrears of interest payments, annuity and jointure arrears, unpaid rents and rates and other outstanding liabilities). Yet the properties to which the petitions applied yielded only an annual gross rental of £665,471. Consequently, the amount the sale of the property would have to fetch on average in order to defray all outstanding claims was just over 18.5 years purchase of the gross annual rent (calculated as the ratio of the actual amount paid to buy the property to the gross annual rent).[52] A later return of petition cases still pending, published in December 1854, shows a continuing high percentage of encumbered properties where a purchase price of 20 plus years of gross rent was required to defray all claims.[53]If net or profit rent (explained below) is used instead of gross rent, then the number of purchase years would be even higher (by at least two to three years).

THE SALE OF ENCUMBERED ESTATES AND THE VARIATION IN DEMAND

Against this background, the Encumbered Estates Act was passed in 1849, administered through the Encumbered Estates Court, to enable indebted estates to be sold to pay off the charge holders. If the interest and annual payments from the charges against the estate exceeded half its income (after payment of head and tithe rents and poor rates), they could petition the Court to arrange for its sale and the proceeds used to repay the debt.[54] The estate owners themselves could also petition the court to do likewise (they submitted 38 percent of the accepted petitions from 1849 to 1858).[55] The sale was conducted mostly through public auctions under the auspices of the Court, though in a minority of cases a private tender was conducted based on the submission of written offers. Significantly (for the type of bidder who tendered for the land), the estate was normally divided into several lots varying in the main from 30 to 500 acres, with an auction or tender conducted for each lot. From 1849 to 1855, the average division was five lots per estate.[56] By 1858, when the Court was superseded by the Landed Estates Court, it had handled the sale of encumbered property worth over £23 million, involving 8,258 conveyances.[57] The Landed Estates Court itself was vested with greater powers, including the conveyance of nonencumbered estates and estates which were subject to only 'trifling encumbrances'.[58] From 1849 to 1855, the heaviest concentrations of sales were found in Counties Galway, Mayo and Tipperary (where land was sold in more than 15 percent of all townlands in each county), followed by Cork, Kilkenny, King's County, Louth and Westmeath (13–15 percent of all townlands).[59]

The demand for land on encumbered estates can be assessed by determining the purchase price paid in the auction or the highest bid price. To assess how expensive or cheap the land was, the actual purchase price was converted into the number of years of purchase. However, as the basis of the calculation, the annual net or profit rent was used. This was the gross rent minus the tithe and quit rents, and most importantly for fee farm grantees and very long-term and perpetual leaseholders, the head rent paid to the fee simple owner. To assess the price of land, a sample of 901 auction sales was randomly selected and examined from 1850 to 1857. The sample included a small number of sales in which the highest bid price was stated in the auction report, but which were adjourned due to the low prices offered. In some adjourned sales, the highest offer was not even stated and so could not be factored into the calculation.

The prices paid in the auctions for encumbered land are given in Table 5.1. The figures show that they varied a lot, but with an overall upward trend over the period 1850–57. In the first three years (1850–52), the price for encumbered land was low, averaging 13 to 15 years of the net rent. Thirty to thirty-eight percent of lots were sold very cheaply, at 12 years or below, while only 12–16 percent were sold at a good price of 20 years or more. It was thus a struggle to obtain a decent price even for good land, and in quite a number of cases, lots were even sold at five years or below. Further weighing down on prices were costly jointures and annuities attached to the land (land lots so affected were usually sold at prices below other lots). The upshot of the low prices was that not all the petitioners could recover their money.[60] Moreover, when auctions were on occasions adjourned due to 'insufficiency of biddings' (in some cases, there were no bids offered), all the petitioners were left empty handed.

Table 5.1 Auctions of encumbered estates, 1850–57

Year	Sample of lot sales examined	Average purchase price/highest bid price	Percentage of sales with purchase price 12 years or less	Percentage of sales with purchase price above 20 years
1850	104	13 years	38	16
1851	130	14 years	34	12
1852	130	15 years	30	16
1853	143	21 years	8	48
1854	132	25 years	12	42
1855	112	24 years	6	70
1856–57	150	22 years	5	41
	Total: 901	Average: 19		

Source: reports of auction sales of Encumbered Estates Court, 1850–57, in *Anglo-Celt*, *Freeman's Journal*, *Nation* and *Nenagh Guardian*.

However, a turning point occurred in 1853. Prices began to rise sharply, reaching averages of 24 and 26 years purchase of the net rent in 1854 and 1855. Often such high purchase prices were above the amount needed to pay off the debt, and occasionally once a sufficient amount was realized, other lots listed for sale by the vendor in the same auction were then withdrawn.[61] The fact that these lots were listed but not sold indicated that the high prices came as something of a surprise. In other cases, though, petitioners were still not able to recover all that was owed to them. Although prices rose steeply, too many land lots still sold at below 20 years purchase (see Table 5.1). This made it impossible to discharge all the debts and liabilities if the estate was heavily encumbered. As mentioned above, many of the petitions which were still pending at the end of 1854 involved such heavily encumbered estates.[62]

Three reasons may be given for the upward trend in demand. Firstly, the prospects of earning a good return from the land improved as the profitability of farming, including grazing, rose. Initially there was concern whether the land would pay in view of current agricultural prices and the price margins for cattle. But as these prices rose and grazing margins increased, buyers become more confident and less averse to risk in tendering for encumbered land, willing to pay in a few instances well over the odds for a land lot.

The other reason for the upward trend was improved publicity and the disclosure of information to would-be buyers. This can be gauged from comparing press notices and reports of auction sales from 1850 to 1857. Initially, sales were not widely advertised, especially affecting potential buyers from England and Scotland. Information about an estate was often patchy (e.g. limited use of independent valuations or lack of clarity regarding whether any lots were indemnified of head rents), making it difficult for those attending a sale to determine an appropriate bid price.[63] As the Encumbered Estates Court became more established and better organized, many of these shortcomings were addressed, enabling a wider circle of interested persons to attend the auctions and allowing them to make more informed judgments in deciding their bid offers.[64]

It should be noted, as well, that a number of estates auctioned in the early years of the Encumbered Estates Court had been neglected and fallen into serious disrepair, often remaining unlet and unused. In an 1851 report, the Encumbered Estates Court stated as much: 'much land has been exhausted or unreclaimed and devoid of suitable buildings, a state of things which would necessarily require a heavy outlay by the incoming purchasers'. In its view, this contributed to the 'depreciation of value' when the estates were sold in those years.[65]

COMMERCIAL INTERESTS IN THE PURCHASE OF ENCUMBERED ESTATES

Those who bid for encumbered land were drawn from various walks of life, but mainly from the commercial and professional classes. Among those from Ireland, two groups stand out as frequent buyers of encumbered property: merchants and lawyers. Merchants were often involved in importing and exporting, supply and distribution (including retailing) and also processing. The goods they traded included corn, seeds, drapery, leather goods and provisions. Located in a nearby town or further afield, they had sufficient capital to readily purchase modest-sized lots of land. And, in many instances, they themselves came from a farming background or had connections to it. In the words of the nationalist politician and newspaper proprietor, A.M. Sullivan, they 'are chiefly mercantile men who have saved money in trade and invest it for a safe percentage'.[66] Likewise, many lawyers—both solicitors and barristers—specialized in and earned a lucrative return from land cases, especially in the Court of Chancery, and were also well informed about land due to their involvement in conveyancing. Among other purchasers were investors in railway companies, surveyors and engineers engaged in land reclamation schemes and land valuation work, and senior clergy of the Catholic Church and the Church of Ireland.[67] This led John Stuart Mill, speaking in parliament in the debate on the state of Ireland in 1868, to refer to the new proprietors as 'strangers—I do not mean to Ireland—but to the neighbourhood of their new properties', who had 'no connection with the tenants'.[68] This was not quite true, since others who purchased were land agents, some of whom had profited from being appointed as receivers for a bankrupt estate, and substantial medium- and short-term leaseholders, including graziers, mostly resident on the estate up for sale. Similarly, some big landowners purchased encumbered estates to expand their own estates (examples were Lords Dunsandle, Clanmorris, Clanrickarde, Lucan and Sligo) or to provide an estate for members of their family.[69]

It is reasonable to assume that a sizeable number of the Irish purchasers were Catholics, given the increasing prominence of the Catholic element among the commercial and professional classes and the stratum of substantial tenant farmers. This was pointed out by Lane, who cites examples of Catholic merchants buying encumbered property.[70] Also involved in purchasing encumbered land were buyers from England and Scotland, drawn from a variety of backgrounds. Of the 159 such buyers between 1850 and 1853, 56 were manufacturers, merchants and manufacturing companies, 7 insurance and land investment companies, and 30 farmers (presumably extensive farmers). But, noticeably, 56 were described as gentry. English and Scottish buyers concentrated their purchasing in Mayo and Sligo, where extensive mountain and moorland estates were acquired.[71] However, the expected inflow of capital from Britain to purchase encumbered land, much heralded at the beginning of the 1850s, did not really materialize. English and Scottish buyers of encumbered land remained a small minority of the total number of purchasers, only 3.7 percent up to the dissolution of Encumbered Estates Court in 1858. The value of the encumbered property they acquired, though, was 13.6 percent of the total value of land purchased, which confirms that they bought the more extensive or highly valued properties.[72]

The influx of new proprietors increased the number of landowners (by 1853 they outnumbered those who were replaced by three to one), and led to a greater proportion of estates which were small or medium-sized, in contrast to the large and sprawling estates of the old gentry.[73] In the process, the landowning class became more diverse, with a greater number of estates owned by individuals from the commercial and professional middle and upper middle classes, alongside the traditional landowners from the gentry. To reflect this, one report to the *Freeman's Journal* in 1853 referred to the 'construction of a middle class' among landowners.[74]

For most of those bidding for an estate from the commercial and professional classes, the purchase of its entirety was beyond their reach, but the division of the land into several lots from 30 to 500 acres, as mentioned above, made purchase feasible. It is significant that of 3,429 lots sold up to March 1853, 46 percent were sufficiently small to be purchased at under £1,000, and 65 percent at under £2,000.[75] With a reasonable amount of capital at hand, some bidders were able to acquire even several lots of land. In referring to the sale of the estate of the Marquis of Angelsey in County Louth in the Encumbered Estates Court in 1857, the *Nation* stated that 'the property was divided in twenty-nine lots to suit middle class purchasers'.[76]

Encouraging the purchase of land by the middle and upper middle class was the Irish Freehold Land Investment Society. Set up in 1850 as a branch of the British National Freehold Land Society, it briefed the press at its inauguration that the Encumbered Estates Court would lead to the establishment of an 'extensive, influential, and thoroughly independent yeomanry class of proprietor'.[77] It confidently asserted that the 'intelligent, industrial classes of the Irish cities and towns will gladly avail themselves of such a means of acquiring property in their own country'.[78] This outcome was encouraged by various leading politicians and administrators, such as Lord John Russell, British prime minister during the Famine years, and Charles Trevelyan, who was a key official in shaping government policy in response to the Famine.

The influx of new proprietors marked a decline in the numbers of the traditional titled families of the gentry as a proportion of the landowning class. Seventy-one such families had parted with all or some of their estates through the Encumbered Estates Court by March 1853, just over two years after the first sales.[79] In the subsequent years of the Court's existence, more of these families relinquished all or some of their land. Of course, the decline in their number was partly offset by the purchase of encumbered property by other local gentry and by English and Scottish gentry, as mentioned above.

Being in the main hardheaded investors, businessmen and commercial farmers, the new proprietors were fixed on one purpose, namely, to make money out of the land acquired and to do whatever was necessary to this end. In the words of A.M. Sullivan, 'they import what the country people call "the ledger and day book principle" into the management of their purchases'.[80] In the same vein, John Stuart Mill, speaking in parliament in 1868, opined that the new proprietors 'bought the land as a mere pecuniary speculation, and have generally administered it as a mere speculation'.[81] Put in a less derogatory light, the intention was to make the estates commercially viable and yield a profitable return. To achieve this was all the more imperative for those purchasers who had borrowed to facilitate the purchase. Raising a loan for this purpose was made possible as a result of granting the purchasers indefeasible land title, which allowed the land to be used as a safe collateral. It is ironic that some of the new purchasers should have become indebted in order to buy out the existing encumbered owners.[82]

The commercial orientation of the new purchasers had two immediate consequences. One was the action taken to realize the rent producing potential of existing tenants of the estate, which resulted in increases of rent. In fact, some of the advertisements were an open invitation to do this. For example, the notice of the sale of one of Lord Portarlington's estates in County Tipperary in 1854 intimated for 16 out 25 lots to be auctioned that the land was let to yearly tenants 'at much below value' or 'at below value'. In providing particulars of each of the other land lots, the notice informed bidders to expect 'a considerable rise upon the expiration of the leases'. For this reason, the estate 'presents particular opportunities to large capitalists'.[83] Among new proprietors who had responded to such an invitation were Henry and Isaac Comerford. On purchasing estates in County Galway in 1856–58, they set about raising rent by 50–100 percent.[84]

The other was the eviction of the small tenants as soon as possible (for tenancies-at-will within a few months, for yearly tenants at the end of the yearly term, and for leaseholders when the lease terminated). The waves of evictions that followed the purchase of the estates were widely recognized. The *Freeman's Journal* put it thus: 'the sale of an estate, and its transfer into the hands of new proprietors, have been generally the certain forerunner of the eviction of tens, or twenties, or hundreds of families, according to the extent of the land sold'. To support this observation, the paper cited from time to time specific instances of a clearance shortly after a property had been purchased.[85]

The eviction figures supplied by the Constabulary lend further support to the link between the purchase of encumbered estates and evictions. Between January 1850, when the first sales were conducted in the Encumbered Estates Court, and 1858, when the Court was dissolved, 39,197 families were dispossessed (excluding those readmitted, which averaged nearly a quarter of the number initially evicted). The peak occurred in 1850, when 14,546 families were cleared, with the number steadily dropping thereafter (in 1858, 720 families were dispossessed).[86] Of course, it is hard to know how many of these evictions were attributable to the new landowners, but it is likely to be more than coincidence that the high if declining rate of evictions from 1850 to 1855 occurred when the Court was at its most active in transferring property.[87]

CONSOLIDATION AND THE ACQUISITION OF LAND BY GRAZIERS

Many of the holdings left vacant either by surrender or eviction during the Famine or after purchase in the Encumbered Estates Court were then consolidated and relet to large landholders. This prompted William Donnelly, the Registrar-General, in his preface to the agricultural returns of 1853, to allude to the 'extraordinary changes in the division of land which have been in progress for several years past'.[88] Most of the large landholders were graziers, with a few who combined large-scale cattle grazing with so-called 'progressive' farming. This could be adduced from the high percentage of usable land on large holdings devoted to pasture (70 percent of holdings of 100–99 acres; 87 percent of holdings of 200–499 acres and 96 percent of holdings of 500 acres or above in 1853).[89] In fact, land use returns in poor law unions in the west of Ireland show that many of these holdings contained at best only a few acres of cultivated land, with some having none altogether.

Evidence of the consolidation in favor of large landholders, especially graziers, is provided from a number of sources. Among those sources are the returns of land occupiers (converted to an estimate of holdings) in 1845, and the returns of holdings in 1851 and 1861, as indicated in Table 5.2. From 1845 to 1861, there was an increase of 31 percent in holdings over 100–99 acres, a 52 percent increase in holdings of 200–499 acres and a 67 percent increase in holdings of 500 acres or more, with correspondingly

Table 5.2 Holdings of different classes in 1845, 1851, and 1861

No. of holdings	1845 (est.)+	1851	1861
Below 5 acres	406,093	158,030	127,030
5–14 acres	564,193	191,854	183,931
15–29 acres		141,311	141,251
30–49 acres		70,093	72,449
50–99 acres	46,457	49,940	53,933
100–199 acres	16,335	19,753	21,531
200–499 acres	5,476	7,847	8,329
500+ acres	954	1,457	1,591

Source: Report from Her Majesty's Commissioners of Inquiry into the State of Law and Practice in respect of the Occupation of Land in Ireland, pt. iv: *Appendix*, 280–3, [672] HC 1845, XXII, 1; *Returns of Agricultural Produce in Ireland*, 1852, iv, [1714] HC 1854, CVII, l; *Agricultural Statistics of Ireland for the Year 1861*, xii, [3156] HC 1863, LXIX, 547. The 1845 return enumerated land occupiers, not land holdings. The numbers of holdings in 1845 were estimated by using the ratio of the numbers of holdings to occupiers within each acreage class in the 1861 agricultural returns.

substantial decreases of small holdings. As shown in Table 5.2, most of the increase in holdings of 100 acres or more occurred during the latter half of the 1840s, but the upward trend continued in the 1850s though at a slower rate. The returns show that these trends were even more pronounced in the western counties. It may be surmised that most of the additional large holdings were grazing farms in view of the extent of pasture on such holdings, as mentioned above.

The establishment or extension of large grazing farms during the Famine and immediate post-Famine years may also be gauged from identifying such farms in townlands, originally well populated, which had then been cleared (with a 90 percent plus decrease of their residents or houses) or had been significantly depopulated (40 percent decrease of their residents or houses). To do this, comparison was made between the census townland returns of 1841 and 1851 in relation to population and houses, with a further comparison with the entries of holdings and houses by townlands in Griffith's Valuation in the mid–1850s. This comparison was made for townlands in three parishes in Clare, two in Mayo and two in Roscommon. Townlands excluded from the analysis were those which had already only a small population and just a few houses in 1841 (less than 30 persons and 5 houses), which often indicated that any large holding in those townlands recorded in Griffith's Valuation was already in existence in 1841. The large holding was identified as one of 100 acres or more or a valuation of £40 or more. Included as well were smaller holdings whose rateable occupants held farms in other (usually neighboring) townlands and smaller holdings with a herd's house (indicating it was part of a grazing farm).

The results of this study are presented in Table 5.3 and show that between 1841 and the Griffith's Valuation of the mid-fifties, the overall proportion of the land area of the seven parishes which was consolidated to create new large holdings was 31 percent. Of the 203 townlands of these parishes, 43 were cleared (90 percent reduction of population or houses), while a further 40 experienced significant depopulation (40 percent decrease of residents or houses). Since many of the large holdings were largely pasture, the figure represents a significant transfer of land to create grazing farms.

Table 5.3 Large holdings in townlands in selected parishes in Counties Clare, Mayo and Roscommon, likely established or extended between 1841 and 1855–57 (Griffith's Valuation)

Parish	Area (statute acres)	Townlands in the parish	Townlands cleared containing one or more large holdings	Townlands significantly depopulated containing one or more large holdings	Percentage of the area of the parish comprising large holdings referred to in the previous two columns
Abbey, County Clare	4,714	13	1	4	28.5
Greninagh, County Clare	4,291	7	2	3	47.0
Oughtmama, County Clare	9,843	20	3	4	39.0
Islandkeady, County Mayo	23,763	57	16	9	31.0
Kilmeena, County Mayo	9,693	59	14	11	30.5
Bulmim, County Roscommon	6,582	24	5	8	20.0
Kilcooley, County Roscommon	3,476	23	2	1	13.5

Source: Figures calculated from *Census of Ireland 1851: Part I, Area, Population, and Number of Houses, by Townlands and Electoral Divisions*, vol. ii: *Province of Munster, County of Clare*, 11–12, 14, HC 1852–53 (1552), XCI, 383; vol. iv: *Province of Connaught, County of Mayo*, 121–23, 128–29; *County of Roscommon*, 208, 210–11, HC 1852–53 (1555), XCII, 515; *Griffith's Valuation: County Clare*, Barony of Burren (part of), 1855; *County Mayo*, Baronies of Burrishoole, 1855; Carra, 1857; *County Roscommon*, Barony of Roscommon, 1857.

Nevertheless, as indicated in Table 5.3, there was considerable variation in the extent of consolidation. In five parishes, the proportions ranged from 20 to 39 percent of the land area, with the proportion in one other parish (Greninagh, County Clare) reaching 47 percent. Only in Kilcooley parish, County Roscommon, was the consolidation to create large holdings limited (13.5 percent of the land area), chiefly due to the number of grazing farms already existing in that parish before the Famine and the amount of consolidation in favor of so-called middle tenants. There was a similar variation between the parishes in the actual number of townlands (as a proportion of the total number in each parish) that were totally or partly cleared to make way for big holdings. In Greninagh parish, nearly all of the townlands were either totally or partly cleared for this purpose.

As further evidence of consolidation in favor of graziers, of the 32 townlands in Mayo subject to group eviction mentioned in the Land League report of witnesses to the Famine and its aftermath (referred to above), 29 were recorded in the Griffith's Valuation as comprising only or mainly one or two large holdings. In more than half of the reports, the witnesses explicitly stated how large grazing farms had been established in their former townlands.[90]

Another source of evidence of the consolidation of land in favor of graziers were the observations recorded in official inquiries, travelogues and press reports. In 1850, the Poor Law Inspector, Arthur Kennedy, referred to the desire of landowners to relet their vacant lands 'to the best advantage' as extensive holdings, and so to ensure that they be tenanted by 'a better and more industrious class of men'.[91] Many of these were cattle and sheep graziers, who wished to take advantage, according to Henry Brett, of the availability of a 'great quantity of grasslands' in the west.[92]

Two observers who separately visited the west of Ireland shortly after the Famine, James Caird, the Scottish farmer, and the physician and traveller, Sir John Forbes, recorded the availability of large areas of grassland, usually in excess of 400 acres, which, in most cases, the previous tenants had only recently surrendered or from which they had been evicted. Caird referred to graziers as now 'the only class of large farmers in Ireland, occupying under a landlord, and really possessed of capital'.[93] This was an exaggeration but contained an element of truth. Similar comments about the conversion of land to grazing farms during this period were made by other travellers to the western counties in subsequent years, based on interviews with local inhabitants and direct observation.

Letters, reports and commentaries in the press during the Famine and post-Famine period paint a similar story. The Western Correspondent of the *Freeman's Journal* wrote in 1849 that 'the universal feeling in the west is to "exterminate" with the view of laying down the land into large grazing farms'.[94] Eight years later little had changed, with a contributor to the *Munster News* in 1857 referring to the way 'hundreds are compelled to depart, expelled by landowners who are consolidating holdings and consigning them to large graziers and others'.[95]

The reallocation of land in the immediate aftermath of the Famine included, as well, several hybrid farmer-graziers, who each leased several hundred acres in the western counties. They combined large scale grazing of cattle and sheep on one part of their land with the cultivation of cereals and root crops on the other part. Some of the produce was used for supplementary stall-feeding of cattle during the winter. At the time, this was labeled 'high' or 'progressive' farming. While those in this category were not numerous, they stood out for using modern methods of farming, improving the land and employing hired labor.[96] Allan Pollock, who purchased a good deal of land in Galway in the 1850s, leased some of it to 'progressive' farmers and farmed the remainder himself along the same lines. The intention was to employ the large number of small occupiers he had evicted (for which he earned the reputation as a ruthless landlord) as hired labor on the 'progressive' farms which had been created.[97]

For the landlords in the Famine period, the graziers offered the prospect of regular rental payments and few arrears to ensure the commercial viability of the estate, even though rents per acre were not necessarily higher, as discussed below. With a myriad of impoverished small tenants and cottiers living on the estate, the opposite was often the case. Typical of the contrast was the estate of Sir James Fitzgerald Mahon at Castlegar, County Galway. In 1849, 307 small tenants, not among the poorest in the west of Ireland, paid in total a rent of £1,150, but with outstanding arrears of £736. To add to his problems, a further £300 of arrears had to be permanently written off in that year. On the other hand, the rents from his 13 graziers under lease, totaling over £2,000, were paid punctually by the gale days, with hardly any outstanding arrears.[98]

Also noteworthy was a discernible increase in the so-called middle tenantry in the western counties in the decade following the Famine. These were small family-based commercial farmers earning a cash income, hiring if necessary one or two farm hands and holding between 15 and 50 acres. Although holdings of 15–29 acres declined nationally between 1851 and 1861, in the western counties they increased—in Roscommon by 17 percent, and in Galway and Mayo by 14 percent. Holdings of 30–49 acres increased marginally for Ireland as a whole, but in Roscommon the increase was 28 percent, Mayo, 24 percent and Galway 17 percent.[99] Unfortunately, returns for these classes of holding are not available in 1845. Moreover, in the sample of parishes referred to in Table 5.3, some of the townlands which had been depopulated were occupied not by graziers but middle tenants holding from 15–50 acres.[100] Lane cites the example of Thomas Richardson, who purchased an encumbered estate of 2,654 acres in Tyaquin, County Galway in 1851, assisted the emigration of destitute occupiers and then divided the vacated land among about 50 tenants in lots of 10–50 acres.[101] Justice Mountfort Longfield, one of the commissioners of the Encumbered Estates Court, testifying to a later parliamentary inquiry, spoke of surrendered or evicted holdings being added to those of the remaining small tenants.[102] Such trends, diverging from those at the national level, point to a strengthening during the Famine and post-Famine years of a commercial middle tenantry in the western counties, alongside the major advance of the extensive graziers.

SOCIAL ORIGINS OF THE GRAZIERS

During the Famine period, the social origins of the graziers were as varied as those of the purchasers of encumbered estates. Many were already well established as graziers who lived in the neighborhood of townlands populated by small tenants and cottiers. They were ready to use their influence so that 'if a poor man's land happens to join theirs [they] may often intrigue with the bailiffs and that class of man generally succeeded in getting the poor man out and absorbing his land'.[103] Sixty years later, Peter O'Malley, a county councilor from Oughterard, recalled the clearances with 'tenants being turned out and whole villages being cleared . . . to satisfy the greed of some covetous neighbour who wanted to make room for his sheep and bullocks'.[104] Others were middlemen, who, after clearing their land of subtenants during the Famine, converted it into pasture for their own purpose of rearing cattle and sheep.[105] This was straightforward enough for those already grazing cattle and sheep alongside letting land.[106] The switch to grazing enabled them to recover the losses suffered when the rental income from their subtenants collapsed.

Grazing land was, as well, offered as a reward to land agents who managed the estate, and bailiffs and drivers who enforced evictions. Furthermore, land agents who then reorganized an estate and converted the land to pasture were in a good position to ensure that they had their share of the vacant land which had been made available.[107] One example was Thomas Blackstock, a land agent for the Geoghegan and Clonbrock estates, resident in Ballinasloe, who leased over 400 acres of grazing land in the early 1850s and continued after that to acquire more land. It is noticeable how many land agents who gave testimony to the Bessborough (1881), Richmond (1881), and Cowper (1887) Commissions had become substantial graziers during the Famine and post-Famine periods.

Another group to take advantage of the availability of grassland were cattle and sheep dealers (often called cattle and sheep jobbers). They were hired to buy and sell stock on behalf of conventional graziers, and were ever present in the sale rings of the major fairs. Alongside this task, they bought cattle and sheep on their own account to be sold a few months later in the hope of securing a quick return. They were essentially speculators and were prepared to take considerable risks in 'playing the market'. It was essential that they had the land to enable them to graze cattle and sheep, so they were keen enough to acquire in particular a temporary or agistment letting, which suited their needs.[108]

Shopkeepers were prominent in taking grazing farms. Of 11 large grocers in Ballinasloe, the Griffith's Valuation shows five to have been landholders in the mid-1850s in nearby townlands. By far the biggest landholder among them was Thomas Browne, a grocer and wine merchant, who leased several holdings which often accommodated a herds house, and comprised in total more than 1,000 acres. It would have made sense for shopkeepers to engage in grazing to supplement their income, since its low labor demand allowed them to stay at the shop most of the time. It also made up for lost income due to the erosion of their customer base during and after the Famine stemming from impoverishment and depopulation.

Another group who acquired large tracts of pasture, mainly in the west, were extensive English and Scottish farmers. The Dublin land agent, Thomas Miller, advertised and promoted Irish grazing farms in England and Scotland, sending out a detailed list of farms and lease forms to any inquirer. In 1853, he reported that he had 'received numerous applications for good farms from 100 acres and upwards, as well as for superior grazing farms and tracts of mountain pasture of large extent'.[109] It was estimated by one land agent that about 800 took up the offer and acquired land under lease mainly in Donegal, Mayo, Galway and Sligo.[110] One was Captain William Houstoun from East Lothian, who came to Ireland in 1851 and acquired a huge stretch of rough moorland pasture, initially 40,000 acres, later increasing to over 70,000 acres, in the Murrisk Barony of County Mayo. The small tenants had been dispossessed by Lord Sligo and the land was let to Houstoun on a 99-year lease at 4.5d per acre.[111] Houstoun, with reportedly a flock size of 23,000 sheep, was a major buyer at the annual Ballinasloe Fair. Another Scottish farmer was James Simpson, who from 1855 leased over 2,000 acres from the Earl of Lucan in Ballinrobe, land which likewise had been cleared during and after the Famine.[112] Such men were attractive to landowners in view of their capital and previous experience of cattle and sheep farming in upland areas, as well as reliability in paying rents.

TENURE UNDER WHICH GRAZIERS HELD LAND

Graziers acquired land during and after the Famine under terminable leases for years or lives. During the late 1840s and 1850s, leases for grazing farms were regularly advertised on the pages of the *Freeman's Journal*, the *Irish Times* and other newspapers. In some cases, the lease term and the conditions of the lease were stated, but in other cases they were not.

Graziers with a long-term commitment to cattle and sheep grazing were attracted by the offer of medium-term leases (21 or 31 years or three lives) simply because it guaranteed security over many years, being a safeguard against unforeseen rent rises and dispossession from all or part of the land.[113] In addition, the right to sell or assign the lease enabled them to terminate before the term had expired, so long as a purchaser or an assignee could be found. Such action was necessary when, as occurred from time to time, serious losses on cattle and sheep were incurred. A further benefit was that the security of tenure guaranteed by the lease made it easier to obtain credit. Such leases were especially attractive in the late 1840s and early 1850s, since rents were low and were then fixed for the term of the lease.

Alternatively, landowners who had cleared their land during the Famine and the post-Famine period, or whose land had been surrendered, often retained it under their direct possession as untenanted land, and let it to graziers as agistment for a grazing season. The tenure of such land was that of a license, not a tenancy, since the terms of the letting only granted the right to use the grass for a season with no other interest permitted. The practice was referred to as 'setting the land for grazing' and was later popularly known as the eleven-month system (as a result of the similarity of the tenure to conacre, it was commonly called 'conacre grazing').[114] For the landlord, seasonal or agistment lettings were sometimes preferable to letting the land under a lease or tenancy, since rents were often higher though less predictable, being closely correlated to fluctuations in market demand. As he only had a right of use, the grazier simply put his cattle and sheep on the land and tended to them as and when necessary. The grass, fencing and other necessities were provided by the landowner. Untenanted grass lettings were publicly advertised in lots early in the year and subject to sealed bids. Alternatively, landowners occasionally came to private deals with graziers to take agistment land. Seasonal grass lettings suited certain types of graziers, such as cattle jobbers and shopkeepers, who frequently bought and sold cattle and sheep as market prices dictated, and accordingly varied the size of their herds and flocks from season to season. They thus required the flexibility to acquire and relinquish land every year. Where they first started to graze cattle and sheep to supplement their income, shopkeepers sought only a small area of pasture let to them on a short-term basis, which subsequently increased as profits from grazing rose.[115]

Certain landowners whose lands had been cleared by them or surrendered by the tenants subsequently engaged in grazing themselves and so became graziers in their own right. Like other graziers, they were attracted by the prospects of profitable returns from cattle and sheep. They were further persuaded to do this in the event of not finding suitable leaseholders or being unable to let the land at an acceptable rent. Whether by necessity or choice, landowners, as one poor law guardian observed in 1849, 'are getting more into grazing'.[116] It is likely that a major element in this group were the purchasers of encumbered properties who were previously substantial tenants and middlemen, and who were already engaged in grazing cattle and sheep. Their natural inclination would have been to use their new property to expand their grazing enterprises.

MOTIVES OF GRAZIERS IN ACQUIRING LAND

Among the considerations of graziers in seeking grazing farms in the western areas during the Famine and post-Famine periods, two are particularly important: the cheapness of land combined with flexible letting terms, and the increased profitability of commercial grazing in the 1850s. Grazing land in the west could be rented quite cheaply at this time. The glut of land for grazing that came onto the market as a result of the surrenders and evictions during the Famine years, combined with further evictions undertaken by those who purchased in the Encumbered Estates Court, obviously depressed rent levels. Reflecting the over-supply, one correspondent of the *Nation* in 1849 wrote of 'several thousand acres of the richest and most fertile land (near Ennis County Clare) lying idle and unoccupied on the hands of landlords'.[117] In addition, landowners under pressure of mounting debts and ongoing liabilities were only too anxious to let land so as to secure a guaranteed income no matter how low the rent might be. Further strengthening the bargaining hand of the graziers, according to the Western Correspondent of the *Freeman's Journal* in 1851, was the advantage that they were 'not tied to the farm by fixtures and improvements in the land' (a common feature of commercial grazing), and thus were 'in a position to force the landlords to equitable terms'. If no agreement was reached, especially if their stock margins were declining, the graziers could 'readily surrender or threaten to surrender coming on May, and draw off their stock'.[118] This particularly applied to short-term leases and seasonal lettings. To prove the point, the correspondent to the *Nation* in 1849, referred to above, stated that 'wealthy and extensive graziers of this country, who paid rents varying from 5,000*l* to 500*l* per annum, have surrendered very many of their farms and are on the point of surrendering still more'.[119]

For these reasons, landowners were prepared to be flexible in arranging letting or lease terms for graziers. Advertisements for grazing farms occasionally were open-ended, with the owner allowing a lease or a letting 'for such terms as may be agreed' or 'for such length of time as may be agreed on'. This flexibility also included lowering rents when supply exceeded demand, an example being the reduction of grazing rents of 25 percent on the Roscommon estate of Charles Coote in 1847, a year when stock margins had declined.[120] Two years later, Henry Brett, speaking to the House of Lords committee on the poor law, stated that 'where [big tenants] are obtained, it is at a great reduction of rent'. Another witness to the committee, Caesar Otway, a poor law inspector and writer, mentioned the unwillingness of graziers from Scotland to take grassland at the previous rents.[121] By 1851, according to the Western Correspondent of the *Freeman's Journal*, the lands under grazing were '40 percent cheaper than they were five years ago' and could be rented for a 'few shillings', presumably with reference to rough pasture.[122]

The second reason for taking grazing land was the prospect of good returns. Most cattle graziers purchased their replacement stock, and so their gross margins (gross income minus variable expenditure which largely consisted of cattle purchases) were determined by the difference in price between the cattle when they were bought-in and when they were sold nine to eighteen months later. That depended crucially upon price margins between stock of different ages. An analysis of the prices at the Ballinasloe fair showed that the margin between stores (second class oxen) and fat cattle (fourth class oxen) jumped from £2 to £3 per head for the years 1847–48, and then increased to £4–£5 per head for the years 1849–52, further widening to £7 for the period 1853–57. From 1847 to 1857, the number of cattle sold at Ballinasloe more than doubled, with a corresponding decline in the number unsold, so reflecting rising demand.[123] According to Thomas Barrington's price index of agricultural produce, the price of young cattle (one–two years old) increased by 50 percent between 1845 and 1860, but that of older cattle (two–three years old) doubled. This points to widening margins for both store and fattening graziers.[124]

This trend is confirmed in the accounts of two graziers, namely, Arthur Henry, of Lodge Park, County Kildare and William Delany of Woodtown, County Meath. Henry's ledger shows that his gross margins for a herd of 50–70 cattle during the Famine period remained quite healthy, exceeding £300 (over 70 percent of variable expenditure). From 1849, they declined sharply, dropping to £134 (20 percent of variable expenditure) in 1851–52, but recovered strongly thereafter, exceeding £700 in 1853–54.[125] William Delany's accounts, which began in 1851, show an average annual gross margin on his herd of fat cattle rising from £477 (£3.19s per head) for 1851–55 to £544 (£4.16s per head) for 1866–70.[126]

CONCLUSION

The Famine and the associated indebtedness of sections of the landed gentry provided opportunities to expand the commercial basis of both land ownership and agriculture. This was made possible by the surplus capital available in the productive sectors of the Irish economy and to a lesser extent the wider British economy, which could be invested in land and commercial farming. The upshot was a more hardheaded and business-minded approach to estate management among both those gentry who held on to their estates and the new proprietors who purchased the encumbered estates. This included consolidating the land which had been surrendered or subject to eviction and then letting it as commercially viable large grazing farms.

Here were the seeds of later conflict. New capital was injected into the rural economy through the purchase of encumbered land, but it was used to pay off the mountain of debts and other liabilities of the former owners. Little of it was used to carry out improvements of estates such as drainage schemes, land reclamation projects, top soiling and manuring, erection of farm buildings and fences and provision of farm equipment. In this respect the new proprietors were not much better, with certain exceptions, than the established gentry. In fact, one landowner critical of the new proprietors spoke forty years later of the confident expectations in the wake of the Famine of 'the improvements to be made by these intelligent capitalists' but whose subsequent management of their estates 'falsified all these roseate forecasts'.[127]

The failure of the new owners to improve reinforced the tenants' claim to an interest in the land, since the burden to improve fell on them. The outcome was the demand for land reform and tenant ownership, which gave rise to the land agitation. The failure to improve was itself linked to letting land in large grazing farms, which required little fixed capital, and obviated the need to carry out capital improvements. The bulk of the physical assets required in the grazing enterprise was circulating capital comprising cattle and sheep bought and sold every six to eighteen months.[128]

In time too, the graziers were seen as having been the beneficiaries of the Famine, taking land whose former occupiers were impelled to surrender or from which they were evicted. A group once respected came to be regarded with resentment. As soon as tenant ownership had been secured, activists' attention turned to the grazing farms, leading to the so-called 'ranch war' of 1906–1912, the seizures of land between 1919 and 1922 and a far-reaching program of compulsory acquisition of grazing land for purposes of distribution. This started with the Land Act of 1909 and was accelerated after independence by several Land Acts, especially those of 1923 and 1933. Here, there may be a paradox: in making their estates commercially viable, the estate owners were prepared to consolidate land not just to create large holdings but also (though to a lesser degree) medium-sized holdings of 15–49 acres, strengthening the middle tenantry of commercial family-based farms, the very group that, from 1879, had been at the forefront of the movement to secure land reform.

NOTES

1. D.S. Jones, *Graziers, Land Reform and Political Conflict in Ireland* (Washington, 1995), 32–41.
2. Fee simple is a perpetual interest, which includes the right of exclusive occupation (entrance into the property requiring the permission of the fee simple holder), the right to alienate the land (by sale, gift or bequest), the right to make alterations and improvements, and the right to determine how the land is used and take profits from that use (profit à prendre). The fee entail holder enjoys all the rights of fee simple except the right to sell the land, which can only be alienated by bequest to his/her heirs. This was a device to retain the land within the family through the line of succession. For fee entail, see Andrew Lyall, *Land Law in Ireland* (Dublin, 1994), 12; J.C. Wylie, *Irish Land Law* (London, 1975), 144.
3. J.L. Montrose, 'Fee-farm Grants: Part I', *Northern Ireland Legal Quarterly* (hereafter cited as *NILQ*), 2 (1938), 195–99; J. C. Wylie, 'Fee-farm Grants—Montrose Continued', *NILQ*, 23, 2 (1972), 285–94, 303–309.
4. Wylie, 'Fee-farm Grants', 296–98.
5. Ibid., 297–99; Lyall, *Land Law*, 250.
6. Elizabeth R. Hooker, *Readjustments of Agricultural Tenure in Ireland* (Chapel Hill, 1938), 27.

7. Lyall, *Land Law*, 558; Wylie, *Irish Land Law*, 147–48.
8. Sean Kelly, 'Crisis in the Countryside: Bohola, County Mayo, 1845–1900', *Cathair na Mart*: *Journal of Westport Historical Society*, 20 (2000), 64, 66.
9. The term 'subdivision' was interpreted in two ways: dividing a property at death among two or more heirs, or subletting the property among two or more subtenants.
10. Jones, *Graziers*, 106–107.
11. Hooker, *Readjustments*, 26–30; J. L. Montrose, 'Fee-farm Grants: Part III, The Relation of Landlord and Tenant', *NILQ*, 3 (1940), 83–86.
12. Robert Scally, *The End of Hidden Ireland*: *Rebellion, Famine, and Emigration* (New York, 1995), 38, 50.
13. David Barr, 'George Henry Moore and his Tenants, 1840–1870', *Cathair na Mart*, 8 (1988), 68–69.
14. Scally, *End of Hidden Ireland*, 21, 25–28, 57; see also Kevin O'Neill, *Family and Farm in Pre-Famine Ireland: The Parish of Killashandra* (Madison, Wisc., 1984), 34–35, 59–62.
15. Hooker, *Readjustments*, 30–31; Margaret MacCurtain, 'Pre-Famine Peasantry in Ireland: Definition and Themes', *Irish University Review*, 4, 2 (1974), 193; Pádraig Lane, 'The General Impact of the Encumbered Estates Act of 1849 on Counties Galway and Mayo', *Journal of the Galway Archaeological and Historical Society* (hereafter cited as *JGAHS*), 33 (1972–73), 51.
16. Thomas Maxwell, *An Outline of the Law of Landlord and Tenant and of Land Purchase in Ireland* (Dublin, 1909), 9–10; Lyall, *Land Law*, 547–53.
17. Maxwell, *An Outline of the Law of Landlord and Tenant*, 9–10.
18. Ibid., 9. For conacre in Roscommon, see Mary Dunn, *Ballykilcline Rising: from Famine Ireland to Immigrant America* (Amherst, 2008), 52–54.
19. *Returns of Agricultural Produce in Ireland in the Year 1850*, HC 1851 (1404), l, 1.
20. *HL Poor Law Comm., 2nd Report*, 37; *4th Report*, 786, HC 1849 (365), xvi, 543; *Select Committee on Poor Laws (Ireland), 2nd Report*, 9, HC 1849 (93), xv, pt. 1, 5 (chaired by Sir John Young and hereafter cited as *Young Comm., . . . Report)*.
21. Kerby A. Miller, *Emigrants and Exiles: Ireland and the Irish Exodus to North America* (New York, 1985), 287; James S. Donnelly, Jr., 'The Administration of Relief, 1847–51', in W. E. Vaughan, ed., *A New History of Ireland, V: Ireland under the Union, 1* (Oxford, 1989), 323–26; Sean P. McManamon, 'Landlords and Evictions in County Mayo during the Great Famine', *Cathair na Mart*, 18 (1998), 128–29; Cormac Ó Gráda, *Black '47 and Beyond: The Great Irish Famine in History, Economy, and Memory* (Princeton, NJ, 2000), 41–45.
22. 'Agricultural Report for the Westport Union, 22 January 1849', in *Young Comm., 14th Report, Appendix,* 281, HC 1849 (577), xv, pt. 1, 177.
23. Kelly, 'Crisis in the Countryside', 67.
24. *Young Comm., 7th Report*, 75, HC 1849 (237), xv, pt. 1, 415. For a similar observation, see *Young Comm., 9th Report*, 86, HC 1849 (301), xv, pt. 1, 647; *13th Report*, 10, HC 1849 (416), xv, pt. 2, 173. See also *the Select Committee of the House of Lords Appointed to Inquire into the Operations of the Irish Poor Law . . . , 1st Report*, 95, 210, HC 1849 (192), xvi, 1; *2nd Report*, 308, HC 1849 (228), xvi, 301; *4th Report*, 786, HC 1849 (365), xvi, 543; *5th Report*, 950, HC 1849 (507), xvi, 927 (hereafter cited as *HL Poor Law Comm., . . . Report*); Miller, *Emigrants*, 294–96.
25. Thomas Barrington, 'A Review of Irish Agricultural Prices', *Journal of the Statistical and Social Inquiry Society of Ireland*, 15 (1927), 251; *Return of Extent of Land under Crops in Ireland, 1852 and 1853*, xxxiii (1746), HC 1854, lvii, 263. The fall in prices was due to the significant rise in imports of grains,

and grain flour and meal (equivalent to 36 percent of the amount produced in Ireland in 1847) from the United States, Britain, France and other countries, and also to a declining number of consumers as a result of mortality and emigration. See *Return of Quantity of Grain and Flour Imported into Ireland, 1839–48; Quantities of Grain, Flour, and Agricultural Produce Imported into Great Britain . . .*, 2, HC 1849 (588), l, 403.

26. For discussion of the clearances, see James S. Donnelly, Jr., 'Landlords and Tenants', in Vaughan, ed., *A New History of Ireland, V*, 336–43; idem, *The Great Irish Potato Famine* (Stroud, 2001), 110–31, 146–47, 152–56; McManamon, 'Landlords and Evictions', 126–33.
27. *Tuam Herald*, 8 July 1848.
28. Sean P. McManamon, 'Irish National Land League, County Mayo: Evidence as to Clearances, Evictions and Rack Renting etc. 1850–1880', *Cathair na Mart*, 24 (2004/05), 86–127; *General Valuation of Tenements, Ireland*: Co. *Mayo*, Baronies of Burrishoole, 1855; Murrisk, 1855; Clanmorris, 1856; Carra, 1857; Costello, 1857 (hereafter cited as *Griffith's Valuation: Co. . . .*).
29. *Census of Ireland 1851: Part I, Area, Population, and Number of Houses, by Townlands and Electoral Divisions*, vol. 4: *Province of Connaught, County of Mayo*, 121–23, 128–29 (1542), HC 1852–53, xcii, 453.
30. Scally, *End of Hidden Ireland*, 50.
31. Ibid.
32. *Returns . . . of the Number of Ejectments . . . and of the Number of Civil Bill Ejectments . . .*, 7, HC 1849 (315), xlix, 235.
33. See *Report from the Select Committee on the Kilrush Union . . .*, 69, 91–92, 151, HC 1850 (613), xi, 529 (chaired by George Scrope; hereafter cited as the *Scrope Comm. Report*); *HL Poor Law Comm., 2nd Report*, 311; *5th Report*, 915; Wylie, *Irish Land Law*, 761–63, 766–71. For recent estimates of reinstatement, see Donnelly, 'Landlords', 343–45; Donald Jordan, *Land and Popular Politics in Ireland: County Mayo from the Plantation to the Land War* (Cambridge, 1994), 113–15, 314.
34. Ó Gráda, *Black '47 and Beyond*, 45–46, 243.
35. *Return, by Provinces and Counties . . . of Cases of Evictions Which Have Come to the Knowledge of Royal Irish Constabulary, in Each of the Years from 1849 to 1880, Inclusive*, 3, HC 1881 (185), lxxvii, 725.
36. *Reports and Returns relating to Evictions in the Kilrush Union*, 8–57 and *passim* (1089), HC 1849, xilx, 315 (hereafter cited as *Eviction Reports and Returns, Kilrush*).
37. Ibid., 10–53.
38. *Scrope Comm. Report*, 217–18, 233, 247–49; see also Donnelly 'Landlords', 146.
39. *Tuam Herald*, 8 July 1848.
40. *Eviction Reports and Returns, Kilrush*, 30, 51. For references to landlords financially assisting small tenants to emigrate, see Miller, *Emigrants*, 296, 303–304, 312, 356; Donnelly, 'Landlords', 337–39.
41. Scally, *End of Hidden Ireland*, 84.
42. Kelly, 'Crisis in the Countryside', 66.
43. McManamon, 'Irish National Land League', 86–127.
44. *Tuam Herald*, 8 July 1848.
45. *Freeman's Journal* (hereafter abbreviated as *FJ*), 4 December 1847; 26 October 1849.
46. See return in *HL Poor Law Comm., 6th Report, Appendix*, 145, HC 1849 (507–II), xvi, 1019. See also Donnelly, *The Great Irish Potato Famine*, chs. 3–5.
47. McManamon, 'Landlords and Evictions', 127–29.

48. L.P. Curtis, 'Incumbered Wealth: Landed Indebtedness in post-Famine Ireland', *American Historical Review*, 85, 2 (1980), 335–38; Marie Kelly, 'Manners and Customs of the Gentry in Pre-Famine Ireland', *Cathair na Mart*, 8 (1988), 48–56; Barr, 'George Henry Moore', 72; Ó Gráda, *Black '47 and Beyond*, 128–31.
49. Curtis, 'Incumbered Wealth', 337–39; Lyall, *Land Law*, 364.
50. Ó Gráda, *Black '47 and Beyond*, 128–32.
51. Pádraig G. Lane, 'The Impact of the Encumbered Estates Court upon the Landlords of Galway and Mayo', *JGAHS*, 38 (1981–82), 48–55; Pádraig G. Lane, 'Land Encumbrances: A Record of the Dillon-Browne Estate', *Cathair na Mart*, 14 (1994), 69–77.
52. *Report of the Commissioners for the Sale of Incumbered Estates in Ireland, as to Their Progress, etc*, 2–3, HC 1850 (1268), xxv, 55.
53. *Report of Her Majesty's Commissioners Appointed to Inquire into the Incumbered Estates Court*... 82–133, HC 1854–55 (1938), xix, 527. For a valuable analysis of this return, see Ó Gráda, *Black '47 and Beyond*, 132.
54. 1849 (12th & 13th Vict.), c. 77, s. 22. This Act replaced the Encumbered Estates Act, 1848, which proved largely ineffective; see 1848 (11th & 12th Vict.) c. 48.
55. *The Nation*, 9 October 1858.
56. *FJ*, 12 June 1855.
57. *The Nation*, 9 October 1858. See also Donnelly, *The Great Irish Potato Famine*, 164–68.
58. Richard MacNevin, *The Practice of the Landed Estates Court in Ireland*... (3rd edition, Dublin, 1859), 1–3.
59. David Butler, 'The Landed Classes during the Great Irish Famine', in John Crowley, William J. Smyth, and Mike Murphy, eds., *Atlas of the Great Irish Famine* (Cork, 2012), 269–70.
60. Pádraig Lane, 'Some Galway and Mayo Landlords of the Mid-Nineteenth Century', *JGAHS,* 45 (1993), 73–78; Lane, 'The Impact of the Encumbered Estates Court', 53–55.
61. Lane, 'The Impact of the Encumbered Estates Court', 55–58.
62. Donnelly, *The Great Irish Potato Famine*, 166; Ó Gráda, *Black '47 and Beyond*, 132.
63. *FJ*, 19 February 1851.
64. *FJ*, 1 April 1850.
65. *Report, dated 3rd Day of May 1851, from the Incumbered Estates Commissioners of Ireland*..., 2, HC 1851 (258), xxiv, 35.
66. A.M. Sullivan, *New Ireland* (Philadelphia, 1878), 195.
67. Pádraig Lane, 'Purchasers of Land in Counties Galway and Mayo in the Encumbered Estates Court, 1849–1858', *JGAHS*, 43 (1991), 95–104.
68. HC Debates, 3rd Ser, 12 March 1868, 190, cols. 1522–23.
69. Lane, 'Purchasers', 95–104.
70. Ibid., 106.
71. *Anglo-Celt*, 9 June 1853.
72. *The Nation*, 9 October 1858; Alvin Jackson, *Ireland, 1798–1998* (Oxford, 1999), 77.
73. *Anglo-Celt*, 9 June 1853; *FJ*, 6 May 1853.
74. *FJ*, 6 May 1853.
75. *Return of Number of Petitions, Produce of Sales, Number of Conveyances and Estates Sold in the Incumbered Estates Court, Ireland*, 2, HC 1852–53 (390), xciv, 599; *Anglo-Celt*, 9 June 1853.
76. *The Nation*, 28 November 1857.
77. *FJ*, 16 November 1850.

78. Ibid.
79. *FJ*, 28 April 1853.
80. Sullivan, *New Ireland*, 195.
81. HC Debates, 3rd Ser, 12 March 1868, 190, cols. 1523.
82. Lane, 'Purchasers', 107–10.
83. *Nenagh Guardian*, 18 November 1854.
84. Lane, 'Some Galway and Mayo Landlords', 73–78.
85. *FJ*, 10 October 1856. For examples of such clearances, see *FJ*, 21 August, 27 December 1850, 24 February, 31 December 1852.
86. *Return, by Provinces and Counties . . . of Cases of Eviction . . .*, 3.
87. Lane, 'The General Impact', 45–51.
88. *Returns of Agricultural Produce in Ireland in 1853*, xi (1865), HC 1854–55, xlvii, 1.
89. Ibid., xi; Lane, 'The General Impact', 67–68; Michael Turner, *After the Famine: Irish Agriculture, 1850–1914* (Cambridge, 2002), 76; Donnelly, *The Great Irish Potato Famine*, 152–53, 158–62.
90. McManamon, 'Irish National Land League', 86–127; *Griffith's Valuation: Co. Mayo*, Baronies of: Burrishoole, 1855; Murrisk, 1855; Clanmorris, 1856; Carra, 1857; Costello, 1857.
91. *Scrope Comm. Report*, 89. For a similar observation, see *HL Poor Law Comm., 5th Report*, 915. See also Donnelly, 'Landlords', 343–45.
92. *HL Poor Law Comm., 2nd Report*, 496.
93. James Caird, *The Plantation Scheme; or the West of Ireland as a Field for Investment* (Edinburgh, 1850), 3, 6, 16–23, 33–34, 44–45, 61–63, 84–85. See also John Forbes, *Memorandums Made in Ireland in the Autumn of 1852*, 2 vols. (London, 1853), vol. 1, 153–54; vol. 2, 35, 389.
94. Reported in *The Nation*, 1 December 1849. The term 'exterminate' was commonly used at the time to refer to mass evictions.
95. The letter was written to the *Munster News* but was reported in *The Nation*, 25 July 1857. For further references to the creation of grazing farms after the land was purchased in the Encumbered Estates Court, and then subject to eviction, see Lane, 'The General Impact', 45–51, 66–68.
96. Lane, 'The General Impact', 53, 56, 66, 68.
97. Padraig Lane, 'An Attempt at Commercial Farming in Ireland after the Famine', *Studies*, 61, 241 (1972), 54–66; Hugh Sutherland, *Ireland Yesterday and Today* (Philadelphia, 1909), 67–68. See also press reports *FJ*, 22 June 1854; 8 May 1856.
98. Rental of Part of the Estate of Sir James Fitzgerald Ross Mahon, Situated in the County of Galway, 1850, National Library of Ireland [NLI], Mahon Papers, MS 8,553.
99. *Returns of Agricultural Produce in Ireland, 1852*, iv; *Agricultural Statistics of Ireland, 1861*, 29, 49, 58.
100. Lane, 'The General Impact', 47, 68.
101. Lane, 'Some Galway and Mayo Landlords', 81–82.
102. *Report from the Select Committee* on the *Tenure and Improvement of Land (Ireland) Act* . . . 28, HC 1865 (402), xi, 341.
103. From evidence of Mathew Harris, *Report from the Select Committee on the Irish Land Act, 1870 . . .*, pt. 1, 271, HC 1877 (328), xii, 1.
104. *Royal Commission on Congestion in Ireland* . . . : vol. 10, 6 [Cd. 4007], HC 1908, xlii, 1 (hereafter cited as the *Dudley Commission*).
105. The fate of middlemen in the 1840s was discussed by Donnelly, 'Landlords', 333–35; Donnelly, *The Great Irish Potato Famine*, 134–36. See also Norman Palmer, *The Irish Land League Crisis* (New Haven, 1940), 35.
106. Lane, 'The General Impact', 64.

107. The involvement of land agents in grazing during and after the Famine was pointed out by the Rev. Joseph Pelly in evidence to the *Dudley Commission*, vol. 10, 166–67.
108. Guardian of the Poor, *The Irish Peasant—A Sociological Study* (London, 1892), 96–97.
109. *FJ*, 9 July 1853.
110. Lane, 'The General Impact', 67–68.
111. Innes Shand, *Letters from the West of Ireland, 1884* (Edinburgh, 1885), 111–12; Bernard Becker, *Disturbed Ireland: Being the Letters Written during the Winters of 1880–81* (London, 1881), 73; Matilda Houstoun, *Twenty Years in the Wild West, or Life in Connaught* (London, 1879), 36, 229, 232.
112. Henry Coulter, *The West of Ireland, its Existing Condition and Prospects* (Dublin, 1862), 151, 173–76; Jordan, *Land*, 113
113. Lane, 'The General Impact', 69–70.
114. Ibid., 66–67.
115. Jones, *Graziers*, 133, 140–41.
116. *Young Comm., 7th Report*, 75. For references to landlords during the Famine who used the land after evictions to graze their own stock, see Caird, *Plantation Scheme*, 19, 23; Shand, *Letters*, 113; Becker, *Disturbed Ireland*, 36–39; George Pellew, *In Castle and Cabin, or Talks in Ireland in 1887* (New York, 1888), 97.
117. *The Nation*, 13 October 1849.
118. *FJ*, 8 August 1851.
119. *The Nation*, 13 October 1849.
120. *FJ*, 22 December 1847.
121. *HL Poor Law Comm., 2nd Report*, 484; *4th Report*, 896.
122. *FJ*, 8 August 1851.
123. *Thom's Irish Almanac and Official Directory . . . 1849*, 487; *1853*, 501; *1858*, 551.
124. Barrington, 'A Review of Irish Agricultural Prices', 251. A similar trend is reflected in 'Prices of Irish Agricultural Produce—1830 to 1879', *Irish Farmers' Gazette*, 1 November 1879.
125. Calculated from Stock Register and Account Book, Arthur Henry, Lodge Park, County Kildare, 1840–57, NLI, MS 23,573.
126. Stock Purchase and Sales Account Books, Delany Family, Woodtown, County Meath, vol. 1, NLI, MS 19,347.
127. Guardian of the Poor, *The Irish Peasant*, 83.
128. Jones, *Graziers*, 7–15.

6 Aspects of Agency

John Ross Mahon, Accommodation and Resistance on the Strokestown Estate, 1845–51[1]

Ciarán Reilly

In April 1847, Major Denis Mahon cleared more than 1,000 families from his 11,000-acre estate at Strokestown, County Roscommon; many of those cleared opted to leave for Canada on a scheme of assisted emigration that he financed. Seven months later, in November, a secret society assassinated Mahon. In a letter to Mahon's heir, Henry Sandford Pakenham Mahon, in October 1849, Pat McLaughlin, a tenant, wrote that John Ross Mahon, his land agent, 'has you strangled in the eyes of the public and the ruin of your Strokestown estate at present can only be compared to the destruction of Troy'.[2] Others too blamed the agent for adopting a 'ruinous and destructive policy' on 'that once splendid estate'.[3] Such representations of Ross Mahon evoke an image of Irish land agents that was well established long before the Great Famine, and only strengthened by it, that is, the agent as a capricious evictor, profiting from the misery of others. Indeed, in the early 1880s, when agitation for land reform intensified, Land League activists regularly linked them to the 'fearful murder committed on the mass of the people' in the Great Famine.[4]

The sterotype of the obnoxious land agent is particularly well represented in the fiction of William Carelton, in which rapacious characters such as 'Yellow Sam' and 'Greasy Pockets' take bribes and cheat tenants and landlords out of money.[5] However, the image of the agent as a simple rent-collector misleads. Agents were expected to make leases, survey land, keep accounts and allot work on the demesne, organize agricultural shows and instruct tenants on new farming methods, all the while keeping the landlord informed of the management of his estate. Many served as justices of the peace or acted as political managers for their landlords, organizing support for them or their favored candidates in elections. In short, then, the agent was a prominent figure in mid-nineteenth-century rural society and politics, and, as evidenced by the Famine-time career of John Ross Mahon, estates not being islands unto themselves and tenants having a range of political and social interests, some tenants were prepared to accommodate themselves to his authority, while others resisted.[6]

STROKESTOWN, THE LAND AGENT AND THE FAMINE

Robert Rundell Guinness and John Ross Mahon formed a land agency in 1836. Run from offices on South Frederick Street, Dublin, Guinness and Mahon soon ranked among the most successful agencies in the country. By 1851, the firm was managing over thirty landed estates, and it was now also involved in banking.[7] But the management of landed estates in the late 1840s and early 1850s was difficult. On the Strokestown estate, which Guinness and Mahon only began managing in 1846, John Ross Mahon and Thomas Roberts, his local under-agent, faced a number of challenges that would only be compounded by the already unfolding Famine. These challenges included endemic subdivision and the prevalence of conacre and subletting. In addition, there had been a breakdown of order in the years prior to their taking over management of the estate. Much of the trouble involved tenants and subtenants resisting efforts at 'agricultural improvement', but there was also a high level of crime against women and children, suggestive, perhaps, of social and cultural dislocation.[8] 'When I became agent to the Strokestown estate in 1846', Ross Mahon later recalled, 'it was covered with paupers. The rental was £9,000 a year, exclusive of the demesne. The average quantity of land each tenant held was three acres one rood plantation measure, without counting under tenants, and almost every tenant had one or two under tenants'.[9] Then, with hunger and disease across the country, the estate was already more than £30,000 in debt and in most cases rents had not been paid since 1843.[10]

In November 1846, when Ross Mahon took over as agent, the Dublin surveyors Brassington and Gale mapped and valued the estate. Upon the advice of these surveyors, the landlord consented to grant a rent reduction to tenants on lands that were considered overset and overvalued. However, after a series of meetings with his new agent, he changed his mind in January 1847. Despite a major relief effort in late 1846, there had been continued resistance to the payment of rent, which the landlord believed to have been inspired by the neighboring district of Ballykilcline, a property leased by the Mahons until 1834, but since vested in the control of government appointed receivers.[11] The Ballykilcline tenants were said to be the 'most lawless and violent set of people in the County of Roscommon'.[12] In Mahon's opinion, many of his own tenants were taking advantage of the potato blight 'in order to allow them to carry out their combination not to pay any rent'.[13] He decided that those who were in arrears prior to 1845 should not be shown any leniency. It was a revealing decision. Local people would later blame the agent for the clearances and emigration schemes, but the landlord was clearly involved in the development of these initiatives. Indeed, on the appointment of the agent, he had explicitly instructed him to submit all plans to him for his approval 'prior to their being carried into execution'.[14]

ASSISTED EMIGRATION

Following the reappearance of blight in 1846, landlords and agents across Ireland had agreed to grant rent abatements. From 1847, however, a different approach was adopted on many estates—tenants and subtenants were to be cleared. So it was at Strokestown. Within the first few months of his agency, Ross Mahon concluded that 'the facts are sufficient without any further remarks of mine to show the impossibility of collecting poor rates or of effecting any change in the condition of the people while the land remains in such small divisions in the hands of paupers unable to support themselves much less to till it to advantage'. Clearing impoverished tenants would allow the estate to be managed *de novo* and 'emigration on an extensive scale', Ross Mahon would later recall, 'was the principal feature of my plan'.[15] Simply put, emigration would relieve the landlord of a financial burden: providing for impoverished tenants admitted to Roscommon Workhouse would cost him £11,000 annually, but a once-off payment of £5,860 would send more than 3,000 people to Canada. In one part of Mahon's properties, comprising 2,105 acres, the agent found 475 families (2,444 individuals), which he estimated was two-thirds more than the number which the land was capable of sustaining. 'I am convinced unless the greater part of the population are removed from your estate', Ross Mahon coldly advised his employer, 'the poor rates of this electoral division will exceed the receipts of rent, and the division being almost entirely your property, the greater part of the poor rate must fall upon you'.[16] He continued: 'while the large pauperized population remained, no plan could be put into place to bring about a change in their condition'. In truth, the agent had been horrified when his census and survey revealed such an 'immense population'. On the townland of Gurtoose, for example, there were some 33 families on little more than 80 acres, which was held by only four lease holders. For Ross Mahon, assisted emigration schemes were a 'conclusive solution to the management of landed estates'.[17]

Some 50–80,000 people left Ireland on assisted emigration schemes during the Famine.[18] Landlords who sponsored major schemes of removal included Earl Fitzwilliam (Wicklow); Charles Wandesforde (Kilkenny); Lord Lansdowne (Kerry); Marquis of Bath (Monaghan); Lord Palmerston (Sligo); George Wyndham (Clare); Sir Robert Gore Booth (Sligo); Francis Spaight (Tipperary) and Lord de Vesci (Queen's County).[19] However, with the exception of the Lansdowne scheme, no assisted emigration program achieved the notoriety of that put in place on the Mahon estate. And yet other schemes were clearly a model for it. In offering advice on how the emigration plan should be put into action, Major Mahon himself suggested that some tenants might be made to emigrate from Sligo, which would be a great saving: 'I hear that Lord Palmerston is doing so and that he states that his plan for the emigration of his tenantry in Co Sligo is going on quite well'. Indeed, in April 1847, he advised Ross Mahon to communicate with his counterpart on the Palmerston estate to see how they operated.[20]

Aware of the controversy surrounding evictions on the Gerrard estate in County Galway in 1846, Major Mahon, like Lord Rosse in King's County, drafted a set of estate rules to avoid any public censure following the removal of tenants.[21] Initially, he hoped that the scheme would include the greatest number of tenants possible, but having failed to secure ready finance for the project, the plan was scaled back to a 'limited number'.[22] Requesting to be informed of the amount of rent due from every tenant who had been selected for emigration, the landlord insisted on giving his final approval in each case. A concern not to lose 'industrious tenants' who would be needed 'going forward' was the key factor here. This concern was well founded: when plans for the scheme were first mooted, many relatively well-to-do tenants had requested to be included. 'I think the first class for us to send', Mahon wrote in April 1847, 'is those of the poorest and worst description who would be a charge on us for the poor house or for outdoor relief and that would relieve the industrious tenants'.[23] If both agent and landlord had to approve those tenants who were to be assisted to emigrate, many tenants were clearly being 'pushed' into leaving. The situation was similar to that on the Fitzwilliam estates in County Wicklow, where the agent, Robert Challoner, ensured that no unmarried people would be admitted to an emigration scheme that removed 5,000 people during the 1840s.[24] It was said of that particular scheme that 'none of them went of their own will but to accommodate the landlord'.[25]

FROM IRELAND TO CANADA

Before a program of assisted emigration could be put in place at Strokestown, the agent's office had a considerable volume of administrative work to complete. Notably, on 21 March 1847 a census was undertaken by Roberts and his team of bailiffs, who carefully recorded the number of persons in each family on the estate.[26] The census complete, the tenants soon learned their fate. According to the agent, most tenants appeared to be satisfied that 'all rent and arrears were forgiven' and in general they 'expressed themselves much obliged and went cheerfully'.[27] However, some tenants were not so acquiescent. And yet they too were to be shipped out.

Tenants selected for emigration had to evict their under tenants, relieving the landlord of that trouble.[28] At the same time, tenants not accepted for the scheme were also now encouraged to quit the estate. These tenants received a number of 'lucrative offers' to convince them to throw down their houses and leave; these incentives included seed potatoes, animals and money, or permission to retain a growing crop. In general, those chosen for the scheme held less than two acres of land. However, some of those 'encouraged' to give up their holdings, surrender land and emigrate were, like Pat Foard, told that they could 'go where you like' upon surrendering possession, that is, it did not matter to the landlord whether they availed of the scheme or not as long as they left Strokestown.[29] Perhaps because the tenants were availing of the emigration scheme, there was little opposition to the estate's auctioning of their crops and animals, which would normally have been the case with the property of evicted tenants. But local, provincial and national newspapers expressed vehement disapproval of developments at Strokestown. In July 1847, the *Roscommon Journal* deplored the clearance of the estate, noting that 'our prisons will be kept crowded; our poorhouse will be kept full; and our streets will be inundated by this "clearance system"—this new mode of depopulating'.[30] Ironically, the *Journal* had printed the civil bills and ejectment decrees received by the evicted tenants.

In July, on completion of the selection process, Ross Mahon warned his employer that secret societies were now plotting to assassinate him.[31] Still, the clearances went ahead, with the agent dividing tenants into three groups—those of means were to be pressed for one year's rent; a second group was pressed to pay a half year's rent; while the third, the poor, would pay nothing. However, much to the agent's disappointment, 'no advantage was taken' by any of the groups. He was particularly aggrieved with those who refused to pay but who produced the rent upon the arrival of the bailiff, sheriff and 'hut tumblers'.[32] And the hut tumblers were busy. In June, Major Mahon, hoping to get rents from 'the better class', had ordered that action should be taken against those who have had already 'plenty of indulgence'.[33] They included Patrick Browne, the middleman of Cloonfad, who held just over 300 acres, and the Castlenode tenants, who were 'what we call snug people'.[34] 'I would have thought with that class of people', the landlord wrote, 'it would have been ample indulgence to have "forgiven the rent due" and let them find their own way out'.[35] At the same time, he also advised his agent that the lands of Cregga would be a good place 'to get out of the hands of so bad a set of [and] such a nest of paupers'. He was, it seems, determined to get rid of the tenants who were 'not improving' and 'badly off'.[36] Middlemen and strong farmers who depended on a host of under tenants to pay their rents were also to be cast out. Those who could support themselves would be allowed to remain.[37]

In all, Mahon chartered four ships (*Virginius, John Munn, Naomi* and *Erin's Queen*) that embarked from Liverpool for Canada during the summer of 1847, carrying over 1,432 people. Passengers on all four ships suffered from cholera and typhus. The *Toronto Globe* thus reported the arrival of the *Virginius* at Grosse Île:

> The *Virginius* from Liverpool, with 496 passengers, had lost 158 by death, nearly one third of the whole, and she had 180 sick; above one half the whole will never see their home in the new world.[38]

Another report described the Mahon tenants as 'ghastly, yellow-looking spectres, unshaven and hollow cheeked', while on the *John Munn* 'the filth and dirt in these vessel's holds creates such an effluvium as to make it difficult to breathe'.[39] To counter such criticism, Ross Mahon wrote to his new employer stressing that tenants were given rations above the government standards and that over £6,000 was spent on their passage.[40] In addition to the government allocation, each passenger over fourteen was given weekly rations of six pounds of sugar; ten ounces of tea; two pounds of shell cocoa; eight pounds of rice; fourteen pounds of oatmeal; a dozen herrings; one and a half pounds of soap; a pint of vinegar; six hundredweight of pepper & salt; children under fourteen received half the supply.[41]

As reports of the condition of the emigrants on arrival filtered back to Ireland, tension increased at Strokestown, and escalated further in October when Denis Mahon ordered his agent to remove recalcitrant tenants from the townland of Dooherty.[42] Then, on 2 November 1847, Mahon was shot and killed as he returned from a meeting of the Roscommon Board of Guardians.[43] It was a sensational incident which sparked a wide-ranging debate involving members of the British parliament, the clergy and even Queen Victoria. Among the many allegations which followed the murder included the claim that the Rev. Michael McDermott, parish priest of Strokestown, had denounced Mahon from the pulpit two days before he was murdered. To McDermott's aid came the Bishop of Elphin, Dr. George Browne. The bishop staunchly defended McDermott against the allegations that he had been directly implicated in the murder, including his alleged remark that Major Mahon was 'worse than Cromwell and yet he lives'.[44]

Anxious to reassert control over the estate, Ross Mahon sought to discredit Browne by highlighting that his own brother, a wealthy middleman, had evicted under tenants at Cloonfad, near Strokestown. In February 1848, Ross Mahon wrote, in a letter to the *Times*, that 'the Bishop's brother expressed a hope of being able to liquidate the arrears if given time' but took advantage of the situation and 'put out every tenant who had not paid up his rent'.[45] Browne held fast. Claiming that he 'would not screen, even a brother, if proved to be an oppressor of the poor', he published a list of over 3,000 people who had been evicted from the estate in the *Freeman's Journal*, albeit omitting his brother's own townland, Cloonfad.[46] Controversy raged. Pro-tenant newspapers, such as the *Journal*, now carried articles deploring 'extermination by the thousand'. While publicly supported by the heir to the estate, Henry Sandford Pakenham Mahon, the agent—having been centrally involved in the emigration scheme—was now a lightning rod for animosity.

EVICTIONS

By 1848, three years of hunger had reduced much of the population in Strokestown to destitution, with many people now appealing for assistance from the landlord and agent. Petitioners stressed that they would adhere to estate policies if they were given immediate relief. For Ross Mahon, however, the deepening crisis was an opportunity to complete the clearance of unwanted tenants, or to press what David Nally has called the 'war on dwellings'.[47] In the wake of Denis Mahon's assassination, he had determined the 'decided measures' necessary to reorder the estate.[48] Now, he commenced eviction proceedings against as many as 1,000 tenants. 'I am happy to say that the *haberes* have been executed without any incident or disturbance', he wrote his employer that August. 'The levelling of the houses has been done most effectively—there is not a wall left standing and the stones are removed to the foundation'.[49]

The evicted included some one hundred families in Dooherty, Cornashina and Leitrim, the pretext for whose removal was their alleged involvement in the assassination. 'We have had a peak number of ejectments', the agent wrote in January 1848; 'in all cases the walls of the house completely levelled'.[50] The tenants of Cornashina pleaded that they were punished 'for the act of the cruel murderer that took away the life of their landlord' and that they were innocent of the deed by 'act or knowledge'. Whatever lenience was to be shown to the Cornashina tenants, Ross Mahon argued that those in Dooherty, where the murder occurred, 'deserve no consideration'.[51] However, he did offer not to evict those tenants if they gave up the culprits, and some tenants did pass information to him.[52]

In addition, these were probably the same people who had given a public display of support at the execution of Patrick Hasty and James Commins in July following their conviction of the murder of Major Mahon, something which the agent noted privately had caused the feeling of the people 'to be as bad as ever'.[53] In October, further eviction took place when Ross Mahon oversaw the throwing down of sixteen houses at Cloonscarie where 'the people in it were peculiarly bad and owed a great deal of rent'.[54]

By the year's end, the frequency of eviction on the Strokestown estate had prompted the *Roscommon Journal* to comment that the 'crusade against the tenantry is daily increasing'.[55] Over 250 ejectments in Strokestown had gone undefended, the editor observed:

> Depopulation is so general that it does not excite surprise or astonishment to hear of hundreds being daily turned to the ditches to famish . . . tenant and small farmer gone to a happier country . . . the poorer classes have either perished or are in the workhouse . . . thousands of acres have not a beast upon them.[56]

RESTORING ORDER

The clearances of the Famine years—intended to make estate management easier—had created as many problems as they solved for the agent. In the years immediately after the Famine, the tenants distrusted each other—and their subtenants—as much as the landlord and agent. The people were said to be 'at war everyday' with each other in 1854.[57] This 'war' owed much to the acquisition of land from which tenants had been ejected in the late 1840s,[58] and also to the process of enclosing and squaring land in which tenants were often 'trampled' by their neighbors.[59]

Against this background, Ross Mahon early resolved to lease sections of the estate to Scottish and English farmers.[60] In April 1849, he informed the landlord that Steward and Kincaid, another major agency, had made arrangements with Norfolk farmers to lease land on estates which they managed, and 'thence others will follow I am sure'.[61] Others too were advocating such a course of action at Strokestown. Later that year, Rev. Thomas Morton, the local Church of Ireland rector, informed Ross Mahon that 'The first thing I think will really [tend] to benefit this County must be an introduction of English or perhaps Scottish tenantry . . . I don't see where in this County tenants are to be got'.[62]

The tenantry, meanwhile, were prepared to oppose such measures.[63] There was a sense of foreboding when plans for leasing sections of the estate to 'outsiders' were announced.[64] Many clamored to be kept on the estate or at least allowed some patch of ground on which they might build a cabin.[65] In September 1848, William Mara had been put to work surveying the estate. In certain areas Mara was directed simply to ascertain who was left; that is who had survived the Famine and clearances. Those who survived were forced to adhere to new estate rules. Tenants were now to be fined for building a second house on their holding, and for subdividing, pairing crops and burning the land. Once again pressure was put to bear on middlemen to clear under tenants. For instance, William Fallon was informed that unless he cleared his numerous under tenants, he would be ejected himself.[66] In addition, the new rules also included stipulations regarding the character of tenants. Where people were found to be engaged in crime or immoral activity (prostitution was said to be rife on the estate) the punishment was to be 'thrown off the estate'.[67] Ross Mahon made some effort to deflect criticism. In August 1849, for example, he decreed that tenants would be ejected during the fine weather only. His actions toward the tenantry were, in his opinion, at all times legitimate—he gave them the opportunity to leave without having to undergo the distress and public embarrassment of having their house knocked. Those who knocked houses of their own accord were remunerated for doing so.[68]

If Ross Mahon was the architect of these policies, his bailiffs felt the wrath of the local population. Indeed, bailiffs were regularly assaulted while carrying out their duties. Michael Madden had his fingers so badly broken that the doctor advised that they be amputated.[69] Others received threatening letters, while rumors were rife with conspiracies to murder.[70] Efforts to 'improve' the estate were constantly disrupted by tenants, even those who had means to pay rent but very often refused to do so. In December 1848, for example, John Robinson distrained the lands of the Rev. Morton of Castlecoote, where arrears amounted to £205. The seizure comprised one bull, five cows, a two-year old heifer, an eight-yearling heifer, two bullocks, two calves, three horses, three cocks of hay, two stacks of wheat, two stacks of oats, three carts, one plough and two reins.[71] Few tenants, however, were as well off as Morton, and across the estate, they resisted efforts to distrain for rent. In particular, tenants now coupled their stock, making it difficult for bailiffs to drive their animals.[72]

In dealing with recalcitrant tenants, Ross Mahon looked to his sub-agent Thomas Roberts. While Ross Mahon was absent for long spells from Roscommon, Roberts was de facto 'lord and master', even residing in Strokestown House in the absence of the Pakenham Mahon family.[73] On occasion, Ross Mahon simply advised that Roberts should do 'as he saw fitting' regarding the estate probably because, as a local, he would have known those most 'deserving'.[74] Aiding Roberts was a team of bailiffs, 'hut tumblers' (or 'levellers') and watchers who provided forensic accounts of the movements and circumstances of tenants across the scattered Pakenham Mahon property. Despite the daily threat of attack, there was no shortage of local men willing to serve notices, throw down cabins and distrain crops and animals.[75] In an effort to better manage the estate, Roberts regularly inquired as to the practice of other land agents and professional land agencies. Martin Kelly, a bailiff, examined the working of the Dublin land agency Steward and Kincaid, on the Pakenham estate in County Westmeath, and noted that they are 'working hard at tenants' and 'making them pay fast'.[76] Kelly was remorseless in his treatment of the Mahon tenants and advocated the wholesale removal of tenants as they were in his opinion 'useless'.[77] Roberts's task was made easier by the constant stream of information provided by tenants about their neighbors. Watchers, or at least those anxious to inform the sub-agent of tenants' movements, included information on neighbors who possessed 'hard money' with which they purchased conacre, cattle and other household materials.[78] In December 1849, for example, Pat Gibbons informed the agent that his neighbor, one John Loughlin, had three stacks of oats in a neighbor's garden and had £5 cash despite his claim that he could not pay the rent.[79]

Ironically, such information reinforced Ross Mahon's desire to create a new tenantry at Strokestown. When the Scottish and English tenants did not materialize in the numbers originally envisaged, Ross Mahon continued to seek Protestant tenants, and local notables encouraged the agency in this regard. For instance, in the wake of the hotly contested elections of 1852, Thomas Roberts was warned by John Hamilton that:

> The priests are at their usual trade of denouncing and more particularly their fury is quite directed to the House of Strokestown. This ought to be a blessing to all Landlords not to encourage Popish tenants; get rid of them and you'll get rid of the priests.[80]

Hence, one finds a family given favor as they were 'good Protestants and have had many trials to struggle through of late years'.[81] Significantly, however, while Ross Mahon generally preferred Protestant tenants, he distrusted the Society of Friends.[82]

Illustrating the agent's power in deciding the fate of tenants was the treatment of the family of Michael Gardiner, who was implicated in the assassination of Major Mahon. In 1849, Ross Mahon decided that the family should be struck from the relief lists of all local committees, thus denying Gardiner's widowed mother access to food.[83] The decision prompted the widow to write to her son pleading with him to spare them of misery by providing information on the murder. Interestingly, as late as the 1940s the social memory of the incident was cited as proof of the rapacity of the Mahon family. The memory of such treatment probably fuelled the 'supposed' desecration of the tomb of Major Mahon by Gardiner when he was released from gaol in the early 1860s.[84]

CONCLUSION

That Ross Mahon was seen as a chief instigator of the clearance was obvious in the number and tone of threatening letters sent to him. In 1852, when blight reappeared in County Roscommon, the Constabulary warned him that although the parties involved in Ribbonism were fewer in number, they still hoped to cause trouble and 'are not all reconciled with you and Mr Roberts'.[85] On another occasion, the language and message was more subtle: 'As to Ross Mahon, the cries of the starved and desolated have reached heavens, after shooting him he is to be hanged and quartered unless he quits Ireland'.[86] Taking the threats seriously, Ross Mahon rarely visited the estate without a Constabulary escort and even then he armed himself with pistols. He had taken a severe stance and few tenants had been shown lenience once arrears had accumulated.

Many agents, and more particularly, land agencies, had little interest in the plight of tenants. Balancing the books was their primary concern. Indeed, some agents had little understanding of rural Ireland. Remarkably, as late as February 1852, Guinness and Mahon confided in Roberts that 'we really do not understand the conacre question'.[87] Ross Mahon managed the estate during a period of enormous change and he would later content himself that he had contributed to the establishment of 'law and order'.[88]

However, he failed to achieve all his objectives. Tenants continued to burn land and subdivision continued; indeed, in 1853, even 'the most respectable tenants' on the estate had under tenants.[89] Moreover, while the threat posed by secret societies decreased, it did not disappear.[90] In 1848, a report on 'colonization from Ireland' concluded that the removal of people from the Mahon estate and others (Spaight, Wandesforde and Wyndham) had resulted in 'increased productiveness, obedience to the law and general contentment', the assisted emigration scheme haunted both the agent and and the Pakenham Mahons. Indeed, even one hundred years after the event, in 1947, the family was at pains to present how they had always enjoyed convivial relations with their tenantry, although no mention was made of the events that occurred during the Great Famine.[91]

NOTES

1. I wish to thank the board of Westward Holdings for permission to consult the Strokestown Park Archive and for their continued support. Likewise, I am also grateful to Professor Terence Dooley, Cathal McCauley, Roisin Berry, Ciara Joyce and the board of the OPW/NUIM Archive and Research Centre at Castletown, County Kildare.
2. Pat McLaughlin to Henry Sandford Pakenham Mahon, 10 March 1849. The material quoted forms part of the Strokestown Park House Archive (SPHA).
3. Harrison to Henry Pakenham Mahon, 14 March 1848, SPHA.
4. Quoted in T.W. Moody, 'Irish History and Irish Mythology', *Hermathena*, 124 (1978), 18.
5. See, for example, *The Works of William Carleton*, 2 vols. (New York, 1880) vol. 1, 1112 and Margaret Chestnutt, *Studies in the Short Stories of William Carleton* (Göteborg, 1976), 112–13.
6. The agent as social and political actor has attracted little scholarly attention, but see Ciarán Reilly, *The Irish Land Agent, 1830–1860: The Case of King's* County (Dublin, 2014); Gerard Lyne, *The Lansdowne Estates in Kerry under the Agency of W.S. Trench 1849–72* (Dublin, 2001) and Desmond Norton, *Landlords, Tenants, Famine: The Business of an Irish Land Agency in the 1840s* (Dublin, 2005).
7. These included, for example, the investment of £2,000 in government stocks in February 1846, on which, see: NLI, Guinness and Mahon Letter Books, MS 32,014.
8. See Ciarán Reilly, *Strokestown and the Great Irish Famine* (Dublin, 2014).
9. *Report from the Commissioners of Inquiry into the Working of the Landlord and Tenant (Ireland) Act, and the Acts Amending Same,* 655 [C. 2779], HC 1881, xciii, 73. See also 'Bond from John Ross Mahon and Robert Rundell Guinness of South Frederick Street in the city of Dublin who promised to pay Denis Mahon of Strokestown House in County Roscommon the sum of £5000, 27 Oct. 1846' and 'Bond from Sir James Mahon of Castlegar, County Galway and John Ross Mahon of South Frederick Street in the city of Dublin, to Denis Mahon of Strokestown House in County Roscommon of the sum of £2000, 27 Oct. 1846', NLI, Pakenham Mahon Papers, MS 48,355/16 (hereafter PM Papers).
10. 'Rental of the Strokestown Estate, 1843', SPHA.
11. For more on the Ballykilcline estate, see Robert Scally, *The End of Hidden Ireland: Rebellion, Famine and Emigration* (New York, 1995) and Mary Lee Dunn, *Ballykilcline Rising: From Famine Ireland to Immigrant America* (Amherst, 2008).
12. George Knox to John Burke, 24 May 1846, NAI, Quit Rent Papers, Roscommon, 1846.
13. Denis Mahon to John Ross Mahon, 21 November 1846, PM Papers, MS 10,102/1.
14. Ibid.
15. John Ross Mahon to Denis Mahon, 21 March 1847, SPHA.
16. Ibid.

17. Quoted in Scally, *The End of Hidden Ireland*, 59.
18. See Gerard Moran, *Sending Out Ireland's Poor: Assisted Emigration to North America in the Nineteenth Century* (Dublin, 2004), 36–38.
19. David Fitzpatrick, 'Emigration, 1801–70', in W. E. Vaughan, ed., *A New History of Ireland, V: Ireland under the Union, I, 1801–70* (Oxford, 1989), 593.
20. Denis Mahon to John Ross Mahon, 2 April 1847, PM Papers, MS 10,102 (1).
21. Newspapers such as the *Roscommon Journal* regularly carried news of the 'Gerrardizing' of the Galway tenantry. In County Clare, Wyndham's eviction policy also received bad press.
22. Denis Mahon to John Ross Mahon, 11 June 1847, PM Papers, MS 10,102 (1).
23. Denis Mahon to John Ross Mahon, 14 April 1847, PM Papers, MS 10,102 (1).
24. 'Memoranda Dealing with Tenancies 1796–1841', NLI, Fitzwilliam Papers, MS 4,948.
25. *Evidence taken before Her Majesty's Commissioners of Inquiry into the State of the Law and Practice in Respect to the Occupation of Land in Ireland, Part III*, HC 1845 (657), xxi, 1, 542.
26. 'Census Recorded on Major Mahon's Estate by the Strokestown Rental Office, Recording Townlands, Parish, Families, and Number of Persons or Individuals 21 March, 1847', SPHA.
27. 'Memorandum of the Management of the Strokestown estate by Ross Mahon Esq. in his First Year as Agent for the late Major Mahon, 8 Nov. 1847', PM Papers, n.558, 928.
28. 'Major Denis Mahon's Emigration Account 1847', PM Papers, MS 10,138.
29. 'Major Mahon's Memorandum of Arrangements with Tenants March 30–6 April 1847, no. 2', SPHA.
30. *Roscommon Journal*, 3 July 1847.
31. John Ross Mahon to Denis Mahon, 23 July 1847, PM Papers, MS 10,102 (1).
32. 'Memorandum of the Management of the Strokestown Estate', PM Papers, n.558, 928.
33. Denis Mahon to John Robinson, 14 June 1847, PM Papers, MS 10,102 (1).
34. John Ross Mahon to HSP Mahon, 18 February 1848, SPHA.
35. Denis Mahon to John Ross Mahon, 11 June 1847, PM Papers, MS 10,102 (1).
36. Denis Mahon to John Ross Mahon, 21 September 1847, PM Papers, 10,102 (1).
37. See, for example, Ciarán Reilly, 'A Middleman in the 1840s: Charles Carey and the Leinster Estate', in Patrick Cosgrove, Karol Mullaney-Dignam and Terence Dooley, eds., *The Rise and Fall of an Irish Aristocratic Family: The FitzGerald's of Kildare* (Dublin, 2014), 178–87.
38. *Toronto Globe*, 4 August 1847.
39. Quoted in Stephen Campbell, *The Great Irish Famine: Words and Images from the Famine Museum* (Dublin, 1994), 41.
40. 'Memorandum on the Management of the Strokestown Estate by John Ross Mahon in his First Year as Agent for the Late Major Mahon, Nov. 8, 1847', PM Papers, n.558, p.928.
41. Ibid.
42. Denis Mahon to John Ross Mahon, 20 October 1847, PM Papers, MS 10,102 (1).
43. For more on the killing of Mahon, see Patrick Vesey, *The Murder of Major Mahon, Strokestown, County Roscommon 1847* (Dublin, 2008) and Peter Duffy, *The Killing of Major Denis Mahon: A Mystery of Old Ireland* (Boston, 2007).
44. For the controversy after the killing, see Donal Kerr, *'A Nation of Beggars': Priests, People, and Politics in Famine Ireland, 1846–1852* (London, 1998), 93–96.
45. *Times*, 23 February 1848.
46. *Freemans Journal*, 29 April 1848.

47. David Nally, *Human Encumbrances: Political Violence and the Great Irish Famine* (Notre Dame, 2011), 161–62.
48. John Ross Mahon to Marcus McCausland, 8 December 1847, Guinness and Mahon Letter Books, MS 32,019 (602–03).
49. John Ross Mahon to Henry Sandford Pakenham Mahon, 3 August 1848, PM Papers, MS 10,103 (5).
50. See John Ross Mahon to Thomas Roberts, 20 January 1848, Guinness and Mahon Letter Books, MS 32,019 (399); John Ross Mahon to Marcus McCausland, 18 January 1848, Guinness and Mahon Letter Books, MS 32,019 (316–17).
51. John Ross Mahon to Mrs Mahon, 24 June 1848, Guinness and Mahon Letter Books, MS 32,019 (433).
52. John Ross Mahon to Thomas Roberts, 7 February 1848, Guinness and Mahon Letter Books, MS 32,019 (931).
53. John Ross Mahon to Thomas Roberts, 12 August 1848, SPHA.
54. John Ross Mahon to Henry Sandford Pakenham Mahon, 16 October 1848, SPHA.
55. *Roscommon Journal*, 13 January 1849.
56. See, for example, Michael Kelly to Henry Sandford Pakenham Mahon, 14 February 1848, SPHA.
57. Thomas Conry to Thomas Roberts, 20 April 1854, SPHA.
58. See, for example, Michael Kelly to Henry Sandford Pakenham Mahon, 14 February 1848, SPHA.
59. James Mahoney to Henry Sandford Pakenham Mahon, 10 July 1848, SPHA.
60. See, for example, Guinness and Mahon to Thomas Roberts, 7 October 1853, SPHA.
61. John Ross Mahon to Henry Sandford Pakenham Mahon, 1 April 1849, SPHA.
62. Rev. Joseph Morton to John Ross Mahon, 2 October 1849, SPHA.
63. Lawrence Kelly to John Ross Mahon, 4 January 1848, SPHA.
64. See, for example, *Liverpool Mercury*, 27 February 1849.
65. See, for example, Pat Wallace to John Ross Mahon, 7 August 1847, SPHA.
66. Martin Kelly to Thomas Roberts, 8 December 1852, SPHA.
67. Guinness and Mahon to Thomas Roberts, 14 April 1852; see also Richard Cowen to Thomas Roberts, 8 July 1852, SPHA.
68. See, for example, 'List of Persons in the Following Townlands from whom Possession was Taken on the 20, 21, 23 September 1848 . . . ', SPHA.
69. Michael Madden to Thomas Roberts, 1 June 1849, SPHA.
70. 'Threatening Letter Sent to John Robinson, Bailiff on the Strokestown Estate', 5 February 1848, SPHA.
71. 'Distress Notice Issued on the Lands of Rev. Morton, Castlecoote, December 1848', SPHA.
72. Daniel Irwin to Thomas Roberts, 6 July 1849, SPHA.
73. After the killing of her father in November 1847, Grace Catherine Pakenham Mahon never returned to Strokestown Park to live.
74. See, for example, the petition of Widow Thomas O'Brien to Henry Sandford Pakenham Mahon, 18 September 1848, SPHA.
75. John Ross Mahon to Thomas Roberts, 23 December 1847, Guinness and Mahon Letter Books, MS 32,019 (9).
76. Martin Kelly to Thomas Roberts, 19 September 1848, SPHA.
77. Martin Kelly to Thomas Roberts, 8 December 1852, SPHA.
78. John McCann to Thomas Roberts, 4 September 1848, SPHA.
79. Pat Gibbons to John Ross Mahon, 13 December 1849, SPHA.
80. John Hamilton, Croswaithe Terrace, Kingstown to Thomas Roberts, 22 July 1852, SPHA.

81. R. Lloyd to John Ross Mahon, 10 May 1853, SPHA.
82. Guinness and Mahon to Henry Sandford Pakenham Mahon, 21 October 1848, SPHA.
83. Copy of letter from Mrs Gardiner to her son, Michael, 22 March 1849, SPHA.
84. 'Statement of Patrick Mullolly, Kiltrustan, Strokestown, County Roscommon', Bureau of Military History, Witness Statement 1,087.
85. Head Constable of the Police, Drumsna, County Roscommon to Thomas Roberts, July 1852, SPHA.
86. *Daily News*, 24 November 1847.
87. Guinness and Mahon to Thomas Roberts, 5 February 1852, SPHA.
88. *Report of Her Majesty's Commissioners of Inquiry into the Working of the Landlord and Tenant (Ireland) Act, 1870, and the Acts Amending the Same*, 1881 [C.2779] [C.2779–I] [C.2779–II] [C.2779–III], 657–58.
89. James Connolly to Thomas Roberts, 22 March 1853, SPHA.
90. See, for example, Nassau Senior, *Journals, Conversations and Essays relating to Ireland*, 2 vols. (London, 1868), vol. 2, 40–43.
91. Quoted in Nally, *Human Encumbrances*, 209. See also 'Notes Prepared for the Coming of Age Speech of Nicholas Hales Pakenham Mahon, 1947', SPHA.

7 'Bastard Ribbonism'

The Molly Maguires, the Uneven Failure of Entitlement and the Politics of Post-Famine Adjustment

Breandán Mac Suibhne

On one of the first days of April 1856, a letter signed 'Patrick McGlynn, National Teacher, Beigha [*sic*],[1] Ardara', arrived for Daniel J. Cruise, stipendiary magistrate, at Wood Lodge, a sizeable countryhouse near the one-street village of Mountcharles, County Donegal.[2] Composed in a fluent hand on everyday writing paper, and dated 31 March, the letter made a remarkable offer: if the magistrate would keep his identity a secret and ensure that he was 'rewarded', the writer would enable him to take members of an illegal combination in the act of commiting a 'depredation', that is, an offense routinely classified by the authorities as an 'outrage'.

> I dare say you are aware of the distracted state of this country occasioned by a party called Molly Maguires.
>
> I write to inform you that I (by means which I shall not divulge) have a means of ascertaining their movements and that I will inform either to you or the police when I become certain that they shall attack a house or some other depredation of the kind. The only means that I see of stopping the career of these villains is by taking them in the act which I think will not only deter the remainder from such acts in future but restore peace to the country.
>
> Knowing that their connexions are very extensive and that my life would be in imminent danger I shall require to receive the reward which you shall think reasonable because the information shall cost me both trouble and expense besides the risk of being suspected is great.
>
> But I shall require from you that not only shall this communication be kept secret but that you shall never divulge my name as in any way connected with any proceedings relating to them. I will if rewarded for the risk obtain such information for the authorities as will make them aware when they shall commit the next depredation and let them capture them in the act but that is all.
>
> I will write to you but I must be certain that it shall never be known who gave the information. Neither will I tell who informed me.
>
> Upon receiving an answer to this I will do all I can to put a stop to their proceedings. Please do not speak to me if you happen to see me in

Ardara nor do not make any enquiries of any person. Should you wish to speak [to] me I will see you at any place you please.

I am sorry for writing to such a length.[3]

The 'distracted state of the county' was indeed well known to Cruise, and so too were the Molly Maguires. Since the mid-1840s, 'Molly Maguires' had become a sobriquet for members of the Ribbon Society, an oath-bound secret society, which, from the 1810s, had built a lodge network across much of the northern half of Ireland, physically confronting the Orange Order, and articulating Catholic nationalist ambition. Or to be more precise, from about 1844, 'Molly Maguires' had been most enthusiastically adopted as a moniker by Ribbonmen in rural areas of West Ulster and North Connacht, among them districts with no history of Ribbon activity, and the appearance of the name was coincident not only with a geographic expansion of the Society, but also with a shift in its social composition and the character of its activities, both of which now became more agrarian.[4]

Various stories have been told to explain the name. It was that of a widow evicted from her farm in Antrim, or that of a woman in whose house Ribbonmen met, or, intriguingly, as it hints at internal conflict over a shift in objectives, it was the name of a 'crazy old woman' in Fermanagh who imagined she commanded a great army, and, after a schism in the Ribbon Society, it had been given in derision to one group by their rivals.[5] But whatever its origin, the preferred form uttered in predominantly Irish-speaking West Donegal was a double entendre that amplified menace. *Clann Mhailí*, Molly's Children, sounds like *clann mhallaithe*, cursed, infernal clan.[6]

On his appointment to Donegal in 1852, Cruise had quickly formed the opinion that the Ribbon Society (aka Molly Maguires) was the 'organized system' behind a wave of 'outrages' in the Glenties–Ardara area in the southwest of the county, the very district from which this letter now purported to have come. Those 'outrages' included attacks on persons and property, midnight arms raids, and intimidation by threatening letters and notices. For instance, at 11.00 p.m. on 2 March 1852, some 40 armed men wearing shirts over their clothes, and led by a man in a blue frock or cloak, with a muffler about his ears, marched through the mountain hamlet of Doohary. Here, John Molloy, standing in his doorway, asked them if they were mummers, but he received no answer. Proceeding north along the bank of the Gweebarra, these men fired a shot to signal to a party on the other side and received a shot in reply. Later that night, there were raids on the houses of Maurice Cannon of Derrynacarrow Far, and Patrick McKelvey and Thomas Duffy of Befflaght. All three were water bailiffs, living in a remote district near the source of the salmon-rich river. Befflaght, close to Lough Barra, was particularly difficult to approach, no road then running north from Doohary to Glendowan. The raiders took guns, powder and shot, but they did no harm to the bailiffs themselves. Indeed, in Cannon's house, they only spoke one word, which he could not or would not repeat.

None of the bailiffs reported the raids, and it was five days before the Constabulary picked up a rumor of what had happened. That same month, some 20 armed men, who had made no effort to disguise themselves, called at night at the house of Patrick McNeilis, a comfortable farmer in Sandfield, a townland bordering Beagh. They fired several shots inside the house and proceeded to dictate the price at which he was to sell potatoes. Leaving Sandfield, this group went some two miles to Ballykillduff, where they broke into the house of another farmer, Francis Shovlin, who they 'slightly carded', that is, scraped his body with paddles embedded with small nails that were used to comb wool. Announcing themselves as 'the Molly Maguires' and 'Sons of Liberty', they here too fired shots inside the house and stipulated the price at which potatoes were to be sold.[7] On some such occasions, the raiders represented themselves as 'Molly's Sons', sent by their mother, to do justice. On others, a man attired as a woman was the leader, who, introducing 'herself' as Molly Maguire, demanded redress for wrongs inflicted on 'her' children.[8] That Doohary-man, therefore, might be forgiven for mistaking the Mollies for mummers, for there was something of the theatricality of mumming (and wake games) in their comportment. But a hard man dressed as a widow conveyed menace never conjured by 'Here comes [*sic*] I Jack Straw, / such a man you never saw'. Bursting into a dark house in the dead of night, 'Molly Maguire' upturned all social and sexual hierarchies. 'Her' very appearance cried havoc.[9]

The raids on the farmers in Sandfield and Ballykillduff accord with the Mollies' self-representation as protectors of the rural poor. The night visits paid the water bailiffs are more complicated, for there had been a dispute between landlords over the fishery, and there had also been contention when the leader of an extensive faction, who gave employment to bailiffs and fishermen, did not have his lease on a section of it renewed. And the bailiffs were far from wealthy: the raiders had no difficulty entering Cannon's house, as 'the door was only laid to, and off the hinges'.[10] At the same time, both the raids on the farmers and those on the bailiffs—like most other incidents in which the Mollies were involved in West Donegal—are difficult to relate to the known 'political' objectives of the Ribbon Society. In his first months in Donegal, Cruise himself expressed the view that it was a group 'without any fixed object but which can at once be used for any purpose'.[11] In this assessment, he was echoing the opinions of local landlords who, conscious of the wider association of the Society with ethno-religious contention and some form of nationalism, felt it necessary to impress on officialdom that it was, in fact, the 'organized system' which they faced. 'There is a kind of bastard rib[b]onism prevalent in the district', John Hamilton, owner of a small estate at Fintown, wrote early the following year, 'which has apparently for its object rather association for outrage & plunder with mutual pledges of aid & support, than any thing decidedly of a political or religious character'.[12] It was the Ribbon Society, officials were being told, but not as they knew it; things were different in Donegal. And yet those officials had been receiving similar reports from other districts for some years, and they had a very clear sense that, with the expansion of the Society in the mid-1840s, it had changed.

Eager to make his mark in Donegal, Cruise had convened a meeting of magistrates in Glenties on 5 February 1853 that successfully petitioned for the Rosses, Glenties (Inniskeel) and Ardara (Killybegs Lower) to be proclaimed under the Crime and Outrage (Ireland) Act (1847), which severely restricted the right to bear arms.[13] Under the proclamation, some 66 guns, 2 blunderbusses, 6 pistols, 8 swords, 76 bayonets, 42 barrels and 1 stock were surrendered at Ardara barracks by 2 April. Most of the guns were probably old yeomanry weapons and fowling pieces held by otherwise law-abiding farmers, many of whom were Protestant and 'loyal', but their surrender prevented them falling into the hands of the Mollies. An additional 17 guns and 2 pistols were given up in Glenties, 12 guns in Lettermacaward, 34 guns and 5 pistols in Dungloe, and 3 guns and 2 pistols in Bunbeg.[14] And yet the 'outrages' had continued unabated, broiling through the mid-1850s.[15]

These troubles, mainly around Ardara, Glenties and Lettermacaward, were part of a Famine-raised surge in 'outrage' in County Donegal as whole, and much of it too was attributed by the authorities to the machinations of the Ribbon Society. This countywide surge was nationally significant. For instance, the 'establishment' (allocation) of Constabulary for the county was 176, but there were 293 constables serving there in 1852, and 360 by summer 1853, a doubling of the force brought about by the repeated drafting of reinforcements to suppress disturbances.[16] Likewise, in 1853–55, the Constabulary offered more rewards for information on 'outrages' in Donegal than in most other counties. In fact, only in Tipperary, a county synonomous with agrarian 'outrage', was more reward money offered in the same period; and the amount offered in Donegal is even more striking given that many other counties were more populous; see Table 7.1.[17] Approaching social unrest, by no means unhelpfully, from the perspective of the Constabulary, the historian W. E. Vaughan observes that Donegal was 'one of the worst counties in the country for agrarian crime of all kinds' in the decade after the Famine: 'if the thirty-two counties are ranked according to frequency of agrarian crime, Donegal was eighth in the decade 1851–60'.[18]

Still, within this 'disturbed' county, the southwest was a particular trouble spot, and, by the mid-1850s, it was a recalcitrant center of Ribbon activity.[19] In late 1855, little over four months before Cruise's receipt of the unexpected letter with its remarkable offer, Dublin Castle had systematically assessed the national, regional and local state of 'lawless and illegal combinations', a category that included the Ribbon Society.[20] From this trawl of intelligence, Duncan McGregor, the Inspector General of Constabulary, concluded that the organization remained in existence, with greater or lesser activity, in the 'whole of Ulster, the northern half of Leinster and the eastern part of Connaught and of the County Clare', but, in general, emigration, an improving economy and better policing had caused it to go into decline: 'on the whole

Table 7.1 Constabulary rewards offered in Ireland, 1853–55

County	Number offered	Sum (£) offered	Population, 1851	Amount per capita
King's	78	1,495	112,076	1.33
Donegal	143	2,930	255,158	1.15
Longford	49	935	82,348	1.14
Leitrim	71	1,180	111,897	1.05
Tipperary	161	3,285	331,567	0.99
Westmeath	46	1,060	111,407	0.95
Meath	61	1,247	140,748	0.89
Carlow	29	600	68,078	0.88
Cavan	79	1,370	174,064	0.79
Kildare	36	685	95,723	0.72
Roscommon	61	1,110	173,436	0.64
Londonderry	60	1,120	192,022	0.58
Mayo	94	1,550	274,499	0.56
Galway	102	1,745	321,684	0.54
Louth	24	580	107,662	0.54
Sligo	40	690	128,515	0.54
Down	84	1,650	320,817	0.51
Clare	63	1,030	212,440	0.48
Fermanagh	30	560	116,047	0.48
Kilkenny	38	755	158,748	0.48
Waterford	43	775	164,035	0.47
Limerick	62	1,165	262,132	0.44
Monaghan	28	625	141,823	0.44
Queen's	34	485	111,664	0.43
Wexford	33	580	180,158	0.32
Armagh	26	585	196,084	0.30
Tyrone	41	655	255,661	0.26
Cork	78	1,430	649,308	0.22
Kerry	27	490	238,254	0.21
Antrim	37	733	359,934	0.20
Wicklow	12	185	98,979	0.19
Dublin	9	110	405,147	0.03

Source: 'Total Number of Rewards Offered and Paid in the Years, 1853, 1854, and 1855', CSORP 1856/17416.

the system is in less active operation now than formerly; its decline being chiefly referable to the absence of some of its promoters, the increased value of agricultural produce, the higher rate of the wages of labour and in some localities, the vigorous application of the Crime & Outrage Act, and the increase of Police'. Registering the increasingly agrarian focus of the Society, and, perhaps, some members' interest in legal and respectable modes of action, McGregor also observed that 'in some parts a better class of persons are being enrolled: the *name* of Ribbonism being abandoned, and that of the "Land System" being substituted; while the members are designated not Ribbonmen but "system men" '.[21]

The situation of the Ribbon Society in Donegal was broadly similar. 'Its spirit [and] system exist all over this county altho' the offences consequent thereon have of late diminished', the County Inspector reported, giving the increase in the number of constables, the suppression of shebeen houses and a drive against the illicit distillation of spirits—the production of *poitín*—as additional factors in its decline. In short, his head constables considered the Society to exist but to be 'in abeyance' in five of the eight Constabulary districts in the county. The exceptions included two northeastern districts, both of which had long been heavily involved in the Ribbon-dominated *poitín* trade, namely, the Carndonagh District (North Inishowen), where the report was inconclusive on account of 'greater secrecy' being observed, and the Ramelton District (Fanad and Downings), where the Constabulary thought it was 'rather on the increase among the lower class of the Roman Catholic population'. The third was the Glenties District (Crolly–Ardara), and here, the head constable worried 'its evil consequences are to be apprehended during the winter'.[22]

•

Against the background of this decade-long movement of Ribbon/Molly Maguire 'outrage', the letter that Daniel Cruise received in early April 1856, if it proved authentic, would be an opportunity for an ambitious man to make a mark. And Cruise was ambitious. A Catholic from a minor gentry family in Galway and Roscommon, he had been part of the first batch of 'stipendiary magistrates', that is, paid officials whom, from the mid-1830s, Dublin Castle had deployed to work with the Constabulary in the administration of law and order, a sudden, effective and often resented superseding of landlords and agents who had voluntarily served as justices of the peace.[23] Although appointed a stipendiary in 1837, Cruise's hopes of finding a higher niche—perhaps the coveted post of county solicitor—had yet to be realized.[24] He now quickly established the authenticity of the signature on the letter by consulting the files of the Commissioners of National Education in Dublin, and proceeded to open communication with Patrick McGlynn, the 24-year-old master of Beagh School. Based on information received from the master, the Constabulary made four attempts to ambush Molly Maguires in the act of committing an 'outrage'. All these attempts failed, as the Mollies did not assemble at the times and places which McGlynn had indicated. At length, in June, Cruise lost patience and threatened him with prosecution unless he gave him a list of Ribbonmen. McGlynn now revealed himself to be a Ribbonman/Molly Maguire (he used the words interchangeably), and proceeded to finger over two dozen members of the Society, mainly around Ardara, but also in Glenties and Fintown, Dungloe, Carrick and Killybegs, that is, spread across five parishes in West Donegal. Among them were men reputed to be not just members but masters of lodges, and also the delegate for West Donegal to the county committee of the Ribbon Society. These men were arrested, and, at the county assizes in March 1857, five of them were convicted of 'having been members in an illegal confederacy . . . known by the name of Ribbonism'. However, their convictions, on the uncorroborated evidence of an accomplice, were controversial in legal circles. Consequently, an arrangement was reached between Cruise and the parish priest of Glenties whereby, at the summer assizes in 1857, other men who had been named by McGlynn pleaded guilty to membership of the Ribbon Society and agreed to take the oath of allegiance. All charges against them were then dropped, and they were bound over to the keep the peace, and released on their own bail.[25] And the government sent the schoolmaster, his wife and two children to Australia.

Although not apparent when McGlynn turned informer in 1856, the movement of 'outrage' that had begun in southwest Donegal in the Famine was as good as over: there would be a spasm of activity in the northwest of the county in 1856–58, when there was a wave of Molly-initiated anti-grazier activity in Gweedore, but, elsewhere in West Donegal, trouble was abating.[26] The story of the schoolmaster and the men whom he betrayed, and the reason he betrayed them, will be told elsewhere and at length. Here, the concern is that Famine-raised wave of Molly 'outrages', its origins and outcomes, the meaning and the memory of it. More specifically, it is the *end* of 'outrage', that is, the shifting objectives of those who engaged in it, and also how, as hunger faded and disease abated, tensions emerged in the Ribbon Society when one element sought to curtail such activity, while another sought, unsuccessfully, to expand it. And in that contention, when the opportunities of post-Famine society were coming into view for some, one glimpses the end, or at least an ebbing, of outrage—in the everyday sense of moral indignation—at the fate of the rural poor.

MOLLY MAGUIRE IN WEST DONEGAL, 1845–55

Molly Maguire's ubiquity in West Donegal in the early to mid-1850s would not have been predicted a decade earlier, for, while well organized in eastern parts of the county since the 1810s, the Ribbon Society had no presence at all in western districts before 1845.[27] That distribution was consistent with ethno-religious politics having caused the rise of the Ribbon Society in the first place. In the east of the county, there was a substantial Protestant population, and there was spasmodic friction between lower-class Protestants and Catholics, most especially in Letterkenny–Milford–Fanad and in Donegal Town–Pettigo–Ballyshannon. In contrast, West Donegal was predominantly Catholic, with only small pockets of Methodists and Churchmen. Certainly, colonial realities were never far from view. If few in numbers, Protestants—in Irish, *Gaill* (foreigners) or *Albanaigh* (Scotsmen)—were visibly advantaged, most families holding more and better land than most of their Catholic neighbors, and their religion and preferred language were those of the state. All the land, meanwhile, was owned by Protestant gentlemen, and only they and their agents got appointed to the grand jury (local government) and commission of the peace (bench). In Irish-language song and story, the *Gaeil* (lit. Gaels, fig. Catholics) gave voice to an abiding feeling of oppression. For instance, a lament composed by Eoghan Óg Mac Niallais (*fl.* 1800–20) of Ardara for Donnchadh Ó Baoill—a member of the family that, before the conquest, had dominated the district—asked rhetorically if it were not better for him that he was dead and buried with his forefathers in Inis Caoil than *faoi chosa Gall, faraor, ag díol cíos leo* (under foreigners' feet, alas, paying rent to them).[28] Still, communal relations were, by and large, good, each side content to let sleeping dogs lie. '[T]here is no bad Party Spirit in it', James Pearson, a Methodist schoolteacher wrote of the Ardara area, in a letter sent to Dublin Castle soliciting relief in a famine in the mid-1830s; 'we can, and do, go in and out with and render to each other all the offices of friendship and good neighbourhood'.[29] Indeed, a half-century earlier, in 1786, when the first Wesleyan preacher arrived in Ardara, and, for want of a choice, took a room in a public house, he found that the two men drinking in the bar were the Catholic priest and Protestant minister. Having established the purpose of his visit—they had guessed he was either a commerical traveler or a gauger (revenue official)—the priest told the young evangelist that he had come to the wrong place: 'You are not wanted here. My friend, the rector, looks after his people, I look after mine, and we get on quietly and nicely together! No one else is wanted'.[30]

By then, the descendants of the pre-conquest élite, if conscious of what had been lost in the shipwreck of the seventeenth century, had long since reconciled themselves to the new captains. Security of tenure and grand jury road contracts, employment as bailiffs and encouragement in business ventures—not least, the establishment of inns from the mid-1700s—and occasional petty indulgences had coopted key families. Many of those families were connected to Dálaigh na Glaisí, the O'Donnells of Glashagh and Ballinamore, the most important—and most self-important—branch of the old ruling family left in West Ulster. Ruairí Rua Ó Dónaill (1763–1841) rode to hounds with the county gentry and got himself made 'sub-constable of the barony of Boylagh', a post that brought a whiff of power sufficient to puff his *mórtas Dálaigh* (O'Donnell pride), and also a stipend that gave an otherwise middling farmer means to live beyond. In short, the O'Donnells of Glashagh and their connections further west—the McDevitts, McAloons and Dunlevys of Glenties, O'Donnells of Letterilly, Craigs of Kilclooney and Maloneys of Ardara—had come through the eighteenth century helping to maintain order, and the long involvement of such notables with the establishment militated against trouble at a lower level with what was, locally, a vastly outnumbered Protestant community. Moreover, if West Donegal Protestants generally were advantaged, they were by no means all better off than these well-to-do Catholics, and, while their deference to the landlords was less ambiguous than that of those Catholics, they were certainly not incapable of sympathy for people of a different religion. An incident early in the Famine stands out. In May 1846, when hunger was beginning to bite, three Dublin boats put into the Church Pool at Narin to purchase potatoes at high prices. 'Countrypeople' assembled in great numbers, and, over several days, crowds attacked and beat farmers carting potatoes to load at Portnoo, and they stoned the boatmen and coastguards who were deployed to protect their vessels; indeed, an attempt was made to scuttle one of the boats by cutting its cable. One of the leaders was a man named Scott, either a Protestant or from a Protestant background, who wrested a pistol from a coastguard, and there is no reason to suppose that Catholics, like the McNeilises of Sandfield and Shovlins of Ballykillduff, raided by the Mollies six years later, were not among the potato sellers.[31]

Another incident earlier in spring 1846, in nearby Summy, that had its roots in brooding sectarian animosity paradoxically also marked the limits of such feeling. That February, the corpse of 70-year-old Sammy Crummer, a Protestant, was recovered from a lake. The investigating magistrate exaggerated when he reported that the corpse—wrapped in a heavy iron chain that was attached to a stone—exhibited 'an appearance of atrocious mutilation, which perhaps the records of crime do not exceed'. Still, the old man had met a brutal end. His chest, all his right ribs and jaw were broken, and his mouth cut, as if by a knife, to his chin. His skull had also been fractured, causing his brains to protrude, and there were cuts and contusions all over his face and body. Crummer had lived with his only son, also Samuel, to whom he had transferred half the family farm when he married. However, when the young man's wife died, and he had converted to Catholicism to marry their servant girl—'greatly to the annoyance and against the consent of all his friends'—the old man had then resolved to leave the other half of the farm to his grandchildren by the first marriage. The couple were early suspected by the friends of the murdered man, who they claimed was often heard to say that his son and daughter-in-law had threatened him, telling him 'the lake would be a bed for one of them yet'. They were soon arrested, and tried and convicted of murder in 1847. Peggy Crummer, whose pregnancy had caused the case to be postponed, was transported to Tasmania. Her husband, 'a stolid, illiterate man', protesting his innocence and alleging that 'some members of his family' were the perpetrators, was to be the only person hanged in Donegal in the Famine. 'Gentleman and ladies', Crummer said from the gallows in Lifford, 'I am going to inform you that I am about to die, and I wish to tell you that I am innocent, and that I never lifted hand or foot to my poor father, nor would I do it, but [name supposedly not heard by the newspaper reporter] of Ardara swore my life away for a little money these hard times. I leave my blessing to my children and all friends, and I forgive all as I hope to get forgiveness myself'.[32]

•

It was during 'these hard times' that the Molly Maguires established themselves in West Donegal, where hitherto the Ribbon Society had been known only by repute.[33] In March 1845, coincidentally the month that people 'kibbed' (planted) their doomed potatoes, Benjamin Holmes, a resident magistrate based in Glenties, heard from a colleague responsible for the north of the county that Ribbon 'delegates' had entered Donegal for the purpose of promoting the Society. Holmes himself initially found no evidence to corroborate this information, and he was inclined to dismiss it. Certainly, around Glenties, he wrote, there was nothing 'indicative of combination or political secrecy on behalf of the People'. But in Mountcharles, a police constable gave him a curious report. He had heard from a 'highly respectable Roman Catholic gentleman', he said, that at mass in Frosses on Sunday 23 February, Rev. Daniel Spence had

> read to his flock the Ribbon Oath and other documents which had been put into his hand by a person who did not wish the dissemination of those principles, that five [*sic*] delegates had come into the parish—one from Donegal, one from Ballyshannon, one from Ballintra, one from Pettigo, one from Ballybofey, and one from Strabane—to spread Ribbonism. He warned his hearers against joining the Society as 'it would be the means of putting a stop to Repeal', and cautioned them to keep private what he had said to them.[34]

The curate and then the constable—and now the stipendiary magistrate and Dublin Castle—had picked up on an effort by what, in Donegal, had been an eastern and urban-centered grouping to reorganize existing lodges and to establish new ones. That summer, 'Molly Maguire' started appearing on threatening notices in the old Ribbon heartlands, around Ballyshannon, Ballintra, Ballybofey and Stranorlar, being particularly common in disputes about land. For instance, on the night of 12 July, a landlord, William Young of Mounthall, Killygordon, had a notice posted under his door, and found another tied to its knocker, both giving him three weeks to get rid of his land steward, and the steward himself received a similar ultimatum, telling him to quit, or Molly would be back 'for his head'.[35] Further south, near Ballyshannon, James Cassidy, a big farmer (and Catholic) who had rented a farm in dispute in Coolcolly, received at least two such letters, one warning him not to evict a subtenant, and another instructing him to dismiss a girl who, in defiance of notices posted through the town telling people not to labor for him, had taken the job of watching his crops:

> James Cassidy if you dont send away this Raskil of a girl that you are in keeping for corrupting, Badness and rascality. This is the second time

> I sent you notice be not under a Mistake if you dont adhere to my Precepts and send away this adulterating witch from your place remember you shortly will reap the benefit—I dont mean to make remarks about this evil carracter or about many other affairs you need not think you have police or soldiers at your back for if you and her was locked in a chest i'll find you out. . . .
>
> Molly Maguire and Sons . . .[36]

If the moniker was new to Donegal in 1845, the posting of such items was well established in the repertoire of popular political action.[37] Since the late eighteenth century, threatening letters and notices, sometimes illustrated with crude sketches of guns or gallows, coffins or graves, had been received by landlords, agents and bailiffs in dispute with tenants about rents, by farmers paying low wages to laborers, by forestallers and shopkeepers deemed to be overcharging for goods and by rectors and tithe proctors, gaugers and cess collectors. In times of political strife, magistrates, yeomen and army officers had received them too. Consequently, some local landowners had been nonchalant about 'Molly Maguire', discountenancing the idea that the use of the name had anything to do with the Ribbon Society proper. One told Holmes that 'the name is made use of by residents who may have any sort of prejudice against persons'.[38] However, some threats were made good: Young's steward was attacked, and six large stacks of Cassidy's wheat and oats (valued at near £25) were destroyed.[39] And while, in the spring of 1845, Holmes himself had not countenanced the prospect of the Society organizing in West Donegal, he shortly got a hint that something was afoot there when, at the harvest fair in Glenties, he purchased *Wonderful Prophecy*. A broadsheet printed in Belfast, it foretold an Anglo-American war, the downfall of England and Ireland's 'divided sons' uniting. It was apparently 'much sought after at all the fairs' that autumn.[40] By the spring of 1846, Molly Maguire was very definitely in Glenties. In mid-February, John McIlheny of Strasallagh found a notice attached to his cow house, threatening to card him—the type of punishment inflicted on the potato-dealer Francis Shovlin of Ballykillduff a few years later. In this instance, it was rumored that McIlheny was 'not acting equitably toward his son who had been married a year or two, and that the son might have had the notice written and posted to bring the father to a fair settlement':

> Take Notice
>
> John McElhenny, get the affair between yourself and your son settle in a short time, dont sleep on it or you will have a party of the Molly McGuire some night about your house that will scratch your backs my honest old friend, the journey is to far for my children to go to settle the

> affairs between you and your son. I dont like to take my oath, but by the City of Dublin if you do not I will give you a hand in the case
>
> Molly McGuire[41]

Over the next few years, the conceit of Molly's sons being brought a long distance to see justice done became common in West Donegal; indeed, as early as 1848, the authorities believed there were several Ribbon lodges in the wider Killybegs area, and that their members were 'well supplied with arms'.[42] Now, across the county, in the dimly lit backrooms of public houses and shops, and in barns, woods and fields, young men were going down on their knees, and, by repeating an oath read by a lodge master, they were being 'made' Ribbonmen:

> I declare and promise in the name of St. Patrick, Patron of this Kingdom that I will keep inviolably all the secrets of this Board, not to leave the society or join any other society, not meaning tradesmen or soldiers. At any of our meetings not to drink to intoxication, nor not to provoke, challenge or fight with any of our Brethren, and if a Brother should be offended or ill-spoken of to aid and assist him with the earliest information. And in dealing to give the preferences to our Brethren so far as circumstances will allow. And that we would not allow or admit anyone of indifferent character into our Society knowing him to be such.

Each quarter, the members would pay the master small sums of money for signs and passwords, by which they could identify their brethren. 'Ireland is in a bad state', a man might say; and a 'brother' hearing it would answer, 'Foreign countries will assist us'. 'May God send a change upon the times', would come the reply, which would in turn elicit the response, 'It was never more required'. And the brothers, if instructed by the master, would commit 'outrages', some of which amounted to nothing more serious than the posting of a threatening notice, while others were attacks of shocking brutality.[43] For instance, in Glenfin, on the night of 16 May 1847, upwards of 100 people headed by a man in a woman's clothes representing Molly Maguire attacked the house of Patrick Doherty, a schoolmaster cum land agent. They got into the building, disarmed him of a gun and two pistols and then took him outside, where they cut an inch off his tongue. Doherty was an informer, and the incident would be vividly recounted in Glenfin into the middle decades of the twentieth century.[44]

Against the background of high food prices and hunger, epidemic disease and desperate emigration in the mid- to late-1840s, the Society did experience setbacks. Notably, in spring 1848, two informers betrayed 15 men in Glenfin, the gateway from southwest Donegal to Ballybofey, Strabane and Derry, and a district in which Ribbonmen were particularly active.[45] Further south, in that same season, another two informers, after converting to Protestantism, implicated some 28 fellow Ribbonmen, mainly in Ballyshannon,

Bundoran and North Leitrim.[46] Among those named here were several men in 'comfortable circumstances'—a publican, a baker and a teacher—and, most significantly, a well-to-do farmer, William Gettens of Portnason, on the outskirts of Ballyshannon, known to the authorities since the 1830s to be a Ribbonman, and by then a leading figure in the Society in the province of Ulster.[47] But the intimidation of witnesses precipitated the collapse of the Glenfin and Ballyshannon cases, and the year 1848 ended with the assassination of a Glenswilly landlord, Dr. Samuel Davis, on his own doorstep in Letterkenny, on 22 December, and, less than a week later, on St. Stephen's Day, an attempt to kill George Wray, the agent of the Townawilly estate, by detonating gunpowder[48] buried beneath the chimney of his living room in Ardnamona. Both Davis and Wray had been evicting tenants for non-payment of rent—'tossing all the houses and wrecking the people', as one pauper in Donegal poorhouse said of Wray—and the attacks were widely credited to Ribbonmen.[49] Within two years, an attack on another landlord caused some 32 magistrates to petition government to 'exterminate the Ribbon System' by proclaiming several townlands in Glenswilly under the Crime and Outrage (Ireland) Act. By this stage, 'disposable men' (detectives) had been working their way through the county's trouble spots but turning up nothing to seriously compromise the Ribbon Society.[50]

In Donegal generally, then, the Society had emerged from the Great Famine strengthened, or 'ramified' as one landlord put it.[51] And its confidence was apparent. On the afternoon of St. Patrick's Day 1850, a procession of 800–1,000 persons—including numbers of 'strangers' who arrived in 12–14 cars from Derry—had marched from Convoy to Raphoe behind three men wearing green caps and ribbons. It was the first such large-scale public display by the Society in Donegal for many years. On coming in sight of a Constabulary party, commanded by the County Inspector, blocking their entry to Raphoe, one of their leaders had raised a cap on a stick, causing the bulk of the marchers to immediately disperse. Some 200 marchers had still proceeded toward town, only dispersing on the Riot Act being read at the Constabulary line. A man was arrested for possession of a pistol, and a Derryman for drunkenness, but the event passed off without any breach of the peace.[52]

This renewal and expansion of the Ribbon Society had several sources. In East Donegal, and, in particular around Ballyshannon, it involved a squaring up to the old Orange enemy, which had been vocal and aggressive during the Famine, in southeast Donegal and other parts of southern Ulster. More widely, it was a product of a deepening sense among the Catholic poor that the state bore ultimate responsibility for the horrors visited on the country and a heightened resentment of landlords. As early as September 1847, the *Ballyshannon Herald*, itself a Tory paper, had grasped the extent to which distress had tightly braided national and class antagonism: 'Social disorganization is nearly complete. The mass of the people are steeped to the lips in poverty. . . . Class is divided against class. The proprietors of the soil are generally regarded as oppressors of the cultivators of the soil. Dreadful hatred of England, of her institutions, is widely diffused among the humbler orders in Ireland'.[53] In this context, the Society was providing an organizational home for young men, who had concluded, in the words of a song carried in the *Londonderry Journal*, that 'we were struck by the rod of an angry God, / for kissing the chains that bound us'.[54] Most immediately, its lodges offered the prospect of direct action to men energized by communal resistance to the state and landlords, whose collectors had come, from 1848, looking for arrears of rent, poor rates (taxes for the support of poorhouses, payable only by people holding land valued above £4 paid) and cess (taxes that funded the county administration), and not getting those arrears, seizing stock, crops and other goods, and, in the case of rent, evicting tenants, while protected by large forces of police. Latterly, elections to the boards of guardians that set rates to maintain poorhouses gave the Society realizable 'political' objectives. In the Glenties Union, in March 1850, 'a large party supposed consisting of 300 armed men' traversed contested electoral divisions at night, and called at the houses of rate-payers (voters), swearing them to support the candidate 'approved of by them'. The following March, when there was another election for the Graffy, Glenties and Glenleheen divisions of the same union and the Constabulary were busy with the census, a company—three officers and 64 men—of the 35th Regiment of Foot was moved into Glenties to preserve the peace, to the 'evident chagrin' of the Ribbon leaders.[55]

A democratic deficit illuminates the intensity which the Ribbon Society brought to these ostensibly petty contests. In 1851, the population of the barony of Boylagh—roughly Ardara to Crolly—was 21,643 (11,165 female; 10,478 male). Thirty-six men in the barony, which was part of the county constituency, were qualified to vote in parliamentary elections.[56] But at least there were elections to Westminster. The most significant local government body was the grand jury, which set local taxes and awarded contracts for road repair projects that employed large numbers of young men, and, consequently, it had a presence in the lives of the poor. However, it was an appointed agency, and, despite some tinkering in the 1880s, it was to remain the preserve of a landed clique until shortly before its replacement by an elected county council in 1898. Hence, in the 1840s and 1850s, a district's board of guardians was the only representative body to which a significant number of relatively ordinary householders could elect people.

This same democratic deficit throws a Constabulary preoccupation, in the late 1840s and early 1850s, with returned emigrants—mostly especially 'disappointed Americans'—into some relief.[57] In these years, before the establishment of the Fenians in 1858, few emigrants are likely to have returned as self-conscious agents of sedition. However, all who returned came with firsthand experience of a society with an extraordinary level of political participation—a broad male franchise for federal (presidential and congressional), state, county, city and township elections—and, more particularly, a place where politicians courted tavern-keepers, contractors and other influential figures in the Irish community. For all returned emigrants, but particularly those who had done well in America, reentry into a colonial society—where, other than the boards of guardians, there was not even a pretense that petty policy bore any relationship to majority will—would have been a cold experience. And crucially, the Ribbon Society would have been a recognizable entity to these types, for the Ancient Order of Hibernians, established as the Society's American branch in 1836—the name was changed from St. Patrick's Fraternal Society in 1838—had, in the Famine, become the largest fraternal organization of Irish workingmen in the United States.[58] A hypothesis here suggests itself: the very Society that rejuvenated itself in Ireland in the 1840s—after the Hibernians had come out of the backrooms and into the light in New York, Pennsylvania and beyond—may itself have been an American parcel. In other words, if the American Hibernians—most especially, the Molly Maguires of eastern Pennsylvania—have been conventionally understood to have imported Irish organizational forms and modes of action, it is still possible to regard the Ribbonmen who reorganized in Ireland from the mid-1840s and who, from the mid-1850s, became something of a Tammany Hall in waiting, as having been shaped by the sister organization on the far side of the Atlantic.[59]

Here, at the intersection of return migration, the rise of Hibernianism in America and the emergence of the Molly Maguires in West Donegal, one family stands out. In 1857, Denis Holland, a Belfast-based republican journalist, toured North and West Donegal, investigating the landlord and state response to the Molly-initiated campaign against Scottish and English sheep-farmers who had leased mountain pasture formerly grazed by smallholders' stock in Gweedore and Cloughaneely. John Doherty, parish priest of Gweedore and a known associate of suspected Ribbon leaders, brought him out to Meenacladdy. There, they chatted with one of the 'wretched peasants', a man named 'Mihil' (Mícheál), who had a wife and 'three or four' children to support. 'This man when describing the misery of himself and his fellows, amid the desolation of the mountain waste', Holland wrote, 'uttered some exclamations in Irish that sounded like oaths'. Effecting to have thought 'that nothing like an imprecation ever escaped the lips of these simple peasants', the journalist remarked on the man swearing to the priest. Doherty smiled, and said, 'I am afraid Mihil learned to curse a little in America'.[60] 'Mihil' was Mícheál Airt Ó Domhnaill (Michael, son of Art O'Donnell), and he was no 'wretched peasant'.[61] He had left Meenacladdy for America in 1844, and he had been doing 'tolerably well'. However, he told Holland, 'the immorality and infidelity they had seen around them—and the spectacle of many ignorant and neglected Irish falling away, amid the temptations of vice, from religion and virtue—had frightened him and his poor wife; and they resolved to make every sacrifice and hurry back to Ireland, with all its miseries again, "for fear the childre [*sic*] would lose the religion"'. Arriving home in 1852–53, he again had taken a holding in

Meenacladdy, where he now opened a public house, that is, the trade which he had pursued in America, and, as evident from Holland's comments, he spoke his mind.[62] Over the next two decades, Mícheál Airt's nephews, who were Hibernians, were central figures in the Molly Maguire troubles in the 'hard coal' region of northeastern Pennsylvania, where they were suspected of involvement in the assassination of mine officials. Indeed, their brother-in-law, Jack Kehoe, a publican and Hibernian master with ambitions in state politics, was dubbed 'the King of the Mollies' by the press. Kehoe was hanged for murder in 1878. But before that, in the early hours of 10 December 1875, one of Mícheál Airt's nephews, Charles O'Donnell, and a niece, Ellen, were shot and killed in Wiggans Patch, when a party of armed men, understood to have been working for the coal company, raided their house. It was thought the raiders were looking for Mícheál Airt's own son, Pádaí, aka Pat O'Donnell (1835–83), a reputed hit man, whose arrival in town a few days earlier had caught the attention of a Pinkerton detective working undercover for the coal men. But Pádaí had already left town. Eight years later, in 1883, he himself came to international attention when, on a ship off the coast of Africa, he identified, shot and killed James Carey, an informer whose evidence had just hanged five men for the sensational assassination of the chief secretary and under-secretary in Dublin's Phoenix Park. Carey had been given an alias by the government and was being relocated to Australia when O'Donnell struck. Convicted of murder, he was hanged at Newgate. It was over a generation since his father, home from America, had looked around Meenacladdy, thought about state and society in Ireland and raged against the injustice of it all.[63]

THE UNEVEN FAILURE OF ENTITLEMENT: A PRELIMINARY ANALYSIS

If the rise of the Mollies in West Donegal in the years of the Famine had many sources, the blowback from hard choices which ordinary people had made to get themselves through the crisis was central to their recalcitrance in the 1850s. The 1831 Census had returned the population of Donegal as 289,149; by 1841 it had risen to 296,448. Allowing for a falling rate of increase, it might have been expected to reach 303–304,000 by 1851; in fact, it fell to 255,169.[64] Notwithstanding widespread and deep privation, two questions confront the historian. First, why was the Great Famine not worse in Donegal? Joel Mokyr has estimated that the excess mortality rate in the county was 10.7/1,000, the ninth lowest rate in the country. The estimated rates for the counties of North Connacht—58.4 in Mayo; 52.1 in Sligo; 49.5 in Roscommon—dwarf it. No less surprisingly, it is the third lowest estimated excess mortality rate in Ulster: the counties with lower rates are Down (6.7) and Derry (5.7). Mokyr's estimates for Armagh, Antrim and Tyrone are 15/1,000; they are near twice as high for Monaghan

(28.6) and Fermanagh (29.2), while Cavan had the highest in Ulster (42.7), four times that of Donegal.[65] And second, why did the poorer agricultural districts in the west of the county not lose a larger percentage of their population? The greatest decline in population was in the prosperous east of the county, while in the west, where in places like Meenacladdy, the valuation of agricultural land per capita was among the lowest in the entire country, some electoral divisions actually experienced an increase in population: see Map 7.1. Obviously, answering the second question goes a long way to answering the first, for the county's experience would be less anomalous if mortality and migration had cut as great a swath of the population in the poorer agricultural districts of the west.

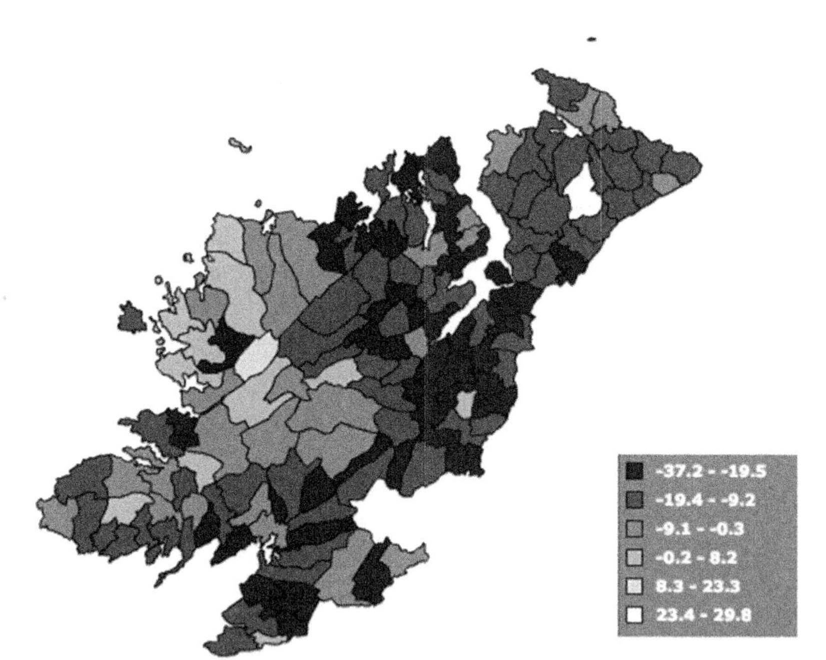

Map 7.1 County Donegal: percentage population change by electoral division, 1841–51

In Gweedore, the population of the DEDs of Meenacladdy and Magheraclogher increased by 5.38 percent and 1.94 percent respectively; most of Hill's property was in the latter electoral division. In the Rosses, the population of Dungloe (3.82 percent), Maghery (3.79 percent) and Rutland (1.64 percent), the greater portion of which was on the estate of the Marquis of Conyngham, also increased. This map was generated using the Online Historical Atlas Portal developed (2011) by A.S. Fotheringham, M. Kelly and C. Treacy of the National Centre for Geocomputation, Maynooth University.

Historians have long been aware of Donegal's curious pattern of depopulation in the Famine, and some have posited explanations. For example, in a history of the poor law administration, Christine Kinealy has suggested that, inter alia, landlord benevolence helps to account for the small decline in the west.[66] However, the two largest estates in West Donegal, accounting for the lion's share of the population, belonged to absentees—the Marquis of Conyngham and Horatio Murray-Stewart—who both, notoriously, did next to nothing to assist the poor, and the population increased on parts of those estates. Kinealy, it seems, had the 'energetic' Lord George A. Hill, then building up an estate of some 24,189 acres in Gweedore, in mind.[67] In 1845, just before the first appearance of blight, Hill had published a pamphlet on his efforts to 'civilize Gweedore and raise its people to a higher social and moral level'.[68] It was widely cited in public commentary on Ireland during the crisis itself, with its 'author' (if it was him, for it is sometimes suggested it may have been James Dombrain) being *almost* universally acclaimed as a 'model' landlord. In April 1846, Tory prime-minister Robert Peel had praised him as 'the public benefactor of his country' while *The Nation*, the nationalist journal, had hailed his 'western oasis of Gweedore'.[69] Indeed, Hill's celebrity had been confirmed at the very beginning of the Famine, September 1845, when a journalist sent by the London *Times* to report on the effect of blight on Ireland contrasted the resident Hill (who, like the journalist, was a Tory) with his neighbor, the absentee Conyngham (a Whig). However, others thought Hill's reputation had been got without merit. In late 1846, when conditions were deteriorating, Hugh MacFadden, the parish priest of Gweedore, wrote a blistering attack on the official preoccupation with making 'property' active, that is, getting landlords involved in relief: 'The landlords leave us to the Govt. and the Govt. leaves us to the landlords; and when they do so they leave us to rest upon a broken reed'.[70] Likewise, in the wake of the crisis, Denis Holland, the journalist who met Mícheál Airt in Meenacladdy in 1857, scoffed at Hill's self-representation, lambasting him as 'a pretentious philanthrope . . . a special blessing on two legs, sent by Providence for the comfort of the neglected Celts of the wilds of Donegal . . . '.[71] In truth, Hill's conduct in the Famine was neither that of the benevolent landlord represented by Kinealy and the Tory *Times*, nor the 'broken reed' described by MacFadden and radical and republican commentators. He was active in relief in winter 1846–47, but not overly active. In his dealings, he never lost sight of the question, 'Does it pay?', and, above all, he was quick to see advantages accruing from the Famine:

> The Irish people have profited much by the famine, the lesson was severe; but so rooted were they in old prejudices and old ways, that no teacher could have induced them to make the changes which this visitation of Divine Providence has brought about, both in their habits of life and in the modes of agriculture.[72]

But, in short, that districts belonging to Conyngham, who all agree was useless, *and* districts belonging to Hill, who was *somewhat* more active, recorded increases in population diminishes landlord benevolence as an explanatory factor per se in population change.

Other historians have focused on what people ate. Notably, the economic and social historian David Dickson has hypothesized that oatmeal had not been completely displaced by potatoes in the diet of the pre-Famine Donegal poor, and that this lesser dependence on the blight-hit crop may help explain the small decline in the population of the county as a whole.[73] The hypothesis can be tested on data collated on the diet of the poor in the 1830s, and it fails the test: these data, at least, suggest that the cottiers, laborers and smallholders of West Donegal were as dependent on potatoes as those of North Connacht, where mortality rates were far higher in the Famine.[74] That said, agricultural returns do show a significant acreage under cereals in the early 1840s.[75] Problematically, however, the bulk of this grain grew in the east of the county, where the population declined, not on the scrap lands of the west, which should direct researchers to the question in the general literature on famine, how did the poor, in normal times, acquire food?

Still, the notion that substitute food saved people persists. If not oatmeal, it has been ventured, fish could have been a factor in pulling the populace through the years of the Famine. Certainly, contemporaries attested to increased consumption of seafood, and *seanchas* (oral tradition) too makes mention of people scouring beaches for seaweed and shellfish. But fish cannot have made much difference. Fishing on a large scale requires capital, not simply for boats and tackle, but also to salt or smoke the catch and thus preserve it, and, lacking capital, the sector was chronically underdeveloped in Donegal. Fishermen could not have suddenly increased their catch to compensate for the loss of potatoes. And, in any event, and regardless of what has been said of bread, man cannot live on fish alone. But, in places, people may have tried. Séamas Ó Gallchóir (b. c. 1867) of Gweedore recalled hearing from people who came through the Famine that the skin of those who ate too much *bia cladaigh* (shore food: shellfish and seaweed) turned yellow, a result of excess beta-carotene and, if disconcerting, in that it mimicked jaundice, not itself a health risk. However, too much *iasc goirt* (salted fish) did cause health problems: in the mid-1900s, other old people recalled hearing that *iasc goirt*, as distinct from *iasc úr* (fresh fish), eaten on an empty stomach in the Famine caused sickness, most especially in children.[76]

Ultimately, it should go without saying, though it is rarely remarked upon, that fish and shellfish of different species were never equally distributed along the coast, that some stretches of coast can be more productively fished than others and that not all coastal communities were equally involved in fishing. Here, a cruel irony emerges: those communities most heavily involved in fishing—Inver, Killybegs, Teelin, Malinbeg, Rosbeg, Arranmore, Downings, Doaghbeg and the Swilly- and Foyle-side parishes of the baronies of Inishowen and Raphoe—all experienced considerable depopulation compared to surrounding districts. The 'cultural economy' of such communities was undoubtedly a factor in this relatively pronounced decline. Thomas Devyr, who fished Donegal Bay for a period in the 1820s, describes it succinctly in a memoir composed late in life:

> The pursuit of fishing gave an adventurous habit that looked down with indifference, or contempt, on the plodding labor of spade and scythe. Worse, it gave a *spending* habit, a contempt for small outlays as well as for small gains. On rare occasions there was not perhaps an experienced fisherman on the coast, who had not realized as much as a pound sterling by one night's lucky fishing. This could only be when there was a very large haul and a very high price, and those two things so rarely met together as to resemble gambling. But the golden memory would remain, and it helped the public houses materially. There is intense friendliness in the Irish people, as well as intense fierceness. The readiest, most convincing way this friendliness can show itself is by 'Come in boys, and let us have a drop.' Conscious of present inability to afford the cost, the next word would be 'the company's health, they're wagging their tails (i.e. the herrings) will pay for this.' And so the fishing, as a staple reliance, did, with an uncertain amount of good, bring very certain amounts of evil.[77]

Fishing villages, then, were hardscrabble places, and in a county that was itself, in a national frame, preeminent in illicit distillation (and, presumably, in whiskey consumption), they were unusually hard-living; there was singing in the town when the boys of Killybegs came rolling home. In such communities, the future was always precarious, and if nowhere yet firmly rooted, the 'natural age-linked and chronological succession of death'[78]—people in mid-life burying their parents—was here more frequently than elsewhere disrupted by the loss of young men at sea. The 'first horror of my childhood', recalled Devyr, was hearing of 'The Drowning in Bruckless Bay'—on the night of 11 February 1813; when he would have been about six, some 200 small boats were caught in a storm, and at least 80 men drowned, mainly from the western districts of Kilcar, Teelin and Malinbeg. Devyr himself did not come from a fishing background—and he had soon seen, suffered and risked enough to be 'put out of conceit with it'—but he learned early that 'each succeeding year brought its average of drowned men and destituted [*sic*] families'.[79] Hence, there were greater numbers of young widows and fatherless children in such communities, and also stepchildren, whose claims on resources may, in hard times, have been ambiguous; some 24 men were drowned at herring fishing in the Killybegs coastguard area in 1835 alone.[80]

More generally, in the largest fishing villages, many families depended not only on the success of their menfolk at sea, which was a function of capital, skill and luck, but on employment ashore that was at once seasonal and catch-contingent. Girls and women gutted and salted fish, and boys hewed and carried. Old women hawked *scadáin ghoirte* (salt herring) through the country, and old men, not fit to fish and without much to farm, contributed a little by mending nets and boats. And they had *comparatively* little to farm. Fishermen's holdings—and most who fished also cultivated potato patches—were smaller than those further inland, and the rent per acre higher. Here, the loss of potatoes in 1845 and 1846—being at once unexpected and, on the second occasion, general—were blows of great severity to people who lived on the edge, who were more integrated than many other smallholders into a *cash* economy and more dependent than most on markets for food—having smaller farms, they exhausted their potato stocks and purchased food earlier in the year—and yet who, being more familiar with death, may not have valued pennies. For many now, there was nothing to fall back upon; and for some, there was nobody, as fishermen were not considered a good credit risk. 'Credit is with difficulty obtained, as there is much uncertainty in the payment for fishing materials', a coastguard officer had remarked of Killybegs in the mid-1830s; 'Industrious fishermen get three months' credit from tradesmen; but they are generally charged usuriously'.[81] And, as argued below, access to credit was central to the survival of the poor in 1845–51.

Above all, fishermen should not be understood as having brought home food; they brought home cash, or at least they went to sea in the hope of bringing home cash, and, in the absence of potatoes, soaring grain prices pushed carbohydrates out of reach. Oral tradition attests to people trading fish for meal in the Famine, and the agents of a Ramelton iodine factory too are said to have bartered meal for kelp across North Donegal in these years. No doubt too, many in the crowds that blackened the shoreline searching for shellfish *sold* much of what they gathered and then purchased meal: for instance, outside Ardara in West Donegal, it was remembered into the 1930s that a young woman came with her children to the townland of Carn at 'the time of the Famine', constructed some form of a shelter on the shore, and supported herself and her family through the crisis by gathering cockles, which she carried some 30 miles east to the inland town of Ballybofey to *sell*.[82]

In the end, numbers speak: again, that those communities which were most involved in fishing experienced *comparatively* high rates of depopulation points to the weakness of the fish hypothesis. Households possessed of the least land (and least stock), and, consequently, most dependent on markets for food, to be purchased with money earned from whatever fish they *might* catch, or from salting and storing, hauling and hawking it, found in particular periods in 1845–51, that they could neither pay for sufficient oatmeal to replace blighted potatoes nor get food on credit. And so hunger, disease and migration swept them away.

An alternate approach to understanding Donegal's curious pattern of depopulation in the late 1840s, and also the recalcitrance of the Molly Maguires in the west of the county in the early 1850s—and one that, in some measure, incorporates insights of Amartya Sen (1980)—emerges from a reading of the memoir of Hugh Dorian (1834–1914). Born into a smallholding family in North Donegal, Dorian's memoir is the most wide-ranging lower-class recollection of the crisis. Horror is described vividly but with restraint: 'in a very short time there was nothing but stillness, a mournful silence, in the villages; in the cottages, grim poverty and emaciated faces, showing all the signs of hardships'. The picture of starvation is stark but authentic: 'the cheek bones became thin and high, the cheeks blue, the bones sharp, and the eyes sunk . . . the legs and the feet swell and get red and the skin cracks'. Here, Dorian articulates a nationalist analysis, blaming Britain for the calamity. He identifies public work schemes as the point where the

> government advisers dealt out the successful blow—and it would appear premeditated—the great blow for slowly taking away human life, getting rid of the population and nothing else, by forcing the hungry and the half-clad men to stand out in the cold and in the sleet and rain from morn till night for the paltry reward of nine pennies per day. Had the poor pitiful creatures got this allowance, small as it was, at their homes, it would have been relief, it would be charity, it would convey the impression that their benefactors meant to save life, but in the way thus given, on compulsory conditions, it meant next to slow murder.

Crucially, however, that analysis frames a more intimate history, and his assessment of the Famine's effects is, in places, unsettlingly callous:

> Arising from death, emigration and dispersion to all parts, the population soon dwindled away. And indeed I hope it will not be any way uncharitable to say [it, but] with the multitude also disappeared many turbulent and indifferent characters who were only a disgrace to the good, the honest and the well-doing, and if there was poverty, there was peace too.[83]

Families or households are central in Dorian's telling, and, the reader is given to understand, all households were not created equally. Most obviously, they acquired food in different ways. Some were dependent solely on agriculture, selling stock or eggs or grain; others supplemented the produce of the land with the proceeds of fishing or *poitín*-making, knitting or sprigging, weaving or tailoring. Some fishermen and kelp-men had little or no land—'Many had no land, no property beyond the cabin they lived in, and to the ocean their chief dependence lay . . .'[84]—and there were other people with no land at all, most obviously, *lucht siúil*—traveling tinsmiths, horse-dealers, hawkers and musicians—but also some artisans and laborers. As regards culture and politics, in its broadest sense, some families were 'good, honest and well doing', and some were 'turbulent and indifferent'. There were households that had influence with clergy or gentry, merchants and shopkeepers; and those that had little or none. Dorian's account, therefore, suggests an analysis of the Great Famine might best proceed by, *a*) establishing which strategies lower-class households were employing to acquire food on the eve of the crisis, and the extent to which those strategies continued to function as it unfolded, and *b*) elaborating how the poor were getting along with others in their own community, and not simply with all-too-often remote and distant landlords, but with merchants, larger farmers and clergy and, indeed, with people in their own social class.

In the years before the blight arrived, the vast majority of families in Donegal depended heavily for sustenance on potatoes, which they grew on rented ground and, as Dorian indicates, they had a variety of strategies to pay their rent (and rates, cess and other demands), and also to carry themselves from the consumption of the last of the old potatoes through to the harvesting of new potatoes, that is, from no later than mid-June—and much earlier for those with the smallest potato patches—through mid-August. In this period, *mí an ocrais* (the hungry month), the lower class generally subsisted on oatmeal. Here, a broad distinction can be drawn between strategies for food acquisition in the east and the west of the county. In East Donegal, the three decades before the Famine had seen the widely organized domestic linen industry exposed to direct competition from cotton which, combined with the mechanization of the industry in the east of Ulster, had undermined the position of weaving households. Weavers' sons had been increasingly unable to replace their fathers at the loom, and many had become cottiers or wage laborers. At the same time, opportunities for women to contribute to household budgets by spinning contracted, while agricultural depression, which favored a return to pasture, capped the demand for agricultural labor and depressed wages. The result was an impoverished, underemployed substratum of society that ever earlier in the year had to resort to markets for food purchased with money earned over the previous months. And that class—most directly dependent on markets for food—suffered immensely when, in 1845–49, wages plummeted and food prices soared.

In contrast, people in the west were not as *directly* dependent on markets for food. The district had never been much involved in linen-weaving, and hence it was not adversely effected by the contraction of that sector. Here, knitting of stockings and seasonal migration had become central to many household economies in the half century before the Famine. The price of a pair of stockings was low: in the early 1830s, the parish priest of Lettermacaward estimated that a woman or child could only earn between a ha'penny and a penny per week knitting stockings. However, the demand was stable all year round and women of all ages could knit. Pregnancy and nursing interfered little, if at all.[85] Moreover, rather than purchasing foodstuffs in *mí an ocrais*, women might receive a quantity of meal as payment for stockings from the merchants. In fact, many merchants routinely exchanged foodstuffs, tea, tobacco or snuff with knitters rather than paying them in cash. Knitters, of course, were a good credit risk. And so too were women with children and early adolescents hired on large farms in the Laggan of East Donegal, often for over six months of the year, or whose menfolk and unmarried young women traveled to Scotland to work at the harvest. Responses to a questionnaire distributed to clergymen as part of the Poor Inquiry in the 1830s give a general impression of local variations in seasonal migration. The question asked—'What number of labourers are in the habit of leaving their dwellings periodically, to obtain employment, and what proportion of them go to England?'—was awkwardly phrased, not least as the reference to England, rather than Scotland, likely threw some respondents. In any event, per the 1831 Census, the ratios of migrants to 'Males 20 Years of Age [and over]' were highest in Lettermacaward (100/472, 21 percent), Clondahorkey (200/1,470, 13.6 percent) and Templecrone (200/1,863, 10.7 percent). Unfortunately, no data were returned for Gweedore, where the rate of seasonal migration was the highest in the county in the late nineteenth century.[86]

One hypothesis, then, is that in the years of the Famine, lower-class strategies for acquiring food did not collapse as completely in West Donegal as they did in the east, that is, that some stocking merchants continued to pay knitters with oatmeal, which they had the capacity to buy in bulk, while seasonal migration to the public works and large farms of Scotland took away hungry mouths in the leanest period of the year, and made those who remained a better credit risk, as they would have family members returning with 'Scotch' pounds after the harvest. And the converse is that in the east, the poor—more dependent than their western counterparts on locally earned wages that fell from late 1845—could not afford to purchase food in the market place. Certainly, for West Donegal, preliminary research points to the persistence of knitting and seasonal migration—and the continued operation of associated credit networks—through the worst years of the Famine. For instance, in spring 1847, when William Bennett, a Quaker relief worker, went into Arranmore, which was then experiencing severe distress, he remarked, 'The feature that struck me most forcibly was, that among this whole population, estimated at 1,500, there was not a single particle of work of any description, that we could see going forward, either inside the cottages, or outside upon the soil, except one old woman knitting'.[87] In truth, it was probably less that old woman knitting who arrested Bennett's attention than the absence of men working in the fields, an absence much remarked upon by English commentators in early 1847—and bizarrely so, given the lack of seed. But the old woman knitting intrigues the historian, for she begs the questions, who had given her the yarn? And what did she get for the stockings? Likewise, the years of the Famine witnessed an expansion in the stocking trade to meet growing British demand. Lord George Hill paid out £70 for stockings and socks at his store in Bunbeg in 1844, and by 1854 he was paying £600, a sum almost equal to the rental of his estate.[88] Hill was a newcomer entering a lucrative trade to meet high demand, that is, getting women knitting who had not knitted before. Hence, the growth of his business in the northwest of the county during the Famine suggests that merchants already in the trade in southwest Donegal—the hub of the industry—may have by then been maximizing local output.[89]

Other factors undoubtedly had some bearing on West Donegal's relatively clean escape from the Famine. Not least of them was the recent experience of localized famine. Repeated weather-related crop failures in the 1830s, when there were reports of deaths from starvation as well as disease across West Donegal, had both honed domestic coping and adapting strategies and familiarized community leaders—priests, schoolmasters, shopkeepers—with the workings of both governmental and nongovernmental agencies that were involved in relief. And that experience stood to them: of £100,000 spent by the semi-official British Association for the Relief of Irish Destitution from January to September 1847, £10,379–6–11 was spent on relief in Donegal; only Mayo (£17,510–11–4) and Cork (£19,506–11–9) received more money. Cavan, where excess mortality is estimated to have been four times higher, received a quarter of the sum spent in Donegal.[90] Furthermore, if most money was spent where the Association's agents traveled in those months and later, it was spent in the west of the county, where the population of some electoral divisions increased.[91] Likewise, that two prominent members of the Relief Commission either owned (John Pitt Kennedy) or had owned (James Dombrain) property in West Donegal can but have helped the district. Finally, that Hill had opened a large store and mill a few years before the Famine was also an unintended asset for a wide area in the worst years: governmental and nongovernmental organizations had a secure place to deposit relief supplies and grind meal. But ultimately, it was microeconomics—seasonal migration to Scotland and knitting at home, and the credit networks which they had called into being—that mattered most.

THE POLITICS OF POST-FAMINE ADJUSTMENT

Glenties Poorhouse was the 'last game of all'[92] for the indigent and the ill, the infirm and the abandoned in a poor law union that comprised the greater part of West Donegal. John Mitchel, who saw it just after its completion, thought its Tudor architecture seemed to mock 'those wretches who still cling to liberty and mud cabins'. To them, 'in their perennial half-starvation', he wrote, it must have appeared 'like a Temple erected to the Fates, or like the fortress of Giant Despair, whereinto he draws them one by one, and devours them . . . '.[93] It could house 800 'inmates', and it had been full, and more than full, at times, in the Famine years. But numbers had fallen as conditions improved from 1849. A week at the beginning of summer, when many people, even in good times, had exhausted their old potatoes, registers the change. There had been 910 people—mainly children under fifteen and infirm women—in the poorhouse in the first week of June 1849, 419 in 1850, 280 in 1851 and 285 in 1852, but by 1854 there were only 117, and if the number rose to 153 in 1855, it would never go that high in that week again in the 1850s; it dipped to 77 in 1856, and hovered around 100 for the rest of the decade.[94]

If 'the Famine', for West Donegal, was, by and large, over by harvest 1849, the immediate legacy of hunger, disease and high food prices was debt. And, crucially, debt included not only arrears of rent, rates or cess—that is, money owed landlords and the state—but also monies owed to local lenders. Prominent in this latter category were mealmongers, to whom the poor, even in good years, resorted for foodstuffs on credit once their potato stocks were exhausted; many of these people were themselves publican-shopkeepers or merchants involved in the butter, egg or stocking trades, who might accept payment in cash or kind. At the same time, people reached a variety of arrangements with better-off neighbors to obtain meal or money, often offering stock, goods or land as collateral.[95] In many instances, debts to smaller local lenders were likely run up in the latter stages of the crisis—1848 and 1849, in particular—when landlords and rate and cess collectors started to press their demands. And, ultimately, the debts to these types too fell due, and, not always being paid, there was conflict. For instance, Seán Mac Calbhaigh of Mín an Lig gave meal on credit to people in the mountain districts above Glenties in *na droch-aimsearaibh* (the bad times), and, in the wake of the Famine, he took legal action against those who had failed to repay him, getting court orders to seize property—cattle and sewn muslin or sprigging—in lieu of cash. A man named Tuathal Ó Gallachóir composed a song, 'Seán na Mine' (Seán of the Meal), that excoriated his meanness, imagining him, with his wee bag on his back ('*do mhála beag leat ar do dhroim*'), being denied admittance to Heaven.

> *Nach Seán atá cráidhte fán triofal bheag gránda*
> *A sgab sé mar cháirde ar a' bhaile seo thíos* . . . [?]
> . . . *Sé Seán bhéas i ngéibheann i láthair an Ríogh,*
> *Fá dtearn sé d'éagcóir thart fá Ghleann Léicín,*
> *Ar bhaintreabhach sléibhe nach rabh aca pighinn.*
> *Thóg sé a gcuid céarsach is chongbhuigh dó féin iad,*
> *Ag dréim le go ndéanfadh siad* proifit *arís;*
> *Acht nuair a rachas sé 'un tsléibhe beidh aithreachas géar air,*
> *Mar nár fhág sé a gcuid ceannrachán uilig aca féin.*[96]

> (Isn't it Seán who is bothered about the wee trifle of grain, / That he scattered for credit on this townland below . . . ? / . . . 'Tis Seán will be in trouble before the Almighty, / For what he did around Gleann Leithín, / On penniless mountain women. / He took their handkerchiefs for himself, / Hoping to make *profit* on them again; / But when he goes to the mountain he will severely regret it, / For not leaving all their cattle to the people.)

This song deploring the profit motive was still 'widely' sung in mountain communities around Glenties in the early 1900s, its insistence on the trouble Mac Calbhaigh's *unchristian* behavior would bring him in the Hereafter an oblique criticism of the worldly Catholic clergy and merchants in the here-and-now.[97] A more overt connection between the same priests and merchants was made by Patrick MacGill, who was born in 1889—two generations after the Famine—on a smallholding outside Glenties. His parents and their neighbors made ends meet by sending their children as laborers to the big farms in East Donegal, Derry and Tyrone while adult males and unmarried women went navvying and tattie-hoking (harvesting potatoes) in Scotland, and the women who remained at home knitted for the McDevitts. In his novel *The Rat-pit* (1915), MacGill gives an account of the rise of that family—here, named McKeown—out of the ashes of the Famine:

> When the black potato blight, with the fever and the famine that followed, spread over Donegal, Farley McKeown saw his chance. By dint of plausible arguments he persuaded a firm of Londonderry grain merchants to ship a cargo of Indian meal to Greenanore and promised to pay for the consignment within two years from the date of its arrival. When the cargo was landed on Dooey Head the people hailed it as a gift from God and the priest blessed Farley McKeown from the altar steps. The peasants built a large warehouse for McKeown, and in return for the work they were allowed a whole year in which to pay for their meal. Meanwhile the younger generation went off to America and money flowed into Donegal and Farley McKeown's pocket. At the end of two years he had paid the grain merchants, but the peasants found to their astonishment that *they* had only paid interest on the cost of their food. They were in the man's clutches, always paying for goods received and in some strange way never clear of debt. This went on for years, and Farley McKeown, a pillar of the Church and friend of the holy priest, waxed wealthy on the proceeds of his business. Then he started a knitting business and again was hailed by the priest as the saviour of the people.[98]

MacGill here misleads a little: the McDevitts had been people of substance—inn-keepers and merchants—in Glenties since the eighteenth century, and long involved in the stocking trade. However, the family was involved in private and public relief schemes during the Famine, and the crisis and its immediate aftermath undoubtedly proved a boon to the family who, adopting new business forms, soon became the dominant local player in knitwear. Little over a decade after the crisis, in 1864, Daniel McDevitt, Jr. entered into a partnership with his brother Hugh, the former investing £1,000 and the latter £600, and this firm soon made them the undisputed stocking kings of West Donegal, and the mountains north of Glenties their demesne. Dealers buying stockings from women at fairs and markets were soon a thing of the past: there was now a more formal relationship between merchant house and knitter. By 1877, the McDevitts were exporting 624,000 pairs of socks and stockings a year (in addition to comforters, guernsey frocks and other knitted goods). In that year, the firm, in estimating the extent of its business, revealed something of its modus operandi and the hold it had on the poor: 'We employ about 1,100 *families* (we mean the female portion), and we imagine that each family would number about three, equivalent to 3,300 persons. . . . As a rule, the younger of each family attend school during the day, and assist the others during the evening and at a night, while at home, at knitting'.[99]

It was in these communities where the stocking trade and seasonal migration had caused credit networks to be most widely elaborated before the Famine—the hinterlands of Ardara, Glenties, Fintown, Doohary and Dungloe—that Molly Maguire 'outrages' were most common in the early to mid-1850s. Here too, a great viciousness—bordering on gratuitous violence—became apparent in 1854–55, when property prices suddenly climbed out of a trough into which they had been pitched in the Famine. There was an extensive trade in 'good will' or 'tenant right' in mid-nineteenth-century Donegal. A tenant was able to sell his interest in his holding or, indeed, in a portion of it. In the course of the Famine, many tenants had divested themselves of land, sometimes entire holdings, in return for food, or else to get cash to purchase food at inflated prices, or to pay rent and rates, or to get an able-bodied young person to Scotland or, if lucky, across the Atlantic. Now, the recovery of land prices left some people feeling cheated, making 'land grabbers' particular targets of the Mollies while also increasing intergenerational tension within families. In Meenagrillagh, adjacent to Beagh, a campaign of intimidation against James Arle, an old farmer, culminated on the night of 21 October 1855, when a party of 12–15 men came to his house. 'They dragged me out of my bed', he told the Constabulary, 'fired a shot and swore they would blow my brains out; they tied a handkerchief over my eyes, put a rope round my neck, [and] led me naked to a field in front of the house'. Having taken him back to the house, they forced him to put out his tongue and threatened to cut it out, then putting him on his knees forced him to swear 'to be good to William Macready [*sic.*] and his family, and if I knew any of the party also to say nothing about the affair or they would visit me at another time as this was only a warning'. William McCready was Arle's son-in-law, who wanted him to sign the farm over to him.[100] A few months later, in late February 1856, a large party of Ribbonmen surrounded the house of Patrick McGroarty, a relatively well-to-do cattleman, in Tievachorky, a mountainous place midway between Glenties and Frosses. They forced an entry, and, firing shots inside the house, inflicted an unmerciful beating on McGroarty with whips, guns and pistols in front of his wife and large family of young children. By the time they left, they had 'completely wrecked' the house, smashed and spilled his milk vessels, shot and killed his dog, punched a servant girl in the stomach with a stick, beaten and threatened to kill his son—at most in his mid-teens—and, finally, forced him to hand over £3, 'to carry them home'. McGroarty was never to recover from the effects of the beating, dying four months later. Although the putative cause of the murderous attack on him was that he had not compensated two neighbors for sheep and geese which his dog had killed, his expansion of his holding in the early to mid-1850s may have given rise to a perception that he had 'grabbed' land.[101]

Importantly, if the Mollies were representing themselves as upholding the rights of the poor, they were themselves not all poor men. The prime suspect in the beating of McGroarty was Neil O'Donnell, a publican cum road contractor later named by McGlynn as master of the Glenties lodge, and James Coyle of Tullinalough, another publican, was one of the owners of the sheep and geese who had demanded the attack. Likewise, Patrick Friel, an Ardara publican, was suspected of involvement in the attack on Arle. And there were many others of the same class—in fact, the same trade—in the Ribbon Society. In December 1855, Edward McGrath of Glenties was stopped and robbed near Raphoe. McGrath used to take goods from Glenties to sell at Derry market, and, on this occasion, he was returning home after disposing of '£53 worth of goods belonging to parties who had taken land for which the tenant right (common in this country) had not been paid by the incoming tenant to the out-goers', that is, he was selling goods for people who would be considered grabbers. Suspiciously, however, McGrath had offered no resistance, and four car-men accompanying him had offered him no assistance. On investigation, the authorities concluded that 'a plan was formed with the connivance of Ed. McGrath to waylay him and take the money from him, under what is commonly called about Glenties a Glenswilly Decree, that is taking by force what cannot be obtained otherwise'.[102] In truth, McGrath was not the simple 'car-man' suggested by extant Constabulary reports of the case, but a well-to-do publican-shopkeeper.[103] Likewise, Patrick McGlynn fingered John Dorrian, Barney Kelly and John Hanlon, all publicans in Ardara, as key Mollies—committee men, who hosted meetings and stored and distributed weapons. Likewise, Neil Breslin, another Ardara Molly named by McGlynn, may have been a publican's son. At a meeting of the lodge in 1855–56, Breslin proposed stealing some sheep belonging to the parish priest, John D. McGarvey, as he had not paid his father for a wall he had erected.[104] In Ardara today, an impressive old stone wall separates the chapel-yard from Teague Breslin's public house, one of only two (out of nine [2015]) licensed premises in the town still owned by the same family that operated it in the 1850s; and in 1855 major work was carried out at the chapel.

The Famine, it is clear, had increased contention within the middle strata of West Donegal Catholic society, between those deemed to be taking advantage of the poor—most obviously, land grabbers and mealmongers—and others, prominent among whom were publicans cum road contractors, who espoused a concern for smallholders. Complicating matters, there were family connections across this small section of society and some publicans, most especially those who kept shop, were likely themselves creditors, and the difference between a 'good' creditor and a 'bad' creditor does not emerge from the sources.[105] At the same time, it was also clear by the mid-1850s that protecting her 'children' was no longer Molly Maguire's sole concern: Molly increasingly wanted something for herself. Even before the Famine, Ribbonmen had come to control much of the *poitín* trade in North Donegal, and people involved in other shady enterprises, such as horse-dealing, found it beneficial to join.[106] Now there were also signs of blatant racketeering. In winter 1855–56, Thomas McMurray of Strabane set himself up in Glenties as agent for some Scottish and English butter merchants, purchasing all the butter brought to him at a higher price than that paid by established local shopkeepers. At 8.30 a.m., on the morning of 23 April, as he was traveling with two servants from Ballybofey to Glenties, three men stopped him at Clogher. One of them struck him twice with a stick, and one of the others, both of whom had firearms, snapped a pistol in his face, and then robbed him of £29 or £30 in copper and silver, and a silver watch valued at £3. The attackers told him to return to Strabane, and not to go to Glenties again.[107] On the same road, at Edeninfagh, men taking cartloads of fish from Teelin to the Laggan were stopped, and their boxes dumped at the side of the road, presumably for not paying protection.[108] Meanwhile, across Donegal, Ribbonmen, by intimidating nonmembers, ensured their 'brothers' were prominent among recipients of grand jury contracts for road-construction and repair: often publican-shopkeepers who employed laborers to carry out the work, the contracts increased their patronage power and secured custom for their houses.[109] And, finally, there were public offices filled by Ribbonmen. Most audaciously, in 1858, William Gettens of Portnason had himself appointed a poor rate collector by the Ballyshannon Board of Guardians. Again, Gettens had been known to the authorities since the 1830s to be a Ribbonman: it was an open secret that he was the longstanding 'county delegate' for Donegal and a key figure in the national leadership.[110] But, from May 1858, Gettens—who had been several times arrested on the word of informers only to have the cases collapse—was regularly taking people to Ballyshannon petty sessions for nonpayment of rates—until, in October 1860, the Board took action against him for withholding monies collected.[111] A farmer cum shebeen-man (he was twice prosecuted in 1855 for selling spirits without a license in Ballyshannon) cum public official (rate collector), the Ribbon leader's name appears as a subscriber in D'Alton's *King James's Irish Army List (1689)* (1855), a reminder, perhaps, that contra his West Donegal 'brothers', the cornerstone of his politics was anti-Orangeism.[112]

In his assessment of the Ribbon Society in late 1855, Daniel Cruise, by then three years in Donegal and most familiar with the west and south of the county, had seen land and little more than land, and the backwash of the Famine: 'the greater part . . . if not all' of the Ribbon activity in his district was 'mixed up with the system of tenant right and to regain possession of lands which some of them have been for several years dispossessed of or sold what they call their good will of and which in many instances they seek to regain . . . '. But based in the northeastern town of Letterkenny, and taking a wider view, the County Inspector emphasized the extent to which the lodges' hand reached into all corners of society and economy. The Ribbon Society, he reported, 'has more or less influence in every transaction, from the occupation or letting of land to the enlistment of a recruit for the Militia'.[113]

Both were right. The magistrate had identified the issue that most animated Ribbonmen—or more accurately, the Ribbon base—in the west and southwest, and the policeman had, no less accurately, discerned the range and scale of their activities and divined the ambition of their leaders. In that, there is nothing unusual: more than one secret society has been the chrysalis of a political machine. East Donegal's Ribbon lodges had undoubtedly become less involved in 'outrage' by the mid-1850s, but the Constabulary had erred on the side of optimism when they judged them to be 'in abeyance'. To some extent, they were simply finding different ways of doing things and different things to do. And a similar reorientation was under way in western lodges, and the tension which it occasioned was a factor in the writing of the letter which Cruise had received from Beagh in April 1856, for Patrick McGlynn, its author, was conscious of strains in his local lodge, and afraid that, in any schism, he himself might be informed upon. Central to the statements which McGlynn swore to Cruise was an account of a meeting in Neil O'Donnell's public house in Glenties on St. Patrick's Night 1855, the purpose of which was to resolve a dispute within the Ardara lodge. This dispute rose from a challenge to the mastership of Little John Breslin of Doohill by Moses Ward of Brackey and Condy Boyle of Meenagolan, who thought that Breslin was 'not breaking enough of houses'. The meeting had involved the masters of lodges in Glenties (Neil O'Donnell), Killybegs (Charles Herroran) and Dungloe (Martin Quigley), and a large contingent of Ardara Ribbonmen. The chairman was James Gallagher of Fintown, delegate of West Donegal lodges to county-level meetings. Gallagher, judging from McGlynn's statement, parried Ward's challenge. Having taken the mood of the meeting, he had pulled a paper from his pocket, and holding it up, he said it was the signs and passwords for the ensuing quarter, which he would give to Moses Ward for 10 shillings. The Brackey-man did not have the money, and, when he failed to raise it over the following week, the mastership for the quarter reverted to Breslin.[114]

A REAR VIEW

An encounter near the end of the nineteenth century may provide a rear view of the contention in the Ribbon Society in West Donegal in the mid-1850s. Seaton Milligan, a 50-something Omagh-man, visited Ardara in 1890. Interested in history, Milligan wanted to see the *ráth* or fort above

Doohill from which the town takes its name. A 'very active old man' who lived adjacent to it was happy to show it to him. Milligan later recalled that

> He was able to get over the ditches as nimbly as I could, and seemed to be possessed of an excellent constitution. In answer to my inquiries, he informed me his name was John Breslin, that he was a linen weaver by trade, and had worked for 60 years on the same loom, and was then 86 years old. The loom itself bore evidence of the truth of his statement, as the seat was almost worn through by friction, and brightly polished from constant use. His dwelling, which I visited, consisted of one apartment, about 16 feet by 12; his loom and bed occupied one side of it, and opposite was the door and window; underneath the latter was a table, and two chairs, the total remaining furniture of the house. A hole in the roof without any chimney brace allowed an exit for the smoke. He never had toothache or any other ache, he never lost a tooth, and bids fair to reach the hundred. He is married to his second wife, a woman 20 years his junior, has no family, is still living as I write (May, 1892), and has now attained 88 years. He writes to London and Dublin for orders for his towels, and seems to have formed a connexion who buys all he produces. I attribute this man's good health and entire freedom from pain and ache to his good constitution, his active life, and to the conditions under which he lives. His house is situated on very high ground, underneath the old Rath, and the large opening in the unceiled roof ventilates the place so perfectly that he breathes a perfectly pure atmosphere, both day and night.[115]

This man (b. c. 1804) was known locally as John the Towel, and it is possible that he and Little John Breslin of Doohill, master of the Ardara lodge in the mid-1850s, were one and the same person.[116] And if they were the same person, then the master of the Lodge, here revealed as an enterprising, individualistic person, stands in even starker contrast to Moses Ward of Brackey and Condy Boyle of Meenagolan than he did on that St. Patrick's Night in 1855, in Neil O'Donnell's in Glenties, when they had the men but not the money to depose him as master. But whether or not the master of the lodge was the towel man, Little John Breslin, being from Doohill, was essentially from the town of Ardara (a mid-eighteenth-century creation), while Ward and Boyle were from mountain-shadowed townlands a few miles south of it. Boyle, in fact, was likely a herd in the hills above Glengesh. The challengers, in other words, were rooted in the most securely Irish-speaking section of the parish where, in the 1850s, rundale, a communal system of land use, sustained notions of the relationship of a family to their neighbors that were different to those which had long prevailed around the town, and which had been strengthened in a wider area by the Great Famine.[117]

But there is no simple opposition here of tradition and modernity. Moses Ward (1826–1912) was still living when Milligan met John the Towel. He had jumped bail in summer 1856, but he had appeared at the assizes in spring 1858, when he pleaded guilty to membership in the Ribbon Society and was released on the same terms as the other men the previous summer. In the early 1860s, he had married Bridget Gavigan and settled on a small-holding in Killasteever, adjacent to Brackey. On it, they reared a family, harvesting and selling seaweed to make ends meet.[118] It was tough, seasonal work, from which he made no fortune. In 1907, when he was still working with his son, he was getting 10 pence for a creel of seaweed. The price is known, as in that year, when he was over eighty, he took a case against a neighbor, Pat Cunningham, under the Small Debts Act, claiming he had refused to pay him 15 shillings due for 30 creels; the case was dismissed. As it happens, he himself had appeared as a defendant in the same court on a number of occasions over the previous half century—charged with trespassing (and cutting and carrying away a stick) on the land of Condy Conaghan in Edergole in 1861; for nonpayment of county cess in 1878; for being drunk on the street of Ardara on Tuesday 14 February 1888; and for nonpayment of seed-rate in 1890 and 1891, an offense that may have been part of an organized campaign.[119]

Not one of these charges concerned a matter of any consequence. Many ordinary decent people were charged with similar and, indeed, more serious infractions. But Moses Ward was an extraordinary individual. Unusually for any person born in his community before the Famine, he could read and write, and literacy was more unusual still for Catholics. In Killasteever (pop. 1901: 23), only one other person over 30 could read and write in 1901. In the electoral division of Glengesh (pop. 1901: 1,368), of which Killasteever was a part, there were then 218 people still living who had been born before the Famine, that is, who were 56 years of age or older. Of these people, 182 were Catholics, and, of them, 139 could neither read nor write; of the remaining 43, 18 could read only, and 25 (13.7 percent) could read and write—a striking contrast with the proportion (24 of 36; 66 percent) of Protestants in the same age bracket (aged 56 or older) returned as reading and writing.[120] Here, among Catholics, it was the children of the 1880s—those born over half a century after Ward—who constituted the first decennial cohort of which a majority grew up literate. No less unusually, while himself a precocious literate, Ward had not disavowed his own cultural background. His children, born in the 1860s and 1870s, grew up speaking both Irish and English. Moses Ward, then, can be said to have embodied an alternate modernity, one in which the achievement of the new (literacy and, indeed, fluency in English) did not necessarily have to involve the abandonment of the old and the particular. And there, in pointing to a future different from that brought into view by the Famine, lay the radicalism of his challenge to Little John Breslin of Doohill: in other words, there was more to Ward—and the defeated majority of Ardara Mollies who sided with him in 1855—than 'breaking houses' and a reaction to loss. David Lloyd's admonishment echoes: 'we should not allow ourselves to imagine that the dead, because their own ways of living were destroyed along with them, were incapable of tracing in their own practices the transformable forms of another life'.[121] And to Lloyd's words of caution nothing need here be added other than that there is no reason to assume that the Mollies of the late 1840s and early 1850s did not prevent more usurious interest rates from being charged, more land 'grabbed', and still more people cleared. After all, the authorities' alarm in the early to mid-1850s suggests that they were making a difference.

No great joy lit Moses Ward's final years. None of his eight children married locally; most emigrated. When he died, aged 86, in 1912, the Ribbon Society, which he had most likely joined about twenty years of age c. 1846, had become the Ancient Order of Hibernians, in many places a de facto branch network of the Irish Parliamentary Party; it was respectable and it was important to the powerful. Indeed, in districts where it had the seal of clerical approval, AOH lodges seemed part confraternity and part political machine. Their rhetoric was of 'faith and fatherland', their banners depicted saints and priests and they marched on St. Patrick's Day and Assumption Day. It is not known if Ward had any truck with the Society in the decades after his arrest. If he had, it had never materially improved his life. He died in a third class house with a bachelor son, Charles, and a spinster daughter, Mary. The rest of his children were either dead or in America. Even before his death, there had been local rumblings against the Party–Church–'Hib' axis, and in the tectonic shift that followed the 1916 Rising, it was, by and large, the poorer, certainly the less respectable, people—people like the Wards of Killasteever—who abandoned the half-a-loaf of Home Rule for republican separatism. Across West Donegal, disputes over access to halls and marching bands' instruments punctuated the years between the Rising and the Tan War, and there were violent clashes between the two factions through the 'troubles'. Indeed, as early as December 1918, Anthony Herron of Lacklea, a 45-year-old Hibernian, died from a gunshot wound inflicted in a fracas after an election rally in Glenties.[122] Friction between the pro-Treaty right-wing Hibs and left-wing Republicans continued to spark through the middle decades of the century, flaring in the 1930s, when the AOH became indistinguishable from the Blueshirts, a group not unfairly dubbed 'imitation Nazis' by their opponents.[123]

In that decade, collectors from the Irish Folklore Commission were calling at houses across West Donegal and, in the glow of Tilley lamps and turf fires, recording songs and stories. It was part of a national effort, unprecedented in size and ambition, to document the oral culture of what was perceived to be a traditional agrarian society on the eve of its demise. In Donegal, in places not unlike Ward's in Killasteever and, indeed, Breslin's in Doohill, old men chortled over what their fathers and grandfathers had done in the mid-nineteenth century. So too did some younger men: in 1936 Johnny Timoney (c. 40) of Mín an tSamhaidh told of hearing from his father how a man named Kennedy from near Narin had informed on a *poitín*-maker named Porter, resulting in a hefty fine and the destruction of a still. Kennedy used to cart goods to Derry market, and once when he was carrying a load of butter out Bealach na gCreach, the Mollies came on him; Porter being a Protestant, Timoney explained that two Catholics had been working for him. The Mollies killed Kennedy's horse, smashed his cart and carried off the *botannaí* ('butts': firkins, wooden containers) of butter. '*Tá mé ag fágáilt*', finished Timoney, '*gur h-itheadh mórán don im a bhí ann an-chómgharach thart fá na dorsacha againn*'. (I make out that much of the butter was eaten *very* close to our doors.)[124] And yet another, more ambivalent note was often struck, namely, that the Mollies somehow 'went bad' or went too far or that violence became an end in itself. Interviewed in winter 1961, Séamas Mac Amhlaigh (b. 1879), who had been reared in the mountains north of Glenties, made a striking analogy with internecine bloodletting that year in the Congo: '. . . the good and bad was in this society. They didn't want anybody to be taking advantage of the poor by overcharging. Even some of the shopkeepers were afraid of them and they daren't charge a penny over the market price. . . . For all these reasons, at the start a whole lot of people had a certain amount of respect for them. In the end they became cruel and they did things like what is going on in Africa today . . . '.[125]

It may be that this notion that the Mollies 'went bad' can be traced to the mid-1850s when hard men, like Breslin, became somewhat more respectable and restrained more militant figures, like Ward, that is, to a time when a leadership decided that what had been done was not to be disavowed but ideally not to be done again.

Ambivalence is ever the end of outrage.

NOTES

Friends and colleagues commented on drafts of this essay or sections of it. I am particularly grateful to Guy Beiner, Claire Connolly, Enda Delaney, Alun Evans, Kevin Kenny, Kerby A. Miller, David Nally, Éamonn Ó Ciardha, Cormac Ó Gráda and Brendan O'Leary. Any error is my own. The award of a fellowship in the Moore Institute, National University of Ireland, Galway, and a visiting scholarship at New York University greatly facilitated completion of this essay.

1. An Bheitheach, place of birches. Beagh, the form adopted by the Ordnance Survey in the 1830s, had appeared on a map of the Conyngham estate, drawn in 1786, which is not apparently now extant. That form was also used in Grand Jury maps and presentments in the eighteenth and early nineteenth centuries. See NAI, OS 88 C 72 [MFP 1/073]. However, other spellings, such as Beigha and Beyha, which are closer to the pronunciation of the Irish-language word, remained common in the mid-nineteenth century.
2. Alistair Rowan, *North West Ulster: The Counties of Londonderry, Donegal, Fermanagh and Tyrone* (Harmondsworth, 1979), 427, describes Wood Lodge as 'a tiny Regency parsonage: three-bay cottage with central attic glebe. Derelict at the time of writing'. The architectural historian's description lacks

context: in 1857, when a typical countryman's house was valued at five shillings for taxation purposes, this 'cottage' was valued at £10 (200 shillings). It was later occupied by Catholic clergymen, and acquired in the early 1900s by Patrick McManus (1864–1929), who had made a fortune in Argentina, where he was a significant public figure; he was a brother of the writer Seumas (1869–1960).

3. For this letter, see NAI, Chief Secretary's Office Registered Papers (hereafter CSORP), 1856/16473.
4. The most incisive analysis of Ribbonism remains Tom Garvin, 'Defenders, Ribbonmen and Others: Underground Political Networks in Pre-Famine Ireland', *Past and Present*, 96 (1982), 133–55. Also see his *The Evolution of Irish Nationalist Politics* (Dublin, 1981), 34–43; Sailbheastar Ó Muireadhaigh, 'Na Fir Ribín', *Galvia*, 10 (1964–65), 18–32; and James S. Donnelly, Jr., *Captain Rock: The Irish Agrarian Rebellion, 1821–1824* (Dublin, 2009), 20–21, 98 fn. 69. On the Molly Maguires in North Connacht, see Jennifer Kelly, 'Local Memories and Manipulation of the Past in Pre-Famine County Leitrim', in Terence Dooley, ed., *Ireland's Polemical Past: Views of Irish History in Honour of R. V. Comerford* (Dublin, 2010), 51–67.

   The complex of ethnic, labor and political troubles that culminated in the Molly Maguire show trials in northeastern Pennsylvania in the late 1870s is the subject of a number of studies, including Wayne G. Broehl, Jr., *The Molly Maguires* (Cambridge, Mass., 1964), Kevin Kenny, *Making Sense of the Molly Maguires* (Oxford, 1998), and, most recently, Mark Bulik, *The Sons of Molly Maguire: The Irish Roots of America's First Labor War* (New York, 2015). Also see George Korson, *Minstrels of the Mine Patch: Songs and Stories of the Anthracite Industry* (Hatboro, Penn., 1964 [1938]), esp. ch. 8. Many of those involved in these troubles were emigrants from West Donegal, and all three books include some commentary on society and politics in that district. For a discussion of the district's connection to northeastern Pennsylvania, see Breandán Mac Suibhne, 'Them Poor Irish Lads in Pennsylvania', *Dublin Review of Books* (March 2015); www.drb.ie/essays/'them-poor-irish-lads'-in-pennsylvania
5. Broehl, *Molly Maguires*, 27–28; Korson, *Minstrels of the Mine Patch*, 240.

   The Molly Maguires in Pennsylvania were members of the Ancient Order of Hibernians. Later, Hibernian apologists portrayed the Mollies as a violent faction that had split from the Ribbon Society in Ireland, and remained separate and distinct from the AOH proper in the United States. T. F. McGrath, *History of the Ancient Order of Hibernians from the Earliest Period to the Joint National Convention at Trenton, N.J., June 27, 1898* (Cleveland, 1898), 52, claimed that, 'In 1825 the name in Ireland was changed from Ribbonmen to that of St. Patrick's Fraternal Society. It is not to be supposed that all these changes took place in harmony, as there was a large number of members who rebelled against those changes and withdrew from the order and continued under the name of Molly Maguires and Ribbonmen, especially in the County Antrim'. Likewise, John O'Dea, *History of the Ancient Order of Hibernians and Lady's Auxiliary* (South Bend, 1995 [1923]), 772, described the Mollies as 'a distinct body from the Ribbonmen . . . men of much violence and poor judgement', who 'brought discredit on the national cause'. Similarly, Michael Davitt, who was no Hibernian, argued that the Mollies 'grew out of and became a rival body to the Ribbon Society' and that they committed 'outrages of a shocking kind that were unjustly fathered upon the larger society'. See *Fall of Feudalism in Ireland; or, The Story of the Land League Revolution* (London and New York, 1904), 43. Traces of these arguments can be found in Kelly, 'Local Memories', 51–67. Focusing on North Connacht, Kelly represents the Mollies as distinct from the Ribbon Society, but having a 'close affiliation' to it, and she argues that 'there was almost certainly some degree of membership overlap between the Ribbon Society and Molly Maguires in pre-famine Leitrim and Longford'. The supposed distinction between the two societies is not clearly drawn, however. Kelly's interpretation runs counter to that presented here for West Donegal. Although the name Molly Maguire emerged as the Ribbon Society became more agrarian in the mid-1840s, there is no evidence that the Mollies were a distinct body in this district. Rather, all sources indicate that the Mollies (aka Ribbonmen) of West Donegal were part of the Ribbon Society proper. At most, the name may be associated with a regional cum agrarian *tendency*, but one firmly within the Society. It is perhaps best understood as a nickname or nom de guerre.

6. I am grateful to Dónall P. Ó Baoill for drawing my attention to this point.
7. Report of Outrage, submitted by John Stuart, Sub-Inspector, 7 March 1852; A. Montgomery to Under-Secretary, 15 March 1852, NAI, Outrage Papers, 1849–52/7/71. Also see CSORP, 1853/2493, detailing ten serious 'outrages' in the district in the year to February 1853. 'Sons of Freedom', a name similar to that used in Ballykillduff, had been adopted by the Dublin Ribbon leader Richard Jones in the late 1830s; see Garvin, 'Defenders, Ribbonmen and Others', 149. However, 'Sons of Freedom/Liberty' had been a moniker of other groups, including the United Irishmen in the 1790s, and the Volunteers in the late 1770s and early 1780s.
8. For an incident in Glenfin in 1847 in which a man dressed as a woman led a group of Mollies, see below, n. 44. For Mollies dressing themselves as women for purposes of disguise, see the attempted assassination of Rev. Alexander Nixon in North Donegal in 1858: *Ballyshannon Herald*, 5 November 1858; CSORP, 1860/15527; NLI, Larcom Papers, MS 7,633.
9. Cross-dressing was common in European carnival and protest; for an influential study of 'symbolic sexual inversion and political disorder', see Natalie Zemon Davies, 'Women on Top', in *Society and Culture in Early Modern Europe* (Stanford, Calif., 1975), 124–51. For the Mollies and mumming, see the useful discussion in Bulik, *Sons of Molly Maguire*, esp. 37–43, 47–50, 99–103.
10. Report of Outrage, submitted by John Stuart, Sub-Inspector, 7 March 1852, Outrage Papers, 1849–52/7/71.
11. D.J. Cruise to John Wynne, 19 December 1852, Outrage Papers, 1849–52/7/434; an excerpt of this letter can be found in CSORP, 1853/2493.
12. John Hamilton to James Stewart, 5 February 1853, CSORP, 1853/2493. For Hamilton's son's reflections on Ribbonism, see especially, James Hamilton to [Under-Secretary], 4 May 1850, Outrage Papers, 1850/7/163.
13. For the meeting requesting the proclamation and related correspondence, see CSORP, 1853/2493.
14. 'County of Donegal, District of Glenties: Arms &c. Given Up to the Constabulary, and Deposited at the Under-mentioned Stations . . . 2nd April 1852', CSORP, 1853/3134.
15. For examples of 'outrages' in County Donegal in 1853–55, not all of which are Ribbon-related, see 'Return of Rewards Offered through the Constabulary by Placard, during the Years 1853 & 1854', dated 29 November 1855, and 'Return of Outrages in which Rewards for Information have been Offered by Constabulary Placards since 1st. January to the 17th November 1855', CSORP, 1856/17416. And for outrages over a longer period in North Donegal, see *A Return 'of the Outrages Specially Reported by the Constabulary as Committed within the Barony of Kilmacrenan, County Donegal, during the Last Ten Years*', HC 1861 (404), lii, 585.
16. See the evidence of Patrick Hobart, County Inspector, in *Select Committee of the House of Lords Appointed to Consider the Consequences of Extending*

the Functions of the Constabulary in Ireland to the Suppression or Prevention of Illicit Distillation, HL 1854 (53), 101–13, esp. 108–109. These figures do not include the Revenue Police, a separate force from the Constabulary. Also see John Fleming to Naas, 6 July 1852, Outrage Papers, 1849–52/7/179.

17. 'Total Number of Rewards Offered and Paid in the Years, 1853, 1854, and 1855', CSORP, 1856/17416. In addition to the sums routinely offered by the Constabulary, the authorities also offered rewards by 'lord lieutenant's proclamation' in cases judged particularly serious; on which see ibid., 'Return of Outrages in which Rewards for Information has been Offered by the Lord Lieutenant's Proclamation in the Years, 1853, 1854, and 1855'.
18. W.E. Vaughan, *Sin, Sheep and Scotsmen: John George Adair and the Derryveagh Evictions, 1861* (Belfast, 1983), 25. Kenny, *Making Sense*, 41, is mistaken when he suggests that 'Donegal was generally known for its peacefulness rather than its violence in the 1850s and 1860s'.
19. From the authorities' perspective, Donegal's great trouble spots had hitherto been Fanad, Glenswilly and Glenfin/Ballybofey, in the north of the county, and Townawilly in the south. All were predominantly Catholic areas that bordered more advantaged Protestant districts. Inishowen, generally, was bothersome for police and magistrates, in part due to the centrality of *poitín* in the local economy, and, there, Clonmany was considered exceptionally resistant to agents of outside authority.
20. In mid-November 1855, Dublin Castle had sent a confidential circular to resident magistrates and chief constables across Ireland, asking if they had detected any 'renewed activity in secret confederacy' in their districts, and—possibly having picked up hints of activity, driven from New York, that was to culminate in the establishment of the Fenians—flagging the likelihood of returned emigrants being involved in such groups. The substantial file containing the responses of the constables and resident magistrates is CSORP, 1855–56/11368; the circular received by Cruise is Edward Horsman to D.J. Cruise, 13 November 1855.
21. D. McGregor to T. Larcom, 23 December 1855, CSORP, 1855–56/11368.
22. Anderson's report and those of his Head Constables are précised in D. McGregor to T. Larcom, 23 December 1855, CSORP, 1855–56/11368.
23. For many landlords and agents, of course, the sting was all the sharper as many of those recruited as 'stipendiaries' were Catholics, like Daniel Cruise, and their appointment was perceived as yet another blow at the old order.
24. On Cruise's early career (and some early [1853] impressions of Donegal), see *Select Committee on Extending the Functions of the Constabulary*, 92–101.
25. For details, see *Belfast Newsletter*, 13 July 1857 and *Londonderry Journal*, 15 July 1857, reporting on the summer assizes in 1857; and *Londonderry Journal*, 10 March 1858 and *Ulsterman*, 8 March 1858, reporting on the assizes of the following spring. On the controversy surrounding the conviction of the men solely on the evidence of the accomplice; see *Irish Jurist*, 9 (1857), 61–62. There was an additional controversy: Condy McHugh of Beagh, named by McGlynn as a Molly Maguire, also swore a statement, admitting to being a Ribbonman and naming others, but he later retracted it. He was later tried on his own statement and convicted. McHugh appealed the decision to the Court of Criminal Appeals, which ruled, by a majority decision, that a statement made by a prisoner with a view to his being examined as a crown witness was inadmissable as evidence against him. See *Reg.* v M'Hugh, reported by P.J. McKenna BL, in Edward W. Cox, *Reports of Cases in Criminal Law Argued and Determined in all the Courts of England and Ireland*, 7 [1855–58] (London, 1858), 483–88.
26. Breandán Mac Suibhne, 'Agrarian Improvement and Social Unrest: Lord George Hill and the Gaoth Dobhair Sheep War, 1856–61', in W. Nolan, L.

Ronayne and M. Dunlevy, eds., *Donegal: History and Society* (Dublin, 1995), 547–82. And for a related controversy, see Vaughan, *Sin, Sheep and Scotsmen*.

27. West Donegal may be here understood as the district west of a line drawn from Killybegs through Fintown to Dunfanaghy. In 1840, when a man with suspected Ribbon connections was arrested near Glenties for burglary, the arresting officer reported to Dublin, that, '*to sow the seeds* of Ribbonism, I am almost certain, was the principal object of his visit to this neighbourhood, *and not being successful* he turned to rob'. See John C. Rodden to Inspector General, 19 June 1840, Outrage Papers, 1840/7/13863; italics added.
28. Énrí Ó Muirgheasa, eag., *Dhá Chéad de Cheoltaibh Uladh* (Baile Átha Cliath, 1934), 184–85.
29. Memorial of James Pearson, Ardara, to Earl Mulgrave, Lord Lieutenant, n.d.; received 17 June 1837, CSORP, 1837/5/48.
30. Charles Henry Crookshank, *History of Methodism in Ireland* (Belfast, 1885), vol. 1 [Wesley and his Times], 411–12. The parish priest was then Patrick McNeilis of Stracastle (d. c. 1812).
31. B. H. Holmes to Under-Secretary, 20 May 1846, Outrage Papers, 1846/7/12225. Although most people of that surname in this particular area were Protestants, two Catholic Scotts can be found in the 1901 and 1911 census—John Scott, a postman in Narin, and Susan Scott, a farmer of Kilclooney. The postman, who spoke Irish and English, gave Scotland as his place of birth, and his year of birth as 1848. Intriguingly, the man involved in the riot with the coastguards in 1846 was reported to have decamped to Scotland. See NAI, Census of Ireland, 1901. There is a significant discrepancy between the age given for the postman in the 1901 (36) and 1911 (63) census forms; I am assuming the latter to be correct.
32. B.H. Holmes to Under-Secretary, 17 February 1846, Outrage Papers, 1846/7/4673; *Ballyshannon Herald*, 27 February 1846; *Freeman's Journal*, 23 February 1846. The trial had been postponed in July 1846, as Peggy was heavily pregnant; see *Freeman's Journal*, 25 July 1846. Peggy Crummer was duly transported to Australia; she arrived in May 1848, received a ticket of leave in October 1854, and a conditional pardon in September 1856. See Trevor McClaughlin, *Irish Women in Colonial Australia* (St. Leonards, 1998), 38. Also see NAI, Transportation Records 6, P 256, and *Ballyshannon Herald*, 19 March 1847. For a report on the hanging, see *Ballyshannon Herald*, 7 May 1847.
33. The expansion of the Ribbon Society into West Donegal from winter 1844–45, and the use from that time of the moniker Molly Maguire, is coincident with the development of the Molly Maguires in Leitrim, as traced in Kelly, 'Local Memories', 55 *et seq.*; there, 'the first threatening notice from Molly Maguire . . . appeared in Cashcarrigan in mid-February 1845'.
34. B. H. Holmes to Under-Secretary, 6 March 1845, Outrage Papers, 1845/7/4715. For a memoir of Spence, see Maguire, *History of the Diocese of Raphoe*, pt. 1, vol. 2, 24–25. He was a native of Stranorlar, an area where Ribbonism was deeply rooted. For instance, see the evidence of Golding Bird, 20 July 1853, in *Select Committee on Extending the Functions of the Constabulary in Ireland*, 52–53, where he refers to 'a strong Ribbon party' as being in existence 'about Stranorlar and that neighbourhood'. O'Connell's supporters frequently argued that rural violence might disrupt progress on repeal.
35. B.H. Holmes to E. Lucas, 19 July 1845, Outrage Papers, 1845/7/15775.
36. B.H. Holmes to E. Lucas, 12 July 1845, enclosing copy of threatening letter, Outrage Papers, 1845/7/15103; B.H. Holmes to Under-Secretary, 29 August 1845, enclosing copy of threatening letter, ibid., 1845/7/18435.
37. For an account of the writing of such notices, see Hugh Dorian, *The Outer Edge of Ulster: A Memoir of Social Life in Nineteenth-Century Donegal*, ed.

Breandán Mac Suibhne and David Dickson (South Bend, 2001), 210–30, and for a discussion see ix–xii, 19–22.

38. B.H. Holmes to Under-Secretary, 7 August 1845, Outrage Papers, 1845/7/16981.
39. For the attacks on Cassidy's property, see B.H. Holmes to Under-Secretary, 6 December 1845, Outrage Papers, 1845/7/28285; Memorial of James Cassidy of Ballyshannon in the County Donegal, Farmer (recvd 23 March 1846), ibid., 1846/7/7273. And for the attack on Young's steward, see Copy of the Information of John McGinty of Meenawau . . . 3rd February 1848, ibid., 1848/7/32.
40. B.H. Holmes to Under-Secretary, 27 September 1845, enclosing *Wonderful Prophecy* (Printed by Henry Watson, Wilson Court, White Street, Belfast), Outrage Papers, 1845/7/20783.
41. B.H. Holmes to Under-Secretary, 20 February 1846, enclosing a copy of the notice, Outrage Papers, 1846/7/5739.
42. T. Blake to Redington, 26 July 1848, Outrage Papers, 1848/7/207.
43. The details are taken from the statement of an informer in the district between Fintown and Glenfin, in 1848: J. Johnston, John Cochran, Johnston Mansfield to Chief Secretary, 3 February 1848, enclosing Copy of the Information of John McGinty of Meenawau . . . 3rd February 1848, Outrage Papers, 1848/7/32. Also see K. Kirkham to Thomas E. Blake, 15 February 1848, ibid., 1848/7/44. For a later account of being made a Ribbonman in the backroom of a public house in Ardara, see the statements of Patrick McGlynn.
44. Reward poster, dated Dublin Castle, 4 June 1847, Outrage Papers, 1847/7/152. *Ballyshannon Herald*, 21 May, 28 May 1847. The newspaper reports suggest the 'savages' had been looking for the agent, Charles Kennedy, not Doherty.
45. J. Johnston, John Cochran, Johnston Mansfield to Chief Secretary, 3 February 1848, enclosing Copy of the Information of John McGinty, Outrage Papers, 1848/7/32.
46. T.E. Blake to T.N. Redington, 21 April 1848; Information of Patrick Mulhern, Innishmacsaint, 20 April 1848; Information of James Gilloway, Innishmacsaint, 21 April 1848, Outrage Papers, 1848/7/130.
47. On his earlier involvement in the Ribbon Society, see Charles Hayden to Inspector General, 7 August 1839, Outrage Papers, 1839/7/7672.
48. The military historian Keith Jeffery thrice refers to the attackers as 'dynamiters' in his *Field Marshal Sir Henry Wilson: A Political Soldier* (Oxford, 2006), 15, 118, 257, even though it was not until 1867 that Alfred Nobel (1833–96) patented dynamite. Jeffery also misdates the explosion to December 1849 rather than 1848. For the subsequent investigation into the smuggling, from Scotland, of casks of gunpowder, and their concealment in Townawilly, see Outrage Papers, 1849–52/7/141, most especially Edward Tierney to T.N. Redington, 26 April 1849, and Information of Hugh Slevin, a pauper in Donegal Workhouse, 25 February 1849. On the recovery of a cask containing 25 pounds of gunpowder on an unoccupied farm in Garvagh, Townawilly, see Andrew Montgomery to W.M. Somerville, 15 September 1849, ibid., 1849–52/7/268; the information that led to the discovery was passed to the authorities by Eugene McCafferty, the parish priest of Donegal.
49. Information of Hugh Slevin, a pauper in Donegal Workhouse, 25 February 1849, Outrage Papers, 1849–52/7/141.
50. For some examples of the use of detectives in Glenfin, see Information of Edward Woods, Constable of Police Acting as a Detective to Obtain Secret Information, 25 December 1850, Outrage Papers, 1849–52/7/379; in Glenswilly and Buncrana, see John Fleming to Chief Secretary, 31 October 1851, ibid., 1849–52/7/315; John Fleming to Chief Secretary, 1 December 1851, ibid., 1849–52/7/343; in Meenacladdy and Dunlewey, Gweedore, see Sub-Inspector

Meredith to Inspector General, 9 December 1852, ibid., 1849–52/7/424 and Meredith to Inspector General, 13 November 1852, CSORP, 1853/14778; and for an appeal for a detective to be sent to Fanad, see John O. Woodhouse to Thomas Larcom, 20 October 1853, CSORP, 1853/10609. For doubts on the efficacy of detectives operating in Donegal, see James Hamilton to Under-Secretary, 5 December 1852, Outrage Papers, 1849–52/7/419, and Coulson to Under-Secretary, 15 April 1853, CSORP, 1853/3451. On the wider use of detectives, see Elizabeth Malcolm, 'Investigating the "Machinery of Murder": Irish Detectives and Agrarian Outrages, 1847–70', *New Hibernia Review*, 6, 3 (2002), 73–91.

51. John Vandeleur Stewart to James Stewart, 2 January 1849, Outrage Papers, 1849–52/7/11.
52. Andrew Montgomery to T.N. Redington, 18 March 1850, Outrage Papers, 1849–52/7/67.
53. *Ballyshannon Herald*, 17 September 1847.
54. *Londonderry Journal*, 12 June 1850.
55. Robert Russell to Marquis of Conyngham, 20 March 1850, Outrage Papers, 1849–52/7/83; Sub-Inspector Stuart to Henry Townsend, 5 March 1851; Montgomery to Redington, 15 March 1851, ibid., 1849–52/7/89; Henry Townsend to Inspector General, 22 March 1851; Sub-Inspector Stuart to Henry Townsend, 20 March 1851, ibid., 1849–52/7/101.
56. 'A Return of the Number of Parliamentary Voters in the Registry of each Barony in the County of Donegal . . . 20th Day of November 1851', CSORP, 1853/1290.
57. Dublin Castle's concern about returned emigrants in 1848 is documented in official correspondence. For examples, see Outrage Papers, 1848/7/193, detailing the arrests of several returned emigrants. T.N. Redington to William Fenwick, 8 August 1848, notes that 'Government are in possession of information stating that a number of Emigrants have returned from America for the purpose of encouraging disaffection'. And for the same concern in the mid-1850s, see the confidential circular to resident magistrates and county inspectors on 'lawless and secret combinations', and the responses from around the country, CSORP, 1855–56/11368.
58. Surprisingly, there is no comprehensive scholarly history of the AOH in either Ireland or America. However, on Ireland, see Garvin, *Evolution of Irish Nationalist Politics*, 95–99, 137–40, and the works cited therein, and A.C. Hepburn, *Catholic Belfast and Nationalist Ireland in the Era of Joe Devlin, 1871–1934* (Oxford, 2008), esp. chs. 4–5. For a recent discussion of the emergence of Hibernianism in America, see Bulik, *Sons of Molly Maguire*, ch. 7.
59. Garvin, *Evolution*, 41, makes an analogy between the Ribbon Society and American political machines. Also see his 'Defenders, Ribbonmen and Others', 150 *et seq*. For a consideration of the moral grayness of machine politics, that might well be adapted to the Ribbon Society, see Peter Quinn, 'Local Politics: Irish-American Style', in his *Looking for Jimmy: A Search for Irish America* (Woodstock and New York, 2007), 101–11, esp. 104–105 and 109–10.
60. Denis Holland, *The Landlord in Donegal: Pictures from the Wilds* (Belfast, n.d. [1858]), 51–52.
61. 'Mihil' is identified as Mícheál Airt Ó Domhnaill, aka Michael O'Donnell, in Dónall P. Ó Baoill, 'Ar Cuireadh Iachall ar Phádraig Ó Donaill Carey a Scaoileadh?', *Scathlán: Irish Chumann Staire agus Seanchais Ghaoth Dobhair*, 2 (1983), 16–32, an exemplary micro-history, which has passed unnoticed in subsequent writing on the Molly Maguires, in Ireland and the United States, and on the career of 'Mihil's' son, Pádaí Mhícheáil Airt (*aka* Pat O'Donnell).

62. On the business acumen of Mícheál Airt and his siblings, see Cití Nic Giolla Bhríde agus Dónall P. Ó Baoill, 'Bunadh Airt Ui Dhonaill', *Scathlán*, 2 (1983), 90–91, which notes their ability to save money, and their investment in taverns and boarding houses in Donegal, Toronto and Pennsylvania.
63. On the Meenacladdy O'Donnells in Pennsylvania, see Ó Baoill, 'Ar Cuireadh Iachall ar Phádraig Ó Dónaill Carey a Scaoileadh?, 28–31. Ó Baoill notes that James McParlan[d], the key undercover detective, later concluded that Pádaí Mhícheáil Airt's visit to his relatives had been a social call. Also see Broehl, *Molly Maguires*, esp. 258–66, Kenny, *Making Sense*, 207–208. And for recent accounts of the assassination of Carey, see Senan Molony, *The Phoenix Park Murders: Conspiracy, Betrayal and Retribution* (Cork, 2006), 233–71, and J. L. McCracken, 'The Fate of an Infamous Informer', *History Ireland*, 9, 2 (2001), 26–30.
64. Data taken from *Return of the Population of the Several Counties in Ireland, as Enumerated in 1831*, pt. 1, HC 1833 (254), 39, and *Census of Ireland for the Year 1851*, pt. 1, vol. 3 (Province of Ulster) (1853), 153.
65. See Joel Mokyr, *Why Ireland Starved: A Quantitative and Analytical History of the Irish Economy, 1800–1850* (Abingdon, 1983), 267.
66. Christine Kinealy, *This Great Calamity: The Irish Famine, 1845–52* (Dublin, 1994), 171, 348–49.
67. Kinealy, *Great Calamity*, 349; also see *op. cit.*, 126, 87–88.
68. The quotation is from a commemorative plaque in St. Patrick's Church, Bunbeg.
69. *Facts from Gweedore, Compiled from the Notes of Lord George Hill: A Facsimile Reprint of the Fifth Edition (1887)*, with an Introduction by E. E. Evans (Belfast, 1971), dust-jacket of 1853 edition.
70. Hugh M'Fadden, parish priest, West Tullaghobegley [Gweedore], to [Sir Randolph Routh], 9 December 1846, NAI, Famine Relief Commission Papers, County Donegal, Kilmacrenan 8,134.
71. Holland, *Landlord in Donegal*, 69–73.
72. See the Introduction to the third edition (1854) in *Facts*, 9.
73. David Dickson, 'The Potato and Irish Diet before the Famine', in Cormac Ó Gráda, ed., *Famine 150: Commemorative Lecture Series* (Ballsbridge, 1997), 1–28, 22. For earlier reflections on the role of oatmeal in the Donegal diet, see Austin Bourke, *The Visitation of God; The Potato and the Great Irish Famine* (Dublin, 1993).
74. *Poor Inquiry* (Ireland), Appendix E.
75. W. J. Smyth, 'Variations in Vulnerability', in Crowley et al., *Atlas of the Great Irish Famine* (New York, 2012), 180–98.
76. Quoted in Cathal Póirtéir, eag., *Glórtha ón Ghorta: Béaloideas na Gaeilge agus an Gorta Mór* (Baile Átha Cliath, 1996), 54–55, 55–56.
77. T. A. Devyr, *Odd Book of the Nineteenth Century* (New York, 1882), [Irish and British Section], 138–39.
78. Massimo Livi-Bacci, *A Concise History of World Population* (Oxford, 1989), 106.
79. Devyr, *Odd Book*, [Irish and British Section], 139.
80. *First Report of the Commissioners of Inquiry into the State of the Irish Fisheries: With the Minutes of Evidence and Appendix*, HC 1837 (77), xxii, 63.
81. *First Report of the Commissioners of Inquiry into the State of the Irish Fisheries*, 69.
82. On kelp, see Póirtéir, *Glórtha ón Ghorta*, 56–57; on Carn, see National Folklore Collection, University College, Dublin: Schools Collection, Beagh, County Donegal, 102–103. I am grateful to Eithne Ní Ghallchobhair for the latter reference.

83. Dorian, *Outer Edge of Ulster*, 210–30, and for a discussion, see ibid., ix–xii, 19–22. Also see Breandán Mac Suibhne, 'A Jig in the Poorhouse: Space and Story, the G-Word and the Issueless Tribute', *Dublin Review of Books* (April 2013), available at http://www.drb.ie/essays/a-jig-in-the-poorhouse An abbreviated version has since appeared in translation (by Chloé Lacoste of Université Paris-Sorbonne) as 'La Zone Grise, le Gros Mot, et de Nouvelles Manières de le Raconter: Quelques Histoires Récentes de la Grande Famine', *Révue Française de Civilisation Britannique*, 19, 2 (2014), 213–38.
84. Dorian, *Outer Edge of Ulster*, 212.
85. Evidence of Rev. Neil Hewston, in *First Report of the Commissioners for Inquiring into the Condition of the Poorer Classes in Ireland, Supplement to Appendix D*, HC 1836 (36), xxxi, 1, 305.
86. *Poor Inquiry (Ireland): First Report from Her Majesty's Commissioners for Inquiring into the Condition of the Poorer Classes in Ireland, with Appendix (A) and Supplement*, HC 1835 (32): Supplement to Appendix A, 320, 324. Two figures were returned for the number of seasonal migrants leaving Lettermacaward. The higher figure (100) given by Neil Hewston, the Catholic priest, is here taken to be more accurate than the number (20) offered by James Kilpatrick, the Church of Ireland clergyman. For the number of males aged over 20, see *Abstract of the Population Returns, 1831*, HC 1833 (634), 246–47.
87. W. Bennett, *Narrative of a Recent Journey of Six Weeks in Ireland* . . . (London, 1847), 73.
88. *Report from the Select Committee on Destitution (Gweedore and Cloughaneely)* . . ., HC 1857–58 (412), xiii, 24, 75, 285, 292–93, 405–406, 472.
89. In southwest Donegal, the decades immediately after the Famine saw the McDevitt family consolidate their dominance of the stocking trade around Glenties, forcing smaller dealers out of the business; see Murrough O'Brien, 'The Condition of Small Farmers in Ireland, and their Position with Reference to the Land Question', *Journal of the Statistical and Social Inquiry Society of Ireland*, 7 (1878), 299–310, esp. 306.
90. *Report of the British Association for the Relief of the Extreme Distress in Ireland and Scotland with Correspondence of the Agents, Tables, &c. and a List of Subscribers* (London, 1849), 139: 'Table 1: Return of Grants made by the Committee and Agents of the Association for the Relief of Distress in Ireland, from January to September, 1847, Inclusive'.
91. Certainly, from autumn 1847 through mid-summer 1848, some £4,982 of £9,171 granted by the Association to poor law unions in Donegal went to the Glenties Union; see ibid., 141, 'Table 2: Return of the Sums Granted by the British Association to various Unions in Ireland from 1st October, 1847, to 8th July, 1848'. Glenties was also the only Union in Donegal where the Association granted cash for the 'relief of general distress'; see ibid., 145.
92. This description is taken from Dorian, *Outer Edge of Ulster*, 223, who was writing with Milford Union Workhouse in mind.
93. John Mitchel, *The Last Conquest of Ireland (Perhaps)*, ed. Patrick Maume (Dublin, 2005 [1861]), 116.
94. Registrar of Persons Admitted and Discharged, 31 December 1851–66, Donegal County Archives, BG 92/32/1; Glenties Poor Law Union Minute Books, BG 92/1/24.
95. See Dorian, *Outer Edge of Ulster*, 215–17, most esp. 217, where he remarks on people 'borrowing' food in small quantities from neighbors.
96. Ó Muirgheasa, *Dhá Chéad de Cheoltaibh Uladh*, 336–37.
97. On one particularly avaricious parish priest, see Breandán Mac Suibhne, 'Soggarth Aroon or Gombeen Priest: James MacFadden of Gaoth Dobhair and Inis Caoil', in Gerard Moran, ed., *Radical Irish Priests* (Dublin, 1998), 146–84.

98. Patrick MacGill, *The Rat-pit* (London, 1915), 20–21. On MacGill's relationship to Catholic clergy, see Mac Suibhne, 'Soggarth Aroon or Gombeen Priest', 150–51, 170–84, and works cited therein.
99. For these details, see O'Brien, 'The Condition of Small Farmers in Ireland', 306.
100. D. J. Cruise to Larcom, 5 November 1855; Information of James Arle, Meenagrillagh, 30 October 1855; Information of James Arle and Jane Adair, Meenagrillagh, 30 October 1855; Information of Jane Adair, Meenagrillagh, 30 October 1855, CSORP, 1855–56/9395. Arle and McCready were Protestants, as was one of McCready's local supporters (Burn [aka Freeburn] of Tullymore); Patrick Friel, a supposed Molly Maguire brought out from Ardara by McCready, was a Catholic.
101. D. J. Cruise to Larcom, 12 July 1856; D. J. Cruise to Larcom, 28 July 1856; D. J. Cruise to Larcom, 12 August 1856; Information of Patk. McRoarty, Tievahorky, Parish of Inver, 1 March 1856; Dying Declaration of Patrick McRoarty, 8 July 1856, CSORP, 1855–56/18243.
102. Considine to T. Larcom, 3 December 1855, CSORP, 1855–56/10193.
103. McGrath (1812–1887) appeared in Glenties Petty Sessions Court on several occasions in the 1860s and 1870s, being then generally described as a publican, and occasionally as a dealer. For instance, on 7 September 1866, his publican's license was revoked on account of his house 'being riotously and irregularly kept'; it was later restored. On 2 November 1866, he was convicted of being drunk on the public street of Glenties on 5 October, and of assaulting a constable in the execution of his duty, tearing his tunic, and on 16 August 1869, a case against him for refusing to surrender an unlicensed pistol to the Constabulary and to close his shop was sent to the Quarter Sessions. See NAI, Irish Petty Sessions, Court Registers: Glenties Petty Sessions Order Books. *Slater's Royal National Commercial Directory of Ireland* (1870), 238–39, returns him as a grocer and spirit and porter dealer. *Slater's Royal National Commercial Directory of Ireland* (1881), 348, returns him as an egg dealer.
104. From the cross-examination of Patrick McGlynn as reported in *Belfast Newsletter*, 12 March 1857.
105. Writing of North Donegal, Dorian, *Outer Edge of Ulster*, 191–92, 227–29, 239–40 *et seq*., remarks on 'genteel' families declining in influence during the Famine, and a new mercenary middle class emerging in their place. Such shifts did not necessarily have any bearing on attitudes to the Ribbon Society. For instance, Neil O'Donnell, named by McGlynn in 1856 as master of the Glenties lodge, was related to the O'Donnells of Letterilly, and presumably, like them, a connection of the O'Donnells of Glashagh.
106. Two of the Sími Dohertys, a well-known traveling family, who traded horses and, as tinsmiths, crafted and repaired the utensils required for *poitín*-making, were exposed as Ribbonmen in February 1857. Cousins, and both named Simon, one was taken in Dunfanaghy for armed extortion for the Society, while the other was arrested in Belfast for horse-stealing. The latter cut a deal for himself by turning informer. Considine to Larcom, 12 February 1857, CSORP, 1857–58/1260. On the place of the family in the cultural life of west Ulster, see Allen Feldman and Éamonn O'Doherty, *The Northern Fiddler: Music and Musicians of Donegal and Tyrone* (Belfast, 1979); also the fine sleeve-notes by Alun Evans in *The Floating Bow* (CCF31; Claddagh Records, 1996).
107. Sub-Inspector to Inspector General, 25 April 1856; D. J. Cruise to Larcom, 13 May 1856, CSORP, 1855–56/14936.
108. For this incident, see Liam Briody, *Glenties and Inniskeel* (Ballyshannon, 1986), 310.

109. On the Ribbon Society's influence on the awarding of road contracts, see the comments of the county surveyor in William Harte to Larcom, 15 May 1858, CSORP, 1858/14388. And for an effort at intimidating a mail coach operator to reinstate a dismissed car-driver, see Wm. Hushoff JP to Larcom, Derry, 3 April 1857, enclosing a copy of a threatening letter signed 'A Son of Molly's' [*sic*], CSORP, 1857/2964.
110. In 1854, when a detective trying to infiltrate a lodge in Liverpool reported the names of four top Ribbonmen, including Gettens, in Ireland, the Dublin authorities simply remarked 'already well known as members of the Ribbon Society'. See Felix O'[Reilly] to Commissioner of Police, 24 October 1854, CSORP, 1859/1959. The other three named were Peter Traynor of Magheramayo, near Dolly's Brae, near Castlewellan, County Down; Edward Smyth, from near Clough, County Down, and Owen McNeill, publican, 13 Mary's Market, Belfast. On the prosecution of Gettens for illegally selling spirits, see NAI, Irish Petty Sessions, Court Registers: Ballyshannon Petty Sessions Order Books CSPS 1/1145 (20 August 1855).
111. NAI, Irish Petty Sessions, Court Registers: Ballyshannon Petty Sessions Order Books CSPS 1/1151 (20 September 1860, as prosecutor); 1/1152 (4 October 1860, as defendant).
112. John D'Alton, ed., *King James's Irish Army List (1689)* (Dublin, 1855), vi.
113. See D.J. Cruise to Larcom, 27 December 1855, and D. McGregor to T. Larcom, 23 December 1855, summarizing the Constabulary reports from around Donegal, and quoting the county inspector, CSORP, 1855–56/11368.
114. Information of Patrick McGlynn, National School Teacher of Beagh . . . [Wood Lodge], 8 June 1856; Further Information of Patrick [Mc]Glynn, Mountcharles, 14 June 1856, CSORP, 1855–56/16473.
115. Seaton F. Milligan, 'Some Recent Cases of Remarkable Longevity', *Journal of the Royal Society of Antiquaries of Ireland*, 22 (1892), 224–36, 234.
116. Lochlann McGill, *In Conall's Footsteps* (Dingle, 1992), 206–207, identifies the man described by Milligan as John the Towel.
117. I address this issue in a work in progress exploring the reasons why Patrick McGlynn turned informer.
118. Among the children were Francis (b. 1865), Charles (b. 1870) and a daughter Mary (b. c. 1871).
119. NAI, Irish Petty Sessions, Court Registers: Ardara, County Donegal, CSPS 1/2: 12 November 1861 (the complainant was Condy Conaghan of Edergole); CSPS 1/7: 9 April 1878 (county cess); 13 April 1888 (drunkenness); 14 February 1893 (seed rate in 1890, 1891); 9 August 1898 (unmuzzled dog); 14 May 1907 (seaweed case);
120. Calculated from NAI, Census of Ireland, 1901: Glengesh DED, County Donegal; of 36 Protestants (56+), only seven could not read, and only five were returned as being able to read but not write.
121. David Lloyd, 'The Indigent Sublime: Spectres of Irish Hunger', in *Irish Times: Temporalities of Modernity* (Dublin, 2008), 39–72, 72.
122. Briody, *Glenties and Inniskeel*, 165. Contention for musical instruments in the Rosses in these years is the backdrop of Seosamh Mac Grianna's novel, *An Druma Mór* (Baile Átha Cliath, 1969).
123. On Hibernian v Republican conflict in west Donegal, see Mac Suibhne, 'Soggarth Aroon or Gombeen Priest', 176–83, and works cited therein. Also see Liam Ó Duibhir, *The Donegal Awakening: Donegal and the War of Independence* (Cork, 2009), 65–68, 73, 80, 82, 84, 89. Michael Sheerin, a member of an IRA flying column in Donegal during the Tan War, later remarked of the pocket of Hibernians around Letterbarra that 'I never met a more conservative body of men'; see Bureau of Military History, Witness Statement 803.

124. National Folklore Collection, Iml. 185: 445, 475–76 Johnny Timoney (40), Mín an tSamhaidh; a story heard from his father, James (b. *c.* 1849); recorded 6 April 1936 by Liam Mac Meanman, Móinín, Clochán, Leifear. The census forms for the family indicate that his father married late (c. 40) to a woman about eighteen years his junior. See NAI, Census 1901: Meenahery [*sic.*], House 5; Census 1911, Meenatawy, House 5. For another reference to the theft of butter on Bealach na gCreach, and the beating of an unnamed man, see Iml. 185: 363, 376: Micí Mac Meanman (68), a native of An Ghlaisigh Mhór, living in Cruach Cholpach, interviewed by Liam Mac Meanman on 2 April 1936. The last question on the form filled out by the collectors asked from whom the story had been heard; usually, the respondents specified a person or said simply *na sean-daoine* (the old people). Here, the collector wrote, *Ní cuimhin leis.* (He doesn't remember.)
125. Quoted in Broehl, *Molly Maguires*, 30–31.

Contributors

John Cunningham is Lecturer in History at NUI Galway. His publications on Irish labor and social history include *Unlikely Radicals: Irish Post-Primary Teachers and the ASTI, 1909–2009* (Cork University Press, 2010). He has also served as editor of *Saothar: The Journal of the Irish Labour History Society*.

Enda Delaney is Professor of Modern History at the University of Edinburgh. He has written extensively on the social history of modern Ireland, including its diaspora. His most recent book is *The Great Irish Famine: A History in Four Lives* (Gill and Macmillan, 2014).

Melissa Fegan is Reader in English Literature at the University of Chester. She specializes in nineteenth-century literature, and she is the author of *Literature and the Irish Famine 1845–1919* (Clarendon Press, 2002) and *Wuthering Heights: Character Studies* (Continuum, 2008).

David Jones is currently a policy consultant. He recently retired as Professor in the Faculty of Business, Economics and Policy Studies of the University of Brunei, and was before then a Professor, Department of Political Science, National University of Singapore. He has published extensively in the areas of political science, public policy and public management. His publications also include several studies of land reform and agrarian politics in Ireland, especially focusing on graziers and land distribution, one of which is his book *Graziers, Land Reform and Political Conflict in Ireland* (Catholic University of America Press, 1995).

Bridget Kelly is a recent graduate in History from the University of Missouri, where she completed a senior thesis on *Ronayne's Reminiscences*. She has since completed a Master's in Social Studies Education at the University of Texas-Austin.

Breandán Mac Suibhne is Associate Professor of History at Centenary College, New Jersey. A founding editor of *Field Day Review* (2005), his publications include John Gamble's *Society and Manners in Early Nineteenth-Century Ireland* (Field Day, 2011), and, with David Dickson, he edited Hugh Dorian's *The Outer Edge of Ulster: A Memoir of Social Life in Nineteenth-Century Donegal* (Lilliput, 2000, 2001; University of Notre Dame Press, 2001).

David W. Miller is Professor Emeritus in History at Carnegie Mellon University. He researches Irish social and religious history, primarily between 1760 and 1870. Among his many publications are *Church, State and Nation in Ireland, 1898–1921* (Gill and Macmillan, 1973) and *Queen's Rebels: Ulster Loyalism in Historical Perspective* (Gill and Macmillan, 1978; University College Dublin Press, 2007).

Kerby A. Miller is Curators' Professor of History at the University of Missouri. He is the author of several studies of Irish and Irish-American history, including *Emigrants and Exiles: Ireland and the Irish Exodus to North America* (Oxford University Press, 1985) and (with David N. Doyle, Bruce D. Boling, and Arnold Schrier) *Irish Immigrants in the Land of Canaan: Letters and Memoirs from Colonial and Revolutionary America, 1675–1815* (Oxford University Press, 2003). His most recent book is *Ireland and Irish America: Culture, Class and Transatlantic Migration* (Field Day, 2008).

Ciarán Reilly is a Research Fellow at the Centre for the Study of Historic Irish Houses and Estates at the Department of History, Maynooth University. His most recent books are *Strokestown and the Great Irish Famine* (Four Courts Press, 2014) and *The Irish Land Agent, 1830–1860: The Case of King's County* (Four Courts Press, 2014).

Ellen Skerrett, an historian of Chicago and its neighborhoods, is a researcher for the Jane Addams Papers documentary history project affiliated with Ramapo College of New Jersey. She is the editor, with Mary Lesch, of the memoir of Francis O'Neill, Chicago's chief of police who collected and published nine volumes of Irish music at the turn of the twentieth century, *Chief O'Neill's Sketchy Recollections of An Eventful Life in Chicago* (Northwestern University Press, 2008).

Index

Printed in Great Britain
by Amazon

36635903R00143